FOAL

"Frankly,
We Did Win
This Election"

"Frankly, We Did Win This Election"

THE INSIDE STORY OF HOW TRUMP LOST

Michael C. Bender

TWELVE

NEW YORK BOSTON

Grand Central Publishing
Hachette Book Group
1290 Avenue of the Americas, New York, NY 10104
grandcentralpublishing.com
twitter.com/grandcentralpub

First Edition: August 2021

Grand Central Publishing is a division of Hachette Book Group, Inc. The Grand Central Publishing name and logo is a trademark of Hachette Book Group, Inc.

The publisher is not responsible for websites (or their content) that are not owned by the publisher.

The Hachette Speakers Bureau provides a wide range of authors for speaking events. To find out more, go to www.hachettespeakersbureau.com or call (866) 376-6591.

Library of Congress Cataloging-in-Publication Data has been applied for.

ISBNs: 978-1-5387-3480-3 (hardcover), 978-1-5387-3481-0 (ebook)

Printed in the United States of America

LSC-C

Printing 3, 2021

For my family

Contents

Introduction

Armed Secret Service agents guarded the secret hideaway inside the U.S. Capitol, where the vice president sheltered with his wife and eldest daughter. A swarm of rioters just outside the room had smashed windows and busted through doors, and now prowled across the waxed sandstone floors beneath the iconic cast-iron dome. It was January 6, 2021, and the symbolic heart of the world's longest-standing democracy was under siege for the first time since the War of 1812. But instead of British troops in red coats, the insurrection was led by an American mob of President Donald Trump's supporters— and they wanted his running mate's head.

Vice President Mike Pence's offense: He had dared to defy Trump's order to violate the U.S. Constitution in an attempt to overturn the results of the November election. The frenzied crowd had already overrun the Capitol Police and the Metropolitan Police Department. Now, Pence's life—and the safety of just about everyone else in the Capitol that day—rested in the hands of the National Guard.

"I want them down here—and I want them down here now," Pence firmly instructed during a private phone call with the nation's top military and defense officials gathered at the Pentagon.

As this book chronicles, the storming of the Capitol was the culmination of one of the nation's most intense and unnerving election cycles, one that tested the foundation of our democratic principles. I initially set out to write a traditional campaign book that would tell the story of how Trump marketed himself to a second term, or how the same traits that lifted him to victory in 2016 imperiled his reelection just four years later. I envisioned this as a deep look at cutting-edge electioneering techniques heading into the quarter mark of the twenty-first century. I anticipated explaining what those tactics told us about the cultural and socioeconomic dynamics that coursed through our politics. I wanted to document the political phenomenon of the Trump mega-rally—from the behind-the-scenes staging to the campaign's collection of personal data from attendees to the motivations of the president's supporters who waited for days outside arenas until he arrived.

But like nearly everything with Trump, there was nothing traditional about this campaign—and the story that revealed itself was far more chaotic and complicated. Without warning, a once-in-a-century pandemic forced millions of Americans to stop commuting to work, log into Zoom, and stay away from shops, restaurants, and even extended family members to avoid a mysterious and uncharted contagion. The electoral kinetics shifted just as quickly and significantly. Trump's reelection bid suddenly hinged more on his response from inside the White House to a complex global health crisis than on how his top political operatives would promote his past successes from campaign headquarters across the Potomac River. My expectations changed, too. Instead of spending the year on the campaign trail with the candidate I'd covered for five years, attending rallies produced by members of his team I'd known for just as long, I only occasionally left my house once pandemic lockdowns started in March 2020.

The result is the story of the final year of Trump's presidency, which opens with his historic first impeachment in December 2019 and extends just beyond his unprecedented second impeachment fourteen months later. It's informed by hundreds of hours of interviews with more than 150 members of Trump's White House, Cabinet, and campaign, as well as friends and outside advisers—and also by my own occasional run-ins, phone calls, and one-on-one interviews with Trump. I traveled to Florida twice after the election, where Trump welcomed me to his Mar-a-Lago resort for a pair of lengthy discussions about the campaign.

Together these accounts reveal the calculations behind the administration's response to the coronavirus pandemic; explain why top lieutenants in Trump World remained in a constant revolving door between exile and repatriation; offer inside-the-room details of the intense battles between Trump and his military advisers over whether to unleash soldiers on civil rights protests in the streets of American cities; and show how Trump spent more than twice as much money on a losing campaign as he had on a winning one. I also spent time with an eclectic group of Trump superfans who regularly slept outside for days to secure their place in the front row of his mega-rallies, and whose stories of how Trump changed their lives help explain his enduring appeal to his base.

The heart of the story, of course, is President Trump himself, whom I covered for the *Wall Street Journal* during the 2016 election, during all four years at the White House, and during the 2020 campaign. As part of my job for the newspaper, I've interviewed Trump inside his corporate office in Trump Tower, on *Air Force One*, and one-on-one in the Oval Office. Trump has praised my wavy hair as being worthy of a job in his administration. And he has complained about my reporting to my elementary-school-age daughter.

Many of my Trump World sources shared their firsthand accounts, internal campaign documents, text messages, emails, and calendars to help reconstruct critical moments during the campaign. Some spoke for the opportunity to share what they had witnessed from their front-row seat to history. Others spoke for protective purposes, concerned that if they didn't tell their story, someone else would. And others still spoke for cathartic and almost therapeutic reasons, eager to try to process the surreal whirlwind through which they had just lived. Many spoke only on the condition of deep background, an agreement that meant I could share their stories without direct attribution.

I agreed to those conditions because my motivation to write this book was the same that compelled many of my sources to speak with me. I have had a remarkable opportunity to watch an astonishing chapter of our history unfurl, and I've been humbled by the chance I've had to speak regularly with the people who shaped it—and were shaped by it. I hope this book adds to our understanding of the people and events that have forever impacted our lives.

—*Michael C. Bender, May 2021*

November 9, 2016

"So, there's good news and bad news," said Mike Biundo, a New Hampshire–based Republican strategist for Donald J. Trump, the day Trump won the 2016 campaign.

"Oh yeah?" Trump pollster Tony Fabrizio asked. "What's that, Mike?"

"The good news is we won," Biundo said. "The bad news is these stupid fuckers are going to think this is the way you win a presidential election."

Prologue

════════════

"I don't think we've ever had an empty seat."
—*Merry Christmas rally, Battle Creek, Michigan,*
December 18, 2019

Saundra Kiczenski packed her Honda Accord before dawn on one of the final days of 2019 and drove five hours from her home in the Upper Peninsula of Michigan, across the Mackinac Bridge, and south along the seam of interstate asphalt stitched down the middle of the giant geological mitten tugged over the Lower Peninsula. She arrived in Battle Creek at 1:00 p.m., two and a half days early for her thirty-first Trump rally.

The fifty-six-year-old worker in the Walmart patio and garden department preferred the familiar comfort of a Wawa or Sheetz convenience store for a quick bite to eat on the road. She wore her straight brown hair in bangs, and dressed in shirts and accessories adorned with Trump's face. Saundra was also one of the founding members of the "Front Row Joes," a group of more than 1,500 Trump diehards who routinely traveled to see the president perform and were almost always among the first few people in line for a rally. Many had attended at least ten Trump rallies by his fourth year in office—several had notched more than fifty.

Trump rallies formed the core of one of the most steadfast political movements in modern American political history, a dynamic that reordered the Republican Party. The president held nearly five rallies a week during his 2016 campaign and averaged one every ten days even after he was sworn in. That perpetual tour attracted a coterie of political pilgrims who traveled across the country and camped outside arenas for days at a time for the opportunity to stand in the front row and, for ninety blissfully frenzied minutes, cheer on the man they credited with changing the country and, in many cases, their own lives.

"You go to the rallies, and he basically tells you that you don't have to put up with 'the swamp' and those kinds of people," Saundra told me, standing outside a rally during Trump's third year in office. "Because of him, I decided not to pay for Obamacare, not pay the fine. And what happened? Nothing. Before, the quiet me would have paid the fine. But Donald Trump told me that we have a voice, and now I stand up for myself."

Saundra and her fellow Front Row Joes described, in different ways, a euphoric flow of emotions between themselves and the president, a sort of adrenaline-fueled, psychic cleansing that followed ninety minutes of chanting and cheering with 15,000 other like-minded Trump junkies. Saundra compared the energy inside a rally to the feelings she had as a teenage girl in 1980 watching the U.S. hockey team beat the Soviet Union, a victory still remembered as the "Miracle on Ice."

"The whole place is erupting, everyone is screaming, and your heart is beating like, just, oh my God," Saundra said. "It's like nothing I've experienced in my lifetime."

After her first rally in 2015, she stopped at a fast-food joint for dinner. Standing in line, she looked up at the wall-mounted television, amazed to see the back of her head on cable news clips from the event that had just ended. She was hooked.

———

Like Saundra, Trump's relentless rallygoers were almost exclusively white. Many were recently retired and had time on their hands and little to tie them to home. A handful never had children. Others were estranged from their families. Several lived paycheck-to-paycheck yet always offered strangers a cold beverage, a prepacked sandwich, or their last cigarette.

Cynthia Barten, who lived in Missouri, relied on disability payments. Her husband, Ken Barten, cut lawns. Jon French sold secondhand items in Kentucky. Kevin Steele quit his job and financed his travels to Trump rallies with a $120,000 family inheritance. To help pay for her trips, Saundra logged into Wonolo or other mobile phone apps to find odd jobs washing dishes or clearing warehouses in whatever town to which she'd followed Trump's traveling circus.

The group included Trump aficionados who had spent decades keeping tabs on his history of political flirtations, tabloid melodrama, and star turns on reality television. But a surprising number had also voted for Barack Obama at least once, attracted to the Democrat's charisma and fed up with Republicans over foreign adventurism and the growing national debt.

Rally regulars stayed connected through Facebook and text messages, pinging one another to see who was attending the next event, who could carpool, and who wanted to split a hotel room. Two of them had already married and divorced by Trump's second year in office.

Even I earned honorary Joe status after attending more than fifty rallies while working for the *Wall Street Journal*. Members of the group would tell me when they heard about the next rally location, almost always before the media had reported the news. Saundra once called me to ask if I'd go half-sies on a hotel room in the Hamptons. She had scraped together $2,800 for a Trump fundraiser ticket but didn't have enough left for lodging. For numerous reasons—work-related ethical issues and likely objections on the marital front—I declined.

Saundra's life had become bigger with Trump. She met new people like Ben Hirschmann, a Michigan legislative aide who posted on Facebook anytime he had an open seat in his car on the way to a Trump rally. She met Brendan Gutenschwager and flew with him to Hong Kong, where they spent twenty-four hours waving their red, white, and blue Trump flags during the protests over China's extradition laws. She occasionally overnighted about an hour outside of Detroit with Judy Chiodo, a fellow Trump rally-trotter, rather than drive all the way home to Sault Ste. Marie.

In Battle Creek, Saundra waited for Judy at Fazoli's, a restaurant chain founded by the Long John Silver's owners and known for its Submarinos sandwiches and Meatball da Vinci. When they arrived at the rally after lunch, they spent their afternoon huddled in Saundra's car near the arena's entrance. It was too soon to get in line, but never too early to monitor for other early birds. Saundra was scrupulous about her campaign queueing.

"We'll just be quiet, and we'll keep an eye on the place," Saundra explained to Judy, who had been to just two rallies before Battle Creek.

As twilight enveloped the small-town streets, they pulled into a nearby parking lot to leave their cars overnight. Snow started falling by the time they returned to the parking lot a few hours later. Undeterred, they unrolled their sleeping bags in their backseats and tried to sleep.

By 6:00 a.m., Saundra was shivering and awake and went for hot chocolate. And by 9:00 a.m., still more than thirty-six hours before Trump would set foot onstage, she and Judy set down lawn chairs on the sidewalk. First in line again! Campaign staffers moved the line into a parking garage connected to the arena, and by that evening, as snow fell steadily along with the thermometer, the gang was all there. Brendan arrived and brought friends. Rick Frazier drove in from Ohio. Richard Snowden called to say he'd be late—typical Richard!—and blamed a snowstorm in Buffalo for his delay. They took turns thawing a block away at Griffin Grill & Pub while the others stayed behind and saved the spots in line. Locals passed out hand warmers, hot soup, and Little Caesars pizza. Saundra was delighted to be around friends and nostalgic for the 2016 campaign when so many of them had first met. That year marked the political awakening for her and other Front Row Joes. They had been among the first Americans to identify the resonance of Trump's political appeal and reveled in the victory for years, recounting the blow-by-blow of that triumphant November evening—right along with Trump—at nearly every rally that followed.

Temperatures dipped below freezing the night before the Battle Creek rally, but the soothing nostalgia helped insulate Saundra as she unrolled her sleeping bag right there at the front of the line on the cement of the open-air parking garage. Others pitched tents. Some switched on their space heaters. A few Front Row Joes recalled how Michigan was the first Trump rally site after Special Counsel Robert S. Mueller III released his report into Russian election interference just nine months earlier.

But Battle Creek was going to be bigger. Trump was getting impeached. And it was about to happen right onstage.

1

Battle Creek

"Are they really going to impeach me?"
—*Conversation with staff, White House, December 18, 2019*

Several hours after Saundra and her friends had taken their places in the front row, President Trump was pacing backstage. Back in Washington, Democrats on the floor of the U.S. House of Representatives were preparing to saddle Trump with the historic and profoundly unpleasant epithet of an impeached president—what for months Trump could only bring himself to utter as "the I-word." But in the Midwestern arena 600 miles from the U.S. Capitol, behind the twenty-foot-tall black velvet curtains and inside a large private room with matte gray walls and a drop ceiling of textured square tiles, the president and Trump World's top lieutenants plotted the path forward. Election Day was less than eleven months away, and his campaign team knew impeachment had some political upside. The first step was to leverage the fortuitous timing of his "Merry Christmas" rally by producing a made-for-TV moment that would steal some of the spotlight from Democrats.

After the House scheduled its impeachment vote for the night of the rally, the plan had been for Trump to burst onto the stage in a defiant display of showmanship, emerging from backstage through a redbrick fireplace—like a MAGA Santa who had come to inspire deplorable boys and girls and put coal in the stockings of every Democrat and disloyal Republican. But once again, Congress was ruining everything. House lawmakers were still yapping, the vote was running late, and it was already a half-hour past the rally's 7:00 p.m. scheduled start.

Inside the hold room, Trump, in his standard blue suit and red tie, grew impatient and snapped about the relatively small size of the Kellogg Arena. With just 6,200 seats, the venue was about half the size of his typical rally.

Michael Glassner, who oversaw production of Trump's mega-rallies as the campaign's chief operating officer, defended the choice as data-driven and strategic. Ronna McDaniel, the head of the Republican National Committee and a former Michigan Republican chairwoman, chimed in that she had warned everyone that the arena was too small. Brad Parscale, the campaign manager, reassured Trump that impeachment was going to help him win reelection. On the other side of the room, White House deputy chief of staff Dan Scavino, the president's longtime aide and social media adviser, scrolled through his phone. Stephen Miller, the White House's senior policy adviser, huddled with Jared Kushner, the president's son-in-law and senior adviser, about how to respond to the impeachment vote.

Trump turned his attention back to the television tuned to Fox News. He'd been in contact with House Republican leader Kevin McCarthy and didn't want to start the rally until the California lawmaker had delivered his party's final speech before the vote. But Trump also wanted to avoid walking out onstage too close to 8:00 p.m., when Fox News host Tucker Carlson was unlikely to cut away from the opening monologue of his show to feature Trump's rally.

He leaned toward Vice President Mike Pence, who stood nearby waiting for the go-ahead to introduce the president. They discussed their options, and finally Trump decided he'd waited long enough.

"Fuck it," he said. "It's going to happen while I'm up there. We're going."

Pence headed to the stage, and Trump pointed a finger at Hogan Gidley, a White House press assistant. He instructed Gidley to make a sign with the final vote and show it to him while he was onstage. Then Trump immediately reconsidered his plan and told Gidley to have Kayleigh McEnany bring him the results. It was a campaign event and McEnany was the campaign's press secretary. Plus, she was wearing a bright orange dress that Trump knew he would be sure to spot from the stage.

At 8:03 p.m., just minutes after McCarthy had finished his speech on the House floor back in Washington, Scavino introduced Trump from the backstage microphone wired into the arena's loudspeakers.

"Ladies and gentlemen, please welcome the forty-fifth president of the United States, Donald J. Trump!"

Lee Greenwood's patriotic anthem "God Bless the USA" boomed through the public address system as Trump waited a beat and then made his grand entrance, smiling and clapping his way through the mock fireplace.* The crowd erupted in applause and cheers so loud that the cresting roar startled several staffers backstage. Trump basked in the moment. He slowly shuffled along the catwalk, and only stopped clapping long enough to pump his fist or point into the crowd as Greenwood's crooning filled the room. Finally, he reached the lectern, flanked on each side by Christmas trees adorned with glossy gold ball ornaments and crowned with a red "Keep America Great" cap.

"It does not feel like we are being impeached," Trump told his devoted followers. "We did nothing wrong."

<hr>

One of Trump's first actions as president—just hours after he was inaugurated on January 20, 2017—was to file paperwork for his reelection. After just thirteen months in office, he hired Brad to manage the campaign. No president had announced a reelection bid that early. That meant Trump never really stopped campaigning. It allowed him to perpetually raise money for his political operation and schedule a rally whenever he needed an injection of adulation or to divert attention from controversy in Washington. Jared, Brad, and Ronna struck a deal that braided the campaign and the White House with RNC operations and enabled them to share resources, including staff and office space. Trump had held his ceremonial campaign kickoff at a rally on June 18, 2019, in Orlando, an event that was indistinguishable from every

---

* Trump's "Merry Christmas Rally" in 2018 included a mini-chimney enhanced with fake snow, which fluttered down from the rafters. The Secret Service had monitored flake production to watch for poison because, as chance would have it, some fake snow landed in the president's mouth. Safety was checked, but not the taste. Trump was so repulsed that snow machines were forever banned.

other rally he'd had: nursing grievances, reliving the glory from the 2016 campaign, and never bothering to outline what a second term might entail.

It was a month after that Orlando rally, on July 25, when Trump picked up the phone and repeatedly pressured Ukrainian president Volodymyr Zelensky to help smear his political rivals. Trump wanted Zelensky to spread misinformation about Russian attempts to influence the 2016 election and investigate Joe Biden, the former Democratic vice president who had opened his campaign to unseat Trump just three months earlier. That phone call—paired with Trump's attempt to force Zelensky's hand by blocking $400 million in military aid for Kyiv—sparked the impeachment inquiry in late September.

The impeachment inquiry, in many ways, marked the actual start of the campaign. It provided purpose and mission to Trump World and offered a desperately needed reason for a fractured Republican Party to unite around the president. Trump always intended to treat his reelection in 2020 as a continuation of his campaign in 2016, even though an incumbent running as a change agent was a tricky feat to pull off. The impeachment allowed the president once again to cast himself as a victim and Washington outsider.

But the prospect of impeachment left him deeply rattled.

═══════

Whenever Trump thought about impeachment—which was often—he would swirl through a narrow range of unhappy emotions: frustration over his helplessness to derail the proceedings in the House; anger that his first three years as president had been almost entirely overshadowed by the Russian election meddling investigation and now eclipsed by impeachment; and bewilderment that his "perfect phone call" with Ukraine had backfired so resoundingly. He said he simply wanted the newly elected Ukrainian president to investigate the political corruption of Joe Biden and his son, Hunter Biden. He never explicitly said it was about the presidential campaign. He constantly peppered aides with questions about whether House Democrats would actually go through with the impeachment proceedings.

"Are they really going to impeach me?" he asked an aide on the morning of the impeachment vote.

If his staff answered affirmatively—and usually that was only Mick

Mulvaney, who was the third White House chief of staff by the third year of the presidency—Trump would unspool a furious diatribe complaining that he was always mistreated.

"They've got nothing on me!" he would complain.

Trump's political team, however, recognized the opportunity impeachment provided and tried to contain the emotional fallout from Trump and his family.

"This is terrible," Eric Trump, the president's middle child, complained during a lunch at the family hotel in Washington with several members of Trump World. "They're going to impeach my father."

"If they impeach the president, it will be awful and it will be a stain on his record," said Richard Walters, the Republican National Committee chief of staff. "But it will nearly guarantee he gets reelected."

When Democratic House Speaker Nancy Pelosi finally stood behind her mahogany lectern and announced opening a formal impeachment investigation into Trump on the evening of September 24, 2019, electricity seemed to pulse through campaign headquarters.

"The president must be held accountable," Pelosi said in the hall outside her third-floor Capitol office. "No one is above the law."

Campaign staffers had congregated around the multiple flat-screen TVs mounted on the dark gray walls behind the communication team's cubicles. When Pelosi finished her speech, Brad turned to Tim Murtaugh, the campaign's communication director. Murtaugh, a slim and serious political veteran, shook his head in disbelief as he watched the screen.

"Okay," Brad said. "Go."

Murtaugh's team of about a dozen aides—his staff would ultimately grow to more than 100—leaped to action. They blasted out a video, prepped weeks earlier, that mocked the Democrats' obsession with impeachment. A small army of Trump World surrogates and social media influencers were armed with talking points that had been prepared for days. Brad put his name on an official statement from the campaign that predicted Pelosi's move would only encourage and energize Trump's supporters and lead to a landslide victory in 2020.

Gary Coby, the campaign's digital director, pushed his team's already aggressive fundraising operation. Their first email after Pelosi's announcement played off a promise from Trump earlier in the day to declassify a rough transcript of his phone call with Zelensky. The email subject line was "Call Transcript" and included a paperclip emoji that suggested an attachment awaited inside. But the only thing included in the email was a link to a donation page.

From Howard Dean to Ron Paul to Barack Obama, online fundraising has always been driven by supporters' passion and small-dollar donations. High-dollar, in-person fundraisers, meanwhile, tended to have a more transactional nature as deep-pocketed donors and corporate executives treated contributions as business decisions. And if emotion was the propellant of online fundraising, impeachment proved to be high-octane fuel for Trump's fiercely loyal tribe that viewed any criticism of him in deeply personal terms. In the first three hours after the House investigation was announced, the campaign raised $1 million. Within twenty-four hours, the number ballooned to $5 million. Over the final three months of 2019, the Trump team's impeachment-themed fundraising appeals helped collect nearly $155 million, one-third of their fundraising haul for the year.

When it came to impeachment strategy, the biggest wild card was Trump himself, and whether he could avoid the self-inflicted wounds that would repel potential allies in Congress. Trump would never win over the Democratic majority in the House, but his team could find a political victory in the defeat by keeping the 196 Republicans unified in opposition. It wouldn't save Trump from impeachment. But losing any Republicans in the House threatened to impede momentum for the White House heading into a Senate trial and undermine Trump's case with voters that the prosecution was a partisan political charade. It was no easy task. More than two dozen House Republicans were retiring in 2020, which meant they couldn't be strong-armed with the kind of political tools that Republican leadership would typically deploy: campaign cash, threats of primary challengers, or a little good old-fashioned online Twitter bullying from the wicked thumbs of @realdonaldtrump.* Several outgoing lawmakers in the House, including Will Hurd of Texas

---

* The fear of getting blasted by Trump on Twitter, and the repercussions from MAGAland that would follow, cannot be overstated.

and Francis Rooney of Florida, had made their disapproval of Trump well known.

Still, plenty of high-ranking officials in Trump World were privately horrified at what Trump had said on that call with Zelensky. They could convince themselves that it wasn't impeachable, but few could justify how Trump had so casually put so much at risk over such a long-shot scheme to discredit Biden. Inside campaign headquarters in September, Brad and his team tried to puzzle together the logic of what seemed to be a completely separate political operation being run out of the West Wing that had encouraged Trump to bring up Biden with Zelensky. The campaign's instinct was to blame the people around the president. And the name that kept coming up was Rudy Giuliani, the former New York mayor with a decades-long relationship with Trump, who was now employed as his attorney.

"This is crazy shit," Justin Clark, the campaign's top attorney, griped about Giuliani's ploy.

But politically, the reelection team couldn't believe their good luck. Two months of Democratic hearings and witness testimony—from members of Trump's own administration—had done nothing to sway public opinion. Even Trump's reliably self-destructive behavior hadn't hurt. But the president wasn't making it easy.

He had broken decades of international precedent when he released a rough transcript of his call with Zelensky the day after Pelosi announced the impeachment inquiry. His West Wing was divided over the decision, and he hadn't even bothered to check with Brad. But Trump pushed ahead, certain that the transcript would convince Democrats to call off the impeachment proceedings. It was the kind of grand, inside-Washington political miscalculation that was proving to be a major weakness of the outsider president. The content of the conversation only emboldened his rivals.

In October, the president publicly called on another foreign power (China) to investigate the Bidens, impeachment proceedings for members of Congress (no such thing), and refused to comply with a single subpoena from the coequal branch of government just a couple of miles down Pennsylvania Avenue (sparking concerns of a constitutional crisis).

In mid-October, Mulvaney openly admitted that Trump wanted to block military aid for Ukraine in exchange for political investigations into his political rivals.

"That's why we held up the money," Mulvaney said in a disastrous news conference.

The White House immediately tried to walk back Mulvaney's candor.* But none of the gaffes seemed to matter.

Just 49 percent of Americans said they thought Trump should be impeached, according to a *Wall Street Journal*/NBC News poll taken after Mulvaney's stunning news conference confessional. Two months later, the same survey showed 48 percent supported the move.

As the inquiry unfolded, Brad hadn't been able to contain his enthusiasm over the thought of a split-screen image on the cable networks featuring, on one side, out-of-touch Washington symbolized by the typical and somewhat tedious C-SPAN shot of lawmakers milling about on the House floor, while, on the other half of the screen, Trump absorbed the adoration from the cheering arena crowd that surrounded him.

Brad's anticipation of the potential political boost from impeachment constantly irritated Trump. But the eager campaign manager was in charge of his first political race, and Trump rallies weren't the sideshow—they were the entire campaign. As chance would have it, Trump was standing onstage the very night of the impeachment vote.

There was no better place for Trump to absorb the impact from the crushing blow over which he'd spent months agonizing than right there in the center of his beloved rally stage. Just him, his pulpit, and the gooseneck-thin microphone he'd reflexively grab at the start of every speech and yank back and forth a few times, as if testing its ability to withstand the flurry of grievances, gossip, putdowns, pranks, understatements, oversimplifications, misrepresentations, deceptions, attacks, counterattacks, self-affirmations, reassurances, promises, hopes, and dreams that he was about to pour into it.

---

* The night before Mulvaney's stunning news conference confessional, he was at dinner in Washington where he boasted to a group of congressmen that he'd finally convinced Trump to let him hold a news conference. Tune in tomorrow, Mulvaney told them, and watch him set the record straight on this whole impeachment nonsense.

Brad was always on the lookout for signs in the stars and listening for what the universe might be whispering. The House's decision to schedule the vote on the night of a campaign rally had to be more than a mere coincidence.

"A happy coincidence," Glassner told him.

Trump was still resisting his fate on the morning of his impeachment when he flipped on *Fox & Friends* and launched his first tweet of the day, inspired by Brian Kilmeade, one of the anchors of his favorite breakfast program. Kilmeade had just lamented that Democrats would impeach Trump over something so trivial.

"Well said, Brian!" Trump typed into his phone.

Twenty-three minutes later, he posted another.

"Can you believe that I will be impeached today by the Radical Left, Do Nothing Democrats, AND I DID NOTHING WRONG!"

And then another.

"A terrible thing. Read the Transcripts. This should never happen to another President again. Say a PRAYER!"

Trump posted forty-three more tweets over the first three hours that morning. As House lawmakers opened the formal debate at 9:00 a.m., Trump was on Twitter interacting with Fox personalities, praising conservative media columnists, and attacking his critics.

When Trump hadn't emerged from behind closed doors by lunchtime, White House reporters started asking what he was doing on that historic day.

"The president will be working all day," said Stephanie Grisham, the sixth of seven White House communications directors during Trump's four years. "He will be briefed by staff throughout that day and could catch some of the proceedings between meetings."

Nine minutes after the statement went out, Trump was back on Twitter.

"SUCH ATROCIOUS LIES BY THE RADICAL LEFT, DO NOTHING DEMOCRATS. THIS IS AN ASSAULT ON AMERICA, AND AN ASSAULT ON THE REPUBLICAN PARTY!!!!"

As Trump prepared to leave the White House for Battle Creek that afternoon, he phoned Tony Sayegh, a communications adviser who was walking out of the White House, for some last-minute feedback on what he'd be saying.

Trump would remain unrepentant. That was never in doubt. But if his vote-counters were right, and House Republicans remained unified in their opposition, he would celebrate that as a win for the party and his movement and a sign of momentum heading into the Senate trial. He just needed to wait for the vote.

The only two other presidents impeached were both at the White House when House lawmakers affixed that political stigma to their permanent record.* Trump, once again, would do things a little differently. He was going to rally the base.

What unfolded over the 121 minutes onstage in Battle Creek would stand as not only the longest rally speech of his career but also one of the strangest. Trump was unapologetic, divisive, and almost immediately off-script. The prepared remarks totaled nine pages for the teleprompter and followed a Trump rally speech's usual construction. They opened with some comments on the news of the day at the very top, designed to catch the ears of cable news anchors and earn some free airtime. At the top of page three, he would mention the list of local Republicans in the audience, whom Trump would usually bring onstage. But Trump started ad-libbing so quickly, the teleprompter

---

* In 1868, President Andrew Johnson relied on messengers scurrying along the Belgian blocks that lined Pennsylvania Avenue to keep him apprised of the impeachment vote. In 1998, President Clinton made a statement in the Rose Garden within minutes of the vote. He apologized, vowed to win back the country's trust, and paraphrased Ben Franklin as he commended his accusers for helping him understand his own faults.

sat frozen. It was more than an hour before Trump mentioned the local Republicans.

Nothing was off-limits for Trump. He attacked the living as well as the dead. He recalled how Senate Democratic leader Chuck Schumer "used to kiss my ass." He called a female protester a slob and encouraged security to rough her up. He was so aggressive that he earned a few groans from the Midwestern crowd when he suggested that John Dingell, a Democratic congressman from Michigan who'd died ten months earlier, had gone to hell.

He condemned low-flow toilets and energy-efficient light bulbs.

He said that his thirteen-year-old son, Barron, could draw bigger crowds than Democratic Senator Elizabeth Warren—ignoring public complaints just days earlier from his wife, First Lady Melania Trump, about dragging her son into politics.

Backstage, Pence watched on the television tuned to Fox News as the votes were tallied back in Washington. Marc Short, his staff chief, and Ronna were by his side. Stephen Miller and his wife, Katie Miller, watched, too. David Bossie, the 2016 deputy campaign manager, paced.

The moment felt surreal for Murtaugh, the campaign's communications director: On one side of the curtain, he stood along with the vice president watching the president of the United States being impeached on national television, while the president himself was just on the other side of the curtain whipping the crowd into a state of frenzy.

Hell yeah, Murtaugh thought, anticipating what the moment would mean politically for Trump.

Pence betrayed no emotion when the House lawmakers voted to impeach Trump. The staff around him scrambled to relay the message to Trump.

Gidley had taken his assignment from Trump exceptionally seriously. He fashioned himself as something of a perfectionist in these arts-and-crafts projects. He had a fanboy's crush on his boss, and he wanted the president to be pleased with the presentation.

Gidley told the team backstage that the sign had to be clear enough for Trump to read from the stage. But it also had to be ready for a prime-time TV audience, just in case Trump wanted to hold up his handiwork for the crowd.

Gidley found some white corrugated plastic board but dismissed the markers that Nick Luna, Trump's body man, offered. No, Gidley knew the marker lines wouldn't be thick enough for Trump to see from that distance. He remembered a printer backstage.

I can print this in huge black letters, Gidley thought.

Stephen Miller's assistant showed him how to use the printer. Gidley went to work on a series of practice runs with the printed-out numbers as Grisham and White House staff secretary Derek Lyons looked on.

Should he put a hyphen between the vote counts? Yes, he should.

Should the board be vertical or horizontal? Horizontal looked better.

How about stacking the vote totals, one on top of the other?

Hmm, Gidley thought.

He went back and forth on this decision. He finally decided to keep the vote counts on the same line. Gidley knew that's what the president would want.

When the vote was announced, Gidley printed out the final numbers and went to work on the board. A small group of White House and campaign staffers gathered around. Gidley set to work, Scotch-taping his black block letters to the whiteboard with Pence looking over his shoulder.*

Lyons offered a last-minute suggestion, but Gidley was too focused and too far along to consider it.

"Look, jackleg," Gidley snapped. "I've been working on this for like a minute. Yeah. So, you back up."

Nervous laughter rippled through the room. Gidley taped down the last number. Pence gave a nod of approval.

Onstage, Trump was still unaware of the vote. When the first impeachment article was approved, he was riffing about selling nuclear submarines to other countries and creating the Space Force.

As the second impeachment article passed, the president mocked Democratic presidential candidate Pete Buttigieg for his "unpronounceable name."

Trump had just referred to Adam Schiff, the California Democrat in charge of the House Intelligence Committee, as a pathological liar when a

---

* Gidley later had Trump autograph the sign for him on the flight back to Washington.

smiling McEnany carried the board into the buffer area, the few feet of space created by the bike racks that separated the crowd from the stage.

"What the hell do I have to do with Russia?" Trump said. "But this guy gets up…Oh, I think we have a vote coming in. So, we got every single Republican voted for us. Whoa. Wow. Wow."

He thanked McEnany—but referred to her three times as "Haley" instead of "Kayleigh"—and described the outcome not as a devastating loss but as a political victory for his party.

"The Republican Party has never been so affronted," Trump continued. "But they've never been so united as they are right there, ever. Never. And I know the senators, and they're great guys and women, too. We have some great women. We have great guys and great people. They love this country. They're going to do the right thing."

Impeachment seemed to energize Trump, and he performed for another hour despite beads of sweat dripping down his face.

At the end, he lingered for several minutes after the opening bars of "You Can't Always Get What You Want," the Rolling Stones' 1969 tune that usually played him off. He clapped and pointed into various parts of the crowd as he paced the stage. He looked into the distance and pumped his fist. He made eye contact with the front row and smiled. He waved as he ambled along the catwalk.

Just before he disappeared behind the backstage curtain hung from inside the giant cardboard fireplace, Trump pointed high into the stands and mouthed the words "Thank you."

⸻

For the Front Row Joes, the rally had delivered. The group's only miscalculation was the extra layers of clothes that had insulated them from the wintery weather outside made an already toasty arena unbearably hot once they were finally inside. The change in temperature—and Trump's late start—took its toll. The group sweated and stripped layers. Judy fell ill and had to bail about forty-five minutes early to check into the Baymont Inn for a decent night's sleep.

The gang met up the following morning for breakfast at Denny's and recounted the highlights from the previous night: How the historic rally had been the first in ages that Saundra and Brandon had attended together, the unusually high number of local news interviews they'd given from the front of the line, and, of course, the impeachment vote—the latest scam!

Saundra unfurled the local paper.

"Hey, Judy," she said. "Here's a picture of you and me in line."

Saundra hit the road by 9:00 a.m., drove straight to Walmart, and punched in just in time for her 2:00 p.m. shift.

2

The Forty-Year Itch

"Why would I want to run? That's not a bad question. When I look at people who have become president, they seem to go out not looking as good as they did going in."

—*Newspaper interview, September 14, 1999*

Donald Trump's first adrenaline rush from the psychological combat of presidential politics pulsed through his veins in 1980 during Ronald Reagan's third bid for the White House, when the former California governor was trying to unseat President Carter. By that time, the thirty-four-year-old Trump had built the sixty-eight-story Trump Tower—replete with a six-story atrium and home to some of the world's top luxury stores. He brought armed bodyguards into meetings with investment bankers and wore maroon suits and matching loafers. He had started deploying the nom de guerre John Barron, posing as his own public relations agent in phone calls with reporters from New York newspapers and tabloids.*

So when Roy Cohn, the preeminent Republican fixer in New York City,

---

* John Barron's first appearance, incidentally, was an attempt to stall a *New York Times* story about why he'd razed a Midtown Manhattan building to make way for Trump Tower. Trump had jackhammered two art deco relief sculptures instead of donating them to the Metropolitan Museum of Art, which he had promised to do after the museum expressed interest in the pieces.

suggested that Reagan's team reach out to the brash builder from the outer boroughs, little additional explanation was required.

"I've heard of him," said a towheaded, twenty-eight-year-old Reagan operative named Roger Stone.

Trump and Stone immediately hit it off. Both were ambitious young strivers resentful of the ruling class whose approval they craved and whose extravagances they were eager to afford. Each viewed being boring as a sin worse than being wrong. They shared an instinct to attack when mere mortals might have been inclined to apologize.

Stone had already established his reputation as a minister of the political dark arts by the time he met Trump. His first dirty trick had been in elementary school, when he misled his fellow pupils by suggesting that John F. Kennedy's opponent supported school on Sundays. He turned to conservatism before he was a teenager and dropped out of college to campaign for Richard Nixon. He donated to Nixon's primary rival in the name of the Young Socialist Alliance—and then sent the receipt to the *Manchester Union Leader*. When the Watergate hearings revealed Stone's role in an attempt to infiltrate the campaign of George McGovern, Nixon's 1972 rival, it cost him his job on U.S. senator Robert Dole's staff.

Stone was setting up a Washington-based consulting firm with Paul Manafort and Charlie Black, two fellow Republican lobbyists, when he recruited Trump and his father, Fred Trump, to raise money for Reagan. The Trumps hit up their subcontractors and quickly raised $100,000, an impressive amount in 1980 for a first-time fundraiser. But to Trump, the contributions were no gift. He now owned a piece of the campaign. He followed the ups and downs like a day trader monitoring his stock portfolio. He checked in incessantly with Stone.

"What's wrong with Carter?" Trump would ask. "Why's he doing this to you?"

When Reagan dethroned Carter, the Black, Manafort & Stone firm expanded and the Trump Organization was included among the group's new clients. The firm eased regulations for Trump's casinos and expedited an environmental permitting process so he could dredge the Atlantic City harbor deep enough to accommodate the *Trump Princess*, his $30 million yacht.

The Trump-Stone business relationship veered into politics again in 1987 as the New York builder prepared to publish his first book, *The Art of the Deal*. As part of the promotional tour, Stone recruited a New Hampshire wood-worker and Republican activist named Mark Dunbar to launch a petition to draft Trump into the presidential race. Stone and the forty-one-year-old Trump flew via helicopter to Portsmouth, where a limousine waited to escort them to Yoken's, an old restaurant that hosted weekly Rotary Club meetings. Dunbar planned for about 200 people. Instead, a standing-room-only crowd of 500 greeted Trump, who spoke for the next forty minutes "with the rhythm of a Borscht Belt comedian," according to a report from the *Philadelphia Inquirer*. Trump's remarks that day would become a template for every political speech that would follow for the next three decades. He promoted his private inter-ests. He hammered away at weak American politicians who were letting foreign powers "knock the hell out of the United States." He signaled his fas-cination with strongmen with a riff about Ayatollah Ruhollah Khomeini, the Iranian leader who had supported holding hostage fifty-two Americans in the Tehran embassy and referred to the United States as the "Great Satan."

"This son of a bitch is something like nobody's ever seen," Trump said. "He makes Gorbachev look like a baby."

Twelve years later, Trump again floated the possibility of running—this time as a third-party candidate. The fledgling Reform Party offered some inherent advantages to a potential candidate like Trump. His status as a tabloid celeb-rity had turned him into a household name, which reduced the need for help from a major political party to introduce him to voters. But an established political infrastructure might not take kindly to a hostile takeover from an audacious outsider like Trump. There would be no such resistance from the embryonic Reform Party founded the previous election cycle by Ross Perot, who in 1992 unsuccessfully ran for president as an independent. Most impor-tant, Trump could spend other people's money. Perot had performed well enough as his own party's presidential candidate four years earlier that the next nominee would be eligible for $12.5 million in federal matching funds.

"You mean I don't have to spend anything?" Trump asked Stone.

Stone was never sure how serious Trump was about the race. Still, together they established an exploratory committee and assembled a policy platform that merged Stone's libertarianism with Trump's market-driven populism. Trump opposed public financing of political campaigns and abortion restrictions. He supported some gun control measures, and came out strong for the Cuba embargo, school choice, missile defense, and a national health care system "that will make Ted Kennedy blush," as Stone promised at the time.

Trump's most audacious proposal was a soak-the-rich tax plan that included a one-time 14.25 percent tax on wealth greater than $10 million, which he said would wipe out the $5.7 trillion national debt.* Trump's platform tested far better in the polls than his candidacy. But he was panicked about his own tax proposal, which would have cost him $725 million of his own money.

"There's no chance this is going to pass, right?" Trump asked Stone as they promoted the plan in a series of phone interviews with reporters. "Because it would be terrible for me."

Stone reassured him that Congress would never vote on it and reminded him of internal polling that showed how well it tested with middle-class Americans.

"It's the only reason you're credible," Stone told him. "You're fighting for the little guy."

But even with a poll-tested policy platform, Trump's standing with a naturally skeptical political press corps had been badly damaged by both his penchant for hype and hyperbole—two main ingredients in *The Art of the Deal*—and the obvious ploy twelve years earlier to disguise a promotional book tour as a possible presidential bid. The reactions to his flirtation ranged from cynicism to open hostility.

In his second TV interview after announcing his exploratory committee, *Today* show host Matt Lauer opened the conversation by immediately drilling into Trump's renown as a womanizer.†

---

* The national debt, incidentally, increased by $7.8 trillion during Trump's four years in office.

† Yes, *that* Matt Lauer.

"The reputation of Donald Trump—the man who dates a different woman every year…" Lauer began.

"I don't do that," Trump interjected. "I mean, I've been with a number of women, but it's been over a fairly long period of time. I've had great relationships with women. The fact that my women are more beautiful than Warren Beatty's women, I guess a lot of people have a problem with that."*

"You've called them your Achilles' heel," Lauer said.

"I don't call it an Achilles," Trump responded, despite having called it that just twelve days earlier in an interview with the *New York Times*.†

Trump understood something about his relationship with the American public that Lauer didn't—nor would much of the political press either then or for the next two decades. His dalliances with women, his casual relationship with the truth, his repeated business bankruptcies were the kinds of questions that would torpedo any other political candidate. But with Trump, everything was on the table—and people commended him for that seeming authenticity.

"I've been more public than the so-called public figures, and I think everything is known about me," Trump told Lauer. "If I go someplace, if I sneak into a room someplace, it's written about. So, you know, you really pretty much know what you're getting. I think you know what you're getting with me much more so than most of the politicians that you deal with."

Trump then filled the rest of the interview with the kind of unconventional ideas and comments that were catnip for TV viewers and political reporters alike. He suggested Oprah Winfrey as his possible running mate. He blasted the media as "a vile lot" save for a single exception—*New York Times* columnist Maureen Dowd. When Lauer cited a CNN poll that showed Trump would get trounced in a matchup against Texas governor George W. Bush and Vice President Al Gore, Trump, with no hint of shame, pointed out a more favorable survey from the *National Enquirer*.

---

* Trump and Beatty had spent the better part of a decade competing for space in the tabloids, and the Hollywood leading man had also just floated the possibility of his own presidential campaign.

† Trump stated in the *Times*, "I've been out with lots of beautiful women, OK? I guess we all have our Achilles' heel."

"Those are the real people," Trump said about the *Enquirer's* readers during one interview with the *New York Times*.

Stone, who was sitting across the desk, put an even finer point on it.

"That is the Trump constituency," Stone said.

While Trump resented the lampooning of his hypothetical candidacy, there were also signs in 1999 that Trump's gift for creating sensational headlines would help conceal the blemishes of his abrasive personal style and unorthodox political positions.

Sean Hannity, then in his third year of cohosting the *Hannity & Colmes* program on Fox News, was particularly fascinated. In one episode shortly after Trump launched his exploratory committee, Hannity repeatedly tried to focus a panel discussion on Trump's interview with Howard Stern a few days earlier when Trump spoke at length about his sex life with his then-girlfriend, Melania Knavs.

"I want to go back to Donald Trump," Hannity said during the show. "He did refer to his girlfriend as a potential first lady, and claimed that he mentally feels her up in public..."

"I don't understand all this shock talk," Russell Varney, the outgoing chairman of the Reform Party, told Hannity.

The panel moved on.

A few months later, Trump declined to run and blamed the unraveling of the Reform Party. The group's most prominent member, Minnesota governor Jesse "The Body" Ventura, had just quit and his exit opened a leadership battle between—as Trump described them—"a Klansman," "a neo-Nazi," and "a communist."

"This is not company I wish to keep," Trump said.

━━━

Trump tested the water a third time during the 2012 election cycle as President Obama was seeking a second term. This time, Trump was almost completely brushed off as a sideshow. But once again, there were signals of his resonance.

Trump was in his eleventh season as host of NBC's *The Apprentice* when he arrived in Washington, D.C., on February 10, 2011, to give a speech to the Conservative Political Action Conference. He walked out onstage to the same theme music as his popular reality show, the 1970s soul tune "For the Love of Money."* The crowd went bonkers—and remained in that state for the thirteen-minute speech that followed.

Trump mocked Ron Paul—the Texas Republican and two-time winner of CPAC's straw poll—as having no chance to win a presidential election. He accused China of manipulating its currency. He ripped American leaders as weak. He bragged about his wealth and the beatdowns he claimed to have put on any people or companies who stood in his way.

"I've won many wars," Trump said.

Baited by repeated rounds of applause and laughter from his audience, Trump soaked up the cheers and waded into the already debunked conspiracy and racist lie that Obama hadn't been born in America.

"Our current president came out of nowhere, came out of nowhere," Trump said. "In fact, I'll go a step further: The people who went to school with him, they never saw him—they don't know who he is."

The crowd erupted in applause.

"Nobody knew who the hell he was," Trump said as the crowd grew louder. "He's now our president!"

Birtherism had bubbled up in 2008, when multiple lawsuits challenged Obama's August 4, 1961, birth at Kapiolani Maternity and Gynecological Hospital in Hawaii. The state health director issued a statement that she had seen the original birth certificate. Both of Honolulu's major newspapers, the *Advertiser* and the *Star Bulletin*, found Obama's birth announcement in their archives. Every lawsuit was dismissed.

Behind the scenes in Trump Tower, the birther issue was too controversial even for Stone. He had warned Trump that he would be viewed as a racist.

"The established media is going to destroy you, because it's going to look like race baiting," Stone told him.

"It's not race baiting," Trump objected. "He's either eligible, or he's not eligible."

---

* Fun fact: The show glorified the dramatic cutthroat competition of capitalism, but the name of the song came from a Bible verse that warned about that very thing: "For the love of money is the root of all evil" (1 Timothy 6:10).

A month later, Trump was the proud face of the birtherism conspiracy.

"Do you think it's an important subject?" Bill O'Reilly asked Trump about Obama's birth certificate during an interview on his Fox News program on March 30.

"Maybe it says he is a Muslim," Trump said. "I don't know."

Hannity, meanwhile, ran with the issue. He used his prime-time Fox News program to discuss birtherism again on April 5, April 7, April 11, and April 13, and in an interview with Trump on April 14 and again in part two of the Trump interview on April 15.

Hannity featured Trump and the birtherism controversy on April 18, and in four blocks of his show on April 19, including his interview with Sarah Palin, the Republican vice presidential nominee in 2008. Hannity returned to it the following night on April 20 and again on April 21, April 25, and April 26. He discussed it again on April 27, the day Obama presented a copy of his long-form birth certificate at the White House.

By then, a CNN poll showed Trump tied for first in a hypothetical Republican primary, and trouncing Mitt Romney, the eventual Republican nominee. But in mid-May, NBC renewed *The Celebrity Apprentice* for another season and said it would find a new host if Trump ran for president. The following day, Trump ended the speculation and said he wouldn't run.

"Business is my greatest passion, and I'm not ready to leave the private sector," he said.

The polls that put Trump at the top of the race seemed to be long forgotten four years later when he finally announced a formal campaign for president of the United States.

The day of Trump's announcement in New York, Hannity asked Jeb Bush, the front-runner for the party's nomination at the time, about the new entry to the race.

Bush laughed.

And then apologized.

"I'm sorry," Bush said with a smile. "I shouldn't have done that."

Each of Trump's successive flirtations with a presidential campaign had taught him something different about how he would run for the White

House. In 1988, the considerable overlap between promotional marketing and politicking played to his natural skills as a showman. The exploratory bid in 2000 signaled that he could exploit the gaping maw between the fragile sensibilities of the media and the underdog pragmatism of the downtrodden to conceal his own blemished character. In the 2012 cycle, he experienced the raw animal magnetism that drew some quarters of the country—and certain corners of Fox News—to a message that the country's racial and cultural identity was under attack.

But Trump's interest was always in running. He thrilled at how the mere act of declaring himself a presidential contender would catapult him into the upper echelons of establishment respectability, and squarely into the state where he was always most comfortable: the center of attention. By the time he finally announced a formal presidential campaign on June 16, 2015, he knew he wanted to win, but he still had never given much thought to exactly how to win—let alone how to govern.

On February 1, 2016, Trump's son-in-law and eldest daughter arrived at the DoubleTree Hilton in Cedar Rapids, Iowa, for the nation's first presidential nominating contest.

They looked around and were appalled.

Trump was one of a dozen major candidates seeking the Republican nomination, and all the other candidates seemed to have hordes of volunteers in color-coordinated shirts standing behind tables with piles of literature about their candidate. The Trump campaign had nothing.

Jared and Ivanka, who was seven months pregnant with her third child, picked up a folding table, carried it across the room, and placed it in the middle of the caucus site. As Iowans approached and asked about caucusing for Trump, the two New Yorkers traded blank stares. Ivanka had recorded a how-to-caucus video for the campaign a few days earlier, but she'd read the instructions from a script. She asked Jared if he knew what to do.

"I have no idea," Jared told his wife.

He pulled out his phone, opened a web browser, and typed out one letter at a time: H-o-w d-o y-o-u c-a-u-c-u-s?

Ivanka delivered an off-the-cuff speech to the caucus goers and promised that "my father will make America great again." Then, she walked a few steps away and called him.

"There's nobody here!" she told her father. "Like, there's no swag. There's no volunteers!"

Jared was furious. Any faith he had left in Corey Lewandowski, the campaign manager, had evaporated. He cursed Chuck Laudner, the director of the Trump campaign in Iowa.

"This is a shit operation," Jared told Ivanka, and vowed to assume the burden of reorganizing his father-in-law's campaign.

But to blame Corey was to forgive Trump for his remarkable lack of preparedness.

Trump had been floating the idea of running for president off and on for thirty years by the time he finally asked Iowans for the Republican Party nomination in 2016. But he had paid little attention to the mechanics of politics, like what a caucus even was or how previous candidates had won. He wanted to win the job without really having to work for it. In an interview after he declined to run in 2000, Trump said his biggest takeaway was how hard it would be to actually campaign for president.

"The other night, I was sitting at Mar-a-Lago in Palm Beach, Florida, watching television and I was watching Gore on a freezing evening knocking on a door saying, 'Hi, I'm the vice president. I'd love your vote.' And he's freezing!" Trump said. "And I'm watching McCain, and I'm watching Bush. And they were all working so hard. And I said, 'You know, it's not such an easy life they have,' as I'm sitting, you know, in 75-degree weather."

But then he made his decision with little actual preparation. He offered Corey, at the time an obscure New Hampshire political operative, the campaign manager's job at their very first meeting, in 2015.

Trump told Corey about his fleet of helicopters and jets, and he asked what his odds were of winning the White House.

"Five percent," Corey told him.

"I think it's ten percent," Trump said. "Let's split the difference."

"Sounds good to me," Corey said.

Trump asked how much it would cost him to run in the first three states to hold presidential nominating contests: Iowa, New Hampshire, and South Carolina. Not how much it would cost to win—just to run.

Corey said that would set him back about $25 million, a fraction of what Mitt Romney had spent in 2012.

"I don't need $200 million for this campaign," he said.

Stone thought Corey was nuts. Stone didn't think anyone could win a presidential campaign by spending next to nothing on television advertising and relying solely on free media from an endless barrage of TV and newspaper interviews. Jeb Bush's political machine was building a $156 million war chest. No way, Stone told them, that anyone could punch their way out of that with one interview after another.

But Stone was wrong. The presidential contest awaiting Trump was as unpleasant as it was unpredictable.

Trump lost the Iowa caucuses, but he won the next primary contest in New Hampshire and never again relinquished front-runner status. He upended the Republican Party, scythed the base from its Washington leadership, and left conservatives at war with themselves—but won the nomination. The political veterans on his team urged him to find ways to unite the party. He would need the entire party's help, they told him, to take down Hillary Clinton, the Democratic presidential nominee who had more money, more political infrastructure, and a more traditionally relevant résumé. But Trump would never atone. Instead, he amplified the divisive intensity.

The general election was a series of dumpster fires and car crashes followed by car crashes into dumpster fires. Trump generated a perpetual news cycle of outrageous statements, vicious political brawls, and previously unthinkable policy positions. And no one could look away.

Not even a scandalous *Access Hollywood* videotape that showed Trump grotesquely bragging about sexually assaulting women proved fatal. The tape from 2005 had surfaced in the *Washington Post* just four weeks before Election Day, and a stream of Republicans immediately rescinded their endorsements or called on him to quit the race. But the next day Trump sat in his Manhattan penthouse and shrugged it off during an interview with the *Wall Street Journal*.

"I never, ever give up," he said.

And Trump won again—a victory that shocked the Trump campaign every bit as much as the rest of the country.

The 5 to 10 percent strategy that he and Corey had sketched out the previous year had worked. Voters said they were horrified by Trump's coarseness and quick temper, but they liked Clinton even less.

———

Inside the White House, Trump's surroundings had changed, but the game plan did not. Allies and critics alike, who had predicted Trump would mature into the job—and that the staggering weight of the office would mold him into a more presidential form—were repeatedly proven wrong. Instead, Trump remained in attack mode and paid little mind to repairing an American electorate riven by a brutally divisive 2016 campaign. That neglect extended to his own team, which had also been shattered by the experience.

While the new president was preoccupied with his baseless claims that widespread election fraud had cost him the popular vote, the tectonic plates in Trump World had shifted violently. He had compiled a bevy of political consultants after a seventeen-month presidential campaign in which he'd cycled through three separate leadership teams, none of which were ever completely eliminated and instead mostly just layered over. He also maintained a wide circle of familial advisers, which most often included his three eldest children plus their spouses and significant others. By the start of 2017, the team was already crawling over each other to take credit for the historic victory—they all claimed possession of a playbook that had never actually existed—and jockey for proximity to President Trump.

Jared viewed himself as one of Trump World's gatekeepers and was often a calming presence who kept Trump—and the team around him—focused on a specific task. He quickly emerged as one of the few Trump advisers whose personal buy-in could help deliver results in an otherwise chaotic West Wing.

But he was also blamed, in part, for the rocky start. He took credit around Washington for the campaign's heavy reliance on digital advertising and social media, a program whose importance he understood much better than the strategy or details that underpinned it. He isolated Corey and David

Bossie, the 2016 deputy campaign manager and longtime conservative activist, making sure neither had roles in the administration. He led the charge to
oust White House chief strategist Steve Bannon, who had been chief executive of the 2016 campaign and could articulate Trump's brand of populism
better than anyone—including even Trump himself. And he retroactively
cast himself as the de facto campaign manager, diminishing the role played
by White House counselor Kellyanne Conway, a fellow New Jersey native
who was installed as campaign manager in the final months of the race and
became the first woman in America to hold that title for a winning U.S. presidential campaign.

In fact, Jared hadn't paid much attention to his father-in-law's presidential
campaign as Trump and Corey had puzzled it together in 2015. But this time
he wanted his hands on the levers of the reelection bid. Jared started laying
groundwork in the early days of the new administration to box out Kellyanne,
Corey, Bossie, and anyone else whom Trump might suddenly decide to put in
charge. Jared described his role to others as protecting Trump from "overcon-
fident idiots." Trump often made decisions in the moment, sometimes based
on little more than reading the faces in the room and making a gut call. Jared
was concerned that management style left him vulnerable to brash promoters,
especially on television.

"You get to run one more time," Jared had told Trump. "So just let me
know what you want to do. This is your campaign, but I'm not going to let you
hire any idiots."

After just thirteen months as president, Trump announced Brad Parscale
as his 2020 campaign manager at Jared's urging. Brad had been digital director for the 2016 campaign, which was the only political race in which he'd
ever been involved. Brad had been living in San Antonio in 2011 when he
low-balled a bid to build a website for the Trump Organization to get his foot
in the door. His ploy worked and the Trumps remained clients until 2015,
when Eric asked him to build a website for his father's presidential campaign.

Brad designed a campaign strategy around a digital marketing funnel
aimed at white working-class voters in the Midwest in much the same way
that the *New York Times* targeted coastal elites. But instead of subscribing to
a digital newspaper, Brad's flood of Facebook ads pushed his targets to go out

and vote for Trump. The digital effort helped Trump overcome a huge cash disadvantage and become the first Republican since Ronald Reagan in 1984 to win Pennsylvania, Michigan, and Wisconsin all in the same election.

Brad had never run a campaign on his own, but inexperience was often viewed as an asset in Trump World. Jared knew Brad's inexperience would make him easier to control—he would later describe him as a mere placeholder—but Brad viewed the promotion as a sign of strength in their relationship. Meanwhile, his elevation infuriated much of the 2016 team, who were blindsided by a move they perceived to be a power grab by Jared. Even Brad didn't know Trump would offer him the job when he arrived in the Oval Office for a meeting on February 27, 2018.

"Do you think you can do this?" Trump asked him. "I heard you were the most valuable player in 2016."

Brad accepted and was immediately shuttled down the street from the White House to a meeting at Trump International Hotel where Jared, Eric, and the president's oldest child, Donald Trump Jr., laid out the rules: Brad needed to divest from any other business, stay in constant contact with them, and remain 100 percent committed to the family. Brad agreed. He asked how they wanted to handle the public announcement, but Jared had already leaked the news to the Drudge Report. Text messages poured into Brad's phone, everything from warm congratulations for landing the high-profile gig to unsettling warnings from friends cautioning that the job would destroy his life.

The dividing lines quickly hardened between Trump's two campaign teams as Brad spent the next year publicly describing the reelection bid as bigger, better, and more disciplined than the ragtag effort in 2016. No more campaign aides having to work on the fifth floor of Trump Tower, where *The Apprentice* had once been taped and sheetrock fell from the walls in 2016. Version 2.0 would be spread across the fourteenth floor of a modern office building just across the Potomac River in Arlington, Virginia, complete with glass-walled conference rooms overlooking the symbols of American democracy that formed the Washington skyline.

The reelection campaign quickly assembled a thick, corporate-style binder with guidelines that covered design minutiae such as font size, spacing, and preapproved colors. Trump Red and Trump Blue were for logos, Trump Gold for special occasions. The detailed book—"Branding Guidelines for the Trump Presidential Campaign"—underscored the new regime's rejection of the seat-of-the-pants style of electioneering that had characterized the first campaign. It specified which images of Trump best conveyed compassion, which showed strength, and, in the case of a photo of the president pointing into the camera, which ones let online donors know they urgently needed to boost contributions.

Corey and Bossie scoffed. They hadn't needed a branding book to win the presidency.

"It's very Trumpian to be understaffed, underfunded, and underestimated as an underdog," Kellyanne told me in June of 2019.

By the start of 2020, the two-year-old reelection bid had a sleek new look and a more professional feel from the outside. But on the inside, the campaign facelift masked the internal tension that had been festering since 2016 as Trump toggled between ignoring the rivalries and encouraging them.

"They're fighting over who loves me the most," Trump told me during a 2017 Oval Office interview when I had asked about the backbiting inside his team.

Also concealed from public view was the unresolved conflict inherent in the setup of the campaign management. Trump put Brad's hand on the wheel, but with Jared steering from the backseat. Each represented competing parts of Trump's own personality.

The thirty-nine-year-old Jared, with dimpled cheeks, a baby-smooth face, and a fondness for slim-fitting suits and skinny ties, was calculating and ruthless and shared his father-in-law's totalitarian approach to business. Jared was married to Ivanka, the president's favorite and most commercially marketable child, and descended from the kind of wealthy Jewish real estate family that Trump admired during his own rise in the industry and even long after he'd transformed his company into a licensing business.*

---

* Trump's fascination was less about race or religion, and more about capitalism and recognition. The Rose family, among the oldest real estate families in the city, were on Trump's short list of true heroes. He was close with Richard LeFrak, one of the largest developers in the New York area. These were people who took huge risks building on some of the world's most expensive real estate. Trump wanted to impress them his entire adult life.

The forty-four-year-old Brad, meanwhile, was a towering six-foot-eight Kansan with a long, bushy beard and an internal compass that consistently led him to the center of the action. He channeled the more primitive pieces of the Trumpian id. Both were restless, truth-stretching salesmen who valued a well-told story over the preciseness of the facts. They shared an instinct for viral branding and understood how to tap into the zeitgeist with merchandising and memes that raised money and generated energy for the campaign. More than 12 million Americans in 2016 said Trump wasn't qualified to be president but voted for him anyway—a data point that reaffirmed for Brad that a well-liked brand could prove more important than a well-liked candidate.

By the end of 2019, the campaign had raised more than $20 million just by selling branded merchandise timed to social media trends and cable news headlines. The campaign pushed Trump-branded plastic straws as Americans complained about environmentally friendly paper straws that always seemed to dissolve upon contact with a cold drink. They promoted a Christmas tree ornament shaped like a red Make America Great Again hat, albeit finished with 24-karat gold as a special treat for the holidays. And when Trump referred to House Intelligence chairman Adam Schiff, the California Democrat leading the impeachment charge, as a "little pencil neck," the campaign quickly printed shirts that lampooned Schiff with a red clown nose and a No. 2 pencil in place of his neck.

But Trump's inability to reconcile his conflicting impulses left his campaign team without a clear roadmap to follow from the very start of the race. Instead, the unresolved questions about control of the campaign and long-simmering internal feuds were carried into the start of 2020, but masked—at least for the moment—by the shiny new campaign operation and an artificial bubble in Trump's poll numbers that had been inflated as his Democratic rivals leaned into impeachment.

"I hit my highest poll numbers since I got elected because the American people and, frankly, people all over the world, know it's a hoax," Trump said at a campaign rally in the opening weeks of the new year. "The Democrats are trying to overturn the last election—we will make sure they face another crushing defeat in 2020. November third—mark it off."

3

Momentum

"The great USMCA Trade Deal has been sitting on Nancy Pelosi's desk for 8 months. She doesn't even know what it says."

—*Twitter, December 19, 2019*

The Battle Creek rally had lifted Trump's spirits, but not enough to completely shake the torment of impeachment. He was more convinced than ever that there was nothing illegal about his call to Ukraine, and that Democrats were only trying to embarrass him. The day after the rally, he barely even noted the moment when the House approved his administration's rewrite of the North American Free Trade Agreement. It wasn't just a major campaign promise: It was one of his only unshakable policy views, the principles of which he had articulated since his very first national TV interview—an October 1980 discussion with talk show host Rona Barrett at the height of the Iran hostage crisis.

"We just sit back and take everybody's abuse," the thirty-four-year-old Trump said at the time.

The revised pact was one of the biggest bipartisan achievements of Trump's term. It passed Congress with more support than his administration's criminal justice reform legislation, which eliminated mandatory minimum prison sentences, and far more than his 2017 tax cut, which about a dozen Republicans voted against. The practical significance of the new trade policy was debatable. The law created more incentives to manufacture car parts in the United

States and improved access to the Canadian dairy market, but the changes were also largely a branding exercise that renamed the pact the US-Mexico-Canada Agreement. Still, the opportunity for a political impact was clear.

Trump's hard line on trade helped explain the unusual appeal for a Republican in the Rust Belt, and his path to a second term started with defending those states, where the new trade law was hugely popular. In 1993, the congressional delegations in Pennsylvania, Wisconsin, and Michigan had opposed the original NAFTA deal, 28–17. Twenty-six years later, House members from the three states—nineteen Democrats, nineteen Republicans, and one independent—backed Trump's US-Mexico-Canada Agreement, 35–4.

But Trump's attention was elsewhere. He posted sixty-eight messages on Twitter that day. Just one mentioned the trade deal, and he used that to criticize Pelosi for not pursuing it sooner. Nearly all the other social media posts focused on impeachment.

"PRESIDENTIAL HARASSMENT!" he wrote.

The next day, Trump and his family bundled up in their winter coats to depart the White House for a two-week vacation at Mar-a-Lago, his winter retreat in Palm Beach, Florida. Trump and his teenage son, Barron, wore matching black overcoats, dark suits, and silk ties—power red for dad, icy blue for son—while Melania attired herself in taupe: a knee-length camel-hair winter coat that matched her cashmere sweater and beige ankle-length dress pants. Her parents, Viktor and Amalija Knavs, who had effectively moved to Washington with their daughter, were on their way, too. The rest of the Trump kids and their families would join everyone in the South Florida sunshine.

The thick, salty South Florida air was good medicine for Trump. He golfed that first morning in Florida and spent fourteen of his sixteen vacation days on the course. He loved to play. There was little else he could think of that was more fun and more relaxing than golfing at one of his eponymous courses, but he hated to admit it. On one hand, he should have been embarrassed; he had relentlessly mocked then-President Obama for the 306 days the Democrat spent golfing over eight years in office—and then Trump nearly matched that total in half the time.

But Trump's shamelessness was his political superpower.

One of the first things Jared realized during the 2016 campaign was the colossal value of his father-in-law's willingness to say and do things other candidates would never dare. There was obvious risk, of course, but every time he thought Trump had finally suffered a fatal self-inflicted wound, his father-in-law would bounce back. And yet admitting a love for golf—or often, that he even played the game—was where Trump drew the line.

I remember being struck by this from the very beginning, in April 2017, when I and a few other colleagues at the *Wall Street Journal* landed the first newspaper interview with Trump in the Oval Office. Trump wanted to memorialize the occasion with some pictures, and as we loitered around the Resolute Desk, Jerry Seib, the executive Washington editor for the newspaper, asked a seemingly casual question.

"How's the golf game?" Seib asked.

"You know, I go to these places, but I don't play very much," Trump said, suggesting that while he was already a frequent visitor to his golf clubs as president, he wasn't actually hitting the links.

Trump's travel between the White House and his courses was a well-documented matter of public record, but the president wouldn't admit he was really playing. At that point—twelve weeks into his presidency—Trump had been golfing nineteen times. Obama, at the three-month mark, hadn't played at all.

Two years and eight months later, during a Christmas Eve call with the troops during the fourth day of his 2019 break, Trump wouldn't even level with Brigadier General David L. Odom, the deputy commanding general of a Marine amphibious force, who asked how he planned to spend his Christmas.

"I really pretty much work," Trump said. "That's what I like to do."

An hour later, Trump climbed out of the black presidential limousine known as The Beast—a specially designed $1.5 million Cadillac that can put out a smokescreen, electrify its exterior handles, and hermetically seal itself to protect the passengers from biochemical attacks—and walked into Trump International Golf Club in West Palm Beach.

On January 2, 2020, the start of what would be one of the most tumultuous years in modern American history, Trump's calendar included some work,
some play, and some campaigning.

After a round of golf that Thursday morning, Trump visited with Jared,
Brad, and Coby. The small crew walked Trump through some early planning
for the new year, including potential rally sites, new merchandise in the pipeline, and the latest campaign ads they were working on—most notably the
hugely expensive Super Bowl ad they were planning. The $5 million thirty-
second spot was roughly 500 times as expensive as a typical national commercial. The ad would later become a flashpoint amid the already vicious internal
backbiting of Trump World. Was the Super Bowl ad—the reelection bid's largest single expenditure—a sign of profligate spending and undisciplined strategy? Or was the purchase—less than 1 percent of the $1.5 billion spent on
his election—an investment in the president's brand and the kind of outside-
the-box thinking needed to reelect an unorthodox candidate?* The most
forceful opponent of the Super Bowl spot was Tony Fabrizio, the campaign's
chief pollster. The sixty-year-old Fabrizio had been in and out of Trump World
for the past decade and involved in politics far longer, ever since working as an
eighteen-year-old on a Long Island congressional race in 1978. Barrel-chested,
bald-headed, and squat, Fabrizio had a reputation for delivering unvarnished
truth to his clients. Raised in an Italian family in Long Island, he could be
a crotchety old bull who was also at turns playful and mischievous. It was
sometimes tough to tell the difference between arguments and affection with
Fabrizio. He drove a powder blue Aston Martin convertible at home in South
Florida and leaned into his reputation as a political brawler. Inside Senator Bob
Dole's 1996 presidential campaign headquarters, where he was chief pollster,
Fabrizio taped his nickname, "The Rat," onto his office nameplate.

Fabrizio had studied the art of applied politics at the foot of legendary
New York Republican Arthur Finkelstein, who groomed a generation of the
party's most well-known operatives, including Roger Stone, whom Finkelstein

---

* Brad was right about one thing: 100 million people tuned in to watch the Kansas City
  Chiefs win their first championship since Nixon—the most-watched television event of
  the year. The second-biggest TV audience in 2020 was 75 million viewers for the first
  presidential debate between Trump and Biden in October.

introduced to Fabrizio in 1978. One of Finkelstein's rules was that it was always a more effective play to focus on your opponent than on your own candidate. And when it came to the Super Bowl ad, Trump didn't even have an opponent yet. The football game was set for February 2, but the first nominating contest in Iowa wasn't until February 3. Even inside the campaign no one was sure which Democrat they might face. The one thing everyone seemed to agree on in January was that Senator Bernie Sanders was going to win Iowa, which was actually won by Pete Buttigieg, the former South Bend mayor. Brad thought Senator Elizabeth Warren was coming on strong. Ronna said Senator Kamala Harris looked like a formidable contender. John McLaughlin, another Trump campaign pollster, and Dick Morris, a former Clinton political strategist who had been quietly advising Trump, warned that former New York mayor Michael Bloomberg could surge to the nomination. Bill Stepien, a senior campaign adviser at the time, pointed to polling that showed Biden was Trump's biggest threat.

But what spooked Fabrizio most was the cost. Inside campaign headquarters in December, Brad had been watching the commercial when he hurriedly gathered in his office senior members of his team to play them a rough cut. Fabrizio, McLaughlin, and Murtaugh watched the chilling spot. Shot in black and white and set to slow, sentimental piano chords, the ad showed Alice Johnson, a sixty-three-year-old Black woman, walking—and then running— out of the federal prison from which she'd just been released and into the open arms of her friends and family. After more than twenty years in prison, Trump had commuted the life sentence she'd received for her role as the kingpin of a Memphis-based cocaine ring. The ad described her crime as "a nonviolent drug offense."

"What do you think?" Brad had asked the room.

"Yeah," Fabrizio said nonchalantly. "It's a good ad."

Brad questioned the pollster's lack of enthusiasm.

"That's a lot of money," Fabrizio said. "Do you know how far that will go at the end of the election?"

Brad waved off the concern. "No," he assured the group. "We're going to have plenty of money."

The fact that the Trump campaign was swimming in cash proved to be the deciding factor. An aggressive, cutting-edge, and boundary-pushing online fundraising operation run by Gary Coby, and a more traditional though equally prodigious fundraising effort by Ronna aimed at high-end donors from the RNC, had together raised more than $460 million in 2019 for Trump's reelection, and the team ended the year with nearly $200 million in the bank. By the end of January, the campaign collected another $60 million. Brad had studied how Obama's reelection campaign collected and spent money in the 2012 race and had adjusted budget projections so that they never had more than $120 million on hand at a time.

"Just think we should keep this around as a quick snapshot of Obama spending," Brad wrote in an email to Jared in December 2019 that included a spreadsheet of how much the Obama team had raised, spent, and had in the bank for each month of 2012. "They matched their spending to what was raised each month after they had a nominee, then released their cash stockpile with any final money raised in the last thirty days. Makes a ton of sense."

At the start of February, just before the Super Bowl ad aired, the Trump campaign had already spent more than $50 million on ads, including $35 million on digital ads on Facebook and Google and another $17 million on broadcast and cable television ads.

Trump was discussing the Super Bowl ad at Mar-a-Lago with Jared, Brad, and Coby when national security officials pulled Trump out of the room.

"Watch your Twitter," he told them. "It's going to get interesting."

Trump disappeared into a secured room in the resort, tuned into a military video feed, and watched as American MQ-9 Reaper drones fired multiple supersonic, laser-guided Hellfire missiles at a pair of cars leaving Baghdad International Airport. Moments later, Qassem Soleimani, the commander of Iran's elite Quds Force, was dead.

After his remote feed cut out after the explosion, Trump returned to the restaurant for a meatloaf dinner with Kevin McCarthy, the House Republican leader. The dining room of Mar-a-Lago during the Trump presidency was a who's who of the conservative landscape—talk radio hosts, members of Congress, and the president. As he and McCarthy dined, Trump noticed conservative radio show host Howie Carr and motioned him over. Carr was based in Boston, but he bought a Mar-a-Lago membership after Trump was elected. Trump immediately wanted to talk about presidential politics.

"Who'd be better to run against?" Trump asked. "Bernie or Biden?"

"Bernie!" both Carr and McCarthy answered. Both men viewed the senator from Vermont as too liberal to win over moderate voters in battleground states.

By the time the ice cream dessert arrived, news of the missile strike was breaking and Trump made the rounds to soak up the adulation. At one point, Trump brought another friend over to the table, Matt Gaetz, a Republican congressman from Florida. Gaetz was shaken by the strike and implored Trump not to get dragged into a war, warning that an escalation would cost him reelection.

Trump looked at Gaetz for a moment.

"Get Tucker on the phone," the president said.

Like Gaetz, Fox News anchor Tucker Carlson opposed American adventurism in the Middle East. Unlike Gaetz, he'd grown wary of Trump's calls. Carlson wanted to be a TV show host, not one of Trump's advisers. He was riding along in a golf cart in Florida when he saw Gaetz calling. He answered only to find Trump on the other end.

Carlson was upset—both about the strike and that he'd been tricked into taking a call from the president. But Trump defended the decision to take out Soleimani and described his calculation as partly based impeachment considerations.

"Sixteen Republican senators were calling me, demanding I do this," Trump told Carlson, keeping Gaetz's phone on speaker mode. "They want me to do this, and they're running impeachment. And, you know, it's really not the time to ignore Republican senators. I had to listen to them."

"Maybe that's why they impeached you in the first place, to neuter your instincts," Carlson told him.

Within days Brad and Coby had pushed out digital ads that boasted about Trump's move to eliminate Soleimani, making slight tweaks to the content as they tested which message attracted the most eyeballs. The best-performing spot, which relied on a loud electric guitar solo and an image of troops in military fatigues, was viewed more than 500,000 times, mostly in crucial battleground states like Florida, Georgia, North Carolina, and Pennsylvania.

Meanwhile, a progressive group, Acronym, had pulled down its digital ads that attacked Trump over impeachment after finding that the spots had actually helped Trump instead of hurting him. The group replaced those spots with clips of Carlson, on his Fox show, criticizing Trump's military action in the Middle East. That dented Trump's approval rating by 4 percent among the key target group.

Yet Trump himself was sure the decision would help his campaign. He mentioned killing Soleimani at almost every campaign rally for the rest of the year.

———

Trump's mood continued to improve on January 15, when he welcomed a Chinese delegation into the White House to formalize the agreement on phase one of his long-sought-after trade deal with Beijing. Some deputies in the White House raised concerns about the wisdom of bringing Beijing officials into the West Wing after China had just alerted the world to a coronavirus outbreak. Dr. Robert Redfield, the director of the Centers for Disease Control and Prevention, had repeatedly contacted his Chinese counterparts seeking more information on the new contagion and offering U.S. assistance, but had gotten nowhere. However, the question about whether to call off the meeting was never raised to Trump's economic and trade advisers. Instead, the show would go on and it would be another week until reporters would ask Trump about the outbreak.

Trump missed his moment on the rebranded NAFTA deal, but almost four weeks removed from the impeachment vote and after a long break in Mar-a-Lago, he was riding high and ready to celebrate. The result was a signature performance in the East Room of the White House, a seventy-five-minute tour-de-force of self-indulgence and back-patting. He ticked through the list of guests in the room—eighty-one different lawmakers, administration officials, and corporate executives—and regaled each one with compliments or by retelling a favorite story about them. The delegation of Chinese officials stood looking on for nearly an hour and a half.

In a nod to history, Trump singled out Henry Kissinger, who, with President Nixon, helped open China to the world in the early 1970s and now sat at the front of Trump's audience. Chinese vice premier Liu He, the chief negotia-tor for Beijing, and other Chinese officials applauded the mention.

The president introduced Lou Dobbs, the Fox Business anchor, as "a man who always liked me, because he's smart, so smart," and noted that Dobbs had compared him favorably to President Reagan.

At one point, Trump appeared irritated that the executives weren't appre-ciative enough of all he had done to help them with his pro-business agenda. After praising a recent earnings report from JPMorgan Chase, he sniped at Mary Callahan Erdoes, the company's chief executive and one of the few women he mentioned during the event.

"Will you say, 'Thank you, Mr. President,' at least?" he asked. "I made a lot of bankers look very good."

He mentioned Sheldon and Miriam Adelson, the casino magnates and Republican mega-donors who privately wanted him to end the trade war, calling them "great people." He joked that Stephen Schwarzman, the chief executive of the Blackstone Group, had been so interested in the deal that the president feigned shock that he merely sat in the audience.

"I'm surprised you're not actually sitting over here on the ledge of the stage," Trump said.

As White House aides ushered reporters out of the room, Trump left them with one parting thought on the relationship between Washington and Beijing.

"The best it's ever been," Trump said.

He could have applied the same verdict to his presidency: His negative approval rating was shrinking, he was neck-and-neck in reelection polls, and he was about to stand trial on impeachment charges the next day in the Sen-ate, where the jury was packed with Republican friends.

4

Acquittal, Part One: The Perfect Call

"I have a 95 percent approval rating. Can you believe it?"
—*Campaign rally, Toledo, Ohio, January 20, 2020*

s Trump celebrated the China trade deal in the East Room, over in the West Wing, White House counsel Pat Cipollone was building the case for acquittal. The Senate trial was set to start the next day, on January 16, and the fifty-three-year-old Cipollone, the slight and bespectacled son of Italian immigrants, had taken charge of the process. Laura Ingraham, the Fox News anchor who had been a Cipollone client, had introduced him to Trump in 2016. Cipollone helped Trump during debate prep in 2016 and joined the White House as its top attorney when Don McGahn, Trump's first White House counsel, departed after the midterms.

Cipollone's task at the start of 2020 was twofold. He had to win acquittal for Trump in the Senate impeachment trial, and he needed to keep Rudy Giuliani at arm's length. The latter would prove infinitely more difficult than the former.

Giuliani and Trump had known each other since the 1980s in New York when the former was a politically ambitious federal prosecutor. In 1988, Giuliani's office had put the squeeze on a man named Robert Hopkins, who was running a gambling ring with mob connections. Hopkins said Trump was helping to launder the money and offered to wear a wire and give up the flashy young developer. Giuliani sent one of his top prosecutors to visit Trump. Weeks later, Trump announced he planned to raise $2 million for Giuliani's campaign for mayor and the investigation into Trump was over, according to Wayne Barrett, a New York journalist who covered both Giuliani and Trump for decades.

Almost three decades later, Giuliani offered tepid support when Trump initially jumped into the presidential race.

"Donald Trump is the epitome of American success," he told Fox News in June 2015, while acknowledging that "people have different impressions of him."

It wasn't until the following April, when Trump had the Republican nomination nearly in hand, that Giuliani formally endorsed him. But by then, much of Trump World had been populated by the Giuliani political family tree.

One of the first additions was Trump's New Hampshire campaign chairman, Stephen Stepanek, who had held the same position in Giuliani's unsuccessful 2008 presidential bid. Jason Miller, the deputy communications director for Giuliani's presidential campaign, was a key adviser for Trump in 2016 and 2020. Giuliani soon joined Trump's campaign as well, where he often spoke ahead of him at rallies. Trump liked having "America's Mayor" vouch for him, and equally enjoyed tormenting his longtime associate. He would needle the former mayor for falling asleep on flights and joke about Giuliani's constant use of his iPad.

"He's looking at cartoons," Trump would say.

Giuliani rarely complained about the treatment. Instead, he seemed to crave the attention and would often physically jockey with other aides and advisers to sit next to Trump at dinner or on the plane.

"Rudy never wanted to be left out," one 2016 aide said. "If you were ever between Rudy and the president, look out. You were going to get trampled."

But Trump wasn't always appreciative of Giuliani's loyalty. When Trump's 2016 campaign was rocked by the release of the *Access Hollywood* tape—a devastating hot-mic moment that captured Trump bragging about forcing himself on women—only Giuliani was willing to go on the Sunday talk shows two days later to defend the candidate. Giuliani did all five shows—the Full Ginsburg as it's known in Washington political circles.*

---

* The expression dates back to 1998, when William H. Ginsburg—the lawyer representing Monica Lewinsky during her sex scandal with President Clinton—became the first person to be interviewed on all five Sunday shows on the same day. Other Trump World

After the shows, Giuliani went directly to LaGuardia Airport, where Trump was waiting on his plane to fly to St. Louis for his second debate with Clinton. When Giuliani climbed up the stairs, he was greeted with huzzahs and high-fives from Trump's aide Hope Hicks, Bossie, and Stephen Miller. When he walked to the front of the plane, Trump barely looked up from his newspaper.

"Rudy, you sucked," Trump said. "You were weak."

Giuliani looked like he'd simultaneously had the wind knocked out of him and taken a kick to the groin.

"What the fuck do you want me to do?" Giuliani said.

After the election, Giuliani was eager for an administration post and assumed he would get one. He privately told friends that he was a lock to be named secretary of state and publicly told reporters that he was being considered for several positions but wouldn't say which ones.

"You don't want the person who's chosen to feel like number two, or number three," Giuliani told me during the transition between Trump's electoral victory and his inauguration.

Giuliani indeed had been considered for several Cabinet positions, but his chances fizzled after even a cursory round of vetting set off alarm bells. Jason Miller met with Giuliani about potential administration jobs and then asked Steven Cheung, one of the communications aides, to pepper Giuliani with questions. Afterward, Cheung spoke with Giuliani's office assistant to check some of the former mayor's answers, then asked Giuliani for a follow-up meeting.

"You said you hadn't been to the Middle East in more than a year," Cheung reminded Giuliani the next day. "Are you sure there wasn't something more recent?"

Giuliani insisted there wasn't. When Cheung said his assistant had relayed he was in the United Arab Emirates only a month earlier, Giuliani's face went blank. He stared at Cheung for a moment, then nodded. Giuliani couldn't

---

denizens who accomplished this feat include Jay Sekulow, a Trump attorney tapped in 2017 to explain the meeting Don Junior and Jared took with a Russian operative, and Secretary of State Mike Pompeo, who did it twice: in 2019 to discuss Trump's attempt to invite the Taliban to Camp David, and in 2020 about Soleimani's killing.

remember whether he had traveled to the Middle East just weeks prior, Cheung thought.

"This isn't good at all," Cheung told Jason Miller.

Giuliani didn't get a job.

Once Trump took office, he continued belittling Giuliani. He berated him in front of others for spitting while he was talking at Treasury Secretary Steven Mnuchin's wedding in June 2017.

"Go stand somewhere else," Trump told him.

And Giuliani did.

But Trump also made clear that only he could degrade the former mayor. In one staff meeting later in 2017, Trump's team started complaining about Giuliani's puzzling television appearances that often veered off-message and created more work for the press shop. Trump barked that at least Giuliani was out there fighting for him. Everyone shut up after that.

In April 2018, Giuliani found a spot on Trump's team of outside lawyers during the special counsel's investigation into Russian election meddling and Trump's potential obstruction of justice. Giuliani seemed to fill a role that was part spokesman, part litigator, and part bumbling strategist. He made contradictory statements to the press and was repeatedly upbraided by Trump.

But Giuliani also had an important side hustle. By late 2018, he was involved in an effort to dig up dirt that might damage Joe Biden. His effort focused on Ukraine, where the former vice president had pressed for anticorruption measures and his son, Hunter, had scored a high-paying job on the board of Burisma, a Ukrainian energy company. Giuliani was providing regular updates to Trump, who made little effort to clue in his own diplomats, national security advisers, or the reelection team.

Hunter Biden's drug problems and reputation for drafting off his dad's political prestige had made him an object of obsession for Republican operatives. A year earlier, in 2018, Hunter had been featured in a book from conservative author Peter Schweizer, *Secret Empires: How the American Political Class Hides Corruption and Enriches Family and Friends*. While Hunter's Burisma job was well known—the company had issued a press release when he joined the board in 2015—Schweizer's book offered some of the most extensive reporting on Hunter's expanding portfolio in China. Schweizer hadn't intended to focus on Hunter for the book—one of his assistants had come across Hunter's work in China while researching Senator Mitch McConnell, who was a main target of the book.

"It was just dumb luck," said a person involved in the project. "It wasn't intentional."

By 2019, when Trump's polling indicated that Biden presented the biggest threat to Trump's reelection, Giuliani understood there was no better way to stay in Trump's good graces than drawing some blood from Biden.

"Rudy was motivated by one thing: How do I fuck up Joe Biden?" a Trump political adviser said.

Giuliani had assembled his own team, including Joe diGenova and Victoria Toensing, married lawyers who were also close to the president, and Lev Parnas, a Ukrainian-born businessman living in Florida. Parnas had become a player in Trump World for no other reason than he started paying his way into fundraisers—a $50,000 check to Trump in 2016 got his foot in the door. There was little vetting before those events, and Parnas was soon working with Giuliani on political side projects in Ukraine.

By the summer of 2019, Giuliani repeatedly appeared on television to single out Ukraine over corruption, which was infuriating both Trump and Zelensky, the Ukrainian president—but for different reasons. In mid-July, Trump ordered his staff chief, Mick Mulvaney, to put a hold on $391 million in military assistance for Ukraine at about the same time one of Zelensky's top aides, Andriy Yermak, called Giuliani and asked him to tone it down. Giuliani's response: Open an investigation into Hunter Biden's relationship with Burisma.

A few days after the Yermak-Giuliani call, Trump watched spellbound as the two-year Russia investigation drew to a close when Mueller testified before Congress on July 24. Washington was electric with anticipation over what the famously tight-lipped investigator might reveal. But the seventy-four-year-old Mueller struggled to answer questions about his report. He repeatedly misremembered his own findings. He stumbled through his answers.

Trump tuned in from inside the White House, even scrapping an economic meeting so he wouldn't miss anything. That night, he was elated when he sat down with campaign aides. He'd beaten Mueller and was confident that he was going to beat any challenger Democrats might nominate. They talked about the convention and went around the room gaming out the strengths and weaknesses of the Democratic field. Polling consistently showed Biden was Trump's biggest threat, but the president always had an avalanche of caveats about why the former vice president couldn't win.

The next morning, a new survey from Quinnipiac University showed Biden ahead of Trump by eight points in Ohio, a must-win state for Trump. But the survey barely registered in Trump World. The president instead spent the morning tweeting that the witch hunt was over and quoting Fox News pundits who proclaimed—incorrectly—that Mueller's testimony "really did clear the president."

"TRUTH IS A FORCE OF NATURE!" Trump tweeted.

After two hours on social media, Trump picked up the phone in the White House at 9:03 a.m. on July 25 and was connected to Zelensky. Mueller's testimony had convinced Trump and his team that they were in the clear, but the president plunged himself right back into the deep waters of legal jeopardy when he prodded the Ukrainain president for what Giuliani had been seeking all along—a little help knifing the Bidens.

"I would like you to do us a favor," Trump told the Ukrainian president.

Trump's phone call—just eighteen hours after Mueller's testimony—would be memorialized months later in House impeachment "Article 1: Abuse of Power."

When Cipollone took over as White House counsel at the end of 2018, he formed a secret pact with Attorney General Bill Barr and their senior staff that if Trump tried to fire one of them for an unjust reason—or tried to force them into an unethical situation—they would all quit. The agreement was nearly invoked during a turf battle over impeachment strategy between Mulvaney, who wanted an outside legal team to run the defense, and Cipollone, who believed his office should handle it. Jay Sekulow, the president's private attorney, told Trump that Cipollone wouldn't work with the other group of lawyers. Within an hour, Trump pulled into his private dining room Cipollone, Mulvaney, other West Wing aides, and dialed in Barr on speakerphone.

"I hear what you're saying," Trump told Mulvaney. "But Pat and these guys say they won't do it, and I need these guys."

In a moment of serendipity for the counsel's office, Pence walked into the meeting. Trump asked for his opinion on whether they should bring in the outside attorneys Mulvaney had requested.

"Well, we have some problems with that," Pence said. "We don't think that's the right idea."

Cipollone successfully wrested control of the impeachment strategy from Mulvaney and contained much of the decision-making to his team of attorneys and advisers. Cipollone cared most about acquittal and worked to keep Trump focused on that goal. But Trump was intrigued by the idea of calling witnesses in the Senate trial. Brad told the president that a lengthy trial with a long list of salacious witnesses would motivate his base, propel fundraising efforts, and, come November, boost voter turnout. Giuliani wanted to put Hunter Biden on the stand. Trump not only went back and forth over the question of calling witnesses, but he also equivocated over the lineup of lawyers who would mount his defense. He'd deliberated over his roster since October, and still wanted to include Giuliani. That arrangement would have been a massive conflict for Trump's legal team.

"Rudy can't do this," Sekulow told Trump. "He's a witness. He's at the center of this whole thing!"

But Trump viewed Giuliani's appearances on TV on his behalf as purely beneficial. The rest of Trump World was perplexed, viewing Giuliani as either problematic or entertaining—but almost always in a purely unintentional way. Officials inside the campaign and White House knew that Giuliani had a direct line to Trump and, with just a quick phone call, could derail any plans they had put in place. Cipollone had an uncomfortable front-row seat as Giuliani moved in and out of the White House during the past year, spinning Trump on convoluted Ukraine conspiracies. But the reserved Cipollone limited his concerns to his team.

"I have a very high regard for Rudy Giuliani as a fellow New Yorker," Cipollone told Trump, then pushed for other high-profile lawyers to avoid adding Giuliani.

Cipollone instead leaned internally on a pair of White House attorneys,

Patrick Philbin and Mike Purpura. For Trump's outside legal team, led by Jay Sekulow, Trump selected familiar faces from Fox News with household name recognition and TV experience—the most controversial selections of which were Alan Dershowitz and Ken Starr. Dershowitz, a constitutional-law professor who famously helped defend O. J. Simpson during his trial on murder charges in the 1990s, was fighting a defamation suit filed by a victim of financier Jeffrey Epstein, who claimed she was forced to have sex with Epstein's friends, including Dershowitz, who had worked on Epstein's 2007 legal team. Starr, also a member of Epstein's 2007 defense, was best known for leading investigations of President Bill Clinton during the 1990s. He had resigned as chancellor of Baylor University in 2016 amid allegations the school mishandled sexual-assault allegations aimed at its football team.

Trump also added Robert Ray, who succeeded Starr as special counsel in the Clinton investigation; Jane Raskin, a veteran of Trump's private legal team during Mueller's probe; and Pam Bondi, a former Florida attorney general. One last-minute addition from Trump was Eric Herschmann, a partner at the firm founded by Marc Kasowitz, who had represented Trump in divorce proceedings, bankruptcy cases, sexual misconduct allegations during the 2016 campaign, and briefly during the Mueller investigation. Attorneys in the counsel's office viewed Herschmann's arrival skeptically, and several believed he was Jared's cousin. It wasn't true, but the misconception lasted for all of 2020 inside the West Wing, fueled by the fact that Jared had brought Herschmann into the White House, and the two were close, both Jewish, and Jared came from a wealthy family and Hershmann drove a Rolls Royce to work. When he arrived in the White House, Herschmann put so many questions to the counsel's office staff that Cipollone soon assigned him a West Wing staffer in order to contain the inquiries. As Trump increased pressure to pursue witnesses, Cipollone handed Herschmann the Hunter portfolio. Herschmann prepared for the possibility that he might examine Hunter Biden with such vigor that he endeared himself to the other attorneys in the office, who didn't want to be bothered with the task.

With the legal team finally in place, an unusual sense of relative calm radiated from all corners of Trump World. The campaign had been using impeachment to attack Democrats with TV ads for two months and to fuel an aggressive digital operation that delivered its best fundraising quarter to date, dwarfing all of the Democratic challengers. Public polls showed that two-thirds of Democrats were worried about the November election, while Republican excitement outpaced Democrats'—and was growing.

The White House wasn't without its internal rivalries. Cipollone had lost confidence in Mulvaney after the news conference gaffe, and he was at war with Grisham, the White House communications director who was furious the attorney was calling his own plays with the media. But the Trump White House was also in a brief period of productivity just before heading into one of the most tumultuous ten-month stretches that any president faced ahead of a reelection.

There were two types of national stories that tended to have the most impact on the public perception of Trump, and neither were in play in those months. As Brad often told the president, his approval only seemed to dip when he was perceived as overly coarse and insensitive, and nothing highlighted those negative traits like his handling of racial issues and the embarrassing chaos created by constant backbiting and turnover in the White House. But for the moment, the pin was in both of those grenades.

A second factor at play was an abiding sense throughout Trump World that they knew what they were doing. That confidence was born out of survival instead of accomplishment. The Mueller investigation, and its daily—often hourly—news cycle that drummed on and drowned out almost everything else for twenty-three of Trump's first twenty-six months in office was over. On one hand, the Mueller investigation netted almost 200 criminal charges, three dozen indictments or guilty pleas, and five prison sentences. But for this White House, it was a resounding victory that Trump was still standing—an outcome that had started to feel inevitable regardless of the size or intensity of the crisis.

During the 2016 campaign, Washington's political class predicted Trump's immediate demise when he misrepresented Republican Senator John McCain's war record and then criticized him over it.

"He's a war hero because he was captured," Trump said at the time. "I like people that weren't captured."*

---

* McCain wasn't universally acknowledged as a war hero simply because he was taken prisoner. The Vietnamese tried to release him when they learned he was the son of a prominent Navy officer, but McCain refused to violate the military's Code of Conduct

But nothing happened.

Trump belittled Khizr and Ghazala Khan, the Gold Star parents of a slain Muslim soldier. He criticized U.S. Judge Gonzalo Curiel for ruling against him in a fraud case against Trump University, accusing the Indiana-born judge of political bias because he was "Hispanic" and "Mexican" and probably didn't like that Trump wanted to build a border wall. Former Miss Universe Alicia Machado said Trump—who owned the beauty pageant—called her Miss Piggy because she'd gained weight and Miss Housekeeping because of her Hispanic heritage. His fellow Republicans wanted him to quit the race after the *Access Hollywood* tape.

He won the election despite all of it.

By the time the White House was heading into the Senate impeachment vote—where the only question about the outcome in a Republican-controlled chamber was how large Trump's victory would be—they were starting to feel invincible.

"We've been through this before," Jared told White House staffers during an impeachment planning meeting.

———

The biggest reason for optimism was that Mitch McConnell was in charge of the Senate, which would ultimately decide Trump's fate. The fastidious and opportunistic Kentuckian, with pillowy jowls and an inscrutable smirk, had methodically swatted away all of Trump's probing questions about a lengthy trial with a parade of witnesses. Trump repeatedly asked about calling Hunter Biden as a witness, hoping to raise doubts about his father. But McConnell was having none of it.

Trump and McConnell were both white Republican men in their seventies who had avoided serving in Vietnam thanks to medical deferrals. But their personalities and political styles couldn't have been more different. McConnell was born in Alabama at the back end of the Silent Generation and was taciturn and goal-oriented. Trump, born four years later in New York

---

for Prisoners of War and insisted soldiers be released in the order they'd been captured. That decision resulted in an extra five years of torture and imprisonment for McCain.

at the start of the Baby Boomer generation, was a loud talker focused on the moment. Trump's first political job was president. McConnell's introduction to Washington was in 1968 as a congressional aide. McConnell endured Trump's frivolity. Trump complained that McConnell wouldn't even crack a smile at his jokes.

In 2017, when the two men struggled to lock down enough votes to repeal the Affordable Care Act, a frustrated McConnell went silent as Trump started chitchatting about a television program he had watched the previous night.

"Mitch?" Trump said. "Are you there?"

McConnell waited another beat.

"Yes, Mr. President," he responded. "Back to the bill…"

McConnell was also frustrated by Trump's refusal to focus on the details of legislation. In one White House meeting, after the president asked for another explaination about a health care provision that McConnell had repeatedly explained at length, the Senate leader's only response was to slowly turn his head and glare at Reince Priebus, then the White House chief of staff.

But by the start of 2020, the two men had forged an odd alliance. McConnell was grateful for Trump's help keeping the Republican majority in the 2018 midterms, and Trump had come to respect McConnell as a hardball tactician. During the three-day government shutdown in 2018—the first of two during Trump's four years in office—the president was considering concessions with Democrats, who had refused to fund the government without changes to his immigration policy. McConnell advised Trump that the Democrats had backed themselves into a corner and would have to cave. Trump took the advice, and the Democrats buckled.

The two also teamed up to install a record number of federal judges, including a particularly acrimonious battle over Brett Kavanaugh's nomination to the Supreme Court. After the opening of Kavanaugh's confirmation hearing, Trump grew alarmed that the moving testimony from Christine Blasey Ford, who had accused Kavanaugh of sexually assaulting her when they were teenagers, would sink the nomination.

"We're only at halftime here," McConnell said, pointing out that Kavanaugh would have a chance to respond to the accusations after the break. "Let's see how Brett does and make an evaluation then."

The nomination was approved by the committee and Kavanaugh was confirmed by the Senate with the Republican majority carrying the day on a largely party-line vote.

On the impeachment trial, McConnell repeatedly pointed to that Republican majority as the most important factor for Trump to keep in mind. Republicans would have enough votes to acquit him, and infusing other variables into that equation created risk, even if it might also provide Trump a chance to embarrass his political rivals.

———

The roughest stretch of the trial came the night of January 26, when the *New York Times* obtained a key passage from the unreleased memoir of John Bolton, who was Trump's national security adviser at the time of his call to Ukraine. The information ran counter to a key Trump defense that he had held up the aid because of broad corruption concerns—not to try to hinder a political rival—and it turned up the heat on some Republicans to extend the trial by calling witnesses.

As White House aides scrambled to figure out how to respond, Trump groused about how Bolton had wanted to be his national security adviser only because he couldn't win the Senate confirmation required for many other senior jobs.

"I should have seen that as a red flag," Trump said. "But instead, I did the guy a favor, took him at his word that this was a good fit, and this is what he did to me?"

For the first time, McConnell's plans for a quick Senate impeachment trial were under threat of derailment. McConnell and his office had been directing the Trump legal team, pointing out which arguments would be important to make during the trial and what would resonate with certain undecided senators. Now the Senate leader exercised a behind-the-scenes campaign in the chamber to keep his members from panicking and breaking en masse from Trump. McConnell told Trump that fence-sitting Republican senators were wary both of crossing the president and of appearing browbeaten by him. They needed to be seen as having made their own decisions. So Trump stayed on the sidelines.

A couple days later, I crossed paths with Trump as he strolled the halls of the West Wing. He was calm and collected, almost bored with talk about witnesses.

"Whatever it is, it is," he said.

The result of the final vote on acquittal, on February 5, was as expected. The details were not. White House officials believed they had all the Republicans locked down—and talked openly about which Democrats would join them.

"Oh yeah, we've got Manchin locked in," Tony Sayegh, one of the communications advisers for the legal team, told associates. "Sinema is 50–50. But Manchin is locked in, 100 percent."

Later that day, every Democrat voted against Trump, as did Romney, keeping Trump from his coveted talking point that every Republican in Congress had opposed his impeachment.

The Romney vote infuriated Trump World, including Don Junior, who was having lunch in Washington. He started gaming out tweets that called on Romney to leave the party, aimed at nothing more than trolling the GOP's 2012 presidential nominee.

"Mitt Romney is forever bitter that he will never be POTUS," Don Junior wrote on Twitter. "He was too weak to beat the Democrats then so he's joining them now. He's now officially a member of the resistance & should be expelled from the GOP."

Instead, the Twitter missive triggered an immediate backlash. Reporters started calling about whether there was a movement afoot to expel Romney. Don Junior also took a call from Ronna, who was Romney's niece.

"You know I can't just kick him out of the party, right?" the Republican Party chairwoman said.

"I'm just fucking with him," Don Junior replied. "This is not some thought-out strategy coordinated with the Republican caucus."

The next morning, the president unloaded on his rivals as "dishonest and corrupt"—doing so at the National Prayer Breakfast, a customarily nonpartisan event in Washington.

There, Trump held up a pair of newspapers with the headline ACQUITTED, and questioned remarks from the previous speaker, Harvard professor Arthur Brooks, who warned of the increasing polarization of the country and urged the audience to "love your enemies." The president took swipes at Pelosi and Romney, the latter a practicing Mormon, who had cited his faith as the deciding factor in his vote for Trump's removal.

"I don't like people who use their faith as justification for doing what they know is wrong," Trump said. "So many people have been hurt, and we can't let that go on."

A new Gallup poll showed a personal best job approval rating of 49 percent, including 94 percent among Republicans, and half of all registered voters saying the president deserved to be reelected.

On the other side of the aisle, Democrats were in disarray. The Iowa caucuses were two days earlier, but they were still another two days away from knowing the results thanks to an embarrassing meltdown in the caucus count, and Biden was six days away from getting trounced in the second consecutive nominating contest.

Trump World felt indestructible.

5

Victory Lap

"A full, complete, and absolute, total acquittal. And it wasn't even close."

—*Campaign rally, Manchester, New Hampshire, February 10, 2020*

On the afternoon of February 10, Trump opened the east door of the Oval Office, stuck out his hand, and checked for rain. He laughed—it was a covered patio—and an aide scurried to grab Trump's black umbrella. With the umbrella extended overhead, Trump shuffled through the wet grass of the South Lawn, waved to reporters who shouted questions from the other side of the grass, and climbed the few steps into an idling *Marine One*, the president's four-blade, twin-engine helicopter painted military green with a white top. The president was heading to New Hampshire for the first campaign rally since being cleared of impeachment charges, and all of Trump World was primed for the victory lap.

Trump had already ousted two key impeachment witnesses: He fired European Union ambassador Gordon Sondland and removed Lieutenant Colonel Alexander Vindman, a Ukraine expert, from the White House National Security Council, along with his twin brother for good measure. He mocked the lone Republican who had dared vote against him during a meeting with U.S. governors just before departing for New Hampshire.

"How's Mitt Romney?" Trump asked Gary Herbert, who was governor of Utah, Romney's home state.

Herbert said they hadn't spoken and continued with his question about the national debt.

"You keep him," Trump said. "We don't want him."

But the rally in New Hampshire was where he could truly revel in his triumph, an endorphin-fueled jamboree with his most entrenched supporters whom he'd been telling for months that were the real targets of impeachment. Trump had been accused of abusing the power of the presidency, but he insisted that what Pelosi and the Democrats in Washington were really trying to do was nullify the 2016 election. The man who had spent fourteen years creating an alternate reality on television had now done the same from the rally stage. Impeachment, Trump argued, was nothing more than the latest attempt from liberals and socialists to shake down Americans for more taxes, take away Christmas, and turn the country into something different than what their parents had wanted for them and what they wanted for their children.

In the biting cold of midwinter in New England, rallygoers started lining up two days early. The first to set up her chair on the icy sidewalk surrounded by piles of newly plowed snow was a founding member of the Front Row Joes, Libby DePiero. Long silver hair sprouted from underneath the hood of her black parka while her black gloves with faux fur trim gripped a sign that read TRUMP'S FRONT ROW JOES. The poster included a picture of her pal Randal Thom's Alaskan malamute, an energetic little pup named Donald Trump.

Libby, a sixty-four-year-old retiree who enjoyed sparkly nail polish, leopard prints, and selfies with Trump campaign officials, had once driven her Ford Focus so far to attend a Trump campaign rally—about 1,000 miles from her home in Connecticut to Indiana—that when she stretched out in bed that night, she thought the twitching in her driving leg was coming from an animal under the mattress.

Front Row Joes maintain instant recall of a particular set of details that effectively establishes their membership in the group and, to a certain extent, determines the internal hierarchy: the number of rallies attended, the farthest they ever traveled for an event, and an excruciatingly detailed story about their first time meeting The Donald. Most of the original Front Row Joes met Trump early in the 2016 campaign during quotidian encounters that became indelible memories to be recounted forevermore with endearing levels of earnestness and pride.

"My first rally was in Nashua, at the Radisson. That was the first time I spoke to him, and I still remember what I said," Libby told me outside a 2019 rally in Orlando as she sat in her aluminum-frame folding lawn chair. A bed pillow softened the seat of webbed nylon straps—red, white, and blue, of course. She wore loose-fitting pants with a snakeskin print, and her black New Balance sneakers bounced with nervous energy.

"It's such an honor to meet you," Libby told Trump.

"What did you say?" Trump asked her.

"I said it's such an honor," she said.

"Thank you," Trump replied.

Libby recalled the memory with a wide smile.

"That's what he said!" she told me.

She'd been to almost sixty rallies by the time she'd lined up in Manchester, returning in part because of the network of friends she'd created at the rallies and in part because she only trusted the president to deliver her the news.

"How else would I know what's going on?" she said.

The next night, as temperatures dropped to 10 degrees, Libby was joined by dozens of other devotees camping out to save their place in line.

———

The reelection campaign planned to flex its muscle in Manchester, a show of strength heading into New Hampshire's first-in-the-nation primary. A swarm of surrogates from Congress and both Trump campaigns attended the rally and would be deployed to polling places on primary day, where they would encourage campaign volunteers and greet voters.

"Getting the band back together!" Louisiana congressman Steve Scalise told Trump on the flight to New Hampshire aboard *Air Force One*.

The remark signaled Trump's strengthening grip on the party. Four years earlier, Scalise had endorsed Trump only after all of his major Republican challengers had left the race.

The splashy display in New Hampshire was designed to run up the score as much as possible on the last remaining Republican primary challenger, former Massachusetts governor William Weld,* who lacked the money and the support to mount much of a campaign. But the bigger obstacle was that the rules of the game had changed. Bill Stepien and Justin Clark had spent much of the past year working to make it as difficult as possible for any potential primary challenger. They had calculated that one of the biggest reasons George H. W. Bush and Jimmy Carter had been one-term presidents was that each had been weakened by difficult primaries.

Stepien and Clark started by holding a national conference call with state party chairs to inform them of the vetting they wanted for convention delegates. Stepien repeatedly told party leaders that there was going to be no drama at the convention. It was a clear message to expel any Never Trumpers where they could. Pro-Trump Republicans were elevated in the ranks in liberal states like Massachusetts. Ken Buck, a U.S. House member and fierce Trump supporter, took over the Republican Party in Colorado, where Trump's unpopularity had splintered the party and resulted in big losses in the midterms. Brad endorsed Laura Cox, a former Michigan state legislator, to take over the state party there. And the Republican National Committee approved a symbolic yet unusual resolution that President Trump had their "undivided support."

It was the kind of backroom arm twisting that Trump had repeatedly criticized the political establishment for doing to insurgents. But one candidate's rigged system was another president's advantage of incumbency. With his nomination all but assured, the only thing left to accomplish during primary season was to deliver historic victory margins, drive up Republican turnout, and unleash a shock-and-awe campaign that would leave little doubt who the favorite would be heading into November.

---

* Weld's candidacy could be summed up in an anecdote relayed by Alex Leary, one of my oldest friends in the business and a colleague on the *Wall Street Journal*'s White House team for the final two years of Trump. Leary was working on a story about the state of the Never Trump movement, and planned to meet Weld for a campaign event at a New Hampshire college. Leary arrived to find Weld and an aide wearing confused looks while standing next to a dozen boxes of pizza inside an empty classroom. Class had been canceled, and no one had bothered to tell Weld.

The effort came with huge costs. In New Hampshire, the campaign char-tered its own planes and planned a massive primary night party at Murphy's Taproom in Bedford for a victory that was never in doubt. Brad had boxes of red campaign hats specially made for New Hampshire: KEEP NH GREAT— 2020 PRIMARY TEAM. Earlier in the month, the campaign had brought everyone to Iowa for a similar showing. In addition to *Air Force One*, they chartered a plane with a manifest so deep that Bossie and Corey, two of the original Trump campaign operatives, didn't know most of the names on the list.

But those expenses didn't matter much at that moment. Trump seemed to be running against all eight of the major Democratic candidates at once, and his team was enjoying the consequence-free campaigning: the adrena-line rush of the fight, but none of the anticipation of an uncertain outcome. Brad intentionally planned to put the rally in Manchester, hoping the presi-dent's extensive security precautions would snarl traffic in the state's largest city and frustrate rival campaigns in the final hours before the polls opened. Traffic was so backed up that my own fifteen-minute drive from the airport to the arena took nearly an hour. It was well past the press deadline to get in when I finally jumped out of the taxi about a mile away and navigated my way through various blockades to the arena, where Emily Novotny, an advance staffer on the campaign, helped me make it past the last few security checkpoints while I was heckled for the last few feet by Corey and Bossie, who seemed quite delighted by the whole spectacle.

Even if the primary result was certain, the outcome in November was very much in doubt in New Hampshire. Trump had lost the state in 2016 by a mar-gin of 0.37 percent, his smallest margin of defeat. But in 2020, Trump had an argument to make: Unemployment in the state was below 3 percent. Wages, which had stagnated during the Great Recession, had been growing under Trump.

The president and his team still hadn't settled on a messaging strategy, partly because they expected Trump to find his secret sauce once Democrats picked their nominee. But Trump was struggling to decide whether to stick with his 2016 theme, "Make America Great Again," or update it to "Keep America Great." Brad urged him to stick with the 2016 MAGA branding, which he argued was now the name of the movement more than anything else. Trump worried that it sounded like he hadn't done the job.

"I made America great," Trump said. "I don't have to make it anymore."

But when it came time to approve the new Keep America Great hats, Trump stalled. He relentlessly tinkered with the flatness of the brim, the size of the font, and the shape of the front panel. At a fundraiser in September 2019 in the Beverly Hills mansion of Geoffrey Palmer, Trump considered several prototypes as he sat behind the desk of the billionaire builder's large study, which was wrapped in gold and maroon floor-to-ceiling curtains and lit by a gold chandelier. Brian Kennedy, the president of Cali-Fame, the Southern California company that had been making the caps since the 2016 race, dripped with sweat as he nervously watched Trump finger the different prototypes while Brad, Jared, Don Junior, Kimberly Guilfoyle, and Treasury Secretary Steven Mnuchin looked on. Kennedy's nerves made Brad overly anxious, and he worried that Kennedy's profuse sweating would distract Trump and further delay a decision about the hats. Brad repeatedly interjected, trying to pinpoint what the president liked and didn't like, but his meddling in the conversation irritated Jared.

"Will you shut up and let him do his job," Jared finally blurted out.

Trump eventually picked one. A week later, he asked for another slight tweak to the font. The repeated changes resulted in multiple "Keep America Great" hats that Trump signed with his name and memorialized by adding "#1" with his black Sharpie.

———

The changes were unusual for Trump. His superstition and paranoia usually meant never changing anything that worked, and he and his team spent much of 2020 trying to re-create the 2016 dynamics. That included holding a rally in the same New Hampshire arena on the same night—the eve of the presidential primary.

It was in New Hampshire four years earlier where Trump had turned his primary campaign around and, the night before, delivered a rally performance that encapsulated the strange chemistry between the performer and his audience that on occasion surprised even him.

"She just said a terrible thing!" Trump had said in SNHU Arena, pointing to a woman in the crowd who had yelled an expletive.

Trump asked the crowd if they'd heard what she called Senator Ted Cruz, his chief rival in the Republican race, and told her to shout it out again. The woman tried, but her tiny voice was hard to discern in the 12,000-seat arena. So Trump amplified it for her.

"She said he's a pussy!" Trump said as he feigned dismay.

The crowd erupted in a deafening roar of approval as Trump surveyed the scene.

"What kind of people do I have here?" He smiled. "What do I have?"

Four years later, *Air Force One* was packed with the president's political aides and allies when it touched down at Manchester-Boston Regional Airport about an hour before the rally. Waiting on the tarmac to greet him was Corey, his first campaign manager, who was based in New Hampshire.

"Welcome home, sir," he said.

Inside SNHU Arena, Representative Matt Gaetz mingled with the crowd, signed hats, and posed for pictures. Onstage, Kimberly Guilfoyle, the former Fox News personality now dating Don Junior, warmed up the crowd. She shouted into the microphone that Trump was "the best president this country has ever seen," pumping her fist into the air with every syllable. The crowd cheered in agreement.

"That felt good, didn't it?" she said, adding, "Gimme some Trump, Trump, Trump!"

Guilfoyle, wearing dark-framed reading glasses with her chestnut brown hair layered over her shoulders, introduced Don Junior as the next speaker. She avoided the kind of vivid descriptions of Don Junior she often used at private fundraisers to give donors an unwanted glimpse into their private lives— how he liked when she wore a cheerleading outfit and was a "naughty boy" when she "let him out of his cage." Instead, she described him as "Braveheart meets honey badger." They greeted each other onstage with a warm embrace and quick kiss.

Don Junior wore a dark blue suit, an open-collared shirt, and a wide smile as he whirled red campaign hats into the audience. The crowd showed their appreciation by breaking into a chant of "Forty-six! Forty-six!"

Trump's son kept chumming the waters with the lumpy red discs in a sea of fervid MAGA fans. When the "Forty-six!" chant broke out again fifteen minutes into his remarks, Don Junior tried to tamp it down with his hands.

His head tilted to the side, and he grimaced. "Wow," he said, briefly letting it pick up momentum. "One step at a time."

He continued, holding his hands in the air. "Let's worry about 2020. That's all we've got to focus on, right? Let's keep winning."

In his next breath, Don Junior started his energetic introduction for Pence, who was warmly received. But there was no special chant for the silver-haired, straitlaced son of Indiana.

Backstage, Marc Short, Pence's chief of staff, and Katie Miller, the vice president's communications director, exchanged a glance.

"That's funny," Miller said.

After Pence walked offstage, he made an awkward joke about the moment to Don Junior and Kimberly. Later that week, Marty Obst, Pence's longtime political strategist, made it known back at campaign headquarters that Pence was never again to follow Don Junior onstage.

"He's just a hard act to follow," Obst said.

≡≡≡

The morning after the rally, Brad pulled up to a cinnamon-colored brick building—weathered and water-stained from the dependably cold and wet New Hampshire winters—that housed the nearly century-old Red Arrow Diner in downtown Manchester. Inside, grizzled old white men, some in puffy winter coats and others in shirtsleeves, were bellied up to the curved, fire-engine-red breakfast counter, sitting on one-legged red vinyl bar stools. The plastic-covered menus had previously been considered by a perfectly adequate roster of celebrity gourmands, including favorite son Adam Sandler, the Barenaked Ladies, and former host of *The Apprentice* and future U.S. president Donald J. Trump.

The diner was a required stop on any candidate's swing through Manchester. But in February 2020, the campaign instead dispersed a group of surrogates, including Brad, on the morning of the primary because Trump was already back at the White House. The president preferred large crowds and cable networks instead of diner stops and local news. He'd made an exception for the Red Arrow back in January 2016 when he slid into a booth and signed autographs. In a dark suit, white shirt, and blue striped tie, he ordered a Diet Coke and a Newton Burger—a ground beef patty with all the traditional burger trimmings, plus a scoop of deep-fried mac and cheese, a grilled cheese sandwich in place of a bottom bun, and a second grilled cheese sandwich as the top bun. It would be immediately rebranded as the Trump Tower.

"Enjoy your burger, racist!" a woman had yelled as she was halfway out the diner door.

Trump had betrayed no reaction and continued the conversation in his booth. But four years later, he sent Brad.

When Brad entered the tiny cafe, it was already cramped at 8:45 in the morning. The tight quarters made him appear even larger as he walked in wearing a dark blue three-piece suit, a fresh New Hampshire–edition campaign cap perched on his head, and his blondish-brown beard neatly combed and styled like an upside-down mohawk. His entourage pushed into the diner and crowded around him: a full camera crew; two young, long-legged assistants; a retired Army special forces soldier now working as a bodyguard; and a press minder. Brad surveyed the scene, his cell phone pressed to the side of his face. It was already his third call that morning from Jared, who would call once more before lunch and send repeated texts. The constant contact was mostly to micromanage Brad's social media profile but also to weigh in on the major political stories.

That morning, the big story was Mike Bloomberg, the tech billionaire and would-be Trump challenger—and father of one of Ivanka's best friends—who was trending on Twitter. An old recording had surfaced of Bloomberg using racial terms to describe the controversial stop-and-frisk policing practice he presided over as New York City mayor. Bloomberg apologized for the policy, but that did little to keep it from ricocheting around the Internet and catching the attention of the president, Don Junior, and Brad, all three of whom did their best to escalate Bloomberg's embarrassment. At 8:00 a.m., Brad tweeted that Bloomberg was "a complete racist" and retweeted another post adding only the hashtag #BloombergIsARacist. But Jared didn't think the campaign manager for the president of the United States should concern himself with juvenile horseplay in the sandbox of social media. Jared wanted the tweets taken down, and told Brad to change the new banner on his Twitter page, which was an old picture of the diminutive Bloomberg standing between Jared and the president. It was cropped so that the heads of Trump and Jared were at the top of the banner, while Bloomberg could barely see over the bottom of the frame. It made Brad chuckle every time he looked at it. He changed the picture, but left the tweets up.

Others in Brad's orbit had warned him to dial down the heat radiating from his social media presence. There were plenty of others around Trump World who would willingly post those kinds of tweets. Don Junior had essentially turned Twitter-flamethrowing into his personal brand. Plus, the campaign already had a network of social media influencers whom they'd blast with text messages suggesting tweets and Facebook posts. The mainstream media had come down hard on Brad the past few years, digging into nearly $100 million in campaign cash that had been paid to his marketing company during the 2016 campaign and millions more when he was named campaign manager in 2018. There was never any evidence of wrongdoing, but that was only half the problem. He'd also bought a pair of million-dollar condos, a $400,000 boat, and another half million in luxury cars, including a Range Rover and a Ferrari. For Trump, who was already prone to conspiracies and triggered by the very thought of people making money off him, the perception that Brad had gotten rich off the back of Trump's political ambitions had fueled a years-long fight between the two men.

Brad could almost always reassure the boss in the moment, but it was only a matter of time before the tensions would erupt all over again. Inviting more attention to himself with divisive tweets seemed inadvisable even to Brad's allies. But Brad would consistently wave off any concern about social media.

"Dude," he said to one colleague. "The person who likes me doing this is Trump."

And sure enough, the Twitter post that had prompted the intervention in the first place would inevitably be retweeted by Trump. Brad understood that a traditional campaign manager would never amplify the kind of incendiary memes and hot takes that poured out of his social media profile. But Trump was no traditional candidate.

"Jared's pissed," Brad said as he scrolled through his phone at Mary Ann's Diner, where he'd order a red velvet muffin—lightly grilled—and unsweetened iced tea. "He doesn't want me pushing the Bloomberg video. But if a video like this came out about Trump, every one of those other campaign managers would be tweeting about it. Jared's just a little more cautious than me. Obviously."

It was a rare admission of any daylight between the two. Brad viewed a significant portion of his job as managing his relationship with the Trump family as much as managing the Trump campaign. And Brad did his part to blur the line between family and business, willingly or otherwise. Born in Topeka, Kansas, on January 3, 1976, he was the eldest son of Dwight and Rita Parscale. Dwight, a former assistant attorney general, spent two decades practicing law, but left the field after getting so upset at a ruling, he told friends, he wanted to "beat the crap" out of the judge. Brad described his upbringing as "not overly redneck."

Dwight had also run, unsuccessfully, for a series of political offices, including a U.S. House seat before Brad was born, and Kansas attorney general in 1990. The two were close. When Brad accepted a scholarship to play basketball at the University of Texas at San Antonio, Dwight moved the family to be close to him.* Dwight had hoped some of Brad's political success in 2016 would help revive his own ambitions, and in 2018, he ran for Republican chairman of Bexar County, Texas. Dwight had been endorsed for the Bexar County position by the outgoing chairman, Robert Stovall, who vacated the seat after Brad endorsed him in a Republican primary for a congressional seat. Stovall and Dwight both lost. Dwight again appealed to Brad for work in 2020, asking his son to have Trump appoint him director of the FBI. When Brad refused, they stopped speaking for a stretch.

Brad would repeatedly find similarities between his father and Trump: Both men were seventy-four years old, prone to conspiracy theories, and had

---

* Brad played for the Roadrunners in the 1996–97 season and put up 26 points and 26 rebounds before getting injured.

businesses that went into bankruptcy* and Brad maintained complicated relationships with each that were often knotted around money.

Brad also had a tendency to view himself as another of the Trump kids. He took it as a sign that while he, Don Junior, Eric, and Jared were all born in different years, their birthdays fell within the same eleven-day stretch between December 31 and January 10.

"That's statistically very rare," Brad told them when he first put it together. "I don't know if it's celestial, but if you're born in the cold weather, it affects how you approach the rest of your life."

Don Junior and Jared were less amazed.

"So what, Brad?" Jared said.

When Brad showed up for work during the 2016 campaign, he didn't own a suit. Eric stopped him before he could get into the elevator at Trump Tower.

"No," Eric told him. "You can't go up and see him without a suit."

Brad walked to Men's Warehouse but couldn't find anything off the rack that fit his unusual six-foot-eight frame. He kept walking to Tom James Company, where he ordered a made-to-measure suit that he wore on his first day at the campaign. Brad eventually had all his suits made at the same shop, including the one he'd worn to campaign for Trump at New Hampshire eateries on the day of the primary.

During the 2016 race, Brad grew close to Jared just as the son-in-law took tighter control of the campaign and showed more interest in exploring the digital side of electioneering. Jared leaned on Brad's background in digital marketing, even though he'd never before worked on a political campaign. Trump asked him to create a webpage for his exploratory committee in 2015, and he was digital director by June 2016, creating and placing ads on social media platforms such as Facebook, developing the campaign's website, and driving online fundraising efforts.

By 2020, Brad viewed Jared like a brother. They had been speaking every day, sometimes multiple times a day, for years. Brad spoke to his own sister twice a year, at best. Jared could wink at Brad from across the room, and Brad

---

* After leaving law, Dwight had an eclectic foray into the business world, including a 3-D animation software company, a scuba shop, and a Western-themed nightclub with a mechanical bull from Fort Worth.

would understand that he needed to take a break and not be so aggressive with Trump.

"I don't think I'm here without him, I don't think he thinks he's here without me," Brad told me once heading into 2020. "We found each other. By the way, let me ask you a question. You've been around for a while. Are two people any closer than me and Jared? We're tied at the hip. Who else has that? Nobody, right? I'm surprised no one has gone far enough to call me a Trump kid."

In the Manchester diner that morning, Brad introduced himself to one patron who showed polite interest, then turned his attention back to his breakfast. Brad glanced around the room, realized no one was trying to catch his attention, and turned to his team.

"Okay, let's get out of here," he said. "I already said hi to all the people."

Later that morning outside Londonderry High School, where voting booths had been arranged inside the gymnasium, Brad dazzled the Republican volunteers, a half dozen senior citizens speakin' in wicked N'Hampshah accents, sporting Patriots coats and MAGA hats. They knew who he was, and were ready for him. So he opened his phone and gave them a behind-the-scenes look.

"You can find events near you, local or national. You can register to attend an event, either an RNC event or a campaign event, register to vote, invite your friends, or host a meet-up. It's everything it takes to be a Trump supporter," Brad told the group, huddled under a pop-up tent with a table of baked goods and Dunkin' Donuts coffee.

"Whoa! Really?" said Liz Thomas, a Londonderry resident on her shift at the polling place. "What's the site?"

"No," Brad said. "It's in beta. But it's nice, right?"

"Did you build that?" she asked.

"Yep," Brad said. "Well, it was my company. But it was my idea. I built Trump World in a lot of ways."

Brad turned to the next group of Republicans who walked up to see him. "Hey! How are you guys? Want a hat?"

"I was in charge of Trump's advertising," Brad added when he was asked what he did before the campaign. "All the advertising and marketing and branding."

Trump would have been surprised to hear that description of Brad's work. The president, when he was upset with Brad, would refer to him as "a guy who makes websites."

But Brad was in his element. He promised one elderly man a half dozen times that he would tell Trump—he would call him that night!—about the need to provide dental care for military vets. He confused one woman in Patriots garb by professing fealty to his beloved Kansas City Chiefs. After a slow start at the diner that morning, Brad was hitting his stride as a man-of-the-people.

"Some people love this part of it—I don't mind it," Brad said as he wrapped up his day of campaigning. "I probably get more handshakes than anyone."

Then he ducked back into the leather interior of the fully loaded black Infiniti SUV escorting him around the Manchester metropolitan area.

"I'm not running for office," he said. "But I think I have it in me."

Brad was creative and hardworking, and loved little more than telling stories. When he thought about the campaign, it was in that context. He was the songwriter, and Jared was the conductor. Another time Brad was the director, and Trump was the artist. Eventually he decided Jared was the director, Brad was the producer, and Trump was the talent.

Brad's optimism and energy on this chilly day in early February was rooted in just how far the Trump campaign had come these past four years. In all of 2016, the campaign spent $42 million on ground game. They'd spent $80 million in 2019, and planned to invest another $492 million in 2020. Brad had worked to develop a close relationship with Ronna at the RNC, and despite Trump's inherent distrust of the establishment of the party he professed to lead, the campaign's partnership with the RNC was closer than it had been with any Republican presidential campaign for as long as anyone could remember. By mid-February it had resulted in more than 80 leadership sessions for volunteers, and 160 neighborhood gatherings for Trump supporters—known as MAGA meet-ups. Volunteers had knocked on 55,000 doors and made 70,000 phone calls. They'd brought out more Iowans to the 2020 caucuses than any campaign since Jimmy Carter.

But Trump would never see Brad as anything more than the guy who made the website.

Meanwhile, out in Los Angeles, Hope Hicks was miserable.

Hope had joined Trump's campaign in 2015 while she was working for Ivanka on her fashion brand. When Trump called her into his office and asked if she wanted to join the campaign, Hope had thought he was talking about a marketing campaign for one of his properties. But she agreed anyway, and became a constant presence at Trump's side in the office, on the trail, on his private plane. In the White House, she was an indispensable aide, a calming presence in a West Wing rocked by one controversy after the next. She left the White House after a little more than a year, in March 2018 as the Mueller investigation was underway. When the investigation concluded the following year, she cried, and called her friends in the White House to tell them how happy she was it was over.

But she also realized how much she missed the dysfunctional adrenaline of Trump's orbit. The transition to Los Angeles, away from her family and friends on the East Coast, was harder than she'd imagined. Her contact with Trump had dropped off considerably when she left, but whenever they talked, Trump told her she was always welcome. Now she was ready to return.

Trump was ready, too. He was admittedly superstitious, and as he looked around his West Wing, he saw that most of his 2016 team was gone. Derek Lyons, his staff secretary, had worked for Jeb Bush, not Trump, during the primary. Mark Meadows, who was effectively chief of staff but who wouldn't formally be given the role for another month, was a late supporter. Jared had kept Corey mostly out of the White House, and always seemed to forget to invite Kellyanne to the political meetings.

"Who was with me when I was there by myself?" Trump would ask.

Hope agreed to come back, carving out a role as a White House counselor. Jared told others she would report to him, but Hope had a direct line to Trump and exerted her influence over the president's schedule with an eye toward reelection. Trump had also just returned Johnny McEntee to the White House. His personal aide on the campaign had been expelled from the White House in 2018, when his growing gambling debts were deemed a security risk to the administration. McEntee was escorted out of the building so quickly that he'd left his suit jacket at his desk.

David Bossie, Trump's 2016 deputy campaign manager, had also returned to Trump World after a months-long exile. Bossie had been cast aside after news reports that one of his fundraising groups collected $18 million during Trump's first two years on the promise to support Trump-aligned candidates, but spent nearly all of those proceeds on more fundraising, administration costs, and salary. Bossie had come into the White House and walked Trump through his expenditures, insisting he had not grifted off the president.

Trump recalled the conversation in the final months of 2019 with his political team during a meeting in the White House Map Room to go over campaign ads. Trump had expected Bossie to spend some of the disputed money supporting Trump's reelection, but complained to others in the room that he didn't like Bossie's political ads.

"You know Bossie," Trump told Larry Weitzner, his lead ad maker and the chief executive of Jamestown Associates, a consulting firm with roots in New Jersey Republican politics. "You should send him some of this footage."

Weitzner told Trump that coordinating with Bossie's group might raise legal problems for the campaign. The president instead turned to Jared and asked him to help improve Bossie's ads. Jared was noncommittal.

"Well, you don't like him," Trump said to Jared.

"I caught him stealing from the campaign," Jared told Trump. "So, no. Typically that wouldn't give me a very high opinion of somebody."

═══

By early February, Trump had much of his old crew back in place and a new poll showing his political stock on the rise. A Gallup poll on February 12 showed that 61 percent of Americans said they were better off than they were three years earlier. That was more than any of the past four election cycles when an incumbent president was running. It put Trump in such a good mood that when he visited his campaign headquarters for the first time on February 13, he made only passing reference to how much the modern office must cost. Instead, he wanted to talk politics. He wanted to talk about which Democrat was going to win the nomination. Another favorite topic was the Alabama

Senate primary, where his former attorney general, Jeff Sessions, was trying to mount a political comeback. The thought of it would ignite a flurry of F-bombs from Trump, who badly wanted to endorse one of the other two main Republican rivals in the race. It took everything in his political team's power to hold him off until the race was down to two candidates.

Trump was also interested in whether he should be meddling more directly in the Democratic primary. The campaign knew that if Trump focused on any particular Democratic candidate, it would drive media coverage and attention from voters. Internal polling showed that Trump performed best against Warren. Brad and others suggested to Trump that if he attacked her, it would convince Democrats to give her a second look and boost her poll numbers. Trump was intrigued, but could never stay on message long enough to make a difference.

————

On February 15, Trump attended a rare South Florida fundraiser outside the confines of Mar-a-Lago. But the price tag was worth traveling a few miles north: The dinner at billionaire investor Nelson Peltz's home raised $10 million for the reelection bid. While the stunning sum made news, attendees would remember it as the first time they'd heard clear warnings from the administration about the contagion in China that had been earning headlines for several weeks.

"It's worse than people think," Robert O'Brien, the president's national security adviser, told a small group of people at Peltz's home. They should be careful where they traveled, he told them.

The next day, Trump opened the Daytona 500 with a lap around the Florida racetrack in the presidential limousine, a first in presidential history.

"So exciting," Trump said.

He then headed off to a four-day campaign swing out West, which may have been the best indication of how good he was feeling. Compared to his predecessors, Trump rarely traveled. When he did, he almost always returned home that night, preferring the comforts of his own bed. His post-impeachment tour would take him through Arizona, California, Colorado, and Nevada, with a pair of fundraisers and three rallies along the way. Each night he would return to his Las Vegas hotel.

The highlight of the trip came on the second day when, after a campaign rally in Phoenix, Trump learned that Mike Bloomberg had been mollywhopped on the Democratic debate stage by Elizabeth Warren.

Trump World was split over the Bloomberg candidacy. Brad dismissed Bloomberg as an unappealing candidate and mocked his strategy of skipping the early state primaries. But not all of Bloomberg's campaign was ripe for ribbing: The New York billionaire was the only candidate besides Trump to spend eight figures for commercial time during the Super Bowl.

Ronna thought Bloomberg's ads were getting better, and his name ID was high. The RNC's data wasn't showing much movement, but no one wanted to discount him because of the huge checks he was writing his campaign.

Pence wasn't so sure, either. Bloomberg had been successful in business, but not even New York politics compared to the national stage.

"I just don't see it," he'd told others in the West Wing.

John McLaughlin, one of Trump's pollsters, and Jared thought Bloomberg could be dangerous. Trump was anxious about Bloomberg, too, and had to be constantly reassured.

"What do you think of Bloomberg?" he'd ask Oval Office visitors.

"Who are you most worried about?" Trump asked Tony Fabrizio in February.

"Buttigieg," Fabrizio said, referring to Pete Buttigieg, the former mayor from South Bend, Indiana, who had won Iowa and nearly pulled off an upset in New Hampshire.

"Buttigieg? That fucking guy?" Trump said. "Nah."

By mid-January, Bloomberg was beating Trump by seven points in Michigan, according to a *Detroit Free Press* poll.

⸻

The Democratic debate began while Trump was still onstage in Phoenix, but the president had been monitoring its progress, with aides providing updates. Now, back on *Air Force One*, Trump cued it up on TiVo. A giddy Trump walked back to the press cabin in the tail of the plane and invited reporters to come watch it with him in his personal cabin at the front.

"Come on, Fake News, follow me," Trump said to the reporters.

He then led about a dozen members of the press through the plane, announcing to his staff along the way, "The Fake News is coming back!"

Don Junior and his girlfriend, Kimberly Guilfoyle, shared a nervous glance from their perch in the room connected to his office.

The reporters fell into the couches lining the wall, and photographers sat on the floor near the television.

"Bring in some shrimp and meatballs for everybody," Trump told his staff. "Put out the little tables."

The flight attendant said there wasn't time for food, since it was a short flight back to Las Vegas. But Trump insisted on at least snacks for his guests, and the staff brought napkin-lined baskets filled with potato chips, which the president washed down with tomato juice and celery.

Jared and Grisham came into the cabin, along with Scavino, who showed Trump the tweets he was posting. Don Junior and Kim stood in the doorway, simultaneously cuddling and commenting on the action.

"I'm hurt they're not talking about us," Don Junior said.

"What's wrong with Chuck Todd's hair?" Kim asked.

While reporters were fixated on the debate, having missed it live while they were at the rally, Trump turned in his seat, facing Jared and Grisham.

"Not as easy as it looks, right?" Trump asked them.

"No, sir. You're so good at it," Jared told him.

Trump then started offering his own color commentary: Bloomberg was smart, but not quick. Biden had an awful facelift. Bernie was sharp, and Warren was nasty but a good debater. He thought Buttigieg was articulate, and seemed to surprise himself with repeated praise for the former South Bend mayor.

But the climax for Trump was Bloomberg melting down when rivals, led by Warren, skewered him over his history of sexual harassment allegations and past support for stop-and-frisk policing. Trump crowed at every stammer he saw on-screen.

"He stutters like Biden!" Trump said.

The flight, as promised, was short, and the plane was soon on the ground. But Trump didn't want the fun to end. He offered to let the reporters walk down the front stairs instead of the back—a treat only Trump would think to offer—but the press had to return to the back of the plane to retrieve their bags. When someone mentioned that it was the sixtieth birthday for Doug Mills, the *New York Times* White House photographer, Trump laughed.

"You mean I'm older than this fucker?" Trump said.

Trump reluctantly let reporters return to their cabin, making them promise they'd finish watching the debate in their hotel rooms.

The president was feeling emboldened. His approval ratings were at the highest point of his presidency, he'd removed or reassigned many of the administration officials who had testified against him during impeachment, and now Democrats were falling apart.

"I'm the president, and I'm going to stay the president," Trump shouted to the reporters as they walked away. "And you're finally starting to realize that!"

Trump returned to Washington before heading out again, this time on a whirlwind thirty-six hours in India, a diplomatic drop-in that was as intense as it was brief. He abhorred international travel and tried to avoid it, frequently sending Pence in his place. He had asked Jared to postpone this trip and tell Narendra Modi, the Indian prime minister, that they'd reschedule after the election. But Jared and O'Brien were eager to make it happen. "You're not going to have time for anything else in your second term other than traveling if you keep postponing these trips," Jared told Trump.

Plus, Modi had taken personal interest in bringing Trump not just to India, but to his home state of Gujarat. It was there, Modi had promised Trump, he would host him for a campaign-style rally.

The rally had initially been planned for New Delhi, but just two weeks before Trump was supposed to arrive, Modi phoned and told Trump he should instead come to Gujarat for a mega-rally inside the world's biggest cricket stadium. There was just one problem. The stadium was still under construction. Trump weighed the risks, considered the optics of a rally inside a 110,000-seat stadium, and signed off.

Nearly everyone in the stadium wore white "Namaste Trump" baseball caps, India's twist on the MAGA campaign cap, which had a visual effect of making the crowd seem even bigger. The same classic rock music that greeted Trump rally crowds in the United States—the Rolling Stones' "Play with Fire," Elton John's "Tiny Dancer," the Beatles' "Hey Jude"—serenaded Trump as he arrived. Trump spoke for about thirty minutes, and was interrupted with applause nearly sixty times. He was thrilled. He praised Modi and complimented the crowd.

"From this day on, India will always hold a very special place in our hearts," Trump said.

After the rally, the Trump delegation departed for a private tour of the Taj Mahal. The ivory-white marble mausoleum built in the seventh century along the banks of the Yamuna River attracts 20,000 visitors a day, but Trump had never been among them. Modi closed it down for the day—and had his government chase off the monkeys known to harass tourists—so Trump could stroll through the gardens unmolested. A motorcade of electric golf carts ferried the president, his family, and his staff on a sunset tour.

Jared snapped pictures on his iPhone of Ivanka, who posted them on Instagram. The president posed for pictures with Melania and asked reporters for questions, before quickly waving them off—a joke signaling he didn't want to sully a memorable visit.

But Trump's victory tour, and the most favorable stretch of his presidency, was about to come to a screeching halt.

For the first three years of his presidency, Trump fixated on two factors that he'd decided would determine whether he'd win another term: the enthusiasm inside his political base, and the strength of the economy. As he left Washington on Sunday, February 23, for India, both of his leading indicators were forecasting smooth sailing on the electoral waters. He had a 98 percent approval rating among core supporters, virtually unchanged during his first thirty-five months in office. The stock market—his preferred economic measure—had been on a steady upward trend during that same time, with gains of more than 40 percent in both the S&P 500 and the Dow Jones Industrial Average. Trump had plenty to boast about, and did. During his four years as president, he tweeted about the stock market more than 150 times, mostly to take credit for the gains. About 15 percent of those tweets came during the first two months of 2020.

But as he boarded *Air Force One* for the eighteen-hour flight back to Washington on February 25, Dr. Nancy Messonnier, the director of the National Center for Immunization and Respiratory Diseases, had just issued a blunt warning at a news conference with reporters about the rapidly evolving and expanding coronavirus situation, warning that "the disruption to everyday life might be severe."

"It's not so much a question of if this will happen anymore but rather more a question of exactly when this will happen, and how many people in this country will have severe illness," she said. She spoke of sitting her children down that morning, to prepare them for "significant disruption to our lives."

The stock market plunged on Messonnier's comments, capping a 1,900-point drop in the Dow, the largest two-day decline on record.

Trump didn't sleep the entire flight home.

6

Covid, Part One: Hyperbole in the Time of Pandemic

"We're prepared and we're doing a great job with it and it will go away."
—*Speaking to reporters, U.S. Capitol, March 10, 2020*

When Bill Stepien first entered Donald Trump's reelection headquarters after the 2018 midterms, he had his choice of any office except for Brad's. It was a drastic change from four years earlier, when he'd been stuffed into the same tiny office as Justin Clark, the deputy political director in 2016. With nearly $1 billion more to spend this time around, the reelection campaign had leased the entire fourteenth floor of the Arlington Tower, nearly 22,000 square feet of modern office space. Stepien looked around the brightly lit expanse, and this time chose to again cram himself into the same office as Clark.

Almost everyone on the campaign who'd been around in 2016 wanted to re-create the same scrappy, underdog dynamic from that first race—and believed they could. But as 2019 came to a close, Stepien, just as he had four years earlier, sat in his shared office and grew troubled about what lay ahead. Stepien was a worrier by nature. The forty-two-year-old kept his sandy blond hair just long enough to part to the side. His fleece vest was always zipped to the top, and his lips seemed permanently pursed. His only opinions were strong ones, which he was careful about sharing and almost never did in a group. He was practically mute in meetings.

But Stepien was spooked by the confidence some of his colleagues carried. He thought Brad outsourced too much responsibility to the Republican National Committee. And mostly he worried about how the White House would respond if a crisis confronted the country before the election and whether Trump could ever rise to the kind of "consoler in chief" approach emergencies required. Stepien had a sense of how it might look—and it wasn't encouraging. He had worked for someone with a similar personality and a comparable political sensibility, and someone who was probably even more stubborn: former New Jersey governor Chris Christie.

Stepien had been Christie's campaign manager in 2009, and was his deputy chief of staff in the governor's office in 2010 when a blizzard blew into New Jersey that year. The storm blanketed parts of the state with three feet of snow, but Christie wanted to keep his plans for a Disney vacation in Florida. Stepien urged him to stay and show voters that his priority was making sure they were safe and secure. Christie wouldn't listen.

"What? Do you want me to stay here and ride on the back of a snowplow?" Christie barked back at Stepien.

Christie headed to Orlando, and the decision was a political disaster. But Christie learned his lesson, and when Hurricane Sandy made landfall in 2012, the governor was a constant presence in his blue fleece, zipped three-quarters of the way up. He left the presidential campaign trail in 2016 when another snowstorm arrived.

"You have to make people be safe and secure," Christie said.

Stepien didn't think Trump had internalized a similar moment. When Trump visited Puerto Rico in October 2017 after Hurricane Maria—after it was clear the administration had bungled the initial response to the Category 5 storm that had ravaged the region—Stepien was White House political director and watched as the boss made a bad situation worse. With power restored to just 7 percent of the island, and some remote corners in need of food and water, Trump landed in San Juan and declared that he deserved an A-plus for his team's response.

The enduring memory of Trump's visit came when he started tossing paper towels into the crowd like T-shirts at a ball game. A few he tossed like he was standing on a free-throw line taking foul shots. Trump was playing for a laugh, but he came off as frivolous and sophomoric amid the emergency confronting 3 million Americans.

"I was having fun, they were having fun," Trump said at the time as he shrugged off the criticism.

The image haunted Stepien, and for good reason.

The crisis that awaited Trump proved more catastrophic than anything else the country had experienced in the previous hundred years. Coronavirus disease 2019 was more commonly known by its abbreviation of Covid-19, although Trump tried to rebrand it at various points as the "China Virus," "Chinese Virus," "Invisible Enemy," "Wuhan Virus," "The Plague," "The Plague from China," and even the "Kung Flu."

From the start of the outbreak, Trump had repeated opportunities to respond in a serious, reassuring, and empathetic way, becoming the sort of wartime commander in chief that some advisers told him would have increased his chances for a second term. But Trump didn't have much interest in putting in the work for a fulsome response, just in how the response would reflect on him politically. Trump's management style was well suited to sales and branding, less so to handling an actual crisis. He turned emergency news conferences on Covid into campaign rallies, and he interpreted the impressive ratings—Americans tuning in for information about a terrifying and rapidly changing disease—as successfully winning a popularity contest.

When it came time to celebrate the Chinese New Year at the end of January 2020, Matt Pottinger had reason to rejoice. A former foreign correspondent who joined the Marines at age thirty-two, he'd been working for a Manhattan hedge fund investigating Chinese companies when in 2016, his old friend Michael Flynn, who was then Trump's national security adviser, recruited him to the White House as the senior Asia policy director on the National Security Council. He and Flynn had served together in Afghanistan. Flynn lasted only twenty-four days on the job, but Pottinger flourished. In three years inside the Trump White House, Pottinger had served under four different national security advisers, record turnover for the seventy-three-year-old security council. Now he was entering the final year of Trump's term as the top deputy at

NSC, arguably the busiest job in the White House. The title of deputy might sound inherently junior, but in a massive political bureaucracy like the U.S. federal government, "deputies are the people who actually do all of the shit," as one White House official once described it to me.

Pottinger arrived at the Chinese New Year party well aware of the virus outbreak in China. He had covered the SARS epidemic in 2002 as a Beijing correspondent for the *Wall Street Journal*, and two weeks earlier, on January 13— just two days before a Chinese delegation would arrive at the White House for Trump's trade deal extravaganza in the East Room—the NSC staff had held preliminary meetings on the outbreak. At the time, Pottinger didn't have enough information to recommend any action. His team had pushed public health officials to be more proactive, and Pottinger told them that they would never receive any conclusive data on a silver spoon, especially from a country like China, which might be covering up a massive outbreak or a leak from a laboratory.

Then, at the party on Saturday night, Pottinger heard more about the grim situation unfolding in Wuhan—new details from people who'd just returned from China, or had family living there. Pottinger wasn't sure what to make of the frightening anecdotes. He returned home that night, dusted off the phone numbers for his SARS sources from almost two decades ago, and started making calls. He reached a doctor who had firsthand knowledge of the situation in Wuhan.

"Should I be thinking about this in terms of SARS?" Pottinger asked.

"No," the doctor told him. "Think in terms of the flu of 1918."

Another source told him that as many as half the people being quarantined in China were asymptomatic. It was a rifle shot in his ear. Asymptomatic spread, he knew, would make the virus virtually unstoppable.

Two days later, on Monday, January 27, Pottinger escalated the issue inside the White House.

"I now have to be convinced as to why we would not immediately impose a travel ban on China," Pottinger told Robert O'Brien, the president's national security adviser. "These are firsthand accounts from citizens, and China is not sharing any of this with us."

O'Brien told Pottinger to do what he needed, that he'd earned the trust to effectively act as White House national security adviser when it came to coronavirus. Pottinger enforced his own authority to summon an emergency meeting of the NSC's deputies committee—a group that included the No. 2s from a dozen agencies, including the CIA's deputy director, the vice chairman of the Joint Chiefs of Staff, the deputy attorney general, and others. Pottinger also made sure that Redfield, the CDC director, would be in attendance, as well as Alex Azar, Trump's health secretary, whose agency encompassed the CDC and the National Institutes for Health.

Inside the Situation Room, Pottinger sat at the head of the table. For about ten seconds. He slid over one seat to the left when Mick Mulvaney, Trump's chief of staff, entered the room and commandeered the primary chair. Pottinger's urgency irked Mulvaney, who could be inclusive to a fault, but also quick with a judgment. The administration was riddled with infighting and incompetence, which made it difficult for Mulvaney to recognize the strengths of the team around him. Pottinger and Mulvaney hadn't worked much together, and the South Carolinian could never quite get past Pottinger's former reporter bona fides.

"He's a journalist," Mulvaney would say, turning the profession into a pejorative.

That tone came from the top. Trump tried to solve issues—or at least sidestep them long enough to survive—with puffery, hyperbole, and salesmanship. It had largely worked, especially when it came to matters of political survival. When Pottinger—followed shortly by Peter Navarro, Trump's anti-China trade adviser—started ringing the alarm bells that this was the one thing that could actually doom the Trump Administration, he and his allies were waved off as alarmists.

Pottinger wanted a complete ban on travel from China, a full stop by the first week of February. At the time, Pottinger was far out in front of the rest of the administration on the issue, and it landed with Mulvaney like an absolutist position. What about the Americans who were still in Wuhan? The cruise ships that would become Covid incubators floating at sea? All the college exchange students? Mulvaney figured he better show up at the deputies meeting before Pottinger implemented a policy that left Americans stranded across the globe.

Pottinger's deputies meeting had been called so quickly that there was no seating chart, none of the usual name cards folded like pup tents along each side of the rectangular mahogany conference table. But word of the meeting had spread rapidly, and bodies were piling into the Situation Room. The first American had tested positive a few days before and the CDC had already warned Homeland Security and the Department of Transportation that inbound flights from Wuhan should be confined to only a handful of airports where passengers could be screened for the virus.

In addition to Azar, Redfield, and Mulvaney, the room included Kellyanne, Dan Scavino, the president's social media czar, and Joe Grogan, the head of the White House Domestic Policy Council. Elaine Chao, the transportation secretary, took a seat near the head of the table. Dr. Robert Kadlec, who oversaw preparedness and response as an assistant secretary of health and human services, sat down, too. Dr. Anthony Fauci, the longtime director of the National Institute of Allergy and Infectious Diseases, joined via video conference. Peter Brown, the president's homeland security adviser, silently observed the meeting from the back corner of the room. At more than thirty people, it was an absurdly large crowd for the Situation Room, a space designed to curtail leaks by keeping conversations to a small group. But coronavirus was on the verge of becoming a major issue, and one that seemed destined to touch nearly every agency.

"I've never seen the Situation Room like that," said one person involved at the meeting. "It was like all the deputies and their plus-ones."

The crowded room fell silent when Pence walked in. Mulvaney, having taken the head seat moments earlier, slid one to his right. The vice president sat down, surveyed the scene, and then, without saying a word, caught a glimpse over his shoulder of the presidential seal hanging on the wall. The insignia signaled the presence of the president, a formality that only Pence, an adherent to the pageantry of politics, had noticed. The room waited as Pence swiveled around, removed the seal, and leaned it against the wall on the floor. It was an act of deference from a vice president who had once during a 2017 trip to the Panama Canal likened Trump's energy and focus to that of Theodore Roosevelt and favorably compared him to biblical figures during a 2018 speech at the Israeli embassy. It was sometimes difficult to tell with Pence where his loyalty ended and his subservience began.

Azar, who sat just to the right of Pence and Mulvaney, dominated most of the first twenty minutes of the meeting. He informed the group they were free to debate policy decisions around the coronavirus outbreak, but that his agency would coordinate daily operations. No one signaled an appreciation for how deeply the virus was about to stress multiple agencies. There was obvious confusion over which agencies had jurisdiction over certain facets of the response.

It was the barest of governmental coordination when a robust, streamlined strategy was imperative. The health secretary wasn't thinking about the chain of command at Homeland Security that travel restrictions would set off to reach Customs and Border Patrol, which handled airport screening, or the Coast Guard to tighten down coastal ports. Immigration and Customs Enforcement and the Federal Emergency Management Agency would need to play key roles, too.

Stephen Biegun, the No. 2 State Department official, mentioned that his agency planned to restrict travel to and from China, and within a day probably ramp it up to prohibiting travel. It took a few moments before the gravity sank in. Both CDC and State could issue travel advisories.

"Wait," Mulvaney said. "Who has the authority to restrict travel to China?"

"We decide," Biegun told him, but deferred when Mulvaney pressed him with additional questions.

Chao warned about restricting travel, noting that passenger planes often contained commercial freight. Her concern came off to some in the room as callous, or too far down in the weeds considering the massive problem they were about to confront. They were talking about stopping air travel to China, and Chao was worried about cargo coming and going in the belly of a Delta flight? Chao would say later that she agreed with others in the meeting that the health and safety of Americans was paramount.

"I don't think this is working," Ken Cuccinelli, the acting deputy secretary for Homeland Security, suddenly barked at the room. By that point, it was clear there was an immense amount of work in front of the administration and that Azar's tone at the outset—that the situation was under control—was ill-informed, at best. For one, few people had been aware of the State Department's pending travel advisory.

"We are failing at both coordination and communication," Cuccinelli said.

Azar was furious. His face turned red, but he remained silent as Cuccinelli finished his rant. Azar then unleashed on Cuccinelli. The two were seated on the same side of the table, but Azar never turned toward him and kept his eyes instead on Mulvaney. Cuccinelli would be barred from the task force a month later.

"This is the first I'm hearing of this," Azar said, complaining that Cuccinelli was questioning his leadership in the meeting instead of seeking him out privately. "It's not consistent with the facts."

Mulvaney saw it was time to break.

"You know what? Let's hold off," Mulvaney said, turning to Biegun and the other State Department officials and asking them to pause any change to China travel advisories. "Let's talk about this tomorrow. Same time, same place and talk through this. In the meantime, I'm going to pulse the president and see where his head is on this and we'll reconvene tomorrow."

Mulvaney ended the meeting by noting that their internal discussion could impact financial markets, and asked for discretion from the two dozen officials in the room.

"What we discussed here needs to stay here," Mulvaney said.

The details leaked the next day.

———

At the same time, Peter Navarro, one of the president's trade advisers, was also shooting off flares about the virus. He had spent the last few years leaning into internal White House fights, willingly disrupting meetings as he pushed for the tariffs Trump had wanted to impose, and then feuding over trade negotiations with China. Navarro was a seventy-year-old economics professor from California who rode a bicycle to work and changed in his office, which was a disaster zone of empty organic trail mix containers, soiled socks, and wrinkled pants strewn on tables and across the floor. He'd run for office in California five times, and lost each race. He found his way into Trump World during the 2016 race when he was recruited by Jared, who was researching trade policy and stumbled upon Navarro's book *Death by China*. The book mixed fairly mainstream recommendations, like helping safeguard U.S. technology secrets, with inflammatory accusations, like calling Beijing "the planet's most efficient assassin."

By the start of 2020, Mulvaney's frustration with Navarro had been simmering for months. Mulvaney told aides he walked in on Navarro working in his boxer shorts, an undershirt, and white socks, and considered the possibility of having White House doctors evaluate the trade adviser's mental stability. He'd already tried to get Navarro fired by having a White House attorney look into whether Navarro was harassing colleagues by yelling in meetings and pounding on tables. Staff complained that Navarro made aggressive, late-night calls to colleagues seeking status updates on his requests, and had called Mulvaney's chief deputy, Emma Doyle, a "globalist bitch." Doyle told her boss that she'd like to have that title memorialized across a coffee mug, which suggested she had taken the slight in stride, but Mulvaney still wanted to punish the bad behavior. The problem was Trump usually protected Navarro—"my Peter," he would call him—and then the report from the White House counsel's office came back inconclusive: Some White House staff said Navarro might be harder on women, but others said he denigrated everyone equally. Mulvaney dropped the inquiry in part because no one wanted to be the one to tell Navarro he had to attend training on respect in the workplace. Still, if Mulvaney couldn't get Navarro fired, he could at least keep him out of the coronavirus meetings.

"Look," Azar told Mulvaney. "I've got four or five people who won't come to the meetings if Peter is there."

Navarro hadn't heard about the Situation Room meeting until later and was furious. He was convinced the outbreak was bigger than China was letting on and that the administration around Trump wasn't doing enough to prepare. Bannon, now on the outside of the White House, urged him to memorialize all of his predictions in a series of memos. But Navarro was hesitant, in part because Trump hated Navarro's memos.

"I'm not even really a part of this," Navarro said.

"Even better," Bannon replied. "Just put 'draft' on it and send it to everybody and ask for their comments."

Navarro hammered out a memo that argued for shutting down travel to China. It estimated the virus could kill nearly 550,000 Americans. Shutting down travel to China might cost $35 billion, Navarro pointed out, but the cost of a pandemic could hit $5.7 trillion.

When no one replied, Navarro removed "draft" from his memo, addressed it to the president, and circulated it again. The documents leaked to the *New York Times* and *Axios* in April.

Trump would deny that he saw the memos, but the documents had been disseminated by the NSC. And it was O'Brien who had elevated Pottinger at the NSC and was close to Navarro—who ultimately helped convince the president to restrict travel from China.

"This will be the largest national security crisis of your presidency," O'Brien told Trump.

Trump treated his decision to ban travel from China on January 31 as if he had all but solved the crisis.

"We pretty much shut it down," he'd say on February 2.

But he knew that the virus was far more severe than he was letting on. In a private interview on February 7, two days after his impeachment acquittal—before his rally in New Hampshire, before his swing out West, where he held three more rallies, and before his trip to India—he'd told journalist Bob Woodward that the virus could be spread through the air—a fact that wasn't widely known at the time.

━━━━━━

Trump's campaign commenced its first major poll of 2020 at the end of February, just before he left for India. It was a comprehensive study of voters in the seventeen states viewed as most likely to decide the 2020 election. Nobody needed a poll to understand Trump was on a political tear. Still, the initial data that rolled in was red hot. Brad couldn't help but keep Trump apprised of the progress. He phoned the president in India, and briefed him as soon as he returned. The final numbers hadn't been crunched, and Fabrizio urged restraint. The request was denied.

Trump and Brad were a pair of momentum junkies whose high-octane and hyperbolic sales pitches would make Billy Mays blush. They viewed themselves as political brawlers with little patience for the fine print. Trump's five decades in real estate, reality television, and politics were guided by his idea of "truthful hyperbole," a phrase he'd coined in his 1987 bestseller, *The Art the Deal.*

Even Jared's most valued trait around Trump World was his optimism. It certainly wasn't his political compass. Jared hadn't even registered as a Republican until his father-in-law had been in office for two years. His previous political experience was as a Democratic donor, spending more than $150,000 to help elect Hillary Clinton, Chuck Schumer, and other liberals in the fifteen years before his father-in-law sought the presidency. When he arrived in Washington in 2017, he claimed to be the brains behind the digital operation that had helped Trump unlock the set of post-industrial Midwestern states that Republicans hadn't won since the 1980s. But he knew little about the mechanics of running a presidential campaign. When a Republican adviser asked him about the digital strategy during the final, frantic stretch of the 2020 race, Jared routed the call to Gary Coby, the campaign's digital director.

"Can you call Gary?" Jared said. "I don't know anything about the digital stuff."

Still, whenever distress and disorder from whatever crisis-of-the-moment threatened to consume the White House or campaign, Kushner was the one who could be counted on to calm the troops.

━━━━━

Truthful hyperbole was an organizing principle for Trump World, and it led to what, by 2020, had become a long tradition of rushing to deliver the boss any and every semblance of good news. Brad understood the dynamic, and he knew Trump would reward him with at least partial credit for the propitious if unpolished polling. The early data showed Trump surging with Hispanic voters, across blue-leaning battleground states, and against the entire lineup of potential Democratic challengers. Trump wouldn't bother asking whether the data were incomplete. For bad polls, Jared told Trump to add five points to his ballot numbers, arguing that pollsters couldn't measure Trump's base. And Trump never questioned a good poll. Even Hope was known on occasion to invent positive polls during conversations in the Oval Office that would help reset the president's mood. In 2018, she testified to Congress that she some-times told "white lies" on behalf of the president. She also told them to the president.

That was the way Trump wanted it. While some executives preferred administrative silos to provide direction and promote focus for the workforce, Trump assembled an extraordinary arrangement of delivery systems that incentivized his team to forage far and wide for bits and pieces of positivity—from news reports, gossip pages, social media posts—that they then fed directly to him. With certain exceptions, it ensured that the most obsequious and submissive staffers lasted the longest. By early 2020, it was widely understood that unquestioned agreement and alignment with Trump meant there were never any consequences for a staffer's mistakes, misfires, or bad advice. But to be proven wrong after even a single disagreement with Trump was to risk for-ever being viewed as disloyal and labeled an idiot, or—in Trump's sarcastic vernacular—"a genius." The result was a constant reading of Good News from the Gospel according to Trump, and he had plenty of disciples eager to recite chapter and verse.

This path to longevity didn't necessarily run parallel with the road to suc-cess for Trump's own political goals. In fact, it was often at cross-purposes with the objectives—and personal ambitions—of the senior staff in his White House. During the final stretch of the 2016 race, for instance, his campaign aides tried to keep him away from Twitter. In his first months as president, press secretary Sean Spicer and chief of staff Reince Priebus discussed shut-ting down his campaign-style mega-rallies. There was also a constant crusade by each of his four White House staff chiefs and all five managers of both presidential campaigns to sequester Trump from his "enablers," a common classification that referred to the pack of troublemakers who would whisper in the president's ear after everyone else had left the room to raise doubts in his mind and ultimately detonate any communication plans, political strate-gies, and policy goals that he'd agreed to just moments before. It was a sur-real, kaleidoscopic corner of Trump World where the colors and shapes often remained the same but the exact scene depended on who looked through the eyepiece. For Brad, this demographic included two of his 2016 predecessors,

Corey and Kellyanne. For Jared, it was Corey, Bannon, and Kellyanne. For Bannon, it was Jared and Ivanka.

The laborious efforts to intercept enablers were viewed as rebellious acts of treachery in Trump World. The Obama, Bush, and Clinton White Houses all kept a narrow list of staffers who could walk into the Oval Office without an appointment. Yet it was free admission to come see Trump. Staffers who didn't barge in would often loiter outside his open door, hoping to catch the president's eye and be waved in for a chat or the chance to pitch a new idea. Trump White House aides frequently tried to sneak in one final word during internal debates by leaving him printouts of unsourced and aggressively biased Breitbart News stories that backed up their own position. Any strategies to restrict access to Trump with the old ways of doing business invariably were solutions aimed at the symptoms instead of the cause and never achieved any long-term success. When John Kelly, a retired, four-star Marine general whom Trump had recruited into his administration, invoked his chief of staff authority to listen in on any call that was patched through to the president from the West Wing switchboard, Trump gave friends the number to Melania's phone to circumvent this official channel.

Information in Trump World obeyed two basic laws of physics: Kepler's laws of planetary motion and Newton's theory of gravity. The first held that every piece of hearsay and every nugget of news—no matter its size, shape, or significance— was effectively its own celestial body in a constant, elliptical orbit around a singular, magnificent Trumpian Sun. The second truth was that the giant orange star at the center of the universe was slowly pulling each object closer.

"Sir," Brad told Trump during one call about the still-unfinished February poll, "you're winning Colorado, you're winning New Mexico. You can win 400 electoral votes."

None of it was exactly true, not to mention highly unlikely. No presidential candidate, Republican or Democrat, had cleared the 400-vote threshold since George H. W. Bush drafted behind two Ronald Reagan landslides and lapped Democrats for a third consecutive GOP win.

Still, Trump was ecstatic. As Brad had anticipated, he interpreted the raw data as proof of Brad's prowess as a decision maker. Trump's judgment was constantly questioned by the press and criticized by his skeptics, including his unusual move to put a website developer turned digital marketer in charge of a $1.5 billion presidential campaign. On the phone half a world away in India, Trump told Brad he might just be the best campaign manager ever.

═══════

Trump had reassured his own supporters during the New Hampshire rally on February 10 that "the virus is going to be fine." A few days earlier, he made comforting remarks to manufacturing workers in Michigan, claiming that "we have it very well under control."

But on February 24, as the World Health Organization acknowledged that it wasn't clear whether the virus could be stopped from spreading across the globe, investors realized that Trump's rosy assessment couldn't be trusted. The Dow dropped more than 1,000 points—its biggest point decline in more than two years—as shares of travel, health insurers, and high-flying technology stock were among the hardest hit. American Airlines Group dropped 8.5 percent, UnitedHealth Group slumped 7.8 percent, and Facebook fell 4.5 percent. The sell-off jarred Trump, at least momentarily.

"Other than yesterday, which was something pretty bad, with respect to the virus, and we'll see what happens," Trump said at an event in India, referring to the stock market crash.

Covid, he added, was "a very serious thing."

But Trump quickly returned to his magical thinking and the message that he'd been drilling home for the past two months, that the virus was "going to go away."

"Things like that happen where—and you have it in your business all the time—it had nothing to do with you," Trump said. "It's an outside source that nobody would have ever predicted. If you go back six months or three months ago, nobody would have ever predicted. But let's see. I think it's going to be under control."

The next day brought another slide in the markets, which Trump blamed on Dr. Messonnier's statement. From the *Air Force One* flight back to Washington from India, Trump called Azar in the middle of the night and threatened to fire the CDC doctor unless he could keep her on message.

"She's scaring the shit out of people!" Trump shouted.

Azar held his own news conference before markets closed that day and said that the virus was "contained." But it did nothing to distract from Messonnier's warning that the virus might force schools to close, conferences to be canceled, and businesses to keep their employees home.

"We need to be preparing for significant disruption," she said.

When *Air Force One* arrived back home at 6:30 in the morning on February 26, Trump knew the stock market was under considerable duress in the seventy-two hours he'd been gone, but he didn't know how to fix it. That evening, after markets closed, Trump held a news conference and contradicted the exact thing he'd told Woodward two weeks earlier.

"This is a flu," Trump said. "This is like a flu."

At the time, Brad was down the street from the White House at the National Republican Senatorial Committee, where he gave a private briefing for senators about the state of the campaign. Still feeling empowered by the validation he'd received from Trump over the polls, he told the Republican senators that they would keep the Senate, and that the Trump campaign would help them do it. He laid out plans to expand the presidential campaign's reach into New Mexico, which Republicans had lost in six of the previous seven presidential contests, and Minnesota, which they'd lost fourteen of the past fifteen.

Later than night, Brad and Scavino sat with Trump watching TV in the private dining room off the Oval Office. When Senator Lindsey Graham called to gush about Brad's presentation, Trump, without telling him, put the senator on speakerphone.

"That kid's a fucking genius!" Graham said.

"Brad?" Trump said.

"He might be the smartest guy in politics," Graham said.

"Yeah," Trump replied. "That's why I got him!"

———

As February drew to a close, Trump took to a campaign rally stage in North Charleston, South Carolina, where he said that recent headlines about his handling of coronavirus were nothing more than the political heir apparent to the Mueller probe and impeachment.

"This is their new hoax," Trump said.

The first report of a Covid-related death came the next day: a Seattle man in his fifties with underlying health conditions—or as Trump described him during a news conference, "a wonderful woman."

Two days later, on Monday in Charlotte, North Carolina—for the final packed arena rally in what was supposed to have been a year full of them—Trump promised a vaccine would be ready "relatively soon." On Tuesday, he said his administration was hustling to develop Covid therapies—"sort of another word for cure."

On Wednesday, he estimated the death rate from Covid was "way under 1 percent" during an interview on *Hannity*.* On Thursday, at a Fox News town hall in Joe Biden's hometown of Scranton, Pennsylvania, Trump falsely blamed Obama for the delay in Covid testing.

On Friday, he signed a $8.3 billion emergency spending package for hospitals and states to fight Covid, falsely claimed that Covid tests were available to everyone who wanted one, called Washington governor Jay Inslee a snake, and said he was opposed to letting a cruise ship full of sick passengers dock because it would add to the national count of coronavirus cases.

That night, he fired his chief of staff.

The morning after Trump was impeached in December, the first item in *Politico Playbook* was news that one of the president's staunchest defenders, Representative Mark Meadows, planned to resign from Congress. Meadows told *Playbook* that he'd spoken to Trump about finding a way "we can work more closely together in the future." He then spent the first two months of 2020 taking meetings and lunches with various Washington power brokers to solicit opinions and advice on how he should run the White House chief of staff's office. His longtime friend, Mick Mulvaney, was still the acting chief—a title he'd had for fifteen months at that point—but Meadows made clear that it was only a matter of when. Still, Mulvaney didn't see it coming.

The night before Mulvaney was fired, Jared had called and tried to warn him.

---

* The World Health Organization had just announced that the global death rate was 3.4 percent.

"For the first time the president actually said, 'Maybe we should go in a different direction,'" the president's son-in-law told the White House chief of staff.

Mulvaney recognized it as a bad omen, but he hadn't been told there was a decision or a pending announcement. There wasn't much time to dwell on what it all meant because, just a few hours later, the White House was alerted that there may have been a coronavirus outbreak inside the Centers for Disease Control and Prevention in Atlanta, where the president was scheduled to visit the next day on his way down to Mar-a-Lago for the weekend.

The White House scotched that CDC leg of the trip, but Covid test results from the public health agency came back negative just as Trump was boarding *Marine One* the following morning. Trump wanted to put the CDC visit back on the schedule.

"Let's just swing by," Trump told his team. "We're flying right over Atlanta."

Deputy White House chief of staff Emma Doyle had just started reassembling plans to return to the CDC when Trump turned to Jared inside *Marine One.*

"Have you told her what we're doing?" Trump asked.

Doyle looked up from her phone.

"No, I didn't want to," Jared said. "I didn't want to violate Mick's confidence."

Doyle had worked for Mulvaney as a legislative assistant in the House of Representatives, as his chief of staff when he was director of the White House Office of Management and Budget, and now as his principal deputy in the staff chief's office. Had Mulvaney known this was coming, she would have been one of the very first people he'd have told.

"You can tell her," Trump said. "Maybe she'll stay."

Doyle was about to have a very different day than what she'd expected.

Trump explained that he thought it was time to make a change. He said he was considering Meadows as a replacement.

"What do you think?" he asked Doyle.

Doyle told the president she knew Meadows as a House member and forced out a few other neutral descriptors. *Marine One* landed at Andrews Air Force Base, and Trump climbed out of the helicopter.

As Trump walked across the runway to *Air Force One,* Jared told Doyle not to say anything before an announcement was ready. It still wasn't clear to her how soon the change was coming. But when she was summoned to the president's cabin on the plane, she saw a draft of the tweet announcing Mulvaney's ouster displayed on his desk.

Doyle pleaded with Jared to hold off until Monday. She happened to have been standing in the chief's office in July 2017 when Trump fired his first chief of staff, Reince Priebus, on the rain-soaked tarmac at Joint Base Andrews—a mortifying finale for what had been a mostly humiliating six months on the job for Priebus. But it might have been even worse for his staff, who had watched with shock as the news played out on television in nearly real time. Doyle was desperate to avoid a similar situation, and she asked Jared for more time so she could prepare the rest of Mulvaney's team—and so that he could be the one to tell his wife and kids. Her request was rejected.

Doyle texted Mulvaney from the plane—they needed to speak in private immediately.

"Today's the day," Doyle wrote.

Trump called Mulvaney later that evening, thanked him for the work done, and told him he could have any job in government he wanted—except the one he had right now. That night, a few minutes past 8:00 p.m.—about ten minutes after he'd arrived at Mar-a-Lago—Trump posted the tweet that announced Meadows would be his next and fourth chief of staff and that Mulvaney would become the U.S. special envoy for Northern Ireland.

"Thank you!" Trump added.

The morning after Mulvaney's ouster, coronavirus cases had been reported in more than half of the states in the union. New York and Washington state had both declared public emergencies. Carnival's *Grand Princess* cruise ship, with more than twenty-one infected passengers and crew, was idling off the coast of California. But that morning, Trump's focus wasn't on the pandemic.

Sitting in his club with a few guests, staff, and Pence, the president showed his visitors a mock-up of a logo for the Republican National Convention, which was still more than five months away.

"I don't really like the way the elephant's nose is shaped," Trump said. "And there are only three stars. It should be five stars. Like a five-star hotel."

Trump cared deeply about the convention, but this preoccupation was something different. One way Trump relieved stress or calmed his nerves was to find trivial issues to agonize over and master. Multiple White House aides had been included in long and painstakingly detailed strategy sessions aimed at picking out the playlist for what classic rock tunes to play over the loudspeakers at his next rally. For a president in the opening days of a pandemic, the harsh truth was there was very little he could easily control. So instead, he crawled into the minutiae of the convention logo, and now he was rolling.

"Jon Voight is coming to the convention," Trump continued. "He's a big star. He was in *Midnight Cowboy*. That was a great movie."

It might have been a bit of a stretch to talk about Voight's stardom in the present tense—the dues-paying member of Mar-a-Lago had starred in *Midnight Cowboy* in 1969.

"Kanye West is going to be the keynote speaker," Trump said. "I had him in the Oval Office with Jim Brown. And even Jim Brown turned to me and goes, 'This guy's a fucking lunatic.' And he is! He's crazy. But he's going to help me win reelection."

As Trump burrowed in on the convention, coronavirus crept right into his club.

═══════

That night, Fox News host Tucker Carlson visited Trump at Mar-a-Lago. Carlson was serious about the virus. He had chastised the media on his prime-time show earlier in the year for spending more time covering the impeachment than the virus. And now Carlson's wife, Susan Andrews, was pushing him to deliver the same rebuke to the president. He had a direct line to Trump and needed to deploy it to focus on the seriousness of coronavirus, she urged.

"This will cost you the election," Carlson warned him.

But Trump shrugged him off and said the virus wasn't as deadly as people thought.

That night, Trump dined with Brazilian president Jair Bolsonaro and a delegation from South America's largest country, seventeen of whom would test positive a few days later, including Fabio Wajngarten, Bolsonaro's communications director, who was photographed standing shoulder to shoulder with Trump at Mar-a-Lago.

Trump ended his weekend in Mar-a-Lago with a packed Sunday night campaign fundraiser that included at least one donor who would test positive for Covid within days.

═══════

Trump suddenly seemed eager to focus on the virus a couple of days later when he returned to Washington, U.S. stocks were in the midst of their worst day since 2008, including a 7 percent drop in the Dow sparked by coronavirus fear and a price war for oil stemming from a clash between Saudi Arabia and Russia. Meanwhile, several Republican House members in Trump's inner circle, including Meadows—the man he'd just named his new White House staff chief—had quarantined themselves after learning that, the week before, they had spent time with someone at CPAC, the annual conference of young conservative activists, who had tested positive for the virus. Matt Gaetz, the Florida congressman, was on *Air Force One* lifting off from Palm Beach International Airport when his staff called to tell him about the exposure. It had been eleven days since his contact, but there still were no clear guidelines on how to handle a potential exposure. Gaetz isolated in the rear of *Air Force One* until the end of the flight, when Trump summoned him back to the front of the plane. Trump wanted to check on Gaetz, who stood in the doorway and refused to enter the president's cabin.

"Do we need to wrap you in cellophane?" Trump asked him.

"I'll jump out of this plane without a parachute if it's necessary," Gaetz told him.

Trump returned to the White House and surprised aides with a sudden resolve to address the contagion.

"I want to do something big," he told them.

That night, Carlson, unsure if his warning had resonated with Trump, did something sure to get the president's attention: He repeated his blunt commentary on the Fox News airwaves.

"People you know will get sick," Carlson said that night. "Some may die. This is real. That's the point of this script—to tell you that."

Carlson didn't mention Trump by name, but explained that the nation's leaders weren't taking the issue seriously.

"People you trust—people you probably voted for—have spent weeks minimizing what is clearly a very serious problem," Carlson said as he stared directly into the camera, as if directing his warning to the president himself. "It's just partisan politics, they say, calm down. In the end this is just like the flu and people die of that every year."

▬▬

On March 11, two days after Trump had returned from Mar-a-Lago, Brad, Fabrizio, and McLaughlin arrived in the Oval Office to share with Trump the final results of their poll.

Their presentation did not unfold as they'd expected.

The map they handed Trump wasn't as optimistic as Brad had first described, but it still showed the president with more than 270 electoral votes and a good chance to exceed the 306 votes he'd won in 2016. Fabrizio explained that voters had long said the economy was in good shape, but more people were now personally feeling the effects from it, and Trump was getting the credit. In 2019, about one-third of voters in the target states said they were better off than they had been a few years earlier. That number was up to almost 50 percent at the start of 2020, and it was making a difference for the president. For the first time, Trump's job approval was a net positive across all seventeen battleground states.

Trump threw the map back at them.

"A lot of fucking good this is going to do me," he told them. "These numbers are all worthless. This China virus is going to wreck the economy, and that's going to be the end of me."

Trump's sulking was about to be put on display for a national TV audience in what would prove to be one of the most significant pivot points of the pandemic.

Just before his briefing with Brad and Fabrizio, Trump had raised the prospect of a national address from the Oval Office to announce new travel restrictions on the European Union, but still hadn't made a decision.

Advisers debated the wisdom of doing so, believing it could lend urgency and weight to one of the most precarious moments of Trump's presidency. The proposal sparked a three-and-a-half-hour meeting with Trump inside the Oval Office with Pence, Azar, acting Homeland Security secretary Chad Wolf, and a bevy of aides, including Ivanka, Jared, and Hope, who all urged Trump to deliver a national address to reassure the country that the administration did, in fact, have a serious response to the rapidly spreading coronavirus. Kellyanne argued against the address. The moment didn't require a prime-time speech, she said, instead urging the president to stick to a more controlled situation, like recording a video he could post on Twitter. As he listened to both sides, Trump was in a serious and somber mood. They were still discussing the best course of action when World Health Organization director-general Tedros Adhanom Ghebreyesus held a news conference to announce that Covid, with nearly 120,000 cases around the world and more than 4,000 confirmed deaths, was now considered a pandemic.

"He seems sad," Derek Lyons, the staff secretary, observed of Trump.

Trump was resigned to restricting travel from Europe, showing none of the pushback that he'd given the team six weeks earlier ahead of the China decision. He said he wanted to give the speech live, but still aides weren't sure it would happen.

"He still has another meeting this afternoon," Lyons said to Jared, pointing out Trump's previously scheduled discussion with executives from some of the country's biggest financial institutions. "I'm not sure he's going to do it."

His meeting with bankers helped focus him on the health concerns and reinforced his inclination to deliver the address. The last few weeks had been a roller coaster for financial markets, and they appealed to Trump's ego in a plea for stability.

"Take care of the health care problem," Bank of America chief executive Brian Moynihan told him. "Because solving the health care problem will help generate confidence."

White House advisers now had just five hours to craft the speech before Trump would return to the Resolute Desk and the cameras would click on. Still, it should have been plenty of time. It was a short speech—just ten minutes—and the administration had significant experience with travel bans, having approved more than two dozen orders that sought to restrict entry into the United States from Muslim-majority countries, from immigrants seeking asylum, from immigrants without health care, and now from multiple countries hit hardest by coronavirus. The task force had also discussed the European ban the day before, and Azar and Fauci both said they supported it. Fauci had urged the task force to go even further and cancel mass gatherings and urge Americans to telework.

"Be drastic," he said. "If we can be drastic and prevent the spike, we win."

Trump wouldn't address those measures in his speech, but a memo later in the week from the White House would urge federal workers to work from home.

When the task force meeting affirmed Trump's decision to announce the new restrictions in a prime-time speech, hardly anyone remained to coordinate the new plan. Mulvaney had been fired. Meadows was in quarantine. Jared had, after three years, left the White House staff with the impression that while he outranked the chief of staff, he wasn't to be bothered with the responsibilities of one. When a late appeal came in from the State Department to exclude Europeans with student and work visas in order to ensure strong diplomatic relations, aides inside the White House wondered aloud who even had the authority to make such a decision. Ultimately, it was Pence's chief of staff, Marc Short, who decided to scotch the request.

Jared, Lyons, and Stephen Miller took over speechwriting duties even though they hadn't been involved in coronavirus strategy. Jared had yet to attend a single task force meeting. Pence joined a large group of aides huddled around Miller as he typed the speech, and while the vice president had been put in charge of the task force, he was far from a public health expert. The doctors were nowhere to be found, and the officials who had been working on the issues for the task force were cut out of the process, leaving them to frantically email in fixes to factual errors.

Instead, however, the errors were fed into the teleprompter and read aloud by Trump, who inserted his own costly mistakes as well. In a prepared line that described how the restrictions would not apply to trade and cargo—the same as Trump's first two Covid travel bans—Trump inserted an extra word, "only," that completely changed the meaning of the sentence.

"These prohibitions will not *only* apply to the tremendous amount of trade and cargo," the president said, incorrectly.

Trump also didn't make clear that the ban only applied to foreign nationals or that there would be some exemptions for Americans who received health screenings.

Trump hadn't prepared for the speech or for the moment. He appeared uncomfortable as he spoke in a hushed monotone, and he offered no words of sympathy to Americans who were suffering from the disease or had lost loved ones. He stumbled over words and twiddled his thumbs. Futures for the Dow Jones Industrial Average fell with almost every word he uttered.

The speech did seem to help change the way Americans viewed the disease, but not in the way Trump's family had hoped. Ivanka and Jared had wanted the moment to reset how Americans viewed the president's handling of the contagion; instead, it only underscored how ill-prepared he was for the job.

Minutes after Trump had finished, actor Tom Hanks posted on social media that he and his wife, Rita Wilson, had contracted the virus while traveling in Australia and would isolate as long as needed. Fifteen minutes after that, the NBA announced it would suspend its season following the first positive test for a player, Rudy Gobert, a Utah Jazz center who a few days earlier had downplayed the disease by touching every reporter's recorder during a news conference.

No single night did more to focus the entire country on the crisis, including, at least temporarily, Trump.

The White House immediately recognized the national address had been a disaster and scrambled to stem the damage. Earlier in the week, Jared had discussed with Short the complicated internal dynamic the vice president was now facing. After returning from India, Trump had asked Pence to take over the task force, which the ever-loyal Pence accepted over the objections of his top advisers and confidants, who didn't want him to become the public face of a deadly virus. Even if Pence was successful, they told him, Trump would resent him for the success. But in trying to impose some order on the chaotic operation, Pence had already alienated some White House staff by cutting some officials out of meetings and usurping other responsibilities from the White House press office.

After the national address, at Pence's request, Jared started to assert himself more on coronavirus issues, a process that would take him out of the day-to-day operations of the campaign for several months. He began by cold-calling tech executives in search of solutions. The short-term answer was a Rose Garden news conference on Friday, two days after the national address, where Trump declared a national emergency over the pandemic, freed up $50 billion in financial assistance for states to address the issue and, with much more fanfare, announced a new partnership with Google to develop a website that would help Americans determine whether they needed a test and, if so, where to find one. The Dow jumped 2,000 points on the news. It showed a new seriousness from the White House, but was far from perfect—or even fully baked. Google executives, for example, were caught off guard by the announcement. There was a website in development, but it was far from finished and would only be available initially in the San Francisco area.

Trump, meanwhile, had taken notice of the plaudits Pence had received for his handling of the task force. The vice president's straightforward, calm approach was remarkable only for how unremarkable it was in contrast to Trump's freewheeling, confrontational style. Pence had also helped to give Fauci a platform at the news conferences, and Fauci's own direct approach was turning him into a star. Trump noted the "rave reviews" both had received, which in the Trump White House was a compliment immediately interpreted as a bad omen. On Saturday, the day after his Rose Garden news conference, Trump attended the task force's news conference, where he announced that he'd finally taken a coronavirus test. On Sunday, he attended a private task force meeting, and then surprised the group's members by saying he would come with them to the press briefing room to help update reporters. He initially said he'd just sit in the front row with the reporters and watch, but he quickly walked straight to the podium and took over the briefing.

Trump was intent on remaining in the spotlight. He held thirty-seven news conferences with the task force in the forty-five days between March 14 and April 27. That stretch started auspiciously enough with Trump focused on combating the virus. Fauci and Deborah Birx had shown him horrific projections from Imperial College in London that estimated millions would die without any action, and Trump decided to back their push for drastic measures to try to get ahead of the contagion. At a news conference with the task force on March 16, the group announced a fifteen-day plan to "slow the spread" by avoiding groups of more than ten people, a move that effectively shut down the economy. The Dow dropped nearly 13 percent on the news, the worst single day for stocks since the Black Monday crash in 1987.

———

The Front Row Joes stared sullenly through the rectangle boxes on their mobile phones and laptops. Coronavirus had claimed the life of the group's first member the day before, on March 31. Campaign events had been suspended because of the pandemic, which meant their only chance to comfort one another was to click a link and join their virtual Zoom memorial. Libby DePiero sat in front of her favorite Trump placards, including the sign with a picture of Donald the dog, and logged in from Connecticut. Randal Thom, a sixty-year-old ex-Marine with a gray Fu Manchu mustache, strapped on red, white, and blue suspenders inside his tiny house on a dirt road bisecting soybean farms and cornfields in southwestern Minnesota. Saundra didn't make it. She had been crushing overtime shifts at Walmart, trying to restock aisles of toilet paper and hand sanitizer that panicked shoppers had depleted. The death of Ben Hirschmann, who was just twenty-four years old, had shaken his friends. At the time, it remained unclear exactly how Covid spread and what all the symptoms entailed. Covid tests were still not widely available. Only 650 Americans had died at that point—and one of the Joes was among them.

Ben was overweight, which significantly increased the risk of severe illness from Covid. But two months earlier, he had found a primary care doctor to help chart his path to physical fitness. He called that same doctor when he started feeling sick in mid-March, just as Trump had issued social distancing measures with his fifteen-day plan to slow the spread. Ben was told he probably had the flu during a telehealth appointment and that some over-the-counter elixirs should help.

But the coughing and chills didn't subside. Ben called the doctor's office again a few days later. Another telehealth appointment. Another order for rest. Another assurance he wasn't sick with Covid.

Ben awoke before dawn the next morning, drenched in sweat and shaking. His mother, Denise, told him to get dressed. No more telehealth. They were going to the emergency room. Ben put on sweatpants, walked out of his room, and collapsed on his parents' living room floor. Denise screamed for her husband and performed CPR on her youngest son. First responders didn't bother transporting him to the hospital. The autopsy would show Ben's lungs filled with the disease.

An outpouring of condolences flooded Ben's home in suburban Detroit. "Ben touched hearts," Randal said on their Zoom memorial.

Ben had met Randal and the other Front Row Joes in 2017 at a Trump rally in Iowa. He had carpooled from Grand Rapids to Cedar Rapids with Shane Doyle, another twenty-something Trump supporter whom he had met at the previous Trump rally in Harrisburg, Pennsylvania. The day Ben graduated from Grand Valley State University in 2018, he drove three hours east to meet the gang on the other side of the state. It was the night of the White House Correspondents' Association black-tie dinner in Washington, D.C., which Trump was pointedly skipping to be with his base. Ben wore his commencement cap and gown to the bar afterward for the Front Row Joes' own "Correspondents Day Dinner." Their guests of honor that night: the Right Side Broadcasting Network crew that streamed every Trump rally online.

"I talked to him more than my own daughter," said Cindy Hoffman on the Zoom call, recounting her maternal relationship with Ben.

Cindy ran a tool-sharpening business in southeastern Iowa, but the cantankerous and combative farm gal had walked to her car when she'd heard about Ben's death, shut the door, and wept.

"I'm sixty years old, and he's just a baby," Cindy said. "When Ben and I would talk—you know all my Trump paraphernalia that I got going on?—Ben would say, 'Oh, you're going to leave that in your will for me, right?' I had that written down, and I was getting ready to redo the will. And then he died before I did. This is so fucking crazy."

"What about me?" Randal asked jokingly, in a voice so coarsened and gravelly it bordered on dysphonic. He and Cindy were the same age, but Randal's years-long struggle to stay sober and out of jail had weathered him beyond his years. "What if I outlive you?"

As the Front Row Joes gathered in cyberspace, they had—for a fleeting moment—faced the devastating consequences of coronavirus, and simply grieved. No attempts to blame a political rival. No dismissing the virus as just another flu. No mask mocking. They'd been floored by the sudden death of their friend and by the uncertainty ahead.

"We pray that everybody in New York and all the hot spots around this country stay safe—we know it's going to grow, and we know it's going to get worse," said Becky Gee, a dairy farmer from Ohio, in the prayer that closed the virtual gathering. "But we just trust that You have a plan, and You're watching out for us. We also ask that You put a heavy hand of guidance over President Trump and his Coronavirus Task Force, and we pray this in Jesus's name. Amen."

As Becky finished her appeal, the group began flicking off their Zoom links.

The mosaic of tiny Front Row Joes faded back into darkness.

7

Covid, Part Two: Retooling the Reelect

"The number one show on television."

—*Phone call with the author, April 20, 2020*

That beautiful wave of political momentum Trump rode into the start of the new year had crested and rolled back by April. The death toll from Covid passed 10,000 Americans the first week of the month, a staggering total just five weeks after the country's first reported fatality. By April 11, the death count exceeded 20,000. Unemployment was at 14.7 percent, up from 3.5 percent in February and the highest rate since the Great Depression. Ohio, Michigan, and other states announced that public schools wouldn't reopen. His approval rating dropped again. And as eager as Trump had been for Democrats to give him a challenger, the one they offered up turned out to be the man he'd tried to convince foreign powers to smear and the one his pollsters had said would be the toughest to beat: Joseph Robinette Biden Jr.

The panic was on, and Trump World fingers were pointing.

Biden secured the nomination on April 8 when Sanders suspended his campaign. The Democrat had pulled off a stunning comeback by quickly coalescing centrist support, but Biden had also just switched campaign managers and was low on cash. His campaign and the Democratic National Committee had socked away just $20 million. Trump and the RNC, on the other hand, had $225 million in cash on hand. Brad wanted to strike before Biden had a chance to reload.

Trump campaign polling showed that Biden wasn't well defined in voters' minds—Americans knew who he was, but not much about him—and Brad's plan was an advertising blitz that aimed to leverage frustration among voters over China's failure to contain the coronavirus by attacking Biden over positive comments the former vice president had made about Beijing. Brad told Trump the ad would appeal to both swing voters and Trump's working-class base and pointed out that a series of Democratic super-PACs had already started attacking Trump. They needed to fire back.

"We gotta be hitting the mick," Brad said about Biden, using a derogatory term to refer to the Democrat's Irish heritage.

Kellyanne was so confident Brad was wrong that she went to both Trump and the press. Brad's idea wasn't unwise—it was unripe, she said. Americans were focused on the pandemic, not the presidential race, and she told Trump his best bet to close the gap was to use his bully pulpit to take on the virus, not Biden. She viewed the political fight over coronavirus as between Trump and Chinese president Xi Jinping. Injecting Biden into that equation risked elevating the former vice president, who was, for now, stuck on the sidelines of the debate.

"Any campaign ads should show the commander in chief, the wartime president, signing $2 trillion in relief for Americans, deploying the USNS *Comfort*, working with Democratic governors and G-7 leaders, standing from the podium flanked by Drs. Fauci and Birx, mobilizing the private sector," she told the *Washington Post*.

But most of the reluctance came from Trump himself, who worried that a flurry of ads against Biden would give the impression that he was afraid of the presumptive Democratic nominee. And he obsessed over the images in the spots. He regularly asked the campaign to find pictures that made Biden look worse, and shots that made himself look better.

"You just spent half the ad making him look fifty years younger than he is," Trump complained.

Trump rejected the China spot three times for that very reason, sending the commercial back to Weitzner, his chief ad maker, because he didn't think Biden looked unappealing enough. Weitzner explained that distasteful images, at a certain point, would make the ads ineffective, but Trump didn't care.

"Use shittier pictures," Trump ordered him.

By the end of the race, the campaign had a "bad Biden" highlight reel of unflattering images of the former vice president that they knew Trump would approve.

<hr />

Trump immediately viewed himself as a wartime president, but he was impatient for progress and frustrated that he was still blamed for not acting sooner. Three days after shutting down the economy, he riffed at a news conference about the possibility that hydroxychloroquine, an antimalarial drug, and remdesivir, an experimental antiviral, could help treat the virus, despite warnings from his administration's doctors that there were still unanswered questions about the safety and effectiveness of both drugs. Shortly thereafter, Trump stopped attending the task force meetings, and he opted instead for a quick briefing from its members before heading into the daily news conference. But even those briefings were subject to the tyranny of the moment with Trump.

On April 20, that moment belonged to Trump, Kellyanne, and me.

I was in the parking lot of a Virginia strip mall, about an hour away from home, and cursing under my breath when my phone rang with a call from the White House.

"Mr. Bender?" asked Molly Michaels, Trump's assistant. "Please hold the line for President Trump."

I had ridden my Vespa out of the city to one of the few computer repair shops in the region that was open and, according to the online form I'd filled out for an appointment, willing to repair a recently cracked iPad—an urgent priority in the first months of lockdowns. But when I arrived, I was informed that the shop did not in fact repair iPads even though, yes, they were aware that that option was still included on their intake form. But now a bigger crisis: I couldn't find my pen and wasn't even sure if I had a notebook, and Trump was waiting on the line. I clicked on the tablet and frantically swiped to find the voice recorder without cutting my fingers on the screen's broken glass.

"What? No, wait—I mean, yes, but stall for me for a minute, Molly," I said. "I need to find a pen. Um, how are things at the White House today?"

"Everything is fine," Michaels said. "The president is waiting. May I put you through?"

I was patched through and Trump's distant voice was a clear signal that I was on speaker. Trump told me that he'd just been informed of an article I'd written a few days earlier in the *Wall Street Journal* about his strategizing with White House and campaign aides over how to respond to criticism of his administration's handling of the crisis. Kellyanne had been cut out of many of those meetings by Jared and Brad and had used my story as payback. She'd directed his attention to the tenth paragraph, which explained that Trump's advisers had concluded that a strong counterargument was that no world leader had been exceptionally well prepared to respond. Kellyanne had countered that this was a ridiculous argument because it acknowledged the original criticism and she had urged the president to call and set me straight. Trump explained this all to me as Kellyanne sat next to him in the Oval Office.

The president's message, he said, was that he'd handled the pandemic perfectly.

"I've saved hundreds, I've saved thousands, actually, they say I've saved tens of thousands of lives," Trump said.

I wasn't interested in litigating a three-day-old story, and I pressed Trump on other topics in search of some news. But Trump mostly wanted to chat. He asked if I'd watched a video he'd posted to Twitter. He mocked a "crazy Charles Blow story" in the *New York Times*. He asked why he hadn't seen me at any of his Covid task force news briefings, and if I needed his help getting in. I viewed it as a generous gesture, but one that made him sound like the bouncer at a club instead of the president of the United States.

But that's how Trump had been thinking about the news conferences.

"The number one show on television," he told me.

He viewed the news conferences as ratings bonanzas, not a crucial public service to impart critical health information to the American people. Trump laughed that the Fox News show *Special Report* had become the top-rated program on the network since he started his news conferences, which Fox carried live and often began at about the same time as Bret Baier's 6:00 p.m. show. Trump asked me what I thought was better: his coronavirus news conferences or his campaign rallies. Then he answered his own question.

"I have a feeling we reach more people this way than the rallies," he said.

"Well," he said, drawing the conversation to a close, "I'm going out there in about fifteen minutes. I took all my time to study. If I do a lousy job, it's your fault, because I didn't have time to read anything."

He laughed and hung up.

After I phoned my editor, I turned my Vespa toward home. A few minutes down the road, my phone rang again with a White House number. I pulled over. It was Kellyanne.

"That's how we roll!" she said.

━━━━

Two days later, Trump's political team presented him with a troubling round of new polling. The president trailed Biden in fifteen of the campaign's seventeen battleground states, including Texas and Iowa. In the other two states, Ohio and Nevada, he and Biden were tied.

The blitz of attack ads from Democratic super-PACs had barely registered with voters. The data showed instead that Trump's news conferences were killing him, especially among seniors. Older voters weren't just an attentive voting bloc, they were also the most at risk for severe health risks from Covid. They were tuning in for up-to-the-minute information about a confusing contagion and instead watching as Trump provided conflicting updates, attacked his opponents, and sparred with the press.

"They're not tuning in for you, sir," Ronna told him. "They want to see their leader. You've said you are a wartime president, and now you have to prove it."

Ronna was among the few in Trump World willing to consistently level with Trump. She and Trump barely knew each other when he backed her bid for party chairwoman in 2017.* But she used her influence sparingly and had become one of the president's longest-running political advisers, particularly among those who didn't inhabit a branch of the family tree. Her own lineage had prepared her perfectly for the job. When Ronna was twenty-one years

---

* One of Trump's favorite rally stories was how Ronna repeatedly called him in 2016 to say he'd win Michigan, her home state, by making just a few more campaign stops there. It was a flattering story, but nary a word of it was true. Ronna had said that Trump could win Michigan, but aside from a brief encounter at a rally that year, the two had never spoken.

old, she worked on the U.S. Senate campaign of her mother, Ronna Romney, who was divorced from her father, the son of former Michigan governor George Romney. But the elder Romney, himself a former presidential candidate, endorsed her mother's primary challenger. Ronna's mother lost.

"There's nothing I've dealt with, even since I've been chair, that was as difficult as that experience," Ronna said.

The family split still manifested itself two decades later. Her mom's side of the family was largely supportive of Trump, and the Romney side less so. Senator Mitt Romney, her uncle and the party's 2012 presidential nominee, said he hadn't voted for Trump in 2016 and wouldn't again in 2020, either. Ronna, who had used her Romney maiden name while campaigning for Michigan state party chair, dropped it when she took the party post in Washington.

Ronna told the president that the news conferences had become less useful and were now hurting him politically. Others on the call, including Jared and Brad, agreed.

But Trump dismissed their concerns and changed the subject.

Three days later, Trump used his news conference to suggest that injecting bleach or other disinfectants might cure Covid.

"Is there a way we can do something like that by injection inside, or almost a cleaning?" he wondered aloud.

The moment was humiliating and became an instant late-night comedy show punch line. But to the relief of many White House and campaign aides, it effectively ended Trump's daily appearances in the briefing room.

⸻

As April drew to a close, Fabrizio grew more frustrated. He sent a three-page memo to Brad that outlined his case for a sustained attack on Biden. The campaign was at its lowest point in a year. While Trump had been hammered by a "triple whammy" of economic collapse, Covid, and his own handling of the contagion, Biden had largely avoided national media scrutiny and taken his message to local markets. The result was that Biden had rehabilitated his image across the board, but particularly with key voting groups, including white independents, suburban women, and Black and Hispanic voters. More than 50 percent of voters said they had a positive image of Biden, according to internal polling, which was up 20 points in just two months. In February, Biden trailed Trump by five points in the campaign's target states. Now the Democrat was up eight.

"We have seen the enemy and the enemy is us," Fabrizio wrote.

"There is little chance that we will find ourselves back in the position we were in February without a full-throated engagement of Biden," Fabrizio wrote. "And there is NO guarantee that in this new post-Covid world, we climb back to where we were."

One reason for optimism for Trump World was that huge swings in Biden's polling during the primary showed that voters could change their opinions about him. But voters had steadfast views about Trump. His approval rating fluctuated, but in a much narrower range than Biden's, a sign that there was little the campaign could tell voters about Trump that they didn't already know or suspect.

For Fabrizio, that meant positive messages about Trump weren't going to move the needle with voters enough to close the gap. The only way to accomplish that was an advertising campaign on television and online that would put their "do or die" states—Florida, Michigan, Wisconsin, and Pennsylvania—safely into their column, and close the gap in the "must win" states of Arizona, Georgia, North Carolina, Ohio, Iowa, and Texas.

Brad agreed and told Fabrizio he'd authorize a few million on TV and a few million for digital.

"Do you have any fear that if I spend too much early, I will be in trouble later?" Brad asked.

Fabrizio told him the job would only get harder the longer they waited. And if the advertising messaging didn't work, they would still have time to adjust. But to know for sure the campaign needed to spend tens of millions on the effort.

"If you're convinced that the campaign will conservatively raise $500–$600 million alone and most all of our ground game costs are paid for by the RNC, what are we waiting for?" Fabrizio asked. "If you don't think we can match Biden dollar for dollar in the final stretch of the campaign, then that might give me pause. But if you think we can, then what is the holdup?"

Stepien, who would be named deputy campaign manager in a few weeks, weighed in with his support, too. He said Trump would have lost in 2016 if that race had been about him instead of Clinton. Right now, Stepien said, the race was entirely about Trump.

"It's not late, but it's not early either," Stepien said. "The White House can't make it a choice and we know the media won't. It has to come from the campaign. I'm with you."

Fabrizio devoted nearly an entire page of his memo to debunking a conspiracy theory that had bubbled up inside Trump World, including with the president, that Democrats were going to steal Biden's nomination at the convention. The rumor had been discussed to the point that Trump had cited it as a reason to hold off on heavy spending against Biden earlier in the month.

Dick Morris told Trump that Biden was too old and too prone to gaffes to be the nominee. McLaughlin agreed it was a possibility. Others said Fox News anchor Sean Hannity expressed concern that Biden would collapse under a sustained attack from Trump. The president, meanwhile, had often complained that his early attack on Warren had damaged her presidential bid, which he regretted because he viewed her as an easier opponent than Biden. Now he worried that a heavy blitz of attack ads would hasten the secret plot being hatched by Democrats, and his mind raced with who they might select in Biden's place.

"They're going to realize he's old, and they're going to give it to somebody else," Trump said during a meeting in April with political advisers. "They're going to give it to Hillary, or they're going to give it to Michelle Obama."

Fabrizio aimed to debunk the theory by outlining the remaining Democratic primaries, in which Biden had no significant challenger, and the delegate math to secure the nomination. Biden would have enough delegates to secure the nomination in just three weeks, Fabrizio explained, and it would be mathematically impossible to steal it in four weeks.

"I know that there is some concern (which I strenuously disagree with) that if we go after Biden too soon, we can collapse him, and the Dems will replace him at their convention," Fabrizio wrote in the April 27 memo. "I know POTUS tends to share this opinion. But whether or not they can steal it from Biden is quickly becoming a moot point. And perhaps, POTUS needs to see and understand the timeline."

===

Brad had been waiting for two years to unleash the campaign's artillery on an opponent, and he used Fabrizio's memo to start assembling a new presentation for the president as he sat poolside in South Florida. He loved working from home. He'd already been home for three weeks when he officially sent the campaign staff home in mid-March. Brad had an apartment near campaign headquarters in Virginia, but he preferred Fort Lauderdale. He took calls from the pool and laughed when the other person on the line could hear him splashing. His daughter, Alexis, came home from college. And he could spend more time with Candice, his wife, and their two Australian Labradoodles, Jackson and Parker.*

But back in Washington, Brad's rivals inside Trump World had started a whisper campaign that used his absence to portray him as disconnected and indolent. Nearly every top lieutenant in Trump World had fought to stay within a few feet of their leader, wary of who might influence Trump in their absence—or shiv them when they weren't looking. But Brad viewed himself as more than just a staffer. He had a strong working relationship with Ronna. He'd nurtured relationships with Trump's children and the in-laws. He told Trump that Ivana Trump and Marla Maples, the president's ex-wives, often phoned to check-in and sometimes share a secret or two about him. Brad described the president to others not as a boss, but as a friend.

The campaign manager missed the growing coup against him in part because he didn't think there was anything to complain about. Trump's numbers were in the tank, but Brad viewed that as a direct result of the president's pandemic response and a problem for the White House. Brad viewed the pandemic as, theoretically, a political advantage for Trump. The lockdowns should have been a much bigger problem for Biden, who was more reliant on in-person fundraisers that the shutdowns made more difficult. He didn't take the Democratic National Committee very seriously, and Biden didn't seem to have any political infrastructure ready. But when it came to Trump's political operations, Brad's feelings matched those sunny South Florida afternoons.

The Trump campaign and the Republican National Committee had spent

---

* Both dogs were named after San Antonio Spurs stars, Stephen Jackson and Tony Parker.

the past several years and invested tens of millions of dollars in collecting email addresses and cell phone numbers from voters. That kind of information was a commodity for almost any private business by 2020, but it was the lifeblood for the Trump reelection effort, and its digital operation was the beating heart pumping information to every corner of the campaign.

While Trump himself struggled with how to handle Covid, the campaign had transitioned quite smoothly. That was largely due to the handiwork of Gary Coby, the digital director. In the first weeks of the pandemic, Coby's team of about 100 people extended their already long tentacles even further into all aspects of the campaign. When the Trump kids and other surrogates stopped holding rallies or traveling on bus tours, Coby's team made sure their online events attracted millions of eyeballs. The digital team fed new targets and information to Chris Carr, who was overseeing thousands of Republican ground troops across the country. But the most important metric was money, and Coby's team—which was blasting more than a million texts and email solicitations every day—was crushing it. They collected a little less than $30 million in March, cleared $36 million, then $47 million in May.

The results exceeded expectations partly because of the makeup of Coby's team, mostly young and hardworking staffers who had moved back home during the pandemic and, without children or any other responsibilities, worked around the clock. Coby, meanwhile, was a thoughtful and hard-charging boss. He was fastidious and goal-oriented, which ran counter to the self-promotional ideals valued inside Trump World. But he was also ultra-aggressive—he'd left the business for a short time in his twenties to play professional poker—and in the wheelhouse of the Trump demo: a thirty-five-year-old white male with a high school diploma and a blue-collar upbringing.

Coby's first break in politics came when he was twenty years old and a member of his church in Bowie, Maryland, a well-known Republican operative named Curt Anderson, helped him land an internship in the U.S. House. Coby worked for various campaigns and private companies until he found himself at the Republican National Committee in 2016. When his boss, RNC chief digital officer Gerrit Lansing, asked if anyone on the team wanted to fly to San Antonio to meet Brad and see the campaign's digital operation, Coby jumped at the chance.

Coby was only thirty in 2016, but when it came to digital advertising, he'd had as much experience as anyone in the business. His résumé dovetailed with Brad's expertise on the creative side of advertising, website building, and digital marketing. The two men dorked out as they dove into the weeds of the digital operations. The next day, Brad was discussing some details with Lansing when he looked up from his computer as if he'd just remembered something.

"Oh," he said. "Gary works for me now. I took him."

"Okay," Lansing said.

Brad never had that discussion with Coby, who just laughed when he heard Brad claim him as an employee. Coby remained on the RNC payroll for the rest of the year, and in San Antonio for much of the next two months. Even when the party's staff was recalled from that city when negotiations broke down over a joint fundraising agreement between the RNC and Trump, Coby remained. The gesture was meaningful to Brad, and negotiations were settled within a couple of days.

The deal divided proceeds from the text messages and digital ads. The RNC agreed to cover the costs and mandated that the party be the permanent home for Trump's growing donor file. The Trump campaign also agreed to use Revv, a private company Lansing had started, to process online payments.

By 2020, Lansing and Coby were partners in multiple companies hired by the Trump campaign. Opn Sesame, which provided text messaging services, sent more than 500 million texts in the final four months, which raised the campaign and the RNC more than $600 million. The company, which earned between seven cents and eight cents per text, was paid about $35 million in those four months, according to internal campaign documents.

The second company was Revv, which Coby invested in after the 2016 race and by 2020 had been folded into WinRed—the Republican Party's exclusive online fundraising program. The creation of the potentially lucrative endeavor launched a battle that pitted Republican data geeks against each other, sparked a year of intraparty legal bickering, and exposed tensions at the highest level of Trump World that finally exploded into an intense argument between Ronna and Jared inside the Trump Hotel.

Jared didn't think the RNC could pull off the new operation and considered doing it himself. He discussed starting a new company with Brad and

Gabriel Leydon, the founder of a California video game company who had informally advised Jared since the 2016 race. Brad said no, and it became increasingly clear that Jared would have to blow up the party to do it.

Ronna also viewed the project in personal terms and had put her foot down. She hadn't decided whether to seek a second two-year term as RNC chairwoman and viewed the WinRed deal as a legacy project that could benefit the party for years to come. Keeping the new company as a nonprofit, she told Jared, would make sure it remained as an arm of the RNC.

Jared wasn't interested. "I don't give a fuck about the future of the Republican Party!" he told Ronna inside the hotel meeting room.

"Good to know," Ronna shot back. "I will be running for chair for a second term, and I will make sure you don't come anywhere near this!"

The eventual agreement formed WinRed. It was a for-profit company but built on Revv's existing fundraising software and anchored inside the Republican ecosystem. Revv owned 60 percent of the company and the other 40 percent stake was for Data Trust, an information warehouse the party had created the previous decade. Data Trust oversaw a treasure trove of information on the voting patterns and consumer habits of tens of millions of Americans that was easily the RNC's most valuable resource.

By early May, Brad finally had Trump's approval to open fire on the Joe Biden candidacy. He was headed to the White House for a round of meetings on May 7, his first face-to-face with the boss in more than six weeks, when he enthusiastically teased his battle plans on social media and compared the campaign to the moon-sized space station equipped with a planet-destroying laser from *Star Wars*—ignoring that the weapon had failed to stop the Rebel Alliance and the station had exploded.

"For nearly three years we have been building a juggernaut campaign (Death Star). It is firing on all cylinders. Data, Digital, TV, Political, Surrogates, Coalitions, etc," Brad tweeted. "In a few days we start pressing FIRE for the first time."

Brad was mocked on social media, but inside the White House, the focus was on what to do about Trump's convention in Charlotte, North Carolina.

Ronna wanted Charlotte to work. They had raised about $40 million for the event, money that would have to stay in the city if the party pulled out. Ronna and the city's Democratic mayor, Vi Lyles, had developed a strong rapport. Their teams had integrated, and more than sixty Republican convention staffers had been living in Charlotte for more than a year making preparations. But Ronna told the president that it was becoming increasingly difficult to raise the final $20 million they needed for the event. Donors weren't convinced a convention could be planned in the middle of a pandemic, and corporations that were furloughing workers couldn't justify cutting a seven-figure check. Plus, the party needed at least another $1 million to cover the masks and other personal protective equipment they hadn't anticipated.

To Brad, that sounded like a green light to start downsizing. He opposed even asking companies for money during the pandemic—he didn't think it was a good look. And the truth was he would have happily canceled those first few days of the convention. He wanted to start building the event around the president's speech, which was the only piece of the convention that he believed would give the campaign a boost.

But Meadows, the newly installed chief of staff, had been in Trump's ear, warning him that North Carolina governor Roy Cooper, a Democrat, would try to use the pandemic as an excuse to shut down the convention. Meadows had represented western North Carolina in the U.S. House for seven years before joining Trump's White House. A sandwich shop owner turned real estate developer, Meadows had shared the ballot during his first race in 2012 with Cooper, who ran unopposed that year for a fourth term as state attorney general.

"Cooper's going to screw you," Meadows told Trump. "He's a bad actor, and he's going to be awful."

Trump didn't want a scaled-down convention. This was his moment, and he wanted the full glory of the coronation that hadn't been afforded to him four years earlier when the four-day convention in Cleveland featured an emotional, public screaming match among several thousand Republican activists over Trump's nomination, Trump distracting from the festivities when he phoned in to Fox News to trash Ohio governor John Kasich, and Melania Trump plagiarizing from Michelle Obama. And that was just day one.

At the meeting with Brad in the White House, Ronna told Trump she would continue pushing Cooper's administration for an agreement on the convention. Brad still had a few items on the agenda, but Trump's schedule was running late, and the campaign manager offered to let Justin Clark jump ahead of him to go through legal issues over Election Day voting. But instead of waiting around, Brad left the White House, hopped on a plane, and flew home. Flight options were limited during the pandemic, and Brad wanted to spend the night in his own bed.

Brad knew the six-week stretch without seeing Trump had been too long. But he figured if he came back to Washington once a week—maybe once every two weeks—that would be enough.

But the ground was shifting underneath him.

On May 21, a group of anti-Trump Republicans known as the Lincoln Project released a political ad focused not on Trump but on Brad. It was unusual, if not unprecedented, for a political advertisement to attack a presidential candidate's campaign manager. But by highlighting reports of Brad's personal spending—and insinuating that he could afford new cars and houses because he was ripping off Trump—the ad had an audience of one: Trump himself.

Trump had been second-guessing his decision to slot Brad in as the campaign manager for the past two and a half years. And his anxiety was almost always about the money, just as it had been in their first fight in 2016 when Trump stormed out of his penthouse on the twenty-sixth floor of Trump Tower, took the elevator down to his campaign offices on the fourteenth floor, and steamrolled past cubicles while wildly waving the printout of a story claiming that Brad's company had collected $96 million from the campaign. But now Trump never came down to the fourteenth floor. He had no idea who was in what office. So he just barked Brad's name as he stomped across the hall.

"Brad!" Trump boomed as he walked right past Brad's office. "Brad Parscale!"

Brad had never before had Trump rip his face from his skull and made the mistake of quickly closing his laptop and running out to meet the boss. Trump unleashed a stream of insults, accusations, and expletives that seemed to defy basic laws of human biology that state every man must at some point pause to take a breath.

"That's my money!" Trump screamed.

Bossie rushed out of his office and directed the two men into the nearby kitchenette to give them at least a modicum of privacy.

"Hey!" Bossie yelled back at Trump, trying to interrupt him.

Kellyanne had now joined the rumpus in the pantry, and she and Bossie explained that Brad's company was paying for the advertising and marketing. That monstrous sum included some profit, but the cash was almost entirely for expenses that were documented on invoices but not in campaign finance reports.

Trump's suspicion that Brad was ripping him off stirred up again in 2019 when a news story surfaced that Brad had been on a shopping spree of South Florida waterfront homes and luxury cars. Trump immediately summoned his campaign manager to his office. Trump hated even the suggestion that someone might be taking advantage of him.

"What the fuck?" he yelled at Brad, again waving a printed-out news story.

He told the president that he and his wife, Candice, had suffered a devastating loss in 2015. Candice had been pregnant with their twins, but the babies were born prematurely—almost three months early—and died after only a few days. Brad had spent much of the following year in New York working on the race, and when he finally went home to Texas, his marriage was strained from the pressure of their overwhelming grief.

What happened, he told Trump, was that he and Candice eventually decided to stay together. Their plan was to sell everything they had—companies, cars, and homes with the furniture, tools, clothes, and everything else in it—and, like so many Americans before them, move to Florida to start over.

Trump sighed.

"I just hate these fucking stories," he told Brad.

Jared spoke up and vouched for Brad. Brad wasn't ripping off the president, Jared explained. If anything, he said, it was the other way around.

"Brad can make a million fucking dollars a month with his marketing skills, and by the way, I'd be the first person to hire him," Jared told Trump. "You're getting him for $30,000 a month. So you need to just calm down."

Trump relented and Brad survived the moment, but the damage was done. Trump would move on, but not from the suspicion that Brad was ripping him off—the only thing he ever forgot was Brad's defense. Trump rarely let an opportunity slip by to let his campaign manager know he was on thin ice. The president constantly asked other Republicans if he'd picked the right guy and tortured Brad with a slightly different, but equally consistent, query.

"What color is that Ferrari again?" he would ask.

The Lincoln Project knew the Ferrari was a pressure point for Trump. Their intent was to rile him to the point of triggering the kind of chaos that turned off voters. Brad was worried it might work.

The group had already put out a series of ads that had captured Trump's attention. Their first spot in March painted the Trump family as profiteers leveraging the presidency for their personal benefit, and highlighted a "billion-dollar bailout" Kushner received from a Qatar-backed investment company to help him pay off a notoriously bad real estate deal. In the first week of May, Trump unleashed a round of furious tweets at nearly 1:00 a.m. after he saw another Lincoln Project spot—this one criticizing his own response to the pandemic—that aired during the Fox News program he had been watching on TiVo. He complained about the spot on social media again later that day, and complained to reporters about it at Andrews Air Force Base.

"They should not call it the Lincoln Project," Trump said. "They should call it the Losers Project."

Before the president arrived for the meeting in the Cabinet Room, Brad had pulled Pence aside to discuss the Lincoln Project spot attacking him. He addressed the vice president by his first name—a striking informality that immediately raised eyebrows.

"Mike, if the president believes this stuff about me, then he better believe what's coming out about Jared," Brad said.

Pence stared silently back at Brad as other aides arrived in the room.

═══

The meeting that morning was with operatives from Trump World and McConnell's team, part of an effort to keep the two sides on the same page in battleground states for both the presidential contest and Senate races. But

Trump was more interested in getting to the bottom of a question he'd been asking for months:

Why couldn't anyone tell him where his most crucial staffer in the largest battleground state had been for the past eight months?

Where was Susie Wiles?

Wiles was among the few experienced political hands around Trump who had compiled a record of success before 2016. But Brad—at the urging of Ron DeSantis, the Florida governor—had sidelined her without telling Trump.

Trump credited Wiles for his victory in Florida in 2016, and winning his adopted home state again in 2020 was always at the top of his priority list. The daughter of legendary NFL play-by-play man Pat Summerall, Wiles had soft blue eyes and short, side-parted silver hair, and she had been a guiding hand in the Republican Party's most important victories during the past decade.

She managed Rick Scott's campaign for governor in 2010—when almost no other operatives in the state would work for him. Scott's hospital chain had paid the nation's largest Medicare fraud fine—and now he wanted to run for governor in the state with the largest share of Medicare recipients in the country.

Wiles helped keep the governor's office in Republican hands in 2018 when she took over DeSantis's bid for governor with six weeks left in the race. Public polls showed him trailing by 5 percentage points, but DeSantis squeaked by Democrat Andrew Gillum by a margin of 0.4 percent.

In 2016, Wiles was in charge of Florida for Trump, but their relationship before the victory had been tense. Less than two weeks before Election Day, Trump was in Florida when Wiles told him they were out of money in the state. She needed him to write a personal check for $900,000 to finish their voter turnout program. Trump was furious, and—as they say in Trump World—he ripped her face off her skull. Every insult he could imagine he hurled at her. Wiles was shaken and repeatedly tried to call Brian Ballard, one of the state's top Republican fundraisers who also ran the lobbying firm where she worked, but he didn't answer. More shouting. She tried to hold back the tears. And finally, she got the check.

The next day, Trump was still steaming at a fundraiser at Mar-a-Lago that Ballard had organized. When Ballard arrived, Trump was waiting for him.

"Your girl doesn't have it," Trump said, skipping any pleasantries. "She's fucking this thing up. We're going to lose."

Ballard chastised him for being such a jerk to Wiles. "You're going to win if you do what she says," he told Trump. "And what are you going to do? We're ten days out. You're going to fold it up?"

"If I lose, it's your fucking ass," Trump said as he poked his index finger into Ballard's shoulder.

Ballard and Trump walked into a ballroom where donors, some of whom had given more than $1 million, had been left waiting for two hours. Trump told Ballard to introduce him quickly—as in seconds.

"Hey, how are you doing?" Trump said to the donors. "We're doing good. We're going to win. But I've got to get back on the plane. I've got to get out of here and go campaign. Anyone have any questions?"

Hands shot into the air.

"No?" Trump said. "Okay. Thanks."

Trump walked out, and the donors asked for their money back. Ten days later, Trump won Florida, and all was forgiven.

Wiles had returned to lead Trump's reelection effort in Florida, but in September 2019, DeSantis and Brad had teamed up to ice her out. DeSantis's team blamed Wiles for a story in the *Tampa Bay Times* that suggested he was trying to sell access to the governor's office. She denied it, and even some of DeSantis's allies couldn't figure out why he'd think Wiles was behind the story. But DeSantis was at the height of his powers as a newly elected governor, and widely expected to seek the presidency after Trump. He leaned on Brad to remove her from the campaign, and he put similar pressure on Ballard to fire her from his lobbying firm. Brad had already openly discussed with others the possibility that he might team up with DeSantis for a 2024 race for the White House. Brad notified Trump World that Wiles had been banished.

"We're done with Susie," Brad told Ronna. "She's out."

Brad never told Trump, but the president asked about Wiles anytime Florida was discussed. When he forgot, Bossie reminded him. When Trump traveled to Florida to visit The Villages retirement community, he asked state lawmakers if they knew where she was. They mostly mumbled.

He called Ronna.

"Why isn't Susie on the ground here?" Trump asked her. "Why don't you have her here?"

Trump's visit wasn't an RNC event, and Wiles wasn't an RNC employee—she had worked for him at the campaign.

"That's not me," Ronna told him. "That's a question for Brad and Governor DeSantis. Because if it was up to me, I'd have her there in a heartbeat."

Eight months later, during the campaign meeting in the Cabinet Room, Pence finally spoke up and said that Wiles had been collateral damage in some of the early jockeying for the 2024 presidential race and internal Florida Republican backbiting. Wiles had worked for DeSantis, but she was closer with Scott, who was also regularly mentioned as a potential presidential candidate. DeSantis may have been trying to clip Wiles and, by extension, Scott. Trump seemed satisfied with the explanation, but he still demanded her return.

"I want her back," Trump said.

⸻

As the meeting broke up, Stepien sidled up to Trump.

"I know you're concerned that Brad has been making money off you," Stepien told him. "I want you to know I would never do that to you."

A few days later, Stepien would be promoted to deputy campaign manager. It was a move that Brad supported—he'd tried to make Stepien deputy campaign manager more than a year earlier—and was designed to help build out some infrastructure underneath the campaign manager for the final five months of the race.

But it was also a move that foreshadowed greater implications, both for Brad and the campaign.

⸻

That afternoon, Trump was aboard *Air Force One* on his way to Michigan again. He'd barely left the White House grounds for two months because of the pandemic, and had been growing restless. The Michigan trip, where he would observe a Ford plant producing ventilators instead of car parts, was one of several strategic trips aimed at highlighting his administration's efforts to respond to the pandemic in key states in the presidential race. As his flight approached the crucial Midwestern battleground, he faced a decision: Should he wear a face mask?

His administration had already reversed itself on mask guidelines. Early in the pandemic, when high-end N95 masks were in short supply, public health officials said masks weren't necessary—a statement designed, in part, to prevent a run on the already hard-to-find N95 masks that frontline workers desperately needed.

"Seriously people—STOP BUYING MASKS!" Surgeon General Jerome Adams had posted on Twitter on February 29.

That recommendation changed as it became clear the virus could be spread through asymptomatic carriers and that simple cloth face coverings, along with social distancing, could slow transmission. Trump announced the the new mask recommendations at his daily coronavirus news conference on April 3, but made clear that he would personally resist the change.

"You don't have to do it," Trump said, undercutting his own administration's message even as he announced it himself. "I'm choosing not to do it."

Trump would take more than four dozen questions over the next ninety minutes. The first one was why he didn't want to wear a mask.

"I just don't want to wear one," Trump said, and added again that it was a recommendation, not a requirement. "I think wearing a face mask as I greet presidents, prime ministers, dictators, kings, queens, I don't know. Somehow, I don't see it for myself. I just—I just don't. Maybe I'll change my mind, but this will pass and hopefully it'll pass very quickly."

At the Ford plant in Michigan, the policy was that everyone on-site needed to wear personal protective equipment, including masks. The car company informed the White House of that requirement ahead of the president's visit. But Trump remained reluctant. He sat behind the chevron-shaped desk in the president's office on *Air Force One* and polled his aides, who were spread out along the leather couch that lined the wall and in the leather captain's chairs on the other side of his desk. Meadows, Scavino, Hope, Derek Lyons, Johnny McEntee, and Kayleigh McEnany all urged him not to wear a mask.

Jared said he thought the mask was a good idea. His daughter, Ivanka, and Melania, the first lady, had both made a point of wearing masks in public.

Trump was intrigued, and he summoned Ronna, who was seated farther back in the plane.

"Should I wear a mask?" Trump asked her.

"Yeah," Ronna told him. "I think you should wear a mask."

Meadows, Scavino, Hope, and McEntee immediately interjected, criticizing Trump for even considering the idea. Trump had made his decision not to wear a mask and, they argued, he could not reverse himself now just because of pressure from the media. They spoke as if the mask contained kryptonite and Trump would lose his superpower with his base as soon he looped one behind his ears.

"The leader of the free world shouldn't wear a mask," Meadows said.

"It's embarrassing," Scavino added.

Ronna was startled. She was also planning the 2020 Republican National Convention, which meant she was closely reading coronavirus guidance and protocols from the Trump Administration and in the states. When she had fallen ill in March with Covid-like symptoms, she had alerted people she had been in contact with that she might have the virus. Testing at that time was not prevalent, and it could take weeks to receive the results. She told her team at the RNC that it was the responsible thing to do and asked for help to spread the word to the people with whom she'd met.

Meadows called her at home. "Ronna, we think it's wrong to share that you're getting this test," he told her.

Now Ronna looked around the *Air Force One* cabin and saw mostly white men prepared to defend Trump to their last breath. Those voters were never going to leave Trump's side.

"Why?" Trump asked Ronna. "Why do you think that?"

"I'm the exact voter you need to win over, and suburban women will love it," she told Trump. "You're going to a state with a high Covid rate, and it will set a good example. They've also asked you to do it."

Jared backed her up. "I think Ronna could be right," he said.

Trump was intrigued by the rare alignment between his son-in-law and the party chairwoman. "Bring me the mask," he said.

He had tried on a white mask before and didn't like it. But the new White House masks were navy blue, with the presidential seal in the lower left corner. He looped the cloth straps around his ears and adjusted the mask over his nose and chin.

"Well?" Trump said. "What do you think, Ronna?"

"Yeah," Ronna told him approvingly. "I think you should wear a mask."

Trump did put the mask on, but only once he was behind closed doors at the plant.

Later, a reporter asked him why he didn't wear the mask on the public part of the tour.

"I didn't want to give the press the pleasure of seeing it," Trump said with the briefest of smirks.

The next week, Richard Walters, the chief of staff at the Republican National Committee, sat in the lobby of Trump International Hotel griping into the iPhone pressed against his ear. It was the second month of lockdowns,* and he was losing his mind over the havoc the pandemic was causing—especially to the Republican convention he was planning.

The convention he and Ronna had spent the past two years planning was falling apart. Cooper's administration in Raleigh had plenty of leverage to require Trump's Republicans to meet every coronavirus protocol that the president was often willfully ignoring. As much as Walters and convention officials tried to negotiate, Cooper wouldn't give an inch.

Walters arrived at the hotel on May 27 for a meeting with Susie Wiles, who had been trying to rebuild a consulting business and was there to meet with Walters and some clients. She saw him on the phone, nodded, and stood off to the side.

"Guys!" Walters yelled into his phone. "It's never going to work in North Carolina. The governor doesn't want us there. He's told us point-blank that it's not going to work."

Wiles knew an opportunity when she saw one.

---

* Except at the Trump Hotel, which could always seem to find an open room for some friends of the president.

"You know," she told Walters. "If things don't work out in Charlotte, we'd love to have you in Jacksonville."

Walters scoffed. Trump didn't want to change cities, and Walters didn't particularly want to go to Jacksonville.

But just a day later, the offer from Wiles didn't seem so funny.

On May 28, Ronna and Walters had reached their breaking point with Cooper. They had a convention meeting scheduled with Trump the next day and decided they needed to bring him some alternatives. The only way changing locations had a chance of working this late in the process was to find a city with a Republican mayor in a state with a Republican governor. They would have to grapple with the pandemic no matter what and wanted to eliminate any risk of partisan flare-ups. But that political calculation severely restricted where they could go. Ronna's convention team considered Orlando, but Orange County mayor Jerry Demings wasn't just a Democrat, he was married to Representative Val Demings, whom Biden was considering as a running mate. Tennessee governor Bill Lee wanted to help bring the convention to Nashville, but Mayor John Cooper was a Democrat. Texas governor Greg Abbott suggested Dallas. Same issue. The one city that they kept coming back to: Jacksonville. Walters called Wiles.

"I know you were joking yesterday," Walters said. "But... were you?"

Wiles made a round of calls, and reported back nothing but optimism.

Ronna and Walters brought the news to the president the next day.

Trump, who had refused even to consider downsizing the convention just three weeks earlier, not only signed off on exploring Jacksonville, but floated the possibility of an even more drastic shift.

"Maybe even something virtual?" he suggested.

Walters felt dizzy. Trump's extraordinary indecision seemed to trigger a momentary bout of vertigo. But the Republican operative collected himself, and booked a flight to Jacksonville for June 1. Ten days later, Trump announced plans to relocate the convention there.

8

Law and Order

"When the looting starts, the shooting starts. Thank you!"

—*Twitter, May 29, 2020*

The sun was setting on a clear and balmy Memorial Day when a forty-six-year-old Black man walked into Cup Foods market at the corner of Chicago Avenue and Thirty-eighth Street in South Minneapolis. He'd been out of work since March when stay-at-home orders cost him his job as a bouncer. He'd been infected with the virus that had caused his restaurant to close. Now he was about to pay for a pack of smokes with a counterfeit $20 bill. And for the briefest of moments, George Perry Floyd Jr. was in the clear.

But when the teenage clerk behind the register spotted the forgery, Floyd refused to return the cigarettes. Soon, four police officers were on the scene, including Derek Chauvin, a white cop with red flags spilling from his personnel file. Chauvin pinned Floyd chest down on the pavement, handcuffed his wrists behind his back, and knelt on the nape of his neck.

"I can't breathe," Floyd pleaded more than twenty times.

Chauvin wouldn't budge.

Less than ten minutes later, Floyd was dead.

Witnesses with cell phones documented every agonizing moment of Floyd's horrific death, from his desperate pleas for mercy to his final cries for his mama. The next day, Minneapolis police chief Medaria Arradondo fired all four officers, and criminal charges soon followed. But that was like bringing a water pail to a forest fire. The nation's loathsome history on civil rights had no shortage of gruesome and tragic events, but it was quickly apparent that the sheer cruelty of Floyd's murder, captured on video for the world to see, would be a breaking point.

From the Oval Office, Trump struggled to calibrate a response to match the enormity of the moment. Few of his top advisers specifically represented—or even really understood—working-class Americans, much less Black Americans. In the White House, the closest Trump had to an adviser on regular Americans was probably Kellyanne, who was raised by her mother, grandmother, and two aunts in a New Jersey working-class home and worked for decades as a pollster for many of the Republican Party's most populist candidates. But even she couldn't come up with the full name of a single staffer when she was asked in 2018 on ABC's *Face the Nation* to identify the seniormost Black official in the Trump White House.*

Trump's response was also impaired by his stunning disregard for history, particularly compared to most other modern presidents. Senior officials described his understanding of slavery, Jim Crow, or the Black experience in general post–Civil War as vague to nonexistent. But Trump's indifference to Black history was similar to his disregard for the history of any race, religion, or creed.

On his way to Paris to commemorate the hundredth anniversary of the First World War armistice, for example, Trump listened as John Kelly, his chief of staff at the time, reminded the president which countries were on which side during the conflict. Kelly continued the discussion by connecting the dots from the First World War to the Second World War and all of Hitler's atrocities.

"Well, Hitler did a lot of good things," Trump told Kelly.

When I asked Trump about the remark, he claimed the conversation had never happened, and he denied praising Hitler. But others said the remark stunned Kelly. The chief of staff told the president that he was wrong, but

---

* Ja'Ron Smith, whom Kellyanne had struggled to recall, was two pay grades below the top ranks. After Kellyanne's interview, Smith asked for a promotion to formalize his role as the West Wing's seniormost Black official and close the $50,000 pay gap. Jared agreed, but then put him off for the next two years.

Trump was undeterred. Trump pointed to Germany's economic gains once Hitler took over as chancellor. Kelly pushed back again and argued that the German people would have been better off poor than subjected to the Nazi genocide.

"Even if it was true that he was solely responsible for rebuilding the economy, on balance, you cannot ever say anything supportive of Adolf Hitler," Kelly told Trump. "You just can't."

Even if Trump hadn't internalized the lessons of history, much of the country seemed to understand the moment and viewed Floyd's senseless killing as only the latest in a shameful series of Black deaths. In 2020 alone, twenty-five-year-old Ahmaud Arbery was killed during a jog near his South Georgia home by two white men, who said Arbery looked like a suspect in several break-ins in the area. Two weeks later, twenty-six-year-old Breonna Taylor was shot dead by Louisville police during a botched raid on her apartment. Floyd's death was a reminder of those tragically avoidable killings, and the countless before them, as well as the painfully debasing racism to which Black Americans were regularly subjected. The frustration and anguish that had accrued after decades of daily racial indignities had been emphatically—finally—cracked open by Floyd's death, and protesters poured into the streets of the nation's capital and major municipalities.

What was unique about the videos capturing Floyd's death were that they also somehow awakened white Americans to what their fellow Black countrymen had long known. The Black Lives Matter protests were joined by large numbers of white men and women, too—young and old, city dwellers and suburban residents—and the demonstrations had support from the vast majority of Americans regardless of race, religion, or economic status. Corporate America rushed to adapt, as Quaker Oats Company canceled its Aunt Jemima brand, NASCAR banned the Confederate flag from its races, and the NFL's Washington Redskins changed their name to the Washington Football Team until they had time to come up with an alternative.

More than 15 million Americans attended protests in the first week. Black men wept on live television. Kaleth Wright, the top Black enlisted airman in the Air Force, spoke publicly about how the sight of blue police lights in his rearview mirror made his heart race "like most other Black men in America."

"Who am I?" Wright posted on Twitter. "I am a Black man who happens to be Chief Master Sergeant of the Air Force. I am George Floyd...I am Philando Castile, I am Michael Brown, I am Alton Sterling, I am Tamir Rice."

But Floyd's death was more significant than even that grisly chronology. If it was racially motivated police brutality that killed him, it was the systemic racism of the nation's economic and health systems that had pushed him—struggling with money and infected with Covid—to that street corner in the first place. Floyd also embodied the disproportionate toll exacted on Blacks from a historic economic collapse and deadly pandemic.

Centuries of racial inequality in the job market meant that Black Americans were more likely to work in the hospitality, construction, and transportation fields, which suffered the highest layoffs during the pandemic. But Blacks were also more likely to be employed as Instacart shoppers, nursing assistants, and other undervalued jobs that were suddenly deemed "essential" to prop up the economy's remains. Long-standing residential segregation and redlining policies meant Blacks were more likely to live in crowded conditions—a problematic situation when the federal government was urging people to stay six feet apart because the virus was so contagious.

Blacks infected with Covid were more likely to experience harsher symptoms since they suffered a higher rate of diabetes, heart disease, and lung disease—three conditions present in a combined 90 percent of Covid-related hospitalizations. Their hospital costs were also less likely to be covered by health insurance. The health insurance gap between Blacks and whites had started to narrow under the Affordable Care Act. But those gains vanished as Trump made it a priority to dismantle his predecessor's signature domestic legislative achievement.

In 2020, Blacks were 2.6 times more likely than whites to be shot and killed by police and 2.5 times more likely to be impoverished. When it came to Covid, Blacks were 1.1 times more likely to be infected, 2.9 times more likely to be hospitalized, and 1.9 times more likely to die from it. For 46.8 million Black Americans, a life-threatening crisis seemed to lurk around every corner. Their deep frustrations over generations of racial tension now had a fresh layer of anxiety stemming from coronavirus.

The country had turned into a tinderbox. And inside the Oval Office was a president who liked playing with matches.

═══════

The groundwork for Trump's response to Floyd's death had been laid years earlier.

Consider the Wednesday evening in North Carolina during the spring of 2016, when loathing and contempt swirled through the rowdy Trump rally crowd at Crown Coliseum, the 8,500-seat home of the Fayetteville Marksmen hockey club. The crowd's candidate was center stage in a dark suit, the knot of his powder blue tie pushed tightly against the top button of his crisp white shirt, but their prolonged and resounding chorus of boos was aimed directly at Rakeem Jones.

A twenty-six-year-old Black man in a white T-shirt with long dreadlocks, Jones, who delivered pizzas for a living, raised his middle finger in the air and followed Cumberland County sheriff's deputies as they escorted him out of his seat.

But as Jones ascended the arena's cement steps, he was blindsided in the right temple by the flying forearm from John McGraw, a seventy-eight-year-old white man in a fuchsia shirt, leather vest, and cowboy hat. Known to friends as "Quick Draw," McGraw made leather gun holsters that he sold at flea markets and had been sitting a few rows behind Jones's group. As they were leaving, McGraw quickly shuffle-stepped down his aisle, past a dozen or so Trump supporters, and reached the steps just in time to slam the stranger viciously in the face.

The crowd gasped as Jones stumbled back. He stayed on his feet, only to be pinned to the ground by four officers once he reached the top of the stairs. McGraw, meanwhile, returned to his seat and watched the rest of the show. Police only arrested McGraw days later when cell phone videos posted online showed him bragging that he enjoyed "knocking the hell out of that big mouth." Trump had used the same language a few weeks earlier in Cedar Rapids, Iowa, when he urged supporters to "just knock the hell" out of any protesters in their midst and promised to pay their legal fees.

The night after Fayetteville, Trump traveled to Chicago, the city with the nation's second-largest Black population, for a rally at the UIC Pavilion. Several progressive groups, including Black Lives Matter, had organized protests outside the arena and sent demonstrators into the event with anti-Trump signs hidden under their clothes. Skirmishes erupted, and Trump eventually canceled the event as security struggled to maintain order. But more violence flared up as protesters celebrated, and Trump supporters grew angry and frustrated. A bottle struck one officer in the head. Dozens were bloodied and bruised. Sopan Deb, an Indian American who had been covering Trump since the start of the campaign for CBS News, was slammed to the pavement and handcuffed without warning by two Chicago police officers as he recorded footage of the protests. When video emerged showing Deb had done nothing wrong, Chicago police dropped the charge of resisting arrest.

Trump refused to condemn the violence, partly because he thought it would invite criticism that he was weak. Experts expected that he would pay a political price for failing to soften his tone. It may have limited his reach, but it never caused the floor to drop. Ten days before the Fayetteville rally, Trump had refused to condemn former Ku Klux Klan leader David Duke. Mitt Romney, the 2012 Republican presidential nominee, reproached him for "disgusting and disqualifying" comments about the KKK, Muslims, and Mexicans. Nearly 100 Republican national security experts denounced him in an open letter over "his hateful, anti-Muslim rhetoric" and "embrace of the expansive use of torture."

None of that mattered to primary voters. They seemed to interpret the attacks as proof of Trump's outsider status. During that same ten days, Trump won seven of the eleven Super Tuesday state primaries, convinced Ben Carson—a Black Republican pediatric neurosurgeon—to drop out of the race and back his campaign, and collected an endorsement from Alabama's Jeff Sessions, the first sitting U.S. senator to back him.

"In this race for the White House," Trump declared at the Republican convention that year in Cleveland, "I am the law-and-order candidate."

But as soon as Trump arrived in the White House, Jared went to work sanding down his father-in-law's hard edge with a push to soften prison sentencing guidelines. It was a jarring contrast with the unforgiving strongman image that the newly sworn-in president had feverishly protected. But the issue was personal for Jared. His own father had spent fourteen months in a federal prison.

=====

Jared was four years old in 1985 when his father was put in charge of Kushner Companies, the family's New Jersey real estate company. Over the next two decades, the company accumulated more than 25,000 apartments, thousands of acres of land, and millions of square feet of commercial real estate. Charlie Kushner became a boldfaced name in state and national politics, wining and dining with Bill Clinton, Al Gore, and Bibi Netanyahu. In 2002, Charlie Kushner was the single largest donor for New Jersey governor Jim McGreevey, who rewarded his financier by nominating him chairman of the Port Authority of New York and New Jersey, a powerful position in charge of hundreds of millions of dollars in development contracts. But Charlie Kushner had to withdraw from consideration as McGreevey was consumed by a controversy that involved cheating on his wife with a man to whom he'd given a cushy government job. McGreevey's paramour, an Israeli national with a work permit, had been sponsored by Charlie Kushner, who had also put him on the family company's payroll as a favor to McGreevey.

Kushner family ties frayed, too. Legal disputes and bickering with his siblings reached the point in December 2003 that Charlie Kushner hatched a plot for a prostitute to lure his brother-in-law to the Red Bull Motor Inn on U.S. 22 in Bridgewater, New Jersey. The plan worked, and Charlie mailed the incriminating videotape to his sister. But a private investigator he had hired to help with the scheme double-crossed him and cooperated with the FBI.

The prosecution was led by an ambitious young U.S. attorney in New Jersey named Chris Christie, and Charlie Kushner ultimately pleaded guilty to sixteen counts of tax evasion, one count of witness tampering, and another count of making illegal campaign donations. He was sentenced to two years in federal prison and released after fourteen months at Federal Prison Camp, a minimum-security jail in Montgomery, Alabama. Jared visited him nearly every weekend.

"This is a great victory for the people of New Jersey," Christie said after the sentencing. "No matter how rich and powerful any person may be, they will be held accountable for criminal conduct by this office."

For Jared, the lesson was that prison sentences were too stiff.

The new administration was barely two months old when Jared held his first meeting at the U.S. Capitol on criminal justice reform. Jared wanted to revive a proposal to reduce mandatory prison sentences that had failed the year before due to opposition led by U.S. senator Jeff Sessions. Sessions, who was now Trump's freshly confirmed attorney general, didn't know about Jared's meeting—Sessions had been preparing for a speech the next day in St. Louis, where he would blame "viral videos" for the tense relationship between law enforcement and minority communities and lay the ground work for his aggressive prosecution of drug offenders.

The striking discrepancy between Jared and the rest of the administration received little attention at the time. When it came to Jared, the story focused on the vast gap between his expansive White House portfolio and his limited amount of relevant experience. Both the Washington establishment and his colleagues in the White House derisively referred to him as "the princeling."

But that was how Jared operated. In a 2015 interview with *Forbes* magazine for its "40 under 40" issue, Jared refused to be defined by the real estate company he was running. Asked about Kushner Companies, he instead pointed out that he had bought a newspaper, the *New York Observer*, and ruminated about his interest in expanding broadband Internet access. He spoke about "creating cultures of results instead of cultures of seniority" and how he could apply that philosophy to any company.

"Every business I do and every transaction I'm involved with teaches me and makes me better in all the other businesses that I'm in," Kushner told *Forbes*.

In the White House, Jared was brokering Middle East peace and would take the lead on U.S. relations with Canada, Mexico, and China. He would oversee issues related to veterans' health care. And he spoke broadly and optimistically about plans to transform the federal government into something smooth, sleek, and corporate. That push to streamline government started by creating a new layer of bureaucracy: the Office of American Innovation.

The new office grew out of an idea that Bannon, as the White House chief strategist, had called the Strategic Initiatives Group, which he had pitched as a McKinsey-style consultancy inside the West Wing to push Trump's campaign promises into law. Jared liked the idea and added his input. He asked for help from Chris Liddell, a former Microsoft and General Motors executive who had joined the administration. Liddell wasn't entirely sure what the new group was supposed to do, so he went and found Bannon's aide, Andy Surabian.

"Did Steve explain to you what this group is doing?" Liddell asked him.

"No," Surabian said. "Not in much detail."

"Dammit," Liddell replied. "I was hoping you could tell me."

The group's early meetings were in Bannon's office, but Jared packed the room with his own loyalists, including Reed Cordish, a Princeton tennis player who parlayed his friendship with Jared and Ivanka into a gig in the West Wing. White House staff chief Reince Priebus panicked that none of his people were included in the meetings and sent his deputy, Katie Walsh. The only senior White House official not present seemed to be Stephen Miller, even though he was always invited to the group's standing 7:30 a.m. meeting. Miller's friends and critics called him many things during the next four years, but a morning person was never one of them.

In the second week of the new administration, a memo circulated inside the West Wing to frame the ambitious new effort, but it also signaled the disorganization that would doom most of the president's policymaking attempts over the next four years. The five-page memo was authored by three staffers, each of whom reported to different bosses, and included two organizational charts.

The meetings quickly migrated from brainstorming sessions in Bannon's office to the Roosevelt Room, where senior aides could schmooze with corporate executives who had started attending at Jared's urging.

Jared's crew floated criminal justice reform, which deflated Bannon's staffers.

"Was that even something Trump supported?" one whispered during a meeting.

Trump's first test at addressing the country's racial tensions came in the summer of 2017. On a Saturday in August, thirty-two-year-old Heather Heyer was killed, and nineteen others injured, when a twenty-year-old neo-Nazi drove his souped-up 2010 Dodge Challenger at about 30 miles per hour into a crowd in Charlottesville, Virginia. Heyer and the others were protesting a white supremacist rally organized to oppose the removal of a statue of Robert E. Lee, a Virginian who commanded the Confederate States Army during the Civil War.

Trump had been golfing at his Bedminster club that morning. He planned to sign veterans' health care legislation that afternoon, and reporters were already scheduled to attend the ceremony in one of the club's ballrooms. It had been about two hours since Heyer's death, and Trump said he wanted to "put out a comment as to what's going on in Charlottesville."

"We condemn in the strongest possible terms this egregious display of hatred, bigotry, and violence on many sides—on many sides," Trump said.

The White House tried in vain to focus cable networks and newspaper reporters on the first words of his statement instead of the final phrase—"on many sides"—that he'd ad-libbed and then repeated. But the obvious question they couldn't answer was how the president could put any blame on the peaceful counterprotesters. His remarks seemed to justify the white supremacist violence, and Trump's silence over the next twenty-four hours unnerved even those around him.

Back at Trump Tower in New York two days later, one of his few visits back home as president, Trump had a news conference scheduled to discuss the nation's infrastructure. Hope and Sarah Sanders, the White House press secretary, urged Trump not to take questions. Trump agreed, then he took the elevator down to the lobby, where reporters were waiting, and promptly invited questions after a brief infrastructure statement.

"If you have any questions, please feel free to ask," he said.

Predictably, nearly every question that followed focused on Charlottesville. Trump criticized executives who'd quit his business councils. He defended his controversial statement and even reread his quote—except for the phrase he'd ad-libbed. He lamented the removal of Civil War statues. He disputed that he had support from neo-Nazis. Then, after the news conference, David Duke, the former KKK grand wizard, publicly thanked Trump for his "honor and courage to tell the truth about Charlottesville and condemn the leftist terrorists."

At one point, Trump pleaded for an infrastructure question.

He again blamed the counterprotesters.

"You had some very bad people in that group, but you also had people that were very fine people, on both sides," Trump said.

The next day, Stephen Schwarzman, a longtime friend of Trump's and chief executive of Blackstone Group, called the president and told him he had disbanded the White House Strategic and Policy Forum. There weren't enough executives left who would stand by Trump after his repeated failures to adequately address Charlottesville, Schwarzman said. Trump hung up and beat his friend to the punch by quickly tweeting that he was shutting down the panel.

Gary Cohn, the president's top economic adviser—and a registered Democrat—was even more despondent. Raised Jewish on the East Side of Cleveland and a longtime New York resident, he stood next to Trump for the infrastructure news conference and grew increasingly alarmed and uncomfortable.

Later, in a private meeting inside the Oval Office, Cohn unloaded on the president. Cohn told Trump that his lack of clarity had been harmful to the country and that he'd put an incredible amount of pressure on people working in the White House. He told Trump that he might have to quit.

No one backed Cohn up. Others in the room, including Pence, remained quiet.

Cohn returned to his office after the meeting broke up. Following a few minutes behind, Pence climbed the flight of stairs and appeared at the threshold of Cohn's door.

"I'm proud of you," Pence told him, safely out of earshot of the president.

━━━━

Trump remained skeptical about Jared's push to change criminal justice laws. Trump worried about upsetting law enforcement groups, whose backing he touted at nearly every campaign rally. He didn't want to create any space for other conservative politicians to criticize him. In a speech about the opioid crisis in March 2018, Trump mocked blue-ribbon commissions tasked with finding detailed solutions to systemic problems like drug abuse. The problem was drug dealers, Trump said, and the only thing they understood was toughness.

"That toughness includes the death penalty," he said.

Trump was one of the few politicians in the country willing to consider capital punishment for drug dealers. Still, Jared remained undaunted.

He appealed to Trump as his children's grandfather and reminded him of his own father's ordeal. He suggested that addressing the issue would bring new support for Trump from Black voters, and he scheduled meetings with conservative politicians who supported prison reform, including Georgia governor Nathan Deal and Florida attorney general Pam Bondi.

But the break came when Jared and his allies used Trump's own language against him and presented it to Trump as if it were another campaign promise kept—even though it was to a pledge he'd never explicitly made.

"You campaigned that you were going to work for the forgotten men and women of this country," Reed Cordish told Trump in a private meeting early in the administration. "And there's nobody more forgotten or underrepresented than people in prison."

"That's right," Trump said, as if the idea had been his all along. "We've got to do something about this."

Trump had mobilized his 2016 campaign around the promise to fight for the "forgotten man." The phrase referred to any worker who felt unfairly treated by a list of imperfect social institutions: government, economic, religious, or otherwise. But it was a generic and pliable rhetorical device that Franklin Delano Roosevelt had most famously invoked during his first presidential campaign in 1932. But where FDR used it to help sell the working class on massive government programs and regulations like Social Security, a minimum wage, and union protections, Trump used it in his bid to dismantle many of those same programs—the "deconstruction of the administrative state," as Bannon described it.

Trump told Jared that any criminal justice legislation required support from the police groups that had endorsed him. Then, in May—two months after supporting capital punishment for drug dealers—Trump's White House hosted its first prison reform summit.

Even during the summit, Trump signaled he wasn't fully on board. He veered off the script and threatened to veto a bad bill, even though the effort was led by his own White House. He recalled how he'd had a friend who once hired three felons, one of whom turned out to be "not the greatest" worker. Near the end, Trump openly questioned his own prepared remarks, which made it clear he hadn't bothered to read the script until it was scrolling through the teleprompter at the event.

"America is a nation that believes in second chances, and third chances, in some cases, and..." Trump said and then paused as he stared at the teleprompter.

"I don't know," he continued. "I guess even fourth chances? I don't know about that."

Nervous laughter rippled through the room.

"That's where I think you and I may differ," Trump said as he turned to CNN political analyst Van Jones and other prison reform advocates Jared had invited to the event. "You know, we'll go two or three, but maybe we won't go that extra length. Okay? You're a little more liberal in that way, but that's okay. But we're both well-intentioned, I can tell you that."

Two weeks later, Jared found the final puzzle piece to unlock Trump's full support: celebrity endorsement.

At the end of May, Jared and Ivanka enlisted Kim Kardashian, the reality TV star whose rapper husband, Kanye West, had voiced support for Trump after the 2016 election and visited the president-elect in Trump Tower during his transition to the White House. In an Oval Office meeting with Trump, Kardashian lobbied the president to release from prison a woman named Alice Johnson. Johnson had spent two decades behind bars after running a multimillion-dollar cocaine operation with ties to a Colombian drug cartel. Kardashian described her to Trump as a grandmother, a first-time delinquent, and an offender of a nonviolent crime.

On June 6, 2018—one week after the meeting with Kardashian and over the objections of White House staff chief John Kelly and White House counsel Don McGahn—Trump granted Johnson clemency. The reelection campaign sent video cameras to record her release from prison. The footage would be turned into Trump's Super Bowl commercial.

<hr />

One of Jared's top priorities for the campaign was expanding Trump's share of the Black vote.

The campaign's focus group testing showed there was some room to grow with minority voters if the campaign explained Trump's policies in a positive and carefully tailored way. Brad viewed that as an opportunity, too, and prioritized the campaign's coalitions department, which was designed to reach out to specific groups of voters, including Black voters, religious voters, and law enforcement officers.

He hired Hannah Castillo from the White House to oversee the coalition-building, making her one of his top deputies, on par with digital chief Gary Coby, political boss Chris Carr, and communications director Tim Murtaugh. Brad tasked Castillo with building a coalitions department that was effectively a series of mini-campaigns inside the broader reelection effort. The major coalitions—Black voters, Hispanic voters, and women—would each be staffed with their own political strategist, communications director, and chief fundraiser to market Trump in a way that would persuade targeted voters. The campaign also created separate websites—and branded merchandise available for purchase—for a lengthy list of other coalitions: evangelicals, Catholics, Chaldean Catholics, Mormons, "Hindu Voices for Trump," as well as veterans, lawyers, truckers, and even felons, or, as the coalitions department referred to them, "Second Chance Voters for Trump."*

Castillo insisted on hiring outside advertising firms to produce the TV spots for Hispanic markets—one for ads in the diverse Latino market in Florida and another for Mexican American voters in the Southwest. She formed advisory boards for the coalitions, but insisted that those spots be given to people who actually wanted to work. Board members were required to raise money, become media surrogates for the campaign, or help recruit volunteers for the grassroots army of ground troops the campaign was building with the Republican National Committee. The coalitions department quickly raised hundreds of thousands of dollars and created contact lists with more than 100,000 emails.

Katrina Pierson, a veteran of the Tea Party movement and Trump's 2016 campaign, had returned to the 2020 campaign as a senior adviser and took an

---

* Just eight states allow some felons to vote after completing their prison sentences: Alabama, Arizona, Delaware, Florida, Kentucky, Mississippi, Tennessee, and Wyoming.

active role in Castillo's "Black Voices for Trump" coalition. The two women believed the president could make inroads with Black voters if the campaign actively reached out and respectfully explained the president's record.

"There's a brand of Black Republican who thinks demeaning Black people by calling them brainwashed by Democrats or stuck on the plantation will somehow resonate—but it doesn't," Pierson told Jared. "It only resonates with white people because it's shit they can't say."

Jared was impressed and in 2019 set up a meeting with Pierson, Castillo, and the administration staff involved in outreach to the Black community. That group included Ja'Ron Smith, the West Wing aide Kellyanne had claimed was the White House's most senior Black employee (Smith also worked in Jared's Office of American Innovation); Nicole Frazier, the White House director for African American outreach; Henry Childs, the Commerce Department's director of minority business development; and Ashley Bell in the Small Business Administration. In the meeting, Jared criticized the White House press shop for what he viewed as a failure to communicate the First Step Act's successful passage. He wanted the group to develop a campaign message for Black voters and assemble a specific and tactical plan to deliver it.

Castillo redoubled efforts on Black Voices, while continuing to roll out other coalitions. The first to be unveiled was Latinos for Trump. For a campaign often fueled on hype, the group's premiere in Miami on June 25, 2019, was something of a plot twist—it exceeded everyone's expectations. Vice President Pence was sent to the launch in Miami, and his team initially questioned the campaign's decision to rent a ballroom in the DoubleTree hotel that could fit 600 people. That was much bigger than the crowds Pence was drawing at his usual stops in Michigan and Wisconsin. But the campaign had already started targeting Latinos, and they had noticed a strong response from South Florida to videos from John Pence, the vice president's nephew and a fluent Spanish speaker. John Pence, who majored in Hispanic Studies and studied abroad in Nicaragua while at William & Mary, had cut so many Spanish-language videos for social media that some on the campaign nicknamed him "Juan Pence."

The Pence team could only shake their heads when they arrived at the Miami airport hotel and found the place packed with an enthusiastic and rowdy crowd decked out in red hats, wrapped in American flags, and wearing bedazzled Trump jewelry pinned to their clothes.

"Mike Pence! Mike Pence!" the crowd chanted.

The sober vice president usually drew older, more milquetoast crowds. His staff was unaccustomed to hearing their boss's name turned into a chorus.

"This is actually happening," one Pence aide uttered.

The event created a buzz inside the Trump campaign and made kickoff events for new coalition groups a high-profile ticket for the campaign's top-shelf surrogates, even attracting Trump family members. Lara, Eric's wife, scheduled meetings with Castillo whenever she was in Washington and set up a biweekly call for progress updates. Lara frequently asked where she could be helpful and made sure that enough resources were available for coalition activities. When the campaign launched its second coalition, Women for Trump, with an event in Pennsylvania—at Valley Forge Casino Resort in King of Prussia—Lara Trump was the headliner. Brad and Pierson showed up, as did Kimberly Guilfoyle, Ronna, RNC chairwoman Ronna McDaniel, and Kayleigh McEnany, the campaign's press secretary at the time.

That event also impressively drew about 1,000 people. But the costs were considerable. The campaign spent tens of thousands of dollars on advertising and even more on building the stage and sound system. Then there were the travel costs and salaries for the senior campaign staff in attendance. It underscored an unusual level of commitment from a Republican presidential campaign—but also raised eyebrows. It wasn't how traditional operatives—like Bill Stepien or Justin Clark, both senior advisers at the time—would have allocated those kinds of campaign resources. Still, no one openly objected.

Campaign officials rolled their eyes whenever Jared would ask about the possibility of collecting 20 percent of the Black vote—no Republican presidential candidate had even broken double digits with Black voters since George W. Bush in 2004. But there was plenty of money to experiment, and Jared's optimism could be infectious. Plus, the coalitions program had become a priority for the family, who jockeyed to launch new groups.

But the splashy blowouts started to drain the coalition budget. When Brad created the coalitions department in March 2019, he set aside $5 million to last until Election Day.

They'd spent it all before the calendar flipped to 2020.

—————

In the early months of the pandemic—before Floyd's death—Trump's team had started picking up positive signals from Black leaders that they interpreted as potential softening on the incumbent president.

The reduction in sentences for crack cocaine offenses, which had disproportionately and unfairly targeted Black offenders, reduced prison time by an average of six years for more than 2,000 prisoners. Of those, 91 percent were Black. Trump's tax-cut bill included specific incentives for investments in poverty-stricken areas, known as opportunity zones. And those incentives were starting to work, according to a study from the Urban Institute. The administration had also made some inroads with historically Black colleges and universities when it canceled repayment of more than $300 million in federal relief loans and made permanent more than $250 million in annual funding.

Al Sharpton, the MSNBC host and civil rights activist, had been secretly calling Trump, promising that his staff would work with the president's team in the White House—even though he'd later ignore the follow-up calls from Jared's team. Jesse Jackson, the Baptist minister and civil rights activist, had phoned a few times, too. White House staffers set up calls with Jackson, ministers, and other groups to provide technical assistance for those seeking coronavirus aid from the Paycheck Protection Program, the package of $350 billion in small business loans that Congress had passed in April. They organized a similar call with Surgeon General Jerome Adams to walk through Covid issues for Black community leaders. And more than 600 Black leaders joined a call as White House aides strategized over a push to codify in federal statutes the opportunity zone revitalization council that Trump had created by executive order.

But none of Jared's efforts to repair Trump's image with the Black community would matter after May 26, 2020, when the video of George Floyd's murder began spreading online.

It was the Tuesday after Memorial Day, and senior White House staff gathered inside the West Wing for a prescheduled meeting about coronavirus. The death toll was approaching 100,000 in the United States, and the administration was scrambling to address a shortage of remdesivir, the antiviral used to treat Covid. The mixed messaging coming from the West Wing as aides touted social distancing guidelines while mocking Democratic governors for not reopening their states faster had created its own problem as local and national news showed horrifying scenes of large Memorial Day crowds gathered on Florida beaches and inside East Coast bars.

"We're getting crushed on Covid," said Alyssa Farah, the communications director.

Jared, who seemed distracted and more aloof than usual in the meeting, interrupted her.

"I'm just going to stop you," he said. "There is going to be one story that dominates absolutely everything for the foreseeable future. I'm already hearing from African American leaders about the death of George Floyd in Minnesota."

Mark Meadows, the White House chief of staff, brushed it off.

"Nobody is going to care about that," Meadows told him.

Meadows disputed that he'd responded that way, but it took another day for Trump to watch the devastating video. By then, protests had spilled across multiple U.S. cities. The first demonstrators had gathered just hours after Jared's warning on Tuesday, creating a makeshift memorial for Floyd outside the convenience store where he'd been pinned to the ground. The crowd of hundreds turned into thousands by that night. They marched two miles from the memorial to the Minneapolis Police Department's third precinct station. Violence erupted as protesters hurled rocks and water bottles, and law enforcement outfitted in riot gear fired flash-bangs and tear gas canisters. Similar scenes were unfolding on Wednesday in Kentucky, Georgia, and California by the time Scavino loaded the Floyd video on his phone and handed it to Trump on *Air Force One*.

Trump sat in the president's suite near the front of the plane. He was returning from Florida, where poor weather had scrubbed SpaceX's attempt at becoming the first private company to launch a human crew into orbit. It was an outing for the whole Family Trump: Melania, Jared and Ivanka, Don Junior and Kim, Eric and Lara, and a collection of grandkids had all come. As Trump pressed Play on the video, he was surrounded by Jared, Scavino, National Security Adviser Robert O'Brien, and his media team.

Trump contorted his face as he watched. He looked repulsed, then turned away, and handed the phone back to his aides without finishing.

"This is fucking terrible," he blurted out.

Trump said he wanted to speak immediately with Attorney General Bill Barr, and dictated a tweet to Scavino, which Trump posted after *Air Force One* landed.

"My heart goes out to George's family and friends," Trump said in the post. "Justice will be served!"

Trump was still shaken by the video the next afternoon when Barr arrived in the Oval Office on Thursday to brief the president about Floyd's death, now three days later. Trump had tweeted the night before that he planned to expedite the probe from the Justice Department. The only effect of the tweet, however, was to politicize the issue and infuriate Barr, who hated the suggestion that his interest in the case was political or the idea that anybody was his boss. It was the opening fissure in the relationship between the irascible and stubborn septuagenarians.

"This is fucked up," Trump told Barr about Floyd's death in a meeting that included Jeffrey Rosen, the deputy attorney general, and a room full of other aides.

Barr pointed to some potential complications, but Trump didn't want to hear them.

"I know these fucking cops," Trump said, recalling stories he'd heard growing up in Queens about savage police tactics. "They can get out of control sometimes. They can be rough."

Trump's assessment struck some in the room as surprisingly critical of police, and the president showed a level of empathy for Floyd behind closed doors that he would never fully reveal in public. Had he tried, it might have helped dial down the tension. But Trump didn't see it as part of his job to show empathy, and he worried that such a display would signal weakness to his base.

———

After his briefing with Barr, Trump told reporters in the Oval Office that afternoon that he didn't like watching the video. When they asked him if he'd spoken to Floyd's family yet, Trump said he hadn't.

"That was a very bad thing that I saw," the president said. "I saw it last night, and I didn't like it."

But Trump's compassion quickly evaporated that night as he watched demonstrators torch a Minneapolis police station and the protests spread to New York City; Denver; Phoenix; Columbus, Ohio; and Memphis, Tennessee.

At nearly 1:00 a.m. on Friday, May 29, Trump made a dramatic pivot from empathy for Floyd's family as he posted a racially charged threat of violence against the protesters.

"These THUGS are dishonoring the memory of George Floyd," he wrote on Twitter. "When the looting starts, the shooting starts. Thank you!"

———

The tweet mortified staff inside the White House and at the campaign. The phrase dated back to the 1960s and the hardline Miami police chief Walter Headley, who aimed it at "Negro hoodlums."

Twitter executives took action. They determined that Trump's post glorified violence, which was a violation of the site's terms of service, and for the first time blocked a message on Trump's Twitter page. That meant other users were prevented from replying to it, liking it, or sharing it with others. The tech company's drastic action was becoming a trend. Just days earlier, Twitter had applied a fact-checking notice to Trump's false claim about voter fraud.

Trump either saw no difference between the peaceful protesters and the rioters or simply didn't care. Inside the White House, Meadows had been chief of staff for just six weeks and a new communications team had been ushered in with him. They frantically tried to convince Trump to walk back his tweet. But there was an art to convincing Trump to reverse himself. He would never admit he'd been wrong, so a different approach was needed. Farah tried to appeal to his political interests, describing herself as the kind of educated female voter who was open to supporting Trump but needed to be convinced.

Trump wasn't persuaded.

McEnany, meanwhile, seemed to have an instinct for communicating with Trump. She framed the fix as merely explaining why the liberal media had either misunderstood or deliberately misconstrued Trump's post. Trump finally sent a second tweet more than thirteen hours after the first.

"Looting leads to shooting," Trump wrote in the post, as he claimed that the first tweet wasn't a threat—it was merely a considerate warning that sometimes lootings are violent.

It wasn't convincing, but at least it was a walk-back.

Trump finally called Floyd's family that day.

"Terrific people," he told reporters Friday afternoon.

But the family remembered the call a little differently. Philonise Floyd, George Floyd's brother, told MSNBC that the call was "so fast" and that Trump "didn't give me an opportunity to even speak."

"I was trying to talk to him," Philonise said during an interview on Sharpton's program. "But he just kept, like, pushing me off, like, 'I don't want to hear what you're talking about.'"

That night, protests erupted for the fourth consecutive time since Floyd's death.

In Georgia, Republican governor Brian Kemp declared an emergency after demonstrators poured into Atlanta's Centennial Olympic Park and smashed windows. Others climbed on top of the large red CNN logo outside the company's headquarters, spray-painted it, and raised a Black Lives Matter flag. In Richmond, Virginia, a police cruiser and a city bus downtown were both set on fire. Violence flared in New York, injuring protesters and law enforcement.

Violence was escalating, but not in a way that Trump World had expected. In Oakland, California, a gunman shot and killed Dave Underwood, a fifty-three-year-old federal security officer guarding a federal courthouse. At a news conference about the murder, Chad Wolf, Trump's acting homeland security secretary, and Ken Cuccinelli, who was Wolf's deputy secretary, talked about Antifa and connected it to the Black Lives Matter protests. But the two men eventually arrested for the killing had ties to the far-right extremist "Booga-loo" movement that sought to instigate a second Civil War. Steven Carrillo, a thirty-two-year-old Air Force staff sergeant, was charged with murder, and Robert Justus Jr., a thirty-year-old he'd met just a few hours earlier, was charged with aiding and abetting.

But Trump had no time for nuance. Crowds were also closing in on the White House, and a burst of violence erupted Friday evening near Lafayette Square, the historic seven-acre park just north of the White House. The park featured President Andrew Jackson's statue on horseback—the world's first equestrian statue balanced solely on the horse's hind legs—and had been used at various points as a graveyard, a zoo, and an encampment for slaves who built the White House.

Law enforcement in riot gear sprayed chemical irritants at protesters in the park who threw water bottles and rocks and tugged at the police barricades. One demonstrator climbed a window ledge at Freedman's Bank Building—a historic building on the edge of the park—and gripped the protective iron bars with one hand while using the other to write "Fuck Trump" in purple spray paint.

When a group of protesters breached a barricade along the Treasury Department fence and the White House lawn at about 7:00 p.m., Secret Service locked down the White House. The president, his wife, and his youngest son, fourteen-year-old Barron, were hurried into a secure underground bunker under the East Wing of the White House—the same shelter that Vice President Dick Cheney had used on September 11, 2001, when authorities feared a plane hijacked by Al Qaeda might be heading toward the White House.

The Trumps remained in the basement bunker for about an hour.

On Saturday morning, Trump tweeted that he'd never felt unsafe. He insisted that he'd watched "every move" of the protests. He never mentioned his retreat to the bunker.

Jared and Brad had been suggesting all week that Trump address Floyd's death with a speech. They wanted to feed him lines that would make him appear more empathetic for the families involved in the senseless deaths and leaven the overly aggressive law-and-order message. But Trump's error-filled Oval Office address about coronavirus a few months earlier was still painfully fresh for too many other White House aides. Trump's advisers also had no new policy proposals to pitch to address the crisis. And ultimately, Trump had no interest in delivering a message of unity.

Instead, the compromise was to insert some lines into prewritten remarks that afternoon at Cape Canaveral, where SpaceX would make its second attempt at the rocket launch.

Trump spent the morning conflating the protesters with the looters on Twitter. In the storm of tweets about how safe he had felt the night before, he threatened to unleash "vicious dogs" and "ominous weapons" on anyone who breached the White House fencing. Critics immediately complained that the violent imagery invoked civil rights era brutality from when police in the 1960s turned dogs and fire hoses against Black protesters. Trump also said he believed that the protests "had little to do with the memory of George Floyd" and called for his supporters to mass outside the White House.

"Tonight, I understand, is MAGA NIGHT AT THE WHITE HOUSE???" Trump tweeted.

Protests were in full bloom in Washington and around the country by the time the president arrived in Cape Canaveral. It was the first weekend since Floyd's death, and the nation seemed to be losing its collective grip. A *Wall Street Journal*/NBC News poll taken that weekend showed that an overwhelming majority, 80 percent, felt like the country was spiraling out of control.

In Dallas that night, a man wielded a machete as he tried to ward off looters—but was instead beaten down by the mob. In Salt Lake City, fifty-seven-year-old Brandon McCormick arrived with a bow and arrow, which he aimed at demonstrators and shouted, "All lives matter." The crowd mauled him, then flipped his car and set it on fire. By 1:00 p.m., Minneapolis mayor Jacob Frey said the peaceful protests had been transformed into "domestic terrorism" and pleaded with residents to stay home. In Seattle, Mayor Jenny Durkan announced a 5:00 p.m. curfew as flames engulfed police cars and looters broke into downtown stores.

The country watched the madness unfold on their television screens, and the protests completely drowned out Trump's speech in Florida, where he struck a drastically softer and more measured tone.

"I understand the pain that people are feeling," Trump said.

White House aides were furious that the cable networks didn't carry the remarks live. But they—and Trump—had missed the moment. It was a rare instance in Trump's four years on the political stage that he'd been overtaken by events instead of the other way around. For some in the White House, Trump's reelection chances seemed to be collapsing in front of their eyes. Senior aides believed Trump's tone-deaf response to Floyd—coupled with his eagerness to shed his responsibility for the pandemic response—fueled lasting doubts about his leadership among moderate voters, who until then had remained open to his economic policies. That same *Wall Street Journal*/NBC News poll showed that by a two-to-one margin, voters were more troubled by police's actions in Floyd's killing than by the violence at some protests.

That night, Trump returned to Washington to a White House that looked like it was under siege. Blockades shut down traffic around the White House, where the National Guard, Secret Service, and the U.S. Park Police reinforced security barricades. Federal and local law enforcement wore reinforced helmets and full-length plastic shields as they patrolled the perimeter. Nearby businesses, like the historic Hay-Adams Hotel just off Lafayette Square, were boarded up.

Bursts of violence erupted along with flash-bangs from law enforcement and firecrackers from demonstrators. Tear gas and pepper spray doused protesters, who set fires around the district and vandalized stores in Georgetown and CityCenter.

The next day, Trump spent his Sunday behind closed doors. But just as the protests had settled in the daylight, Peter Baker and Maggie Haberman at the *New York Times* broke a story that Trump had spent part of Friday night hunkered down in the basement bunker. For Trump, the humiliation was deep.

The story not only undercut the president's strongman image but directly contradicted his tweets from a day earlier that his safety was never in question. Trump lashed out as aides did their best to avoid him. The White House was already relatively vacant due to Covid, and the protests emptied it further. Meadows had been out of town, too. He was on his way back from Georgia, where his daughter had held a large wedding in violation of the state's social distancing guidelines.

That night, protesters smashed basement windows and started a fire inside the historic St. John's Episcopal Church, which was among the few remaining original buildings around Lafayette Square. The flames damaged just one room, but the moment took on outsize importance around Washington and beyond. The pale yellow church with a steeple that encased a 200-year-old bell cast by Paul Revere's son was only about a quarter mile away from the White House, just on the other side of the park. Every president had worshipped inside its four walls since its doors opened during James Madison's second term in 1816 when the nation's fourth president wanted to be treated like a regular parishioner and chose to sit in Pew 54. The church reserved that pew for presidents for the next 200 years, even though Lincoln opted instead for Pew 89. That was the last pew in the back corner beside the door, and he could slip in and out unnoticed.

There was some hope inside the White House and campaign that the violence would turn public opinion away from the protests. Brad and Jared discussed how frustration with the rioters might allow them to appeal to suburban women and seniors. Meadows added that he'd heard more concern about the damage at St. John's than anything else during the protests.

"He's going to end up on the right side of these riots," Brad told Jared. "They've gone too far, and there are too many Americans that want to get back to work. But he needs to pivot back to the economy and stop talking about protesters as Antifa."

But Trump wasn't about to pivot. He was fixated on his image and furious about the bunker story. He was going to swing the law-and-order message like a hammer at anything that remotely looked like a nail.

9

Anarchy and Chaos

"I wish we had an occupying force."

—*Conference call, Situation Room, June 1, 2020*

B y 3:00 a.m. on the morning of June 1, law enforcement had chased the last few protesters from Lafayette Square. Remnants of tear gas and pepper spray hung heavy in the air above the park as smoke scattered rays of light from police beacons, floodlights, and open flames. A block away, the powerful spotlights that typically illuminated the world's predominant symbol of presidential power and American democracy had been switched off. The White House sat in darkness.

Inside, Trump stewed over the bunker leak. But security concerns at the White House extended beyond the preventative trip to the underground safe house. Additional safety precautions included moving senior administration officials who lived in Washington into hotel rooms in Virginia and assigning security details to aides who needed to commute to the West Wing.

Trump's top military, law enforcement, and West Wing advisers knew he must have been upset when he summoned them to the Oval Office for a meeting first thing in the morning—several hours before he usually emerged from the residence.

Those suspicions proved correct. Trump boiled over about the bunker story as soon as they arrived and shouted at them to smoke out whoever had leaked it. It was the most upset some aides had ever seen the president.

"Whoever did that, they should be charged with treason!" Trump yelled. "They should be executed!"

Meadows repeatedly tried to calm the president as startled aides avoided eye contact.

"Okay," he said, over and over. "I'm on it. We're going to find out who did it."*

Trump's advisers told themselves he didn't *really* want to execute an aide, and Trump told me later through a spokesman that he never made such a threat. But those who said they'd heard the president issue that warning had interpreted the outburst as a sign of a president in panic. Trump's chief political worry was appearing weak. Yet while his team silently understood the problem, there was no clear agreement on a solution.

Some White House aides mentioned a plan from Park Police to install unscalable fencing beyond Lafayette Park, which would push the perimeter even farther from the White House. There was no opposition to that plan in the room, which included officials from the Pentagon, Department of Justice, and Department of Homeland Security.

But Trump wanted more. He didn't think the administration had been tough enough with the protesters. Pence mentioned the Insurrection Act, an obscure federal law that enabled the commander in chief to deploy troops within U.S. borders. The act was passed in 1807 when President Jefferson feared rebellion brewing within the fledgling nation. But George Floyd wasn't Aaron Burr, and the protesters weren't Confederates. Pence's casual advice unnerved others in the room.

Are you freaking kidding me? one senior administration official thought.

The Insurrection Act had been discussed a year earlier inside the White House when Stephen Miller proposed invoking it to enlist troops in his personal war against illegal immigration. Now that Pence had again broached the subject, Trump became fixated on it.

Barr, Trump's seventy-year-old attorney general, was George H. W. Bush's forty-one-year-old attorney general the last time the Insurrection Act had been invoked—in 1992, when violence erupted after the acquittal of four

---

* Trump's fury burned for days, and he repeatedly asked Meadows if he'd found the leaker. Meadows, in turn, obsessed over tracking down the source. It was the lasting memory of the ordeal for many West Wing aides.

police officers in the beating of Rodney King, a Black man brutalized during what should have been a routine traffic stop. Barr explained to Trump that Bush invoked the act only after consulting with California governor Pete Wilson, who supported the move. He cautioned Trump against taking such a step.

"It's not really necessary in this situation," Barr told Trump. "It's a break-glass-in-case-of-emergency option."

But Trump could still have a strong show of force, Barr said. He suggested a plan to put one law enforcement officer on the street for every two protesters—not to react to demonstrators but to control events. There were plenty of National Guard reserves to backfill where needed. Barr said that that sort of presence would "dominate the streets" and immediately reduce violence.

Trump said he wanted to put the nation's highest-ranking military officer in charge of the effort: Mark Milley, an Army general and the Joint Chiefs of Staff chairman. But Milley was the president's military adviser—he wasn't in command of troops or the National Guard. Milley told the president that it would be highly inappropriate for him to lead the effort. The Pentagon could provide support to a civilian agency but wouldn't oversee the response.

"I can't be in charge of this," Milley told Trump.

Barr backed him up.

Milley had been alarmed by the talk of the Insurrection Act. The chairman of the Joint Chiefs of Staff understood the precise difference between sending active-duty troops into the protests instead of the National Guard: One group was trained to take land and kill the enemy, and the other had been taught riot control and quasi–law enforcement techniques.

The sixty-two-year-old Milley viewed the unrest around Floyd's death as a political problem, not a military one. He told the president there were more than enough reserves in the National Guard to support law enforcement responding to the protests. Milley told him that invoking the Insurrection Act would shift responsibility for the protests from local authorities directly to the president.

Milley spotted President Lincoln's portrait hanging just to the right of Trump and pointed directly at it.

"That guy had an insurrection," Milley said. "What we have, Mr. President, is a protest."

The same debate would play out repeatedly inside the Oval Office all summer as civil justice protests flared up across the country: Trump would push to deploy troops, while Milley, Barr, and Mark Esper, the defense secretary, would push back against the president and any other voices of support in the room.

When protests in Seattle and Portland drew attention from cable networks—along with the so-called police-free zones in those cities—Trump's language became increasingly violent as he argued inside the Oval Office for the U.S. military to take over major American cities.

Trump would highlight videos that showed law enforcement getting physical with protesters and tell his administration he wanted to see more of that behavior. "That's how you're supposed to handle these people," Trump instructed his top law enforcement and military officials. "Crack their skulls!" He told his team that he wanted the military to go in and "beat the fuck out" of the protesters. "Just shoot them," Trump said on multiple occasions inside the Oval Office.

When Milley and Barr pushed back, Trump would tone it down. But only slightly. "Well, shoot them in the leg—or maybe the foot," Trump said. "But be hard on them!"

Stephen Miller chimed in during one Oval Office debate with an apocalyptic vision of tumult tearing through the streets. He equated the scenes unfolding on his television screen to those in a third-world country. Major American metropolises, he said, had been turned into war zones.

"These cities are burning," Miller warned.

The comment infuriated Milley, who viewed Miller as not only wrong but out of his lane. The Army general who had commanded troops in Iraq and Afghanistan spun around in his seat and pointed a finger directly at Miller.

"Shut the fuck up, Stephen," Milley snapped.

A Boston-area native who played hockey and had earned two Ivy League degrees, Milley understood the kind of hotshot attitude that permeated the ranks of Trump World, and he had no trouble keeping up. He also made it a point to arrive at every White House meeting armed with the kind of precise and straightforward data that often made a difference with Trump. As Miller nursed his wounds in the back of the room, Milley informed Trump that civil unrest was an issue in about a half dozen of roughly three hundred American cities with populations of more than 100,000 people. Among those half dozen cities, only a tiny fraction of the total population participated in the protests.

"No, Mr. President, they're not burning the cities," Milley said.

Milley represented the last career military man in the Trump World orbit, even though Trump had surrounded himself with highly decorated officers at the start of his term. He put John Kelly, a retired Marine general, in charge of the Department of Homeland Security before making him his second chief of staff. Army lieutenant general H. R. McMaster was White House national security adviser for most of Trump's first fifteen months in office. James Mattis, another retired Marine general, had commanded Trump's Department of Defense.

But Trump didn't know any of them when he asked them to join the administration. Where previous presidents arrived in office flush with contacts from their days in Congress, relationships from governors' associations, and longtime donors eager to offer suggestions, Trump had always kept a tight circle around him of mostly friends and, by 2016, fellow septuagenarians whom he knew from real estate and marketing. Bannon, himself a former Navy officer, knew Mattis and Kelly by reputation and pushed for them. Trump liked the idea of military generals coming to work for him and spoke of them possessively, as if the stripes on their shoulders were transferable.

"My generals," he would say.

But the idea of selfless service embedded into each military branch's bedrock values was anathema to the solipsism at the center of Trumpism. Trump's generals viewed the job as service to the country, not to him, and it frustrated Trump.

Under President Obama, Milley had leaned into his Ivy League credentials—rattling off details from the deep cuts of military history as well as minutiae from the back pages of briefing books piled on his desk—and quickly rose in the administration. He was deputy commander in Afghanistan for about a year before Obama put him in charge of the U.S. Army Forces Command, the largest of the service's four commands, with more than 750,000 soldiers. Nine months later, Obama promoted him to Army chief of staff. Milley was a sports fan who could sit at any bar with football or hockey on the TV and hold a conversation. He had a loud and bombastic side that gelled with

Obama's successor. And after serving two years with Trump, Milley was elevated to chairman of the Joint Chiefs of Staff, a panel of the nation's top military leaders. Trump promoted Milley during a surreal Oval Office interview on December 7, 2018, that would set the tone for their final two years together.

Just before that meeting, John Kelly, who was still White House chief of staff, told Milley that Mattis had pushed to install him in an overseas post—but Trump was inclined to give him the chairman job.

Milley asked Kelly what he himself would do. But Kelly hated working for Trump and his departure had been rumored for months. The following day, Trump would announce that he and Kelly had finally agreed to part ways by the end of year.

"I would get as far away from this fucking place as I fucking could," Kelly told Milley.

Kelly and Milley walked into the Oval Office, but Trump talked mostly to his chief of staff.

"What's that other job that Mattis wants me to give him?" Trump asked Kelly. "Something in Europe?"

"That would be SACEUR," Kelly said. "Supreme Allied Commander Europe."

"What's that guy do?" Trump asked.

"He is in charge of all the U.S. things in Europe," Kelly said.

"Which is the better job?" Trump asked.

"Oh," Kelly said. "Chairman is the better job."

"Well, what do you think?" Trump asked Kelly as Milley sat silently nearby.

"Pick Mark," Kelly told Trump. "He's the best we got."

"Okay," Trump said, turning to Milley. "I want you to be my chairman. What do you think?"

"I'll do whatever it takes," Milley said.

Even as the lone active service member surrounded by political strategists in Trump's Oval Office, Milley was considered a savvy operator. He displayed that skill during his first White House meeting as Joint Chiefs of Staff chairman in October 2019.

At that time, Trump faced a fraught decision about whether to leave American special operations forces in northern Syria amid a likely attack from Turkey—a NATO ally—or remove the troops and abandon the Kurds, a key partner for Washington in the fight against ISIS.

"Well, what are we going to do?" Trump asked a room full of military and national security advisers.

Milley stood up, walked around to Trump's side of the Resolute Desk, and unfurled a map of the Middle East's troubled region in front of them both. Milley frantically drew on the map where he thought U.S. forces should be positioned. As he explained his reasoning, Trump listened, decided that would be the plan, and abruptly ended the meeting.

"Okay," Trump said. "That's what we're going to do."

After the meeting, Trump's national security adviser, Robert O'Brien, immediately confronted Milley as Esper and Secretary of State Mike Pompeo stood nearby.

"Never do that again," O'Brien said. "Don't brief the president from behind the Resolute Desk without going through us."

Milley flashed the palm of his hand at O'Brien.

"Who the fuck do you think you are?" Milley said. "It is my legal responsibility to advise the president of the United States on military matters. So, if I have to throw a fucking map in front of the president, that's what I'm going to do."

━━━━━

On the morning of June 1, the final compromise inside the Oval Office was to rely on the National Guard to keep the peace in Washington—a win for Barr, Milley, and Esper. But Trump could also claim victory by calling up the 82nd Airborne Division and stationing them at Joint Base Andrews in suburban Maryland. The elite unit had last been deployed in January—amid the escalating tensions with Iran over the killing of General Soleimani. Another two hundred military police were deployed from Fort Bragg, North Carolina, to Fort Belvoir, Virginia, about twenty miles southwest of the White House— just in case.

Trump's aggressiveness in the Oval Office spilled into his 11:00 a.m. teleconference with fifty state governors. Seated in the Situation Room with Barr, Milley, and Esper, Trump exaggerated claims about the violence and alarmed officials both on the call and in the room by announcing he'd just put Milley "in charge." He said police should respond to protesters throwing rocks the same as if they were firing guns. He urged the governors to use the National Guard to knock out protesters "like bowling pins."

He sounded at times like he was narrating the call instead of leading it.

"It's like we're talking about a war," Trump said.

Tim Walz, the governor of Minnesota, said he'd already called up the National Guard and asked Trump to explain to the American people that the guardsmen were there to help keep the peace and not as an occupying force sent to take over cities. But Trump liked the more hostile imagery.

"People wouldn't have minded an occupying force," Trump told Walz. "I wish we had an occupying force."

Trump also reprised some of Barr's points from his earlier meeting, but his shorthand came off as callous and insensitive.

"You have to dominate—if you don't dominate, you're wasting your time," he said. "You have to dominate, and you have to arrest people, and you have to try people, and they have to go to jail for long periods."

When Barr had talked in the Oval Office about dominating the streets, he meant increasing the number of law enforcement officers. But Trump simply ordered the governors to "dominate," repeating the word six times in the first ten minutes of the call in a way that sounded more physical and aggressive than anything Barr had suggested.

Barr, who was in the Situation Room with Trump, added some context. He urged the states to create a "strong presence" with law enforcement. The National Guard, he said, could help control the crowd and free up local law enforcement to go after the troublemakers.

"There are very few people who are running around lighting fires," Barr said. "They have to be taken off the streets and arrested and processed."

Barr suggested a federal-state partnership modeled on the Joint Terrorism Task Force, which had been in place for decades to coordinate state and federal investigative efforts.

But a few minutes later, Trump seized on Barr's suggestion and referred to the protesters as "terrorists."

"These are terrorists," Trump said. "They're looking to do bad things to our country. They're Antifa and the radical left."

After the call had gone on for nearly an hour, Illinois governor J. B. Pritzker, a Democrat, pointed out that no mention had been made of George Floyd or any civil justice issues at the center of the protests.

"I've been extraordinarily concerned about the rhetoric that's been used by you," Pritzker told Trump. "It's been inflammatory, and it's not okay for that officer to choke George Floyd to death. But we have to call for calm."

Trump immediately snapped back. He criticized Pritzker's handling of the coronavirus, an issue that they hadn't discussed at all on the call, and touted the "great compassion" he'd shown after Floyd had been killed. Then Trump lost the thread and referred to the Minnesota man as "Officer Floyd" and spoke passionately about the launch of the SpaceX rocket he'd watched a few days earlier.

Trump responded the way he often did to stress, which was to control the minutiae of someone else's job. The president, who would often act as his own White House communications director and chief of staff, suddenly worked like the conference call operator.

"Okay, who's next, please? Hashtag two," Trump said, using Twitter jargon to describe the phone keypad buttons—the pound key, and then the number two—that the governors needed to press to speak.

"Hashtag two, please," he repeated.

"We have no one in queue at this time," the operator said.

After the call, Milley confronted Trump about his role. He was an adviser, and not in command.

Trump had had enough.

"I said you're in fucking charge!" Trump shouted at him.

"Well, I'm not in charge!" Milley yelled back.

"You can't fucking talk to me like that!" Trump said.

The argument continued to escalate between the native New Yorker and his Boston-born military adviser. Few New York-Boston disputes had ever held in the balance such profound consequences.

"Goddamnit," Milley said to others in the Situation Room. "There's a room full of lawyers here. Will someone inform him of my legal responsibilities?"

"He's right, Mr. President," Barr said again. "The general is right."

Barr, Milley, and Esper left the White House after the teleconference, and Trump returned to the Oval Office. When an internal White House email circulated that afternoon ordering staff to evacuate the building by 4:00 p.m. due to the protests, Trump had already been plotting his exit.

He huddled that afternoon with Jared, Ivanka, and Hope and continued to vent about the media coverage of the protests and his handling of the unrest. Trump wanted to counter that footage of the darkened White House and show he wasn't cowering in fear. With Park Police planning to push the perimeter farther back, the White House had notified the Secret Service that the president was interested in walking through Lafayette Square to inspect damage at the park and to speak to law enforcement in the area. But inside the Oval Office, Trump discussed two other destinations to demonstrate he was out of the bunker and in control. Both were politically compelling backdrops, but each offered a distinctive subtext.

One option was the Lincoln Memorial, a short motorcade less than two miles from the White House. Demonstrators had gathered for the past few nights at the ninety-eight-year-old neoclassical temple honoring the Great Emancipator. A group of Howard University students had held a prayer vigil at the memorial. It might project a sense of unity for Trump to stand next to the symbol of American excellence etched into white Georgian marble.

The other choice was St. John's Church, just a short walk from the White House. The chapel where Lincoln had prayed was a powerful symbol of faith in the heart of Washington, and a visit from Trump would be an unmistakable communiqué to the evangelical base the president had wooed for years. Two weeks earlier, Trump had told his team he wanted to be the face of the effort to reopen churches shuttered by the pandemic. He had watched a Fox News report about disputes between church leaders and Democratic governors. He'd then held an impromptu news conference to declare that churches, mosques, and synagogues were "essential services" that needed to remain open and threatened to override governors who refused. When asked what authority the president had to issue such a warning, White House press secretary Kayleigh McEnany had dismissed the question as a "hypothetical."

Trump loved the idea of walking to the church. He spoke to Kellyanne about the plan, and she asked whether he was bringing a coalition of evangelical and Black supporters with him. She reminded the president that Jared had said he'd reach out to Black leaders after Floyd had been killed.

"I thought those calls were being made already," Kellyanne said.

═══

That evening, Barr, Milley, and Esper returned to the White House. They had little idea what they were walking into—but they also never should have been there in the first place.

Barr and Milley had spent the afternoon at the Washington Field Office, an FBI bureau about two miles from the White House, where the administration set up a de facto command post for law enforcement agencies maintaining order in the nation's capital. They could see on the television sets that Park Police still hadn't widened the perimeter around the White House. Some communications equipment in their operations center needed to be rebooted. A sense of restlessness seemed to sweep through the room.

Milley suggested heading back to the White House where they could see what was going on in the park and joked about swinging by to see if Trump wanted to have dinner—and Barr, somewhat astonishingly, agreed.

Milley had planned to eventually head in that direction. He was dressed in combat fatigues with the intention of visiting with law enforcement and guardsmen on duty that night, including those on patrol near the White House. But even in jest, the suggestion of casually dropping in on the president was distressing—and memorable—for others in the room.

Barr later told others that he had planned to debrief the president at some point that evening. But he hadn't visited the Oval Office without an appointment in months.

Esper, meanwhile, had been at the Pentagon, where he called the governors of Maryland, Pennsylvania, and Virginia to start moving National Guard units toward Washington. Esper was on his way to the command post at the Washington Field Office when Milley called and said they were headed to the White House. Esper rerouted directions to his driver, and he was surprised to find a large group of White House officials in the room just outside the Oval Office when he arrived at nearly 6:30 p.m.

"Where's the meeting with the president?" Esper asked.

There's no meeting, he was told.

Trump was about to speak to the media, and then they would all walk to the church.

⎯⎯⎯⎯

Reporters had been summoned to the Rose Garden at about 6:00 p.m., roughly the same time the convoys for Barr and Milley had pulled into the White House drive. As reporters lined up outside for the remarks, Barr and Milley walked directly to Lafayette Square to greet the law enforcement officers lined up along the security perimeter on H Street. Milley crossed paths with Major Adam DeMarco, a D.C. National Guard officer who was among the most senior military soldiers on the scene.

"How many protesters?" Milley asked.

"More than two thousand," DeMarco said.

"Keep the troops calm," Milley told him. The guardsmen were there to respect the demonstrators' First Amendment rights, he added.

Barr, meanwhile, walked down the line of Park Police and D.C. guardsmen and then toward the statue of President Jackson. He was surprised to see that Park Police still hadn't expanded the security perimeter. But DeMarco, who had been briefed by Park Police when he'd arrived on the scene about ninety minutes earlier, had understood that they wouldn't clear demonstrators from the park until 7:00 p.m., when a curfew imposed by Washington's mayor, Muriel Bowser, went into effect.

At about 6:15 p.m., a round of cheers erupted from the protesters on H Street, on the north side of Lafayette Square. Protesters had watched law enforcement take a knee and assumed it was a show of solidarity. That was incorrect. The officers were simply putting on their gas masks.

At the same time, cable TV cameras showed Milley standing in the park on his phone. In combat fatigues and surrounded by officers outfitted from head to toe in riot gear, the scene looked like an Army general commanding his troops. Milley later told colleagues that he'd taken a call from his wife, who had seen him on TV. She called to ask what in the world he was doing.

Trump's team was watching, too. The group of White House officials whom Esper would find a few minutes later outside the Oval—Pence, Meadows,

O'Brien, Jared, Hope, McEnany, Farah, and others—had crowded into the small office where two of the president's assistants sat, glued to screens as on-air reporters tried to make sense of Barr and Milley in the park and the timing of Trump's unscheduled speech, which was already several minutes late.

But one had little to do with the other. Inside the West Wing, Trump had only decided to walk over to St. John's moments before reporters had been called to the Rose Garden. At about the same time, Meadows told Tony Ornato, a deputy White House chief of staff for operations, to notify the Secret Service that Trump would walk to the church after his Rose Garden speech.

When Alyssa Farah heard Meadows tell Ornato that the area needed to be secured for Trump, she reminded the chief of staff that news reporters were mixed in with the protesters. The daughter of two journalists—including Joseph Farah, the editor in chief of *WorldNetDaily*, a right-wing website known for promoting conspiracy theories—Farah cautioned that their plan would backfire if clearly marked reporters were roughed up by law enforcement. She asked to send word to the front line to watch for press credentials.

"Yeah, that's not going to happen," Meadows said with a laugh. Meadows later disputed the exchange.

<hr/>

Milley and Barr were walking back to the White House as black-clad officers from the Secret Service civil disturbance unit positioned on the park's northeastern corner were the first to push to expand the security perimeter at about 6:20 p.m. They started pushing protesters away but quickly stopped, according to hours of cable news and social media video compiled and analyzed by the *Washington Post*. Protesters at that corner of H Street and Madison Place responded by hurling water bottles, candy bars, and eggs—not bricks and stones, as law enforcement later claimed.

At 6:22 p.m., a voice on a loudspeaker from behind the police line asked for the protesters' attention. Park Police said the message was a warning to clear the area, but footage showed protesters couldn't hear the loudspeaker through the crowd noise.

Six minutes later, the National Guard and other law enforcement officers advanced on the crowd.

Park Police on horseback backed up Secret Service agents on the northeastern corner of the park. Members of the Bureau of Prisons special operations response team arrived wearing riot gear and armed with pepper ball guns and canister launchers. Officers again started to push the perimeter.

At 6:35 p.m., a chemical grenade rolled down H Street. Reporters waiting for Trump in the Rose Garden heard the explosions two blocks away.

The protesters had turned and ran. A Park Police officer swung his riot shield into the stomach of an Australian TV cameraman, Tim Myers, who was in the middle of a live shot for 7News, one of the country's most watched news channels. Viewers of the Australian breakfast program, including Australian prime minister Scott Morrison, watched from a stunning first-person angle as the officer then punched his fist directly into the camera lens. Another officer struck 7News correspondent Amelia Brace with his baton.

"Whoa!" 7News anchor David Koch said as he watched Myers get slugged. "Amelia, are you okay? Or your cameraman?"*

Officers from the Bureau of Prisons shot pepper ball guns at the fleeing crowd, and Park Police continued to roll tear gas bombs and sting ball grenades down the street. By 6:38 p.m., the police line had surged past St. John's Church.

At 6:43 p.m., Trump exited the Oval Office alone, walked along the colonnade, and down the steps to the lectern awaiting him in the Rose Garden. For six minutes, he spoke over the sound of exploding tear gas canisters as officers continued to push demonstrators down the final half block to I Street.

"I am your president of law and order," Trump said. "And an ally of all peaceful protesters."

He reprised many of the conversations that had taken place behind closed doors earlier that day. He accused Antifa of domestic acts of terror. He announced he'd mobilized "thousands of heavily armed soldiers" to keep the peace in Washington and threatened to deploy active duty troops to other cities. He vowed to restore order to help business owners.

"Thank you very much," Trump said as he closed his remarks. "And now I'm going to pay my respects to a very, very special place."

---

* Morrison quickly called for an investigation. Park Police never identified the two officers and said their investigation was still ongoing a year later.

Inside the outer Oval, aides erupted in high-fives. The cheering confused Barr and Milley, who hadn't been briefed on Trump's plans that evening.

─────────

After his Rose Garden statement, Trump turned and climbed the red-carpeted steps behind him. He resisted the temptation to answer shouted questions from reporters. Instead, he snuck a quick side-eyed glance at the media after he reached the top step and turned left under the covered pavilion toward the Oval Office door, which aides opened for him.

In a traditional White House, the chief of staff would have been duty-bound to apprise Cabinet secretaries and the Joint Chiefs chairman of a plan that included a walk through a days-long protest to a church for a photo op. But Meadows didn't chief the staff as much as staff the president.

Trump saw his senior military and law enforcement officials and motioned for the group to follow him.

"Come on," Trump said. "We're all going."

"What are we doing?" Esper asked.

No one answered Esper as Trump walked toward the North Portico door of the White House. Esper and Milley looked at each other.

"Let's go and see if we can find the troops," Esper said.

"Yeah, good," Milley said. "Okay."

─────────

Trump emerged from the White House just as Mayor Bowser's 7:00 p.m. curfew went into effect.

Generally considered to be the White House's main entrance, the North Portico door, crowned by an intricate stone carving of Double Scottish Roses, was rarely used. Instead, the West Wing's main entrance was the usual entry for staff and White House guests. But on the night of June 1, a parade of two dozen Trump World palace squires and constables poured through the door behind their president: Milley, Barr, Esper, Jared, Ivanka, Hope, Meadows, Scavino, Farah, Cipollone, Ornato, Kayleigh McEnany, Robert O'Brien, Stephen Miller, staff secretary Derek Lyons, deputy press secretary Hogan Gidley, personnel director Johnny McEntee, the president's personal assistant Nick Luna, and Keith Kellogg, who was Pence's national security adviser.

They trailed behind Trump for the one-block trek to the church, past a graffiti-covered building in the park, stepping over tattered signs and walking around days of detritus from demonstrators whom police had dispersed only moments earlier.

At 7:08 p.m., the procession reached St. John's, where plywood sheets covered the front door and windows. Trump stood alone in front of the chapel's stone steps, his hands at his sides and a blank stare on his face. Ivanka reached inside her white Max Mara handbag and handed her father the Bible she'd carried with her from the White House.

Milley had thought Trump wanted to speak with guardsmen as he had done earlier and only realized how wrong he'd been as he watched Ivanka pull that anonymous Bible out of her soft Italian leather handbag. With its adjustable strap and double zip, it was big enough to carry the Holy Scripture, but not to contain the shame of a four-star Army general.

At the same time, Milley noticed that the White House press corps had rushed to the church to document the moment.

"What the fuck?" Milley muttered as Ivanka stepped toward her father with the Bible.

Milley grabbed his aide and they backed away from the church. They took a circuitous route back to the White House to avoid any more TV cameras, climbed into their car, and drove away.

———

Trump initially held the Bible down at his side. After a few seconds, he started posing with it. He propped it up with two hands, the cover facing the cameras, just in front of his belly. He examined the spine and shook it a few times as if it might have been a secretly hollowed-out box. Finally, he gripped the bottom edge of the Bible in his right hand and raised it into the air.

"That the family Bible?" asked Steve Holland, a veteran White House reporter for Reuters.

Trump tried to ignore the question because the honest answer was that it was a fluke that this particular Bible ended up in his hand. Earlier that afternoon, an aide had scoured the West Wing, the East Wing, up and down the White House, and any other nearby offices gathering Bibles. The aide presented the prettiest versions to the president, and he picked the one Ivanka had carried in the $1,500 purse she brought to the tear gassing. Other than that, the only thing Trump knew about the version he had in his hand was that its dark navy-blue cover matched his suit; the gold embossed lettering on the spine spelled HOLY BIBLE; and it had a red ribbon bookmark bound with the pages. Not that Trump had ever absorbed much of the Good Word. In an interview with my then-colleagues at Bloomberg Politics in 2015, Trump had refused to reveal any of his favorite Bible verses.

"I wouldn't want to get into it because to me, that's very personal," Trump said at the time. "When I talk about the Bible, it's very personal. So I don't want to get into verses."

When he was asked if he was an Old Testament or New Testament guy, Trump punted again.

"Probablyyyyyy, equal," he said. "The whole Bible is incredible."

The crowd of college students at Liberty University laughed when he mispronounced a book of the Bible during a campaign stop there in 2016. Trump read the line on the page as "Two Corinthians," instead of how the frequently referenced scripture was spoken in Christian churches across America, which was "Second Corinthians."

But the Bible was a powerful political symbol for Trump. He had carried his own copy to the Value Voters Summit in 2015, a political rally where he showed a rare, boyish exuberance as he told the crowd about the book his mother had given to him.

"I brought my Bible!" Trump said.

Trump opened the book to one of the front pages and recalled how his mother had written his name and address, almost seeming a little flushed at the memory, as if he couldn't believe someone had cared enough about nine-year-old Donald to plan for a scenario in which he might lose the gift. He brought it again to his inauguration in 2016, where he made the very Trumpian move of being sworn in on double Bibles. Melania held the stack that included Mary Anne Trump's gift for graduating from Sunday Church Primary School at First Presbyterian Church in 1955 and Abraham Lincoln's

Bible. The only other time someone other than Lincoln had used that Bible was to swear in the nation's first Black president.

Trump was also convinced that the Bible had been the common thread between his two closest competitors in the 2016 Republican primary. He was terrified of Ted Cruz's appeal with evangelical voters and continuously attacked the Texas senator as a hypocrite, a pretender, and a prevaricator. "Lyin' Ted," Trump said about Cruz at almost every mention in early 2016.

"He holds the Bible high, and then he lies," Trump often quipped.

Just two weeks before his walk to St. John's, Trump insisted that Ben Carson—the Cabinet secretary who had briefly overtaken Trump in the 2016 Republican primary polls—had used the Bible the same way.

"I had to run against him, and he was very tough," Trump told Cabinet members seated on May 19 around a long mahogany table in the West Wing. "And he was even tougher when he'd run onto a stage holding a Bible up in the air. That was tough."

Neither Carson nor Cruz ever made a habit of holding up a Bible. The two Republicans enjoyed talking about the central role religion played in both their politics and private lives and would have jumped at the chance to discuss a Bible verse of their choosing. But they weren't known to publicly flaunt a Bible—high in the air or otherwise—on the campaign trail. Aides to both men insisted such a thing never happened.

After Trump ignored Holland's question in front of St. John's, NBC's Kristen Welker immediately followed up.

"Is that your Bible?" she asked.

"It's *a* Bible," Trump said.

On the walk back to the White House, Trump halted just before he reached Pennsylvania Avenue. He'd gotten out ahead of the press pool and wanted the cameras waiting at the gates to record his triumphant return home.

Trump walked back into the White House, again through the North Portico door, and the rest of the team followed at 7:18 p.m.

⸻

The whole scene had been exhilarating for Trump.

"Pretty great," he said after leaving the church.

He told his team back at the White House that the administration had to do "more to reopen churches like that," ignoring the fact that St. John's remained as boarded up when he left as it was when he arrived.

Still, he had a veritable choir of conservative supporters to back him up. Inside the White House, the digital video team went to work editing a thirty-second supercut of Trump's fifteen minutes in the park to underscore the president's narrative as an enforcer of law and order and a champion of religious freedom.

"It was illustrative that rioters won't prevail," Kellyanne told me for a story in the *Wall Street Journal* that day.

But other supporters tempered their reactions.

"I don't know what the purpose of the trip was," Senator Lindsey Graham told the *Journal*. "I mean, to show appreciation for the church? I don't know. You'll have to ask him."

"If your question is, 'Should you use tear gas to clear a path so the president can go have a photo op?' The answer is no," Senator Tim Scott told *Politico*.

Trump had walked to St. John's as a show of strength. But the president had put as much planning into his walk as most people would put into taking a stroll to the corner store to pick up a few snacks. Trump had created a new moment for the networks to talk about, but it was backfiring. Cell phone videos recorded every possible angle of violence perpetrated on indisputably peaceful protesters for Trump's benefit. There was also cause for concern in how Trump comported himself at the church, which some allies worried had hurt him with some evangelical voters. According to internal polling, Trump's support among Republicans was already starting to soften.

Had Trump consulted more closely with the evangelicals on his senior staff, including Meadows, McEnany, and Farah, they would have urged him to open the Bible and read a verse—or not carry it at all. Holding the Bible in the air like a trophy was politicizing the holy book and would be received like a slap in the face to many mainstream evangelicals. But to the extent that Trump bothered to consider the particulars of his walk—or what he would do when he got there—he had only consulted with Ivanka, Jared, and Hope. The three were trusted confidants who wanted the best for him—or at least more than many did in Trump World. But Hope was raised by Catholics in Connecticut.

Jared and Ivanka were practicing Jews from New York who kept kosher and observed the Sabbath. They weren't immersed in evangelical culture, nor did the Trump White House have a track record for successfully planning events to deliver a clear political message.

Jared's lack of familiarity with evangelicals had been pointed out recently in the West Wing by Meadows. A devout Christian who homeschooled his children, Meadows believed the Lord had called him to run for a western North Carolina congressional district in 2012 that, by the grace of God and the Republican majority in the state legislature, had just been redrawn to tilt so heavily in favor of Republicans that the incumbent Democrat, a famous college and professional quarterback named Heath Shuler, resigned. Meadows won the primary that year by fourteen points, in what would be his closest race during his seven years in office.

"A Jew growing up in Manhattan, I never thought I would meet and be such great friends with so many evangelicals," Jared said to Meadows during a West Wing chat. "You are just some of the best people. Paula White? She's incredible."

"Whoa," Meadows told Jared. "Never tell any mainstream evangelical that Paula White is your gold standard."

White was the thrice-married pastor of a prominent Florida megachurch but better known as a popular televangelist on whose show Trump occasionally appeared dating back to 2006. She had been condemned as a heretic by other Christian leaders and was a proponent of prosperity theology, which teaches that a believer can increase their material wealth by, among other things, increasing their donations to religious causes.

═══

If Trump's messaging to evangelicals ultimately was a few teleportations short of a rapture, when it came to the military, his march to St. John's was like planting political land mines along the path he'd spent four years clearing for veterans, troops, and their families to find their way back to his campaign.

Milley was furious to be pulled into a political photo op without any warning. He channeled his rage Monday night by patrolling Washington's streets with law enforcement. Esper joined him for part of the night, and the two men made a pact. They realized that things had changed that day, and that they had to recalibrate their political antenna so as not to get caught in that situation again. From now on, they would double-check the details behind every trip to the White House. Esper declined multiple invitations to the White House during the next five months.

For Milley, who described the sequence of events to colleagues as "complete fucking bullshit," the whole ordeal left him with the petrifying thought that everyone involved had thoroughly botched their role in the decision-making process. Two days after the march to St. John's, turmoil permeated the administration.

Barr was now enraged that the West Wing had effectively blamed him for the violent clashes in Lafayette Square and was furious that the Washington press corps wasn't willing to give him the benefit of the doubt. He had been aware of the plan to expand the perimeter around the park. But that hadn't been connected to Trump's walk to the church.

"The troops didn't invade the Philippines just so fucking MacArthur could walk on the beach," Barr complained to colleagues. "No. One thing happened, and then another thing happened."

Meanwhile, Trump was still fixated on the bunker, insisting that he'd only been examining the stronghold's safety features.

"I was there for a tiny little short period of time," Trump said in a Fox News radio interview.

At about the same time, Esper gathered defense reporters to the Pentagon for a news conference to give his version of events, which would send White House aides scrambling.

Esper told reporters that he hadn't been briefed on law enforcement's plans to disperse demonstrators and that he had left the White House with Trump that evening with the impression that they were going to inspect damage in Lafayette Square and the park.

"I was not aware a photo op was happening," Esper told reporters. "And look, I do everything I can to try to stay apolitical and try and stay out of situations that may appear political."

Esper's comments led every cable network. Trump was furious.

West Wing aides privately referred to Esper as "Yes-per," a nickname aimed at belittling the defense secretary as weak and unable to hold his ground. Now even that takedown seemed too soft "because he's really more of a Nope-er," one senior West Wing official said.

Kellyanne told Trump that Esper's most significant mistake was that he referred to the event at St. John's as a "photo op," which she viewed as parroting the media's word-of-the-day.

Meadows called over to the Pentagon and laid into Esper over the defense secretary's news conference and warned that Trump was upset.

"He's infuriated, like foaming-at-the-mouth mad," Meadows said.

Esper and Milley were due in the Oval Office that morning to brief Trump on the situation in Afghanistan. Esper knew the president would rip his face from his skull as soon as he walked into the Oval Office. He had drafted a resignation letter. He wasn't going to quit but he wanted to be ready if Trump asked him to step down.

When Esper and Milley entered the Oval Office, Pence, Pompeo, Cipollone, and O'Brien were already seated in four of the six chairs arranged in a semicircle in front of the Resolute Desk. The others immediately looked away as soon as the two Pentagon officials walked into the room. They knew the bloodshed that awaited the two military leaders—they'd been given a sneak preview of the butchering a few minutes prior.

Esper took his seat, and Trump didn't bother waiting for Milley. The Army general was still pulling his chair away from the desk to sit down when Trump exploded on Esper with a verbal assault so brutal and intense it would have embarrassed the foul-mouthed drill sergeant from *Full Metal Jacket*.

To the surprise and admiration of others in the room, Esper attempted to explain his thinking. But it just further fueled Trump's overheating motor. When Esper interrupted again, Trump went nuclear. The velocity and volume of the president were both awe-inspiring and terrifying to others in the room.

But then, as suddenly as he'd started, Trump stopped. It was over. He didn't speak to Esper for the rest of the meeting—nor did Esper try to chime in—but just moved on to the Afghanistan briefing without another word about what had just happened.

A day later, troops from the 82nd Airborne started returning to their base.

Milley publicly split with the president the following week during his graduation speech at the National Defense University. The Army general

apologized for his presence in the photo op, which, he said, "created a perception of the military involved in domestic politics."

"I should not have been there," Milley said.

Trump confronted Milley a few days later in front of other aides in the
Oval Office.

"Why did you apologize?" Trump asked him. "That's weak."

"Not where I come from," Milley said. "It had nothing to do with you. It
had to do with me and the uniform and the apolitical tradition of the United
States military."

"I don't understand that," Trump said. "It sounds like you're ashamed of
your president."

"I don't expect you to understand," Milley said.

=====

With Trump's relationship with military leaders fraying, some in Trump World
saw another opportunity for the president to display some racial sensitivity
and leadership with a seemingly comfortable victory: renaming the ten military bases named in honor of Confederate officers.

Trump had long resisted the change, including in the summer of 2017
when a similar issue sparked the racial violence in Charlottesville, Virginia.
At the time, Trump said eliminating memorials to Confederate leaders risked
the "history and culture of our great country being ripped apart."

In the aftermath of the St. John's debacle, David Urban—a well-connected
Washington lobbyist before Trump's election and a bona fide K Street Sultan
after the inauguration—urged Trump to reconsider his opposition.

"It's a ready-made campaign event," Urban told him.

The president didn't always follow Urban's guidance, but Trump almost
always listened to his bull-necked, bald-headed, and blue-eyed adviser. The
president credited the fifty-six-year-old Urban for the 2016 campaign victory
in Pennsylvania.

Once Trump took office, Urban proved to be a pipeline for critical positions in the new administration. Two of his recommendations were fellow cadets from his West Point class of 1986, both Esper and Pompeo, who

became Trump's first CIA director and spent the final thirty-three months of the administration as secretary of state.

For Urban, removing the monuments was a guaranteed political win. Other than the Confederate officers, no other bases were named after military leaders who attacked the United States. Urban framed it to Trump as a rebranding opportunity. Use the bases, he said, to memorialize Medal of Honor recipients instead of insurrectionists. The change would give him a political tailwind and help cool the temperature of an already overheated racial debate.

"That's a pretty good idea, actually," Trump said.

"It's a great fucking idea," Urban responded.

Esper also signaled his willingness to change the base names, the first time the military had opened the door on the conversation. Then Trump slammed it shut. He'd heard from other aides, including Meadows, that changing the base names would hurt him with his base.

"Our people hate this," Trump told two Cabinet officials. "Changing the names? We're not doing that."

After the Senate Armed Services Committee, with bipartisan support, approved a measure that would strip Confederate names from the bases, Trump posted on Twitter that he would veto the military spending bill if lawmakers included the action.

In 2016, Trump built his law-and-order message on three main pillars: stopping illegal immigration, confronting China to bring high-end manufacturing jobs back to the United States, and pulling the plug on endless wars.

It was a powerful pitch for military voters and particularly persuasive for the families, friends, and loved ones of soldiers who died fighting in Afghanistan and Iraq, and it may well have tipped the balance to Trump in 2016. In a little-noticed research paper seven months after that election, two university professors, who had spent a decade studying the socioeconomic gap between military families and the rest of the country, showed that Trump dramatically overperformed in disadvantaged communities where voters have shouldered a disproportionate burden of the human cost of national security.

Bannon told me after the 2016 race that the campaign had targeted blue-collar communities with a high rate of combat casualties, using social media advertising and Trump political rallies.

"It was one of the most important things we did," he said.

Trump had kept the country out of any new armed conflicts. Still, he'd insisted on bringing 1,600 active-duty troops to Washington to fight his political battles—and that number would have been closer to 10,000 had it not been for the pushback from Milley, Esper, and Barr. In the days after St. John's, Mattis, Trump's former defense secretary, loudly criticized the scene as an abuse of executive authority, and he accused Trump of creating a "false conflict between the military and civilian society." Two days later, John Kelly—by then out of the White House and a vocal critic of Trump—said he agreed with Mattis. Kelly said there was no "mature leadership" in the White House and that Trump wasn't even trying to pretend to unite the country.

"The partisanship has gotten out of hand—the tribal thing has gotten out of hand," Kelly said at the time.

Military veterans still preferred Trump over Biden, but not by the margins Trump needed to win reelection. Exit polls ultimately showed that his seven-point margin against Biden in 2020 was down from twenty-seven points against Clinton in 2016 among veterans.

10

Juneteenth, Observed

"I did something good—I made Juneteenth very famous."
—*Interview with author, Oval Office, June 17, 2020*

By early June, as Trump stewed amid negative coverage of the worsening pandemic and deepening recession, it was clear to campaign aides that they needed to get their candidate back on the road again, and soon. Brad had suggested a drive-in rally in Florida, but Trump hated the idea. Brad then pushed for an outdoor event in the state, but Trump told him that Florida Governor Ron DeSantis didn't want to host a rally at that point in the pandemic.

Brad had been scheduled to present the campaign's plans for TV advertising on June 9, and Trump said he wanted the meeting to also include an update on potential rally locations. The discussion in the White House Map Room included about a dozen aides, plus Trump, Pence, and Mike Lindell, the Minnesota entrepreneur who had overcome a crack cocaine addiction, founded the MyPillow company, and been a vocal Trump supporter in 2016. He'd become a close adviser to Trump heading into the reelection.* Trump admired the success Lindell had selling pillows with infomercials, and Brad wanted Lindell there to attest to the brilliance of the advertising campaign.

---

* Lindell's advertising company, LifeBrands, had multiple meetings with the Trump campaign during the first half of 2020 to compare marketing notes. Lindell attended one, but turned it into a planning session for a speaking tour of Minnesota fairgrounds he had wanted to piece together for the summer.

"You need to go in there and you need to tell the president that the TV team is doing a good job," Brad told Lindell before the meeting.

Brad's prep work paid off. Trump turned to Lindell as soon as the presentation had finished.

"Mike, are they doing a good job?" Trump asked.

"Yes, they're doing great!" Lindell said. "I've talked to them before, and they're talking to my team."

The meeting then turned to a discussion about rallies, and Brad presented a list of eleven potential locations in six different states: Arizona, Florida, Michigan, Oklahoma, Pennsylvania, and Wisconsin. Nearly all of the sites were outdoors. Brad pushed again for Pensacola. He told Trump that he'd spoken to DeSantis, and that the governor would back down if the president called him again. But Trump didn't want to make the call. Florida was off the table.

Pennsylvania, Michigan, and Wisconsin were all governed by Democrats and Trump World didn't want to repeat the problems they'd had planning the party's convention in Charlotte. They didn't blame Covid for their convention issues. They blamed Roy Cooper, the state's Democratic governor.

Trump and his team were convinced that Democratic governors in battleground states were playing politics with social distancing guidelines, refusing to loosen protocols in a way that would let him hold the kind of mega-rallies that had become a physical manifestation of his political strength.

But waiting until the pandemic was under control was simply not an option.

Scale back rallies? Hope would tell him he'd be mocked for capitulating to critics in the media. Models from the scientists showing Covid deaths increasing would draw sneers from Meadows. "You look weak in a mask"—that was the refrain from Johnny McEntee.

That left Tulsa, Oklahoma, which had landed on Brad's list after he asked Pence earlier that week about which state, governed by a Trump-friendly Republican, had the fewest Covid restrictions.

Tulsa also had the smallest coronavirus caseload of any of the options, reopening efforts were the furthest along, and the Mabee Center—the 11,300-seat arena Brad proposed that day—had been the location of a Trump rally during the 2016 campaign.

Trump was sold.

An indoor rally, however, immediately raised the question of face masks. There was debate about whether they would require masks, and Brad suggested printing a few thousand face masks with campaign branding. Trump rejected both ideas.

"No, we don't need to give out masks to everyone," he said.

Brad recommended holding the rally on June 19. He loved Friday night events, but rallies those nights were rare because the campaign often had to find open days between concerts, basketball games, and other traveling road shows that had been booked months in advance. Brad floated the date inside the campaign, but not to an extensive circle. No one on Brad's team flagged that day—or that combination of time and place—as potentially problematic. Had Brad bothered to ask Katrina Pierson, the highest-ranking Black staffer on the campaign and a close friend of Brad's, she could have told him that June 19 was Juneteenth, a significant holiday for Black Americans that commemorated the end of slavery.

She also would have told him that Tulsa, as most Black Americans are well aware, had been home to one of the bloodiest outbreaks of racial violence in the nation's history. She'd have explained that it had only been two weeks since Floyd had been killed, that protests over police brutality, which disproportionately had fatal consequences for Blacks were still boiling over across the country every night, and that holding a rally in the middle of a civil rights crisis on Juneteenth in the same city as the 1921 Tulsa Race Massacre was unwise.

Meanwhile, in the White House, Ja'Ron Smith—the West Wing's seniormost Black official—had been working on an executive order for Trump to declare Juneteenth a federal holiday. But no one had thought to ask him, either.

When Richard Walters heard about the plans on a conference call that day with the campaign, the Republican National Committee's chief of staff's eyes widened. Walters, who started out with a low-level job at the party as a twenty-three-year-old out of college, grew up in the Deep South, about fifteen miles east of the Mississippi state capitol and some three hours south of Oxford, where he attended the University of Mississippi. He wrote his college thesis on the effect of systemic racism on education policy, and he knew what the Juneteenth holiday meant to Black Americans. And he didn't need *Wiki-pedia* to know that some 300 people were killed in Tulsa—and an entire Black neighborhood, including 1,200 homes, destroyed. He urged the campaign to reconsider immediately, and Ronna, as she often did, had his back.

"Don't do this," Ronna told Brad. "The media is not going to give us the benefit of the doubt, especially now."

There was time to change the date, or reconsider plans entirely. The campaign hadn't yet signed contracts with vendors or the arena, or even publicly announced the event. But Brad dug in. What he lacked in campaign experience, he filled in with overconfidence in what he viewed as his own unlimited ability to win hearts and change minds. If Juneteenth was such an important holiday, Brad reasoned, then Trump should be at the center of the festivities.

"This is a holiday that's supposed to be about celebration and acknowledging that slavery is over," Brad said. "I'm not going to let the media frame that narrative."

Brad discussed it later with Jared. Neither one told Trump.

The next day, June 10, Trump had a single item on his public schedule: a 12:30 p.m. intelligence briefing. But, as was often the case with the Trump White House, that changed suddenly without any significant notice. At 3:30 p.m., the White House summoned whichever reporters hadn't wandered too far from their briefing room desks and quickly ushered them into the Cabinet Room, where Trump sat with Jared and, as Trump described them, Black friends of his. That included Ben Carson, Trump's housing secretary; Darrell Scott and Kareem Lanier, the founders of the Urban Revitalization Coalition; and Republican gadfly Raynard Jackson, who had sued the party over the trademark for "Black Republican Trailblazer Awards Luncheon," which he believed that he, not the GOP, owned.

"We're with friends of mine and members of the African American community," Trump said. "And we're going to be talking about law enforcement, education, business, health, and various other things."

For the next half hour, Trump didn't articulate any particular policy that would address any of those issues. He condemned the "defund the police" movement growing out of the Black Lives Matter protests but said little else that would indicate any consideration of future policymaking.

The one thing Trump did talk about most extensively that afternoon: his return to rallies. It's where he turned the conversation immediately after introducing the group as his Black friends, but before mentioning a single one of their names.

"We're going to start our rallies back up now," Trump informed the press. "The first one, we believe, will be probably—we're just starting to call up— will be in Oklahoma."

As reporters were ushered out of the room, one journalist asked Trump when he was going to Tulsa.

"It will be Friday," Trump said. "Friday night. Next week."

Juneteenth.

Trump's pronouncement put the campaign on high alert but, at least initially, not because of the date. They hadn't signed the contract for the arena yet or finalized a slew of other details. But that drama would soon be overtaken when Democrats went on the warpath. Trump, they said, couldn't be more insensitive to the world erupting all around him. If you weren't hunkered down inside your own home hiding from Covid, you were probably out on the streets protesting police brutality. Trump seemed to be thumbing his nose at both with a campaign rally on Juneteenth.

The backlash shocked Trump. He started quizzing everyone around him.

"Do you know what it is?" Trump would ask.

He didn't have a single Black senior adviser around him to ask.

"Nobody had heard of it," Trump told me in an interview just days before the rally.

During the interview, he was surprised to find out that his own administration had put out statements in each of his first three years in office commemorating Juneteenth.

"Oh really?" he said. "We put out a statement? The Trump White House put out a statement?"

Each statement, put out in his name, included a description of the holiday.

The day after announcing his Juneteenth rally, Trump escaped Washington and flew to Dallas for a fundraiser with about two-dozen attendees, collecting about $10 million for the reelection effort. He woke up in Bedminster the following morning as the cable networks continued hammering him for the Juneteenth rally. That night, Trump turned to a Secret Service agent, who was Black, and asked him about Juneteenth.

"Yes," the agent told Trump. "I know what it is. And it's very offensive to me that you're having this rally on Juneteenth."

At 11:23 p.m. that night, Trump posted on Twitter that he wanted to change the date. In the tweet, and later to me during our Oval Office interview, Trump would exaggerate the number of people who'd personally asked him to reconsider.

"Many of my African American friends and supporters have reached out to suggest that we consider changing the date out," he posted on Twitter.

Trump moved the rally back a day, to Saturday, June 20, but never considered canceling it.

The electric, capacity-crowd Trump rallies had become the signature events of his conservative movement. And the potential to bring even hundreds of thousands of people to Tulsa—at a time when there were no baseball games, no concerts, no large gatherings of any kind—would serve as a potent reminder of the fervor and passion that Trump commanded across America.

―――――

On the afternoon of June 17, the Wednesday before the Tulsa rally, my phone vibrated with a call from the White House. By the third month of work-from-home orders, I was healthy, but fully ensconced in lockdown mode. Face unshaven for two months and hair unsheared for twice as long, I wore a pair of grungy khaki shorts and a tattered orange T-shirt from a long-ago family reunion. My afternoon cup of coffee almost finished, I was hustling to file a front-page story for the *Wall Street Journal* from my bedroom. The room my wife and I had once used almost exclusively for sleep now doubled as our cramped home office during the day, as well as a sort of clandestine cafeteria where we regularly ate lunch in order to escape the grabby fingers of a toddler in our nanny share on the first floor, and to not disturb my nine-year-old on the second floor, who was spending much of her summer synchronizing iPad games and FaceTiming with her friends.* The White House call pierced the sanctuary of my bedroom-turned-workspace.

"Any chance you could get to the White House, like, now?" asked White House communications director Alyssa Farah. "The president just asked for you."

I quickly showered, slipped on a dark suit, and knotted a tie around my neck for the first time since March 10, my last day in the office. Within thirty minutes I arrived at the north gate of the White House where a staffer from the medical unit awaited visitors from inside a canvas tent. He checked my temperature, inquired about any experiences I may have had with a list of symptoms, and waved me through. Inside the West Wing, the crew of young, unmasked White House press assistants mocked my long hair and bearded face. A military paramedic asked me to sign a consent form, explained the pros and cons of the Abbott testing machine approved under the Emergency Use Authorization, and told me a positive test, God forbid, would be relayed "all the way up to POTUS."

He held up a swab. I held my breath.

As the machine that resembled a cross between a photo printer and a hand-held credit card reader analyzed my nasal secretions, I sat in the West Wing lobby frantically scribbling questions for the most powerful man in the world.

After twenty minutes, White House press secretary Kayleigh McEnany appeared and flashed me a warm, wide, and toothy smile.

"You saved the day," she told me.

At the time, I wasn't sure what she meant. I interpreted her comment simply as appreciation that I'd rushed over to the White House on a moment's notice, which was, in fact, the one thing I'd asked them not to do to me. Two months earlier, when the president and Kellyanne had called to dissect one of my articles, Trump had invited me to the White House for an interview. That sparked weeks of back and forth with McEnany and Farah over schedules, my request to bring other *Wall Street Journal* reporters with me, and whether we could have cameras in the room. But after more than a month of struggling to

---

* Complicating matters, my partner, Ashley Parker, was also a competitor on the beat, covering Trump for the *Washington Post*. In full disclosure, I'm not totally sure she considers me a competitor. She's won a Pulitzer Prize, moderated a presidential debate, and scooped me every time we chased the same tip.

get straight answers on any of those questions, I ultimately retreated to a single plea: Please just don't call me in the middle of my work-from-home nightmare and give me a five-minute notice. Yes, Farah had assured me, that's a completely reasonable request.

But I had no time to quibble. More pressing was the question of why I had been so suddenly summoned. I'd interviewed Trump as a candidate in the corner office of his eponymous New York skyscraper, as president on *Air Force One*, and in multiple rooms of the White House. He knew me at that point, and we had a perfectly fine relationship. He liked that I worked for the *Journal*, a business-centered publication that has a reputation for playing with a straight bat in its news pages. During an exchange in the Oval Office during take-your-child-to-work day in 2017, Trump told my oldest daughter that I was an accurate reporter "about 80 percent of the time." High praise from this president—though it perplexed my daughter, who later quizzed me about the other 20 percent of my work. But the key to my relationship with the president: He admired my hair.

I first realized this during a flight on *Air Force One* to Washington after a rally in Cedar Rapids, Iowa, as I and a few other reporters chatted with Trump in the press cabin of the plane. He was in a good mood, as he usually is after ninety minutes of continuous affirmation, but still feeling his way through the new job and having a hard time hiring a press secretary.

"I have ten people for every job," he said. "Who wouldn't want it?"

I merely raised my eyebrows in doubt of his claim, but Trump seemed to possess a biological sonar that senses disapproval, like a bat bouncing high-frequency sound waves off nearby objects. The president picked up my subtle signal of skepticism and pivoted his six-foot-three frame to face me.

"Would you take it?" he asked me.

It seemed like a joke, but you could never be too sure with Trump. In either case, there was only one answer.

"No," I told him.

Trump smiled.

"You have that beautiful head of hair," he said, ogling the unruly auburn mop atop my head, which I wore long enough that it confused my buttoned-up grandfather but delighted my more spirited and extroverted grandmother. My peers erupted in laughter.

"You'd take it in two seconds," the president said.

That moment would define our relationship for the next four years. Even when he wanted to be upset with me, he'd remember he liked my hair and his internal conflict over those competing emotions would save me from some of the vicious takedowns other reporters suffered at his hand. He verbalized it most clearly during an event in the Roosevelt Room of the White House in 2019. His staff was trying to escort reporters out of the room, and I kept asking questions. Sarah Sanders, then the White House press secretary, snapped at me, but Trump interrupted her.

"He's one of the tough ones," the president explained to the other administration officials in the room. "But such beautiful hair."

More than a year had passed since we last sat down. As McEnany and I walked to the Oval Office, she turned her head toward me.

"Do you know what you want to ask?" she asked. "News of the day, or something? Just some general topics I can tell him beforehand?"

What struck me was that her question answered my own: There was no particular message the president wanted to drive, or news his team wanted to break. There was no strategy for bringing the *Wall Street Journal*'s senior White House reporter into the West Wing. The output from the next hour would be completely determined by what questions I wanted to ask, and whatever was on the president's mind.

"Okay," McEnany said as we entered an otherwise empty Oval Office. "We'll be with you in sixty seconds."

I was then left alone, in the Oval Office, for the next thirty minutes.

A few pages of tan-colored paper were stacked in the middle of the Resolute Desk. Ice cubes slowly melted in a half-filled glass of Diet Coke deserted on a shelf. Farah's cell phone lay facedown, silent, on a chair near the desk.

"Hey, Michael!" Vice President Pence punctured the silence as he entered the room from behind me.

Pence earnestly asked about my family, remembering that my wife, Ashley, and I had had a baby a little over a year prior. He encouraged me to come travel with him on the campaign trail, and he ticked through his schedule for the next couple weeks.

"There's a lot of enthusiasm out there," he said. He squinted his eyes and repeated the point in a hushed, distant whisper: "A lot."

And plenty of Covid, I thought to myself.

"Anyway," Pence said. He returned to a normal indoor voice that brought us back into the moment. "I saw you in here and just wanted to say 'Hi.'"

I thanked him, briefly considering asking him to shut the door on his way out, but thought better of the joke. Pence viewed himself as a serious person, and my dry attempts at humor had fallen flat with him before.

"It was really nice to see you," I told him.

And I meant it. After a few months at home, it was nice to be out again with Pence, even if that meant enduring constant skepticism from his chief of staff, Marc Short.

I sat back down.

As soon as I opened up my notebook, Dan Scavino burst into the room. Scavino was a ubiquitous presence in Trump World. He'd known Trump since he caddied for him as a teenager in 1990, and had been continuously employed by Trump since 2004, when he took a job as assistant manager at the same course they'd first met. Scavino was now Trump's chief social media strategist, which effectively meant traveling everywhere with the president and drafting posts for Facebook, Twitter, and Instagram. Scavino was the only man Trump trusted to tweet for him.

"Bender!" he said as he glided through the room. "Enjoying the peace and quiet?"

I joked I was just trying to get a little work done. A man of few words, Scavino didn't break stride as he walked from Trump's private dining room, across the Oval, and disappeared behind the lobby door.

"One more minute," Farah promised as she reappeared in the Oval. "I just need to grab my phone."

McEnany scrambled past.

"He should be out in just a moment," she said. Finally, at 6:00 p.m. on the dot, Trump emerged.

"Hey, Michael, I'm sorry," Trump said, sitting down. "How are you?"

"I'm good," I told him. "How are you?"

"We're doing good—I just got some good poll numbers," he said.

Where Pence and I had chatted about our families just a few minutes earlier, that kind of small talk—or curiosity about another human being's personal life—rarely occurred to Trump as something to discuss. When it did,
it mostly bored him. So it was no surprise he interpreted my initial question
to him—*How are you?*—as a political one. What surprised me was that he
wanted to start the conversation with his poll numbers. Every reputable public
poll at that point showed a plurality of Americans, if not a majority, did not
like him, and hadn't for quite some time now. The four-point gap between
him and Joe Biden a month earlier had swelled to more than eight points in
national polls, and he'd fallen further behind in the biggest battlegrounds:
Florida, Michigan, Pennsylvania, and Wisconsin.

But Trump ignored all of that. He was, in his view of the world, doing well
against Biden. "I think," he added.

And really, if you thought about it, he continued, the campaign was only
just beginning. You couldn't spend too much time thinking about it, he
seemed to be telling me, but if, even for just a minute, you could open your
mind to consider unconventional possibilities and alternative facts, then you
could maybe see how very few things that had happened in the past were
relevant to the moment we're in now, and where we're about to go. Where we
end up—the future—is, in a sense, all that truly matters.

"I mean, we haven't started campaigning, you know," Trump said, inviting me into his vortex of logic, a space-time continuum where he could bend
the fabric of truth to make whatever point he liked. "I have not, essentially,
started.

"I guess," he added, "you could say it starts on Saturday."

Saturday?

Trump was three days away from bringing thousands of people together for
an indoor rally as the deadliest infectious disease in more than 100 years ripped
through a nation defending itself with only cloth face masks, improvised hand
sanitizer, and a rudimentary understanding of social distancing. But the president didn't want to talk about the potential health consequences for his superfans. He thought about it as the kickoff for his reelection campaign.

That state of mind required a certain suspension of disbelief. His campaign team had spent a half-billion dollars on the reelection effort at that point. Trump had effectively kicked off his reelection campaign in each of the first three years of his presidency. A year earlier, on June 18, 2019, I was at the rally that Trump and his campaign had billed as the official kickoff. Supporters traveled to Orlando, Florida, from all over the country for the event.

"Tonight," Trump said from his rally stage that night, "I stand before you to officially launch my campaign for a second term as president of the United States."

Two years earlier, on February 27, 2018, Trump had announced Brad would manage his reelection campaign. This was the moment Trump's lawyers considered his campaign officially launched. Much to their chagrin—and more than a year earlier than they were hoping—Trump's White House attorneys now had to be mindful of potential violations of the Hatch Act around the West Wing. The law prohibits federal workers—short of the president, vice president, and a few other technical exceptions—from engaging in most forms of political activity. If you had a campaign manager, you had a campaign, and having a campaign very clearly meant there would be political activity.

But even earlier than Brad's announcement—three years before the Tulsa pseudo-kickoff—Trump's team had filed his initial reelection paperwork with the Federal Elections Commission. That was on January 20, 2017. The same day as his inauguration.

So having a fourth annual kickoff to his presidential race made a certain sense. Even if only for the sake of symmetry, he would have to do it again.

In a few days, Trump would tell his latest audience to forget everything that had come before. "So we begin, Oklahoma," the president would tell them. "We begin. We begin our campaign."

But the truth was the campaign had begun long ago.

What was actually beginning now, for Trump, was the end.

11

The Last MAGA Rally

"The event in Oklahoma is unbelievable—the crowds are unbelievable."
—*Speaking with reporters, South Lawn, June 20, 2020*

By the time Trump announced his après-pandemic Tulsa rally—six months before the first American was vaccinated—the Front Row Joes had pinned the death of their friend Ben Hirschmann on Michigan governor Gretchen Whitmer. Their justification was that Ben had been misdiagnosed with flu symptoms via a telehealth appointment—the kind of Zoom medicine that Whitmer, a Democrat, had encouraged by trimming some regulations in response to the pandemic.

But an in-person visit also might not have caught Ben's coronavirus, and Whitmer's orders hadn't shuttered hospitals—her actions were similar to steps the Trump Administration had taken. But by June, "that woman from Michigan," as Trump referred to her, had evolved into one of the president's chief foils in his abrupt pivot from social distancing to reopening the country, and the Joes were following his cues.

By mid-June, the irreparable split between the president's base and the rest of the country—including his fellow Republicans—was increasingly apparent, a fissure riven by what was fast becoming the central issue of the election. In a *Wall Street Journal*/NBC News poll the first week of June, just 6 percent of Trump's base said he deserved at least some of the blame for the spread of coronavirus, compared to 60 percent of the country as a whole.

Masks had even started to split the Front Row Joes, just as the question of face coverings had divided Trump World. Brad had told Fox News that he would wear a mask to the Tulsa rally just hours before White House spokeswoman Kayleigh McEnany said she wouldn't. Randal Thom mocked masks as cowardly and weak even though his good friend Libby DePiero wanted to wear one to protect her husband, Brian, who was battling cancer. Ultimately, sixty-five-year-old Libby decided the risks were too significant and avoided Tulsa.

"She wasn't brave enough to come," Randal said.

For Randal, not even a deadly pandemic would stand between him and his idol. A heavy smoker who was significantly overweight, he had fallen severely ill earlier in the year with high fevers and debilitating congestion. He was convinced he had coronavirus but refused to go to the hospital; he didn't want to take a Covid test and potentially increase the caseload on Trump's watch.

"I'm not going to add to the numbers," he said by way of explanation.

Early in the pandemic, Trump had said that he wanted Covid-stricken passengers to remain on cruise ships just off the coast of California because he didn't want to increase the virus case count inside the United States. "I don't need to have the numbers double because of one ship that wasn't our fault," the president said.

And ardent supporters like Randal had internalized his concern.

Now, just as Trump's supporters trusted him as he knowingly underplayed the severity of the contagion, they also took him at his word as he overhyped predictions of the massive crowds that would greet him in Tulsa. So they adjusted their schedules to beat the traffic, and the first wave of Front Row Joes descended on Oklahoma's second most populous city a full six days before Trump's rally.

They were also motivated by the prospect of a reunion. Three months had passed since the last rally, and they missed each other. They missed Trump. Randal was astonished when he rolled into town after a ten-hour drive from Minnesota in his Toyota Sienna minivan—more than three days before the rally—to find that others had been there for three days already. Randal, who arrived in black wraparound sunglasses and a red, white, and blue cowboy hat, was a bit embarrassed.

"I guess I could have gotten here a little earlier," he said.

m Detroit a little later Wednesday. She had been

of her home but had given herself a pep talk.

she said.

1 her last will and testament and the instruc-

ayed the documents in plain sight for whoever

red herself that her affairs were in order. She

she'd left them a mess.

e told friends before leaving. "But this might be it."

ra. Antifa did.

ould be crawling with members of the shadowy,

ilitants whom Trump had obsessed about round-

"Maybe I'll get back to the hotel from the venue," she told her friends. "Or I may not."

The reality was that Saundra experienced an impressive display of hospitality from Oklahomans from the moment she arrived, a fitting welcome from the cradle of American congeniality. Locals brought coffee, donuts, and breakfast sandwiches every morning to the Front Row Joes camped out on the pavement around the arena. Pizzas arrived every night. A troop of Boy Scouts wheeled out coolers of water, ice, and a seemingly endless variety of sodas.

On Thursday evening, Saundra returned from her daily stroll around the arena—a precautionary exercise she referred to as "taking my measurements" that entailed familiarizing herself with every potential entryway into the arena—and found law enforcement trying to move the Joes from the shadow of the arena. Tulsa mayor G. T. Bynum had imposed a 10:00 p.m. curfew at the urging of the Secret Service. But the cops and Joes struck a deal that they would line up on the sidewalk by the start of curfew and not wander around the city.

On Friday, the Front Row Joes were moved farther away from the arena as security installed a "sterile zone," a phrase no Trump supporters seemed able to repeat without a thick slathering of sarcasm. The sounds of crews installing nine-foot unclimbable fencing around the perimeter roused Saundra awake from inside her sleeping bag on the sidewalk at 3:00 a.m. that night. The boundary would be patrolled by the National Guard and serve as a barrier between rallygoers and protesters.

Law enforcement slowly wheeled away a section of the security fencing at the front of the line around 11:00 a.m. Saturday. Officers barked at the Trump fans to stay in line. Rallygoers at the front shouted at the people behind them to stop pushing. Then the days-long wait was over, and the line surged forward. Inside the fence, Trump supporters zigzagged through a maze of barricades until they reached a group of nurses who greeted them from under white canopies with face masks and temperature checks. A successful health screening was rewarded with a green paper wristband that, once fastened, ensured entry to the next set of lines forming in front of a row of metal detectors. Through the security checkpoint, the first Front Row Joes immediately broke into a sprint for the final block to the area. Running was never one of Saundra's specialties. She was in pain, and the block felt more like a mile. But she reminded herself that she was almost there and tried to stay positive and keep slugging it out. It was sunny and in the mid-80s, but Saundra would swear it was 100 degrees for that final stretch between the security sensors and the campaign aides awaiting them at the arena with more masks and hand sanitizer.

"I came in second place," Saundra said.

Once inside, it was one final scurry along the arena's gray cement floor to the bike racks serving as barricades about ten feet from the stage. Saundra was once again front row and center. She hoped that maybe the buffer zone between the fence and the stage would decrease her chances of catching Covid. She wouldn't be as crowded as the people just behind her.

No one beyond the president himself needed Tulsa to be a success more than Brad. He'd been taking the heat for Trump's dismal poll numbers and had known for months that he was on borrowed time on the campaign, and the anxiety, combined with his enthusiasm, led him to make some interesting bets.

Michael Glassner, the chief operating officer of the campaign, was a slight, bald, and curmudgeonly political operative who counted among the campaign's original four hires in 2016 and who had for years been something of a Trump rally czar. Glassner had suggested returning to the 12,000-seat arena in Tulsa that the president had visited in the past. But Brad had eyed the newly renovated BOK Center, with more than 19,000 seats, as the best option. Instead of sending RSVPs to supporters living in a fifty-mile radius of the venue, as Glassner had done for previous rallies, Brad had blasted the RSVPs to the campaign's nationwide list. The sign-ups started pouring in, but from unlikely corners of the country, including countless sign-ups thanks to a chaos campaign orchestrated by mischievous TikTok users and K-pop's teenage fans who were hoping to overload the Trump system with requests so that actual supporters wouldn't get tickets.

Don Junior had noticed the prank happening in real time on social media and fired off a text to senior officials in the week before the rally.

"Sending to Glassner," one of the officials wrote back.

The Republican Party's data operation immediately started flagging the high number of fake RSVPs coming into the system. According to internal records, the campaign received 1.4 million ticket requests, but less than half were distinct sign-ups, and only one-fourth, or about 338,000, could be matched to the party's voter file, which includes information on effectively every living American who has ever been registered to vote. Only 55,500 of the RSVPs were from Oklahomans.

That data set off alarm bells in some corners of Trump World. It was already nearly impossible to travel. Campaign aides with friends and family interested in attending the rally bailed once they couldn't find flights in and out of Tulsa. Few wanted to stay in hotels overnight, concerned about the spread of the virus, which reduced the distance people were willing to travel.

But Brad hadn't wanted to hear it. A little more than a week before the rally, he referenced the top-line number of a million RSVPs and said he wanted to announce it. The campaign had never before published the number of RSVPs.

"If you say that number, then you better be able to deliver that number," Hope told Brad. "And if you can't, you don't need to say it."

But afterward, Jared told Brad to call Trump and tell him the numbers. It would make him happy, Jared told him. Everyone wanted to make Trump happy.

Brad reached Trump on his cell phone at the golf course. "Put it out," Trump told him. Brad relayed some of the reluctance he'd heard on the campaign call that morning, but the president talked over him. "Get that out, Brad," he told him. "Get it out wide."

At 9:30 a.m. on Monday, June 15, Trump tweeted that he'd received nearly 1 million requests for tickets to his Tulsa rally. Ninety minutes later, Brad followed with his own tweet that ticket requests had surpassed the 1-million mark. Expectations were growing out of control.

Trump had told everyone who would listen that 1 million people were trying to get tickets to the mega-rally, four times the magnitude of Dr. Martin Luther King Jr.'s March on Washington, in 1963, and twice the size of the women's march in the nation's capital in 2017.

"Almost One Million people request tickets for the Saturday Night Rally in Tulsa, Oklahoma!" Trump tweeted five days before the rally.

Brad had taken the extraordinary step of constructing a second stage outside the arena to accommodate the crush of expected Trump junkies. He also considered paying for a *third* stage before canceling the contract the day before the rally. A plane was chartered to fly Trump campaign surrogates into Tulsa. Brad boasted about hiring a satellite company to snap pictures of the crowd from space.

The morning before the rally, Brad went on to Fox News to continue raising expectations, pointing to "an outer perimeter fence that's going to allow a much larger amount of people to come."

"This is more of a festival," he said. "Almost like a convention." That night, he tweeted a picture of the outdoor stage being built: "If you come to the rally and don't get into the BOK Center before it's full, you can still see the President in person!"

That afternoon of the rally, the Trump campaign's worst fears came true. Instead of testing staffers off-site before arriving at the arena, the campaign administered Covid tests inside the arena. That meant that when six staffers tested positive, it didn't take long for word to spread, and then leak. NBC broke the news at 1:00 p.m., just hours before doors were set to open to the public. For Oklahomans on the fence about whether to attend the event, that was more than enough incentive to stay home and watch the speech on Fox News. If Trump couldn't keep his own staff safe, how would he protect civilians? Testing the staffers on-site also meant the virus was already inside the arena. Ronna was in Jacksonville in a meeting with fellow convention planners when she saw the news alert on her phone and knew the rally was in trouble.

But no one had yet told Trump. Back in Washington, the president stopped to speak to reporters before leaving the White House, telling them he was hearing "the crowds are unbelievable—they haven't seen anything like it."

In Oklahoma, Trump's staff already knew better. The crowds weren't anything close to expectations. They would be lucky to fill half the arena. Realizing he had no other options, Brad abandoned the second stage and canceled the entertainment he had planned for outside—and knew he'd dodged a bullet by bailing on the third stage.

"It is what it is," he told some staffers, and then headed to lunch with his wife and some friends three blocks from the arena at the Daily Grill, connected to the Hyatt Regency Hotel in downtown Tulsa, which had shut down the back of its restaurant for the group of VIPs. Brad was on his phone almost the entire time. The group finished eating a couple hours later, just as Trump emerged from the White House on his way to Tulsa. On his way out of the restaurant, Brad crossed paths with a reporter who tried to ask a question about the rally. "No, no," Brad said. "I'm too busy."

By the time *Air Force One* touched down, the second stage was being dismantled. The swarm of faithful, red-capped followers never materialized. Don Junior was right: The TikTokkers had been pranking the campaign, trying to drive up the estimated crowd size to scare off the real rallygoers. When Trump walked into the 19,000-seat arena, just 6,000 people were on hand. The most renowned audience member in the sparse crowd was arguably Herman Cain, the former CEO of Godfather's Pizza, and the 2012 fly-by presidential candidate who famously supported a "nine-nine-nine" tax policy that seemed ripped from a commercial for a used car dealership.

But still, no one had told Trump. On the flights to rallies, White House aides usually inflated crowd sizes for Trump once they were told a capacity crowd was inside—15,000-seat arenas always seemed to have at least that many fans waiting outside by the time the president landed in a rally city, or at least that's what he was told. Brad said he'd spoken to Trump after the president had boarded *Air Force One*. But inside the plane it wasn't clear that the disappointing news had registered, and aides debated how to break it to him on the way to Tulsa. It wasn't until Trump was backstage and turned on the television that he realized the arena was two-thirds empty. Trump was irate and only interested in finding one person in the building.

"*Braaaaaaaad!!!*" a campaign aide called into the headset in a shrill voice that chilled other staffers on the feed. "Can you come backstage?"

Brad had hightailed it out of the backstage area a few minutes earlier when he saw Trump and the White House entourage approach, ducking into the arena where he grabbed one of the many available seats. He stood up once he'd been called, but before he could reach the aisle, Trump had scrapped the summoning. The campaign had cleared almost everyone from backstage after the staffers had tested positive for Covid-19 that morning, and they couldn't be sure who else might have been infected. Brad sat back down.

Onstage, Trump was unhinged. He abandoned plans to use the moment to commemorate Juneteenth. He abstained from offering a gesture toward the passing of Floyd. Instead, he railed about left-wing radicals, referred to the pandemic as the Kung Flu, and said he told his team to slow down Covid-19 testing—which he called "a double-edged sword"—in order to manipulate the case count.

"Here's the bad part: When you do testing to that extent, you're going to find more people, you're going to find more cases," Trump told the rally crowd. "So I said to my people, 'Slow the testing down, please!'"

The cable networks, which broadcast the events live, hung it around his neck. Even the Drudge Report couldn't resist chiding the president, featuring pictures of the empty rows inside the arena and stripping an all-caps headline across the website: MAGA LESS MEGA. Following the rally, *Marine One* deposited Trump at the White House at 1:00 a.m. He emerged from the Nighthawk helicopter disheveled and seemingly shell-shocked. If he was confident about reversing fortunes for the country and his campaign, he hid it well. His trademark red silk tie hung unknotted from a white shirt collar stained with makeup residue. He meandered across the South Lawn, raising his right hand to gingerly wave to a few reporters while his left clutched a crumpled red MAGA hat.

Outside the Bank of Oklahoma Center, there was no Antifa waiting to harass Saundra after the rally. But there were angry neighbors back home in Sault Ste. Marie.

In the days before the rally, the front of the line was a frequent target of news reporters seeking interviews with the people willing to brave a pandemic for a political rally. By the time the gate opened, Saundra's interviews with Reuters, one of the world's largest news agencies, and the *Guardian*, a British newspaper with one of the world's most visited news websites, had hit the Internet. Saundra started receiving Facebook messages from neighbors accusing her of endangering their isolated town that, so far, had relatively few Covid cases. Emails from the local listserv—where the typical drama entailed snitching on drivers heading in the wrong direction around local roundabouts—questioned her decision to travel to Tulsa.

She was unnerved by the social media messages and emails, but she told herself that she wasn't the only person to have left Michigan since the start of the pandemic. She didn't recall seeing any of the Black Lives Matter protesters being harassed like this. She wore her mask on the airplane and inside stores. She thought it was unfair to be talked about like a one-woman superspreader on her way home to Sault Ste. Marie.

"I didn't realize how awful this town is," she said.

Saundra flew into Detroit, drove to the Upper Peninsula, and headed straight into work. But instead of punching in, she went and found her boss. She'd been rehearsing her speech the entire drive north on Interstate 75. She'd called in sick precisely one time in the past three years, but now she needed some time. She feared for her safety and didn't want to cause a scene in the lawn and garden department if her enemies tracked her into the store.

"I'm not afraid of the virus," she told her boss. "I'm afraid of the evil people on this planet."

Her boss told her not to worry, that she didn't need to come in.

She explained her theory that the hatred against her was probably coming from one nemesis in particular, whom she had blocked on Facebook months ago.

"This is a guy who hasn't accepted the results of the 2016 election," Saundra said.

"Yeah," her boss said, offering a soft laugh and smile.

⸻

After the rally, Parscale scratched himself from the *Air Force One* manifest and flew home to South Florida instead of back to Washington as he had planned. He told colleagues it was because he might have coronavirus. But he'd used that excuse to explain why he disappeared back in March, and other senior campaign staff was skeptical. Whatever the reason, it looked like Brad was trying to avoid the president and nurse his bruised ego in private. The change in travel plans fed into the growing narrative that Brad was spending too much time poolside at home, and not enough behind the desk.

When he arrived back in Florida, he called Eric Trump. Political Twitter was on fire with speculation that Brad would be sacked, and he offered a half-hearted joke about how it might happen.

"So which one of you is going to call me and fire me?" Brad asked Eric. "I'd really like to know how that's going to go down."

Eric tried to reassure Brad, as he had dozens of times before.

"No one is going to fuck you," he told him.

⸻

Back in Washington, the embarrassment arrived at a particularly difficult moment for Trump. The night after the rally, John Bolton, his former national security adviser who had stepped down the year before, pilloried the president during an ABC News prime-time special. Trump's Justice Department was in full crisis mode, too, as they tried to remove the U.S. attorney in charge of the Southern District of New York—the nation's most prominent federal prosecutor's office—who had investigated many of the president's allies. The Supreme Court had just delivered a trio of stinging defeats by blocking Trump's attempt to reverse workplace protections for LGBTQ employees; rejecting the challenge to sanctuary-city laws in California; and halting a push to cancel legal protections for undocumented immigrants brought to the United States as children. Civil rights protests rippled across the country.

Underscoring all of that drama: Joe Biden's lead over Trump in the national polls—which averaged around five points for most of the first six months of 2020—broke double digits for the first time that weekend.

By Monday morning, two days after the Tulsa debacle, Trump sat alone in the White House with a toxic mix of frustration, anger, and anxiety brewing inside him. He was inconsolable. Father's Day didn't cheer him up. Nor did a round of golf. He couldn't escape the headlines and wouldn't turn off the television, so he dialed through a list of friends and advisers into the night and again the next morning. One topic consistently dominated the conversations: Who should take over his campaign?

Trump dialed one adviser after the next. Ike Perlmutter, the former chairman of Marvel Entertainment. Home Depot cofounder Bernie Marcus. Blackstone Group CEO Steve Schwarzman. Casino magnate and longtime Republican backer Sheldon Adelson. Andrew Stein, the New York business consultant.

The feedback fell mostly into two categories: The most obvious change was that Trump needed to show more discipline. These advisers urged him to forget about the campaign, because the voters he needed to convince didn't care about another rally—they wanted him focused on the job in front of him. Others had simpler advice: Fire Brad.

Never one to be too hard on himself, Trump started workshopping possible changes.

He solicited opinions on Karl Rove, the strategist for former President George W. Bush whom Brad had been bringing around the White House. Trump was also trying to reel in Nick Ayers, the Georgia-based operative who had been Pence's chief of staff and had refused Trump's repeated offers at the end of 2018 to be his White House chief of staff.

On the Monday after the Tulsa rally, Trump offered the job to Ronna.

"You just run it all," an exasperated Trump told her.

It wasn't clear how the party chairwoman would also serve as campaign manager. She'd almost certainly have to step down from the RNC. But the details were never discussed—she quickly rejected the offer out of hand.

"Absolutely not," Ronna told him.

Trump got word to Steve Bannon, whom he had banished to the wilderness after a multitude of sins back in 2017, including stealing the boss's spotlight and speaking ill of his family. Even Trump's myriad triggers would never eclipse his desperate desire to win.

But not even Bannon wanted the job.

By the summer of 2020, Bannon had reestablished himself in the right-wing media landscape. When Trump exiled him, Bannon also lost his perch at Breitbart News, an aggressively right-wing news site he'd helped build and turn into one of the top conservative click-bait sites on the Internet. But now he was back with an equally popular podcast from which he'd been warning all year about the threat of coronavirus. The president's fury with Bannon had faded with each TV hit where he defended Trump. Yes, the Goldman banker turned Hollywood filmmaker had publicly compared Ivanka's brainpower to that of a brick and predicted Don Junior would be broken like an egg by federal prosecutors, but Trump liked how Bannon defended him on the shows. Evocative and energetic, Bannon articulated Trumpism in a way few others could—or would. He amplified the populism, nodded to its nationalism, and framed the movement in a global context with an existential importance. Trump had started trying to bring Bannon back into the fold after watching him rhapsodize about the president's push to contain China during a Sunday morning on Maria Bartiromo's show on Fox Business.

"Donald Trump is the hammer," Bannon said on the program. "And American capital and American technology is the anvil."

Trump had Jason Miller reach out to Bannon to gauge his interest in coming back inside the tent. Miller found Bannon on board the *Lady May*—a 151-foot, $28 million superyacht owned by Chinese billionaire Guo Wengui, a high-profile Communist Party dissenter and dues-paying member of Mar-a-Lago. The only thing Bannon had to do, Miller told him, was go on TV and publicly profess his desire to return to the campaign.

"No fucking way," Bannon said. "I'm not coming in and bailing out Jared Kushner at the last second again."

Bannon, who had spent seven months as Trump's White House strategist, viewed the campaign as a sideshow. For him, reelection was always going to be won or lost from the West Wing, not whatever was being plotted from inside campaign headquarters. Bannon had been telling everyone from the very start that the path to victory was a laser-like focus on policy—plugging away, one at a time, week after week, month after month, at each and every campaign promise Trump had made in 2016. But no one listened. Jared buried him instead. The whiteboard in Bannon's West Wing office where he had sketched out that battle plan had been wiped clean three years earlier. And now, with a little more than three months left in the race, Bannon saw no way to win.

Based on how Trump and the West Wing were responding to Covid, Bannon was convinced the race was already over. Peter Navarro, one of Trump's top advisers in the White House, had told Bannon that hardly anyone from the West Wing had worked a weekend since Memorial Day.* Trump's refusal to wear a mask showed he wasn't taking the pandemic seriously, and the public's exasperation would only get worse when parents realized there was no plan for their kids to return to school in the fall, Bannon said. In Bannon's estimation, Trump was surrounded by the worst staff in the history of the White House.

He saw no sense of urgency from Trump—or his team—to respond to what was a full-blown national crisis. And Bannon himself—as he sipped coffee amid the white marble and bleached oak interior of the *Lady May* and read his books out on the boat's teak deck—certainly felt no call to help.

"I'd rather fight Biden for the next four years," Bannon said. "I can do that. But I'm not going to do this."

Trump also floated the idea of moving Kellyanne from the West Wing to campaign headquarters, offering her the same kind of chairman role he was considering for Bannon or Ayers to oversee strategy. The president had asked both Stepien, then the deputy campaign manager, and Jason Miller, his communications strategist, about the idea.

"Stepien loves you," Trump told the fifty-three-year-old Kellyanne. "They both want you over there, honey. But I don't know. What do you think?"

Kellyanne was noncommittal. Like Bannon, she viewed the White House as the center of power in a reelection campaign. And she wasn't about to leave the president alone with Meadows, McEntee, and the other senior staffers she considered to be the West Wing's "Covid deniers."

---

* That fact both alarmed and delighted Navarro. With no one in the White House on the weekends, he was free to walk around shoeless in his running shorts and a T-shirt.

Jared had soured on Kellyanne during the 2016 campaign. He tried to limit her exposure to Trump and had the campaign lasted two more weeks, he told colleagues, he would have fired his fellow New Jersey native. But that was probably easier said than done. Kellyanne had established her own following among conservatives, and her own relationship with Trump. She had known Trump since 2001, when she and her husband, George Conway, were newlyweds and moved into a condo at Trump World Tower in Manhattan. Her knack for snappy quotes as she leaned into her role as most prominent female defender of Trump in 2016 only expanded her following.

Trump's victory made Kellyanne the first woman ever to manage a winning presidential campaign. She was stung that Jared had downplayed her role, and was furious when Brad launched a media tour in 2017 to promote the role he played as digital director, boasting that he had harnessed the power of Facebook and activated Trump voters in places like Michigan, Wisconsin, and Pennsylvania. When Jared installed Brad as campaign manager so early without consulting her, let alone giving her first right of refusal, it ensured that their relationship would remain volatile for the entirety of Trump's term.

But after his father-in-law started thinking about putting Kellyanne back at the campaign, Jared was suddenly over-the-top nice to her. It was a disorienting turn of events for staff who witnessed the exchanges during White House meetings. Others described it as nauseating.

"Oh, that's brilliant," Jared told her in one meeting.

By their fourth year in the White House, Kellyanne was mostly fascinated by Jared's about-face. But the steely-eyed brawler from New Jersey wasn't going to miss an opportunity to turn the screws.

"What I said was pretty basic and obvious," Kellyanne deadpanned. "But I'll give you a nudge when I say something brilliant."

Trump hadn't directly consulted with Jared about bringing back Bannon or moving Kellyanne. He was doing everything he could to avoid his son-in-law at that point. He was furious with him. He knew it was Jared who had talked him into hiring Brad. And he still blamed Jared for the dismal public approval of his response to the civil unrest. Trump had privately told advisers in June that he wished his response to the protests had been stronger from the start.

"I've done all this stuff for the Blacks—it's always Jared telling me to do this," Trump said to one confidante that weekend. "And they all fucking hate me and none of them are going to vote for me."

At the end of June, Trump canceled a trip to Bedminster at the last minute. Jared was already at the New Jersey golf course for the weekend, and Trump wanted to avoid him. The president also wanted to better understand what was going wrong with his campaign, and decided to hear what was going on without Jared's filter. Trump would never push Jared out of the fold, but he didn't need to consult with him on every move, either.

Jared understood what was happening and gave his father-in-law space to get to the only choice he was ever going to make. It was clear to Jared now that he could no longer protect Brad.

In campaign meetings, Jared was increasingly short with Brad and constantly snapped at him. He mocked his ideas, and even shushed him. It was another shocking twist. Aides who had been bewildered by the string of saccharine accolades Jared had suddenly showered on Kellyanne were now embarrassed by his shortness with Brad. Brad was well liked across Trump World, aside from Kellyanne and a few other exceptions, and to see him humiliated made everyone uncomfortable. It also sent a clear message about where things were headed.

Trump's constant questions about replacing a staffer or how his White House or campaign was being run sometimes signaled a change was coming, and sometimes it didn't. While Trump's reluctance to fire someone himself was well known, there was less appreciation for how long it took for him to make the decision—even if it was always going to be someone else who had to deliver the news. Sensing this, Jared proactively urged Brad to step down from the job in early July.

Sitting in his West Wing office—a cramped space just on the other side of the president's private dining room, where he kept a picture of Ivanka, another of his grandparents who had survived the Holocaust, and framed *New York Times* articles signed by his father-in-law in thick black Sharpie*—Jared told Brad that he probably had only three options.

One, he said, was that Brad could try to keep the campaign manager's job

---

* "JARED GREAT JOB- THANKS- DONALD J. TRUMP."

he'd already held down for the past twenty-eight months and stick out the last sixteen weeks. But that was a risky bet, Jared told him, and would almost certainly result in the second option, which was getting fired. But there was a third way, Jared explained. Brad could willingly take another job in the campaign. Jared's suggestion was to return to his roots, which was digital marketing and advertising.

"That's the best option for you," Jared said. "There are a lot of people trying to kill you right now for all kinds of reasons, and this gives you the opportunity to focus on what you're best at."

Brad immediately objected. He didn't want to lose his job, and he viewed a demotion to be on par with being fired. He also knew that he couldn't be fired. The websites, the email system, the campaign app—it all ran on a system that he had designed. If they got rid of him, it would all disappear.

"Layer me, just layer me," Brad pleaded. "Put somebody over me that takes over the political role, and let me run the day-to-day operations."

Jared was noncommittal, but Brad had survived another day.

=====

As Jared tried to get Brad to fall on his sword, the campaign's pollsters were just coming out of the field with a fresh round of polling. The new survey showed Trump trailed Biden by one percentage point in a survey of seventeen battleground states, down from a five-point advantage for Trump in those same key states in February. But that gap would have been wider had it not been for lingering optimism over Trump's handling of the economy. Even though a plurality of voters in battleground states said the economy was headed in the wrong direction, a majority of voters, 54 percent, still trusted Trump over Biden with the task of rebuilding.

Trump had bet his political life on the economy, and it was the only issue keeping him in the race. But for how long? Brad and Jared believed the pandemic would peter out by the end of the year, at which point the economy would surge back and become the top priority for voters. But the race wasn't playing out that way. Their new polling showed that coronavirus remained the issue that was confronting Americans most directly: By the summer of 2020, 60 percent of voters in battleground states told Trump's pollsters in July that they knew someone who had tested positive, compared to just 38 percent in May.

And Trump continued to test poorly when it came to the pandemic. The percentage of persuadable voters in battleground states who disapproved of Trump's handling of coronavirus was seven percentage points higher than those who approved.

But the most troubling number for the campaign in that summer poll: 65 percent of voters in Trump's target states said the country was on the wrong track, more than double the 27 percent of voters who said the nation was headed in the right direction. In the campaign's February poll, the question split voters almost directly down the middle.

But by July, after the pandemic had killed 150,000 people, the poll showed that voter sentiment, when it came to Trump's reelection bid, increasingly ranged somewhere between foul and hostile.

Trump's own mood fell somewhere on that spectrum, too.

═══

The tipping point for Brad came on Sunday, July 12, in a front-page story from the *Washington Post*. The article weaved together all of Brad's troubles and succinctly articulated—in a way Trump never could—exactly what had the president tied in knots over his campaign manager. The story pointed out that Brad had been featured in a TV ad for the campaign and had paid for Facebook to promote digital ads on his Facebook page instead of Trump's, which raised questions about whether he was purposefully raising his own public profile. There were embarrassing leaks from a private political meeting where Brad had struggled to answer questions about the campaign's budget, which suggested he either didn't know what was going on or perhaps was trying to hide something. Maybe the most devastating detail of all: Brad had flown home to Florida—again!—the week before while other senior aides, including, interestingly, a prominent mention of Stepien, had remained in Washington working on the campaign.

Each paragraph was like a sledgehammer to every trigger point for Trumpian tantrums.

TRUMP FRUSTRATED WITH CAMPAIGN MANAGER PARSCALE AMID FALLING
POLLS, read the headline of the article.

If it wasn't true prepublication, it certainly was now.

———

At a political meeting in the White House on Monday, July 13, Trump could
barely bring himself to look at Brad. The president seemed willing to acknowledge his campaign manager only to belittle and embarrass him in front of colleagues. When Brad presented a digital rendering of the stage design for the
Republican National Convention—usually one of Trump's favorite things to
discuss—the president shot him down.

"Okay, sure, Brad—show me your picture," Trump sneered. "And why don't
you explain to me how you're going to make sure it's not another Tulsa!"

Tensions in the room were already high after Ronna had floated downsizing the convention. When Trump had moved the convention a month ago,
Florida was averaging about 1,300 new Covid cases per day. Two weeks later,
the seven-day rolling average had spiked to 6,300 new cases per day and Jacksonville officials had, just that morning, implemented a mask mandate. The
spread in Florida was now worse than in North Carolina.

Ronna pitched a plan that would move most of the convention outdoors
and made Covid testing available. The biggest crowd would be 5,000 people at
an outdoor venue for Trump—a huge reduction from the 20,000 Trump had
expected—but Ronna pointed out that the plan had flexibility to allow for
more people if caseloads started to fall.

Trump seemed agreeable, and Brad quickly signed off. Pence raised no
objections either, and Stepien, as usual, said nothing. But there was pushback
again from Hope, Meadows, and Johnny McEntee.

"I've just got to chime in here," Hope said. "I don't know why we're even
doing this if we can't have 12,000 people in the room every day."

Hope equated downsizing the convention to caving to media pressure.
Trump had been loudly calling for schools to reopen in the fall. The media
would torch him for hypocrisy if he then went and limited participation at his
own convention.

"If you do this, you're saying you can't have rallies and you can't do anything outdoors," she said. "You can't do any campaigning. You're just conceding and giving in."

Ronna took the criticism, and worried that her plan was about to be derailed. She fought back, arguing that she'd rather endure a one-day story for doing the responsible thing than withstand months of coverage as delegates suffered the effects of Covid.

That sounded like an argument to get rid of any testing, Hope shot back. "People should know what's good for them," she said. "If they're that old and sick, then they shouldn't be traveling."

Walters warned that daily coverage of Covid issues at a full convention could overshadow even the president's speech—a similar dynamic to what had played out in Tulsa after campaign staffers who tested positive.

"If we have 10 percent of people test positive every day, that's a massive media story," Walters said. "That will end up scaring people out of coming to the president's speech on Thursday."

Meadows was skeptical of Walters's numbers, and demanded to know his source. Walters and Ronna had been consulting regularly with both Deborah Birx and Anthony Fauci, the two top doctors on the White House's coronavirus task force.

"Oh," Meadows said as sarcasm dripped from each syllable. "If it's coming from Dr. Birx, it must be true."

"If it's coming from an infectious disease expert, then I'm going to believe that individual over you," Walters shot back.

Unfortunately for Brad, the meeting turned back to convention programming. The programming had always been the campaign's responsibility, but he was in full defense mode now and turned on one of his closest allies in Washington.

"I thought Ronna was going to do that," he said. "The RNC dropped the ball."

"If I would have picked the speakers and crafted their speeches, you would have been horrified," Ronna said. "You have the polling. You're the one who should know the message for your candidate. That is not what the RNC does."

Ronna was right. But Hope did a double take. The convention was six weeks away.

"Nothing's been done?" she asked.

"We were always going to wait until we got a little closer," Brad said.

Trump had heard enough.

"You don't even know what you're talking about," he barked at Brad. "Just stop!"

━━━━

The following night, July 14, Stepien was summoned to the White House for a private meeting with Trump. The invitation made clear that Stepien needed to arrive as quickly as possible. The meeting, he was told, was to be off the books.

When Stepien was offered Brad's job, he immediately volunteered to cut his own salary to show the job was more important to him than the money. Trump asked about the other Republicans for whom he was working.

"You've got a lot of clients," Trump said.

"The clients I have have been helpful to you," Stepien replied.

"I need your focus," Trump said.

"You have it," Stepien assured him.

━━━━

The next morning, Wednesday, July 15, Brad was demoted.

Jared arrived at campaign headquarters in the morning and asked Brad to come into his office.

At 1:00 p.m. that day, Jared and Brad sat alone in his campaign office, the White House tranquil in plain view through the office window behind them.

"Brad, you're demoted," Jared told him. "Bill is now the campaign manager, and you're digital director."

Jared's ice-cold approach crushed Brad. No one told him why he'd been replaced, and he took it personally. He blamed Trump, and he told friends that he'd been punished for following orders. He had wanted to have an outdoor rally in a swing state. Summoning his inner Trump, he insisted that he'd had no missteps. There was the tweet that wildly overestimated the crowd size of the Oklahoma rally, but like a true Trumpian, he blamed the media for amplifying his post.

"Other than that, I have no other mistakes," Brad told friends.

Regardless, his fate was sealed. At least for the moment. A rapid rise in Covid cases put Oklahoma into the pandemic's "red zone," which forced reopening measures there to be reversed. Herman Cain was hospitalized with a Covid infection eleven days after the rally—an infection that even some campaign officials privately believed he'd contracted during the event—and died from the disease before the end of July.

Brad decided to head home to Florida. He'd get some rest, punch the clock for a while at the campaign, and plot his way back to the top.

12

Stepien's Shot

"I'm not losing."

—Fox News Sunday, *Oval Office patio, July 19, 2020*

On the morning of July 16, Stepien and Brad—the new campaign manager and the newly demoted one—assembled the staff outside the manager's office for a symbolic passing of the torch. Brad had been crushed by the demotion—so badly that Lara, Ronna, and other friends exchanged nervous texts to make sure someone was checking in on him. He'd had a few drinks that night and emotions were still raw the next morning when he woke up on the office couch. The staff, nearly all of whom Brad had hired, was divided over whether he should have been put in charge from the start. But there was wide agreement that he'd been scapegoated by Trump and Jared—and plenty of suspicion that Stepien had helped.

"I just want this man to win," Brad said of Trump as he choked back tears.

The staff erupted in applause for their former manager. But then Brad turned and left. The plan had been for him and Stepien to stand in front of the team—the first all-staff meeting of the campaign—in a show of unity. Stepien was furious that Brad had undermined that message by making for the exit.

Still, Stepien tried to rally the troops. Trump had trailed Clinton at the exact same point in the summer of 2016, he said, and remained behind her in 213 of the next 226 public polls—until the day he won.

Stepien promised 2020 would be no different. The upside, he said, was that internal campaign numbers also showed the race within the margin of error.

"We're just going to keep doing our jobs," he continued.

But that wasn't exactly true. They couldn't just keep doing their jobs. The internal polls showed a toss-up when all seventeen battleground states were averaged, but the state-by-state numbers showed Trump trailing in the electoral vote count and trending downward. Something drastic needed to change quickly.

Stepien just didn't know what.

Hundreds of millions of dollars had already been spent building a campaign he believed was fundamentally flawed. He thought Brad ceded too much power to the Republican National Committee. That joint operation was underpinned by a digital program that Stepien didn't fully understand and relied on voter data he didn't fully trust. He was surrounded by Trump family members and White House senior staff who had little political experience, but he was rarely willing to confront them.

At the age of forty-three, Stepien was in command of just the seventh presidential reelection bid to occur in his lifetime, with a swanky new title that would be affixed forevermore to his every public mention. But as he stood on that mountaintop and peered out at the final 109 days of the campaign, he saw nothing but black, swirling rain clouds closing in from every direction.

"I need to land a plane that doesn't have any wings left," Stepien would tell confidants in the weeks to come.

———

Intensely private and naturally suspicious, Stepien knew he wasn't as likable as his chatty and outgoing predecessor. He had always been edgier and more reserved than most. Still, he could be coaxed out of his shell with talk about hat tricks, one-timers, and slap shots. Stepien loved hockey and one of his first high school jobs during the early 1990s in northwestern New Jersey was at Chimney Rock Ice Rink as a skate guard—effectively a hallway monitor on ice. The Zamboni driver was a college kid named Mike DuHaime, whose father was a Passaic County freeholder and his mother a small town mayor. Stepien wasn't old enough to drive and didn't much care about politics.* But DuHaime would soon bring him into the family business.

Stepien was enrolled at Rutgers playing club hockey and struggling with math classes for his accounting degree when DuHaime, then twenty-three, convinced him to volunteer for the state Senate campaign he was managing.† Stepien agreed, their candidate won, and plans for an accounting career were quickly abandoned.

Stepien graduated from Rutgers in the spring of 2000, but his more meaningful education came that fall when DuHaime hired him as the wheelman for U.S. Senate candidate Bob Franks.‡ Franks was a legendary figure in New Jersey Republican circles who mentored countless young operatives during his two-dozen years in politics as a state lawmaker, state party chairman, and congressman. Stepien drove Franks around in a beat-up car with hockey gear stuffed into the trunk and strewn across the backseat.

Franks ultimately lost to Democrat Jon Corzine, but came within three points—far closer than anyone expected—and nearly overcame a massive ten-to-one fundraising gap.§ The Franks campaign also launched the careers for a quartet of New Jersey Republicans: Stepien, DuHaime, a campaign lawyer named Bill Baroni, and David Wildstein, who had launched an anonymous blog, *PoliticsNJ*, to generate positive news clips for Franks—but quickly became a must-read for New Jersey political junkies. For those four, the Franks campaign was like the dead body that Gordie, Vern, Chris, and Teddy in *Stand by Me* went to see on a lark—and then turned into one of the defining events of their lives.

In 2003, Baroni brought the band back together for his own campaign for New Jersey Assembly. Stepien was campaign manager, DuHaime the chief strategist, and Wildstein the unnamed house organ pumping out praise for their brilliance under the pseudonym, "Wally Edge." And it looked like he

---

* If Stepien had been paying attention to politics in high school, he no doubt would have noticed a wild local race for Morris County freeholder his junior year that ended with the election of a brash young Republican named Chris Christie.

† Stepien earned all-American honors from the club league in both his junior and his senior years.

‡ Mobbed-up Jersey vernacular for what most other Americans would simply call a driver.

§ The losing streak for New Jersey Republican Senate candidates now stands at sixteen consecutive races over forty-two years after Cory Booker was comfortably reelected in 2020.

might be right. Baroni was the only New Jersey Republican that year to defeat a Democratic incumbent.* But the other big story was Stepien, who had found his footing as a political number cruncher. He manically combed through data in the district trying to find the Democrats who were open to voting for Republicans, armed Baroni with addresses for doors on which he needed to knock, and then walked with him marking down who was and wasn't home. The young campaign manager then returned to the office, adjusted his numbers, and, more often than not, ended the evening in a shouting match with the campaign's grassroots coordinator, an equally ambitious operative named Stacy Schuster.

DuHaime and Stepien became a package deal in Republican politics. In 2004, President George W. Bush hired DuHaime to run the northeast region of his reelection bid, and DuHaime installed Stepien as his man in New Hampshire. During Bush's second term, DuHaime was named political director at the Republican National Committee. He hired Stepien to oversee the party's get-out-the-vote efforts.

Meanwhile, Wildstein was breaking a ton of political news on his website.† It had become an undeniable political force in New Jersey by 2007, when it was acquired by a would-be media mogul named Jared Kushner. Jared had branched out from the family real estate empire, bought the *New York Observer*, and added Wildstein's blog to the publishing empire he envisioned. After the sale, Wildstein sent a few thousand bucks to Stepien, DuHaime, and Baroni as a thank-you for the help they'd given him at the start.‡

Even as a Jared property, Wildstein continued promoting Stepien and DuHaime, who teamed up again on the 2008 presidential campaign for Rudy

---

* Baroni caught some breaks that year, too. When his opponent attacked him over a false claim that he was a Hamilton native, Baroni admitted he'd been born in another state—but adopted by Hamilton residents. The silver-tongued Republican lobbyist was suddenly transformed into a sympathetic orphan.

† "Wally Edge" helped launch the careers of some widely respected political journalists, including MSNBC's Steve Kornacki, *Politico's* Alex Isenstadt, and the *Boston Globe's* James Pindell.

‡ The three Republicans helped "Wally Edge" rank the state's top operatives, which also just happened to always include their names. A decade later, DuHaime's bio page at Mercury Public Affairs—the global consulting firm where he's a partner—still notes that he's been named to every annual power list put out by *PoliticsNJ*.

Giuliani, the early Republican front-runner who ultimately ended his bid without winning a single delegate.

In 2009, Stepien took on the most important job of his fledgling career: managing Chris Christie's campaign for governor. Christie's Democratic opponent: Jon Corzine. Nine years later, the Franks friends had their chance for revenge.

Stepien ran the day-to-day of the campaign with maximum intensity, sending emails at all hours and locking staffers out of early morning meetings if they arrived late. DuHaime was Christie's lead strategist. Baroni, now a state senator, endorsed Christie early. But Wildstein was rowing in the wrong direction. With *PoliticsNJ* now wholly owned by Jared, the website turned into an attack machine aimed directly at the Republican who had put Jared's father behind bars. Still, Christie defeated Corzine by 3.6 percentage points—the first New Jersey Republican in a decade to win a statewide seat.

Stepien was soaring. The weekend after the campaign, he was married.* Then Christie named him deputy chief of staff in the governor's office. His friends joined the administration, too. Baroni took a job as deputy executive director of the Port Authority of New York and New Jersey, a powerful post that oversaw hundreds of millions of dollars in contracts. Wildstein left the website and joined Baroni at the port.

Stepien's professional hot streak continued through Christie's first term. He lived and breathed the job. Stepien showed up before 7:00 a.m., and he made clear that he expected that kind of dedication from his team, too. Aides late to staff meetings were paraded in front of the group or sometimes sent home for the day.

His mission was to deliver a landslide reelection victory in 2013—an overwhelming win for a Republican governor in the increasingly Democratic state to convince presidential primary voters and conservative donors that Christie was a top contender for the White House in 2016.

---

* Stepien surprised some friends that year when they found out that not only was he engaged, but that his fiancée was Stacy Schuster, with whom he'd sparred during Baroni's 2003 campaign.

Stepien covered his office walls with state maps dotted with push pins to identify towns where voters were most likely to split their ballots between the two parties. He set to work collecting endorsements for Christie and was furious when Democratic mayors like Jersey City's Steve Fulop wouldn't play ball. He instructed Wildstein to not even return Fulop's calls to the Port Authority.

"Ice him," Stepien ordered.

The silence irritated Fulop, which, in return, pleased Stepien.

"He's getting a little snippy," Stepien told Wildstein. "Good."

Stepien had built a reputation as a political data whiz, but after a few years in Trenton, that proved to be only part of the story. From his perch in the governor's office, he'd also proven himself to be a skilled practitioner of old-fashioned, meat-and-potatoes patronage politics. When it came to political stylings, Stepien had developed a persona that was part accountant and part hockey goon. He could read the numbers as well as anyone but was also willing to twist an arm to help his team.

But the silent treatment for the big-city mayor hardly compared to the fate awaiting the little town of Fort Lee, whose mayor, Mark Sokolich, had also refused to endorse Christie.

In many ways, Donald Trump's path to the White House was cleared at 7:34 a.m. on Tuesday, August 13, 2013. By then, Stepien had taken over the reelection campaign and the person he'd hand-picked as his replacement in the governor's office—Bridget Kelly, whom he had also been dating—sent Wildstein an eight-word email.

"Time for some traffic problems in Fort Lee," she wrote.

"Got it," Wildstein replied a minute later.

The emails ignited one of the state's most memorable political scandals: Bridgegate. To many, Bridgegate was a brash plan of political vengeance designed to inflict pain on a small town mayor who refused to endorse Christie. For others, it was a big misunderstanding. But in the end, the result was a devastating blow to Christie's political future—and one that destroyed the team around him.

On Monday, September 9, just before rush hour on the first day of the school year, the Port Authority shut down two of the three lanes dedicated to Fort Lee motorists on the insanely busy, twenty-nine-lane George Washington Bridge. The lanes were shut down for five days and the bottlenecks caused huge delays for commuters, school buses, and emergency responders. New York's appointee to the Port Authority, Patrick Foye, emailed Baroni that the closures violated both federal and state law. Baroni had publicly claimed that the lane closures were part of a traffic study, and he scrambled to keep a lid on the tension. When *Wall Street Journal* reporter Ted Mann called Baroni questioning the cause of the traffic, Stepien blew it off. When Mann published Foye's email to Baroni, Stepien wasn't so calm.

"Holy shit," Stepien texted Wildstein about Foye. "Who does he think he is, Capt. America?"

Pressure was mounting from New Jersey Democrats, who had opened an investigation in Trenton into the lane closures based on Mann's reporting in the *Journal*. The investigation quickly cost Wildstein and Baroni their jobs. When Wildstein resigned, Jared offered a word of encouragement to his former blogger.

"I thought the move you pulled was kind of badass," Jared wrote.

But the full picture of the scandal was still coming into view as Christie cruised to a twenty-two-point victory, the widest margin in twenty years in the state and the best showing for any New Jersey Republican in twenty-four years. The successful reelection bid was also the biggest career achievement for Stepien and Christie. Stepien opened his own consulting firm, Nassau Strategies, naming it after the street he lived on in Princeton. Christie installed him as his top political adviser at the Republican Governors Association and endorsed him as the next chairman of the New Jersey Republican Party, a powerful position that would give Stepien access to the party's most important donors and allow him to influence candidate selections and the direction of the party.

"Bill Stepien is the best Republican operative in the country," Christie crowed.

But the very next day, it was Stepien who would be iced.

On January 8, a batch of Bridgegate texts and emails that had been subpoenaed by the State Assembly were published in the media. The messages included Kelly's famous "Time for some traffic problems" note. Baroni's story about a traffic study seemed less credible. Stepien was intimately involved in the coordination between the players.

Stepien repeatedly phoned Christie, but the governor refused to answer. Instead, it was DuHaime who eventually returned his messages, and asked to meet at the Panera Bread in Princeton. Surrounded by the aroma of Asiago cheese bagels and the dulcet tones of classical music playing from overhead speakers, DuHaime told Stepien what Christie could not bring himself to say: He was out.

The two would barely speak again for years.

"I was disturbed by the tone and behavior and attitude of callous indifference that was displayed in the emails by my former campaign manager, Bill Stepien," Christie said at a news conference. "It made me lose my confidence in Bill's judgment. And you cannot have someone at the top of your political operation who you do not have confidence in."

Stepien wasn't just fired. He was banished. He couldn't find work anywhere. From Lake Hopatcong to the Jersey Shore and back to the Delaware River, Christie had salted the state of New Jersey with warnings not to hire Stepien. He insisted that Stepien had lied to him.

One of the few New Jersey Republicans willing to stick out his neck for Stepien was Ocean County GOP chairman George Gilmore, who helped find Stepien work with GOPAC, a 527 group where Gilmore was on the board of directors.* Still, Stepien struggled to make money and moved back home. In a handwritten note to the state Division of Revenue and Enterprise Services, he changed the address of his Nassau Strategies firm to his family's house in Washington Township.

Stepien had hit rock bottom. By 2015 he was divorced, politically excommunicated, and a constant topic in pretrial motions. That fall, his twenty-six-year-old brother, Shane, an Iraq War veteran, died in an early morning car accident.

His friends Baroni and Kelly were eventually convicted, and ultimately

---

* The goodwill would be returned when Stepien successfully lobbied Trump to pardon Gilmore for felony convictions over falsifying a loan application and failure to pay taxes. Trump issued the pardon on his last day in office.

received prison sentences of more than a year, while Wildstein struck a plea deal and avoided jail.

Stepien's name was invoked more than 700 times during the trial—Wildstein testified in court that Stepien had been aware of the plot, its retaliatory nature, and the cover story—but he was never charged and was never called as a witness.

Christie, meanwhile, pressed forward with his presidential aspirations, but Bridgegate clipped him badly. As a first-term governor, Christie had brilliantly deployed town halls and social media to project his forceful personality. He was Donald Trump before Donald Trump, only with a command of the issues and an approval rating in the seventies. It's impossible to know for sure, but multiple Trump World operatives and others close to Christie remain convinced that Trump would never have run for president had Christie maintained those kinds of numbers heading into 2016. But Bridgegate changed everything. And while it was impossible to see at the moment, it was Stepien—and not Christie—who would be preparing for life in the White House by the end of 2016.

Standing inside a hotel ballroom in eastern Iowa in 2016, Jared was convinced that blame for Trump's caucus defeat to Ted Cruz should be pinned squarely on Corey. The day after the caucuses, Jared called Ken Kurson for ideas on whom he could find to replace Corey.

Kurson was a longtime friend of the Kushners whom Jared had installed as editor of the *Observer* in 2013. But before that, Kurson had worked for Rudy Giuliani's 2008 presidential campaign, and later, Jamestown Associates. When Jared called that night in February, Kurson pointed him to Stepien, even though the Bridgegate trial was still ongoing.

"Look," Kurson told Jared. "He's a little radioactive right now. But if you want somebody who's still available with so many candidates in the race, it's going to be somebody who's got a little bit of hair on them. Otherwise, they would have already been hired."

The silver lining was that Stepien had been double-crossed by Christie. He and Jared would at least have a political enemy in common.

Jared immediately called Stepien.

Stepien viewed Trump as a paycheck, but also as payback. Christie finished Iowa with less than 2 percent and hadn't hit 5 percent in the national polls. Without a strong showing in New Hampshire, he was finished. And Stepien was eager for the opportunity to trounce him.

On his call with Jared, Stepien walked through his approach of estimating the total turnout of an election, and then reverse-engineering a strategy. It was a model he'd learned at the foot of Bob Franks: figure out which message appeals to which voters in order to end up with at least one more vote than 50 percent.

"That's what running an election is all about: a ground game," Stepien told Jared. "You can't do that if you have a bad candidate. But if you run a great ground game, that can help you with two or three points."

Jared was impressed. Stepien's approach seemed to take the emotion out of the equation, or at least minimize it in a way that felt right to Jared and contrasted with Corey's fondness for backroom brawling. But Jared underestimated Corey's skill set. Corey caught wind of Jared's meddling and got Christie on the phone himself. Even though the New Jersey governor was a competitor in the Republican primary, Corey told Christie that he—not Jared—was considering bringing Stepien into the fold. Christie said that Stepien was a skilled campaign technician but added that the Bridgegate trial was still unfolding.

"I can't tell you what his involvement was with Bridgegate—I can't vouch for him," Christie said.

Corey relayed Christie's warning and, two days after the Iowa caucuses, Trump shelved Jared's plan.

"Let's not take the risk," Trump told Jared during a campaign stop in Arkansas.

Trump demolished all his competitors in New Hampshire, including Christie, who finished a distant seventh place, dropped out of the race, and, two weeks later, endorsed Trump.

It wasn't for six more months—after Corey was fired in June—that Jared found the space to bring Stepien into Trump World as the campaign's national field director.

Stepien was put in charge of state directors for the 2016 Trump campaign. While Brad had merged fairly seamlessly with the Republican National

Committee's digital team, Stepien clashed with his counterparts at the RNC from an adjacent office in Trump Tower. Stepien complained to colleagues that Brad was ceding too much to the party. Officials from the regional political teams for both the Trump campaign and the RNC complained they were working at cross-purposes and on the verge of a civil war.

Three weeks out from Election Day, RNC chief of staff Katie Walsh and Chris Carr, the RNC's political director, approached Stepien about setting up a joint call to show a united front to the troops. Stepien refused to commit, and Walsh escalated the issue to Bannon, the campaign's chief executive.

"I don't know what the fuck this guy's problem is," Walsh told Bannon.

Bannon, like Brad, viewed the RNC as a crucial tool, from fundraising to political infrastructure to, most important, its data operation.

"This is ridiculous," Bannon told Walsh, and ordered Stepien to fall in line.

But Stepien continued to keep Walsh and Carr at arm's length. Emails went unanswered. He refused to schedule a meeting and complained that his team was already overburdened with conference calls.

"Maybe we can get through this week, and I'll introduce the idea this weekend to them," Stepien told Walsh.

Walsh unleashed a flurry of expletives that caught the attention of others in the office. "I have multiple email exchanges with Steve telling you to do joint calls!" she shouted. "I've printed them out, and they're getting leaked the day after the election unless you get on the fucking phone."

The state director call was held the next day.

After his promotion to campaign manager in the summer of 2020, Stepien moved into Brad's office. Stepien's elevation made a certain amount of sense. He had been deputy campaign manager. Trump was familiar with him. And he and Jared were close.* But it was never clear what problem he solved for the president's reelection bid.

It had been obvious for months to many in Trump World that the reelection team's vulnerabilities were disparate messaging and de minimis strategizing. The messaging issue always came with high risk and high reward in

---

* Jared was dazzled by Stepien's mastery of analytics and had tried to hire him at Kushner Companies in 2016 when Corey and Trump blocked Jared's first attempt to bring Stepien into the campaign.

Trump World. And yield on that bet had been terrible for most of the summer. In the week Stepien was hired, Trump surprised his team by threatening to ban TikTok, the popular Chinese video app; equated Portland, Oregon, with Afghanistan as he complained about bursts of violence at Black Lives Matter protests; and boasted about passing a cognitive test—a simple exam meant to detect dementia—in an attempt to attack Biden.*

The issue of strategy, on its face, seemed solvable. Even Brad, who had the closest view of the campaign's strengths and weaknesses, had begged Jared to bring in an experienced strategist who would give him air cover to finish building out the campaign. The decision to install Stepien was its own acknowledgment that such a person no longer existed in Trump World—or wouldn't take the job.

Stepien was a veteran political operative, which was no small thing in Trump World. The personnel departments in the White House and campaign often seemed to more closely resemble a public bus stop: Just standing in the right spot at the right time was mostly all it took to catch a ride. Stepien had paid his dues running and winning campaigns. But Christie's 2013 campaign had cost $11.4 million, just a bit more than double what Trump had spent on a single Super Bowl commercial earlier in 2020. And Stepien had never been the big-picture strategist with the sweeping vision that guided tactical decisions. That had always been Mike DuHaime's role. Even for Christie's two races, Stepien had been campaign manager but DuHaime was the top strategist, consulting from the outside.

Stepien and DuHaime had barely spoken since Bridgegate, but the night Trump offered the job to Stepien, he phoned DuHaime and asked his old friend for advice. The skate guard and the Zamboni driver from Chimney Rock Ice Rink rehashed some of the good old days, what worked and what didn't. They talked strategy and tactics. They compared notes on motivating staff and maximizing the talent on the team. The two men continued the conversation over the remainder of the campaign.

The thing Stepien wanted most was structure and logic. He had an

---

* "So it's 'Person, woman, man, camera, TV.' Okay, that's very good," Trump boasted during a Fox News interview, explaining how he'd passed the cognitive test by repeating back five words. "If you get it in order, you get extra points."

Election Day countdown clock prominently displayed in campaign headquarters. He scheduled weekly senior staff meetings and daily check-ins with a tighter circle of deputies. He drew up a new organizational chart, and immediately implemented a strict chain of command around himself, telling his team that he wouldn't speak to more than ten people per day. Otherwise, he would lose focus and become less efficient. He joked that he suffered from obsessive compulsive disorder, but there was a kernel of truth in his self-deprecation. Stepien kept his desk highly organized. He wrote everything down, and he tracked all the details. His own checkbook was perfectly balanced. It had made him anxious to watch staffers flow in and out of Brad's office all day long.

Stepien's first move was to elevate Justin Clark, his comrade for the past four years in Trump World, to deputy campaign manager. A forty-five-year-old attorney, Clark was a father of four and grew up in a middle-class home in West Hartford, Connecticut. He was as affable as Stepien was curmudgeonly. Clark drank beer, ate barbecue, and played linebacker on the same high school football team as Brett McGurk (defensive line), who had held national security positions in three consecutive administrations.

Clark was undoubtedly the only member of the Trump campaign who was also a veteran of Al Gore's 2000 presidential bid. Clark had helped with accounting issues on the former Democratic vice president's campaign before converting to the lonely life of Connecticut Republicanism and working on a series of unsuccessful statewide campaigns, including the failed 2012 U.S. Senate bid from future Trump Cabinet member Linda McMahon. He'd worked closely with Stepien since the two met on the 2016 campaign, including two years together in the White House.

Stepien also promoted Nick Trainer, his thirty-year-old protégé with a bald head and bushy red beard, as well as a keen ability to keep many of his colleagues at the campaign irritated. The biggest reason for the griping was his unenviable position as Stepien's enforcer.

Trainer denied requests for more staff or more money. He clapped back at state directors who talked to the president without clearing it first through headquarters. But he also often executed with an air of self-importance that drove some staffers crazy. Some colleagues privately referred to him solely by the awkward title of battleground strategy director as if it was his name: "Mr. Director of Battleground Strategy."

The traditional strategist job under Stepien mostly fell to Jason Miller, just as it had for roughly two months before Brad's demotion. Stepien and Miller had both worked for Trump in 2016, and they knew each other from Giuliani's presidential bid. Miller, a rotund forty-five-year-old with a black goatee, was a methodical communications operative whose career seemed perpetually on the brink due to a proclivity for misbehavior and hedonism.

Trump had expected Miller, who was married, to join him in the White House as communications director in 2017 until his affair with a campaign adviser spilled into public view—and remained there for much of the next four years. A fellow Trump campaign adviser, A. J. Delgado, became pregnant with Miller's son while Miller's wife was also pregnant with their second daughter. Miller reconciled with his wife, but Delgado repeatedly sued him over failure to pay child support and accused him of trying to secretly drug her with an abortion pill slipped into a smoothie. When Miller sued for $100 million claiming Delgado's accusations had ruined his reputation, he ended up acknowledging in a deposition for the case that he'd been a frequent customer of massage parlors in New York, lap dances in Tampa, and escorts in Washington. The judge ruled against him. The feud between Miller and Delgado then turned to issues of child support, again playing out in public. Trump constantly needled Miller about it and complained to others that he just needed to pay Delgado and make the problem go away.*

Miller declined the White House job, landed a $500,000-per-year job as a managing director of Teneo, but then appeared to lose the gig with the global strategic communications firm when he fired off a series of obscene tweets at House Judiciary chairman Jerrold Nadler, a New York Democrat. In the aftermath, Miller announced that he and the company had agreed to sign a formal "separation agreement and general release." But behind closed doors, Miller and Teneo quietly signed a new deal for the same amount of money that he'd

---

* Marital fidelity was one thing Trump admired about Pence. And he had an amusing, Trumpian way of describing it—as if it hadn't occurred to him to be faithful until Pence mentioned it. "He was like thirty years ahead of his time on the woman thing," Trump told one friend. "If the rest of us had listened, we would have had a lot less problems."

be paid as a consultant, according to the *Guardian*. By the summer of 2020, Miller had firmly reestablished himself inside the campaign and proved to be something of a Trump whisperer. He awoke before dawn, organized talking points, prepared a political briefing, and delivered both to the president every morning. By July, Miller was largely credited both inside the White House and at the campaign for Trump's good days. He parlayed that goodwill into a top post at the convention, which he oversaw from the production trailer parked outside the convention center, and a more influential role overseeing the content of the campaign's television advertising.

———

Within forty-eight hours of Stepien's promotion to campaign manager, he sought to get firmer control of the budget. He canceled more than $10 million for billboards and to fly banner ads over beaches on Labor Day. Stepien's team found at least one no-show contract worth $15,000 per month and terminated it. He reduced staffing at events, limited the number of aides who could fly on *Air Force One*, and banned the use of charter flights to fly the team to rallies.

To better understand the campaign's TV advertising, which was one of the most significant costs, Stepien scheduled a conference call on his second day on the job with Jason Miller and the political advertising team, which included the campaign's pollster, RNC staff, an outside ad buying agency, a data analytics firm, and staff from American Made Media Consultants, which was the in-house ad-buying company the campaign had created to avoid vendor commissions and conceal spending details.

"Okay," Miller said to start the call. "How are we targeting TV?"

The seemingly simple question triggered a series of assumptions, arguments, and sidebar conversations that exposed layers of tensions inside the campaign. Staff for American Made Media Consultants, which had been set up by Brad, Lara, and others, were suspicious of why their former boss had been demoted. They closed ranks quickly and made it virtually impossible for Miller to see inside the operation. Miller had previous political ad-buying experience, but that had predated the availability of some of the analytical tools Brad had been using, and much of the ad team had dismissed Miller as a dinosaur.

Miller's question about TV targeting was one any new department head would have asked. But he also viewed analytics as hocus-pocus. The campaign had spent tens of millions of dollars on law-and-order campaign ads that summer, and Miller had been told that the spots tested well. But the spots had failed to improve Trump's poll numbers. When Miller's team looked into the testing, they determined that the sample sizes were much too small. In some cases, Miller told Stepien that advertising decisions had been based on responses of fewer than ten undecided voters out of sample sizes of around 200 respondents.

The ad testing was being done by Deep Root Analytics, a political data company the RNC had brought in to test ads and monitor the effectiveness of political messages across television markets and online audiences. Brent Seaborn, a Republican operative and one of the company's founders, defended the work product on the call. He told the group that the RNC had used Fabrizio's polling data to build a universe of voter targets, which he then had used to test the spots. The campaign's pollster reacted like he'd been backed into a corner. Fabrizio questioned the wisdom of intertwining the two data sets, saying his polling data was based on survey questions that differed from what the RNC asked in their surveys.

The call left the campaign with more questions than answers. Miller was concerned about the results coming out of the analytics company, but Stepien was also suspicious of the RNC data being fed into the algorithms in the first place.

"I think this data is shit," Stepien told Miller after the call.

"Then what the fuck are we paying attention to it for?" Miller said.

Fabrizio suggested a secret poll of the RNC's universe of persuadable voters—the group of Americans the party had determined were open to supporting Trump. Stepien agreed. The next week, the results showed just 15 percent of respondents said they were undecided. It seemed to confirm Stepien's hunch.

"Their data is shit," Fabrizio told Stepien.

An alarmed Stepien called another meeting. The goal was to assess any breakdowns occurring in Brad's data operation. It quickly became clear to Stepien that he'd inherited a mess. But Brad caught wind that his advertising plan was under pressure and started to fight back. He complained to Jared and Trump that the data program was being undermined over internal grudges, and misunderstandings about how it had been built. The struggle over data reflected the vastly different personalities, management styles, and political approaches between the two men. From a certain angle they had complimentary skills, and, to their credit, they had discussed a deputy campaign manager role for Bill earlier in 2019. The conversation didn't go well, and Bill declined.

The bigger problem was that Trump had asked Brad to build a political campaign based on marketing, advertising, and branding, and then hired Bill to run it like an accounting firm. The problem wasn't as much that one was wrong and one was right. It was that they had been forced on each other, and neither liked it.

To help him straighten out the data program, Stepien brought in old pal Bill Skelly, a fellow New Jersey native whom he'd met during the 2004 cycle when both worked at the RNC. Skelly would be teamed up with Matt Oczkowski, who Brad fought to bring into the campaign. Before he was demoted, Brad had been on the verge of hiring Oczkowski to oversee the data program and start predictive modeling of Election Day scenarios. Even Brad's allies shook their heads in disbelief that the campaign hadn't put those critical pieces in place months earlier.

Yet Oczkowski was controversial, too. He had worked with the Trump campaign in 2016 when he was head of product at Cambridge Analytica, a data company that shut down in 2018 after allegations about its misuse of Facebook data. Trump campaign officials denied they used Cambridge's Facebook data in 2016, or the psychographic targeting the company had said it could perform based on personality types. Instead, Brad said he relied on Cambridge to help find persuadable voters and track polling. But the company's modeling had been off in a big way—it had predicted an almost certain defeat for Trump on Election Day.

Fabrizio's view of Oczkowski's operation was similar to Miller's perception of Deep Root—a slightly more sophisticated form of witchcraft. For Fabrizio, Oczkowski might as well have been trying to dunk voter data in water to see what floated. Oczkowski, in return, didn't really believe in Fabrizio's polling.

It also became clear to Stepien that Trump World had competing plans for how to collect 270 electoral votes, which effectively meant that there was no plan. The RNC had its path to 270, which differed from Fabrizio's plan, which conflicted with Oczkowski's. Fabrizio's polling showed Trump had issues that needed to be fixed with white independent males. But that assessment confused the analytics team—with no party registration in places like Michigan, that meant nearly every male in Michigan was a white independent male. Fabrizio's universe included more than two million people. Oczkowski's universe of persuadable voters was closer to 100,000 people. He'd also identified white independent males—just not all of them. Meanwhile, the RNC was focused on a group of Republicans they referred to as "disengagers"—conservatives who had moved away from Trump.

The competing opinions meant that the RNC thought the campaign was responsible for persuading disengagers, while the campaign thought that the RNC was turning them out. Instead, no one from Trump World was consistently talking to one of the most important subsets of the electorate—a major gap in the voter universes of which almost no one had taken ownership.

While Brad had stood up various independent pieces of the campaign, he hadn't been able to pull them all together. Ideally, the data modeling team and pollsters would work hand-in-glove to build a universe of persuadable voters to target, test the messages that those voters would find most persuasive, and continue to refine the targets and sharpen the pitch. But Fabrizio and Oczkowski looked at the same data and drew different conclusions. Fabrizio thought he'd proven his point when he tested Oczkowski's universe of persuadable voters and found that—similar to the RNC's universe—nearly 80 percent said they were definitely going to vote for either Trump or Biden. But Oczkowski viewed the results as validation of what they all knew already—Trump was losing, and the campaign needed to persuade voters who were planning to vote for Biden to switch to Trump.

But the campaign still wasn't sure what its message was for Trump, or which voters to target. Stepien was swamped. His team was also telling him that the campaign was on pace to spend $200 million more than they were projected to raise, so pulled down almost all of the campaign's advertising from television. Stepien also halted the campaign's use of Deep Root to target campaign spots (despite the company's contract already having been paid) and went about rebuilding the data operation—with just three months left in the race.

When Stepien took over, he had to move quickly to install his team, because Trump—who insisted he was his own best chief of staff, communications director, and military adviser—had also been moving personnel like pawns across a chessboard. He'd grown frustrated with Jared as the situation with Brad had worsened, but the only punishment he'd inflicted upon his son-in-law was to take matters into his own hands.

Trump had opened frequent communication with Dick Morris, the former Clinton political strategist whose father had been Trump's real estate lawyer and was a cousin of Roy Cohn, the hard-charging anticommunist who was also Trump's mentor. Morris started providing friendly advice to Trump in April, but it picked up in the summer and the two men were in daily contact for the last two months of the race.

Morris was soon emailing Stepien's inner circle and campaign pollsters with suggested survey questions and pointed critiques. Jared had also started sharing polling with Morris, as well as with Meadows and former House Speaker Newt Gingrich, but had failed to mention it to Stepien.

Morris, Meadows, and others, including White House policy adviser Stephen Miller, had also started suggesting their own poll questions. The queries ranged from testing transgender issues to questions about expelling Chinese students from the country after the Covid outbreak, which was one of Morris's pet issues. There were so many poll questions being proposed from outside the campaign that they were assembled into what the political team referred to as the "peanut gallery survey." The questions then would be polled through an "IVR" poll, which was a relatively short automated call that carried little weight with top campaign officials—but it helped to placate the president and the people around him and bought Stepien a little more time to try to get the operation under control.

Another consequential personnel move by Trump that summer was to bring back Jeff DeWit, who had been a part of the 2016 campaign and later served in the administration as NASA's chief financial officer. DeWit was the Arizona state treasurer in 2015 when he met Trump at a South Carolina conference. After the two chatted, DeWit offered to endorse Trump's presidential bid. Although the burgeoning campaign wasn't ready to roll out endorsements,

DeWit became an unofficial adviser to Corey, and raised his profile with Trump when he helped organize what became one of Trump's biggest early campaign rallies: more than 4,000 people at the Phoenix Convention Center.

In May 2016, DeWit was in his office in Phoenix reading the news that Corey had just been fired as Trump's campaign manager when his phone rang with a call from Jared.

"How soon can you get to New York?" Jared asked.

DeWit told him he needed just a day, even though he was working as Arizona state treasurer, a job he'd been elected to in 2014. He arrived at Jared's New York office having been told little else other than they had a 9:00 a.m. meeting inside Trump Tower, about three blocks away. DeWit had been in and out of Trump Tower for much of the past year and had pitched Jared on an unpaid job as chief operating officer. He'd noticed that phones weren't being answered and mail had gone unopened and wanted to help make the campaign more efficient. But when they arrived in Trump Tower, DeWit was brought to a small conference room outside the office of Allen Weisselberg, the chief financial officer of the Trump Organization. When Jared and DeWit walked into the conference room, Weisselberg was grilling Rick Gates, a senior campaign adviser who would later be sentenced to 45 days in jail as part of Mueller's Russia probe.

"Where's the fucking money, Rick!" Weisselberg barked at Gates.

The money in question was more than $730,000 that had been transferred from the campaign to a new Delaware-based company called Left Hand Enterprises. Gates denied any wrongdoing, and said the money had been spent printing and mailing campaign flyers to voters. Weisselberg wanted to know what he knew about the new LLC—who was running it, what his connection was to it, and where it had come from. They went back and forth for nearly an hour until an exasperated Gates threw up his hands and asked his interrogators what exactly they wanted him to do.

"Well, that's why he's here," Jared said, pointing to DeWit. "He's the new CFO and you're not touching the money again."

DeWit seemed confused, and finally spoke up to tell Jared that he had wanted to be chief operating officer, not chief financial officer.

"Oh, sorry," Jared corrected himself. "He's the CFO and COO."

DeWit walked out of the meeting unsure about what had just happened.

Jared's advice was to go run the campaign. "It's down on the fifth floor," he told him. "You know where it is."

On the fifth floor, DeWit announced himself as the new COO/CFO and looked for a desk. The only one he could find was in the office that Corey had just vacated. He went in, sat down, and almost immediately staffers started funneling through asking for his input on decisions. A couple of months later, DeWit was headed to the Republican National Convention in Cleveland and asked Sean Dollman, his chief deputy back in the Arizona treasurer's office, to come out to New York to cover for him.

"Here's what you do—just sit at that desk and people will run in and ask questions," DeWit told Dollman. "Just choose the best option, and it will all work out—and you'll get to know everybody."

Dollman thought his boss was crazy. But it worked, and he was soon named deputy chief of operations for the Trump 2016 campaign.*

DeWit, meanwhile, had been asked by Jared to travel to San Antonio to negotiate a contract for Brad. He had been earning a 12.5 percent commission on the campaign's digital advertising, and costs were starting to accumulate. DeWit returned to New York with a contract that reduced Brad's commission to 1.5 percent.

But DeWit was suspicious of Brad's invoices. Brad's company was charging the campaign for use of the staff back in Texas, but DeWit wasn't sure those staffers existed. With approval from both Trump and Jared, DeWit began preparing to travel back down to San Antonio to audit Brad's team.

A few days after the election, Brad stormed into DeWit's office screaming about the 1.5 percent commission. He felt he'd been ripped off. He had earned about $900,000, but insisted that the digital director of a winning presidential campaign should have made more than ten times that. DeWit pointed out that he'd been working without a salary the entire time, and offered to switch places.

Shortly after, DeWit took a phone call from Rick Dearborn, who had been named executive director of Trump's transition team. Trump and his family had just won the White House. Any interest in DeWit's audit was gone.

---

* Dollman was named operations director of Trump's reelection in 2017 and became chief financial officer of the 2020 campaign.

===========

They were curious again in the summer of 2020.

As part of Trump's attempt to get a handle on his own campaign after Tulsa, he made it clear that he wanted DeWit back in the fold. DeWit flew in from Arizona to meet with Trump at the White House, and then was taken to Jared's office, where, along with Brad, they discussed a new role for DeWit.

Brad would later tell people that DeWit was desperate for the chief operations officer title, even though it had been held by Michael Glassner—who had been working for Trump for five consecutive years. DeWit would tell Glassner that the idea came from Brad, who wanted to shift blame for the Tulsa rally to Glassner, who had been in charge of campaign rallies for years. Regardless of whose idea it was, Brad, Jared, and DeWit all agreed: Glassner would be demoted to a role overseeing the campaign legal bills, and DeWit would break the news to him.

Glassner, eating lunch at his desk inside the campaign, knew what was coming when DeWit walked into his office.

"I'm out, aren't I?" he asked.

"Yes and no," DeWit told him.

"Fuck," Glassner replied.

They agreed that Glassner would move his belongings out of the office that night, after the other staffers had left for the day. When campaign aides arrived the next morning, DeWit was seated at the desk, ready to weigh in on any decisions that needed to be made.

DeWit got to work analyzing the campaign budget, and within ten days provided Jared documents that showed the reelection campaign was trending into debt: between $100 and $200 million in the hole by Election Day. Jared was upset about the finding, and initially blamed DeWit, ordering him to run the numbers again. When DeWit came back, he told Jared the problem was that the campaign was underestimating the costs of fundraising—and was spending too much money trying to raise more. Brad was out a few days later.

DeWit turned next to a review of Brad's campaign income, which he believed was a duty that fell to him as chief operating officer. But the blowback turned on him first.

After Brad was demoted, news leaked from *Business Insider* that DeWit's real job had been to perform an internal review of the campaign spending. The story set off alarm bells around Trump World.

Pointed questions about Brad's income had always been most useful as an internal cudgel to help undermine him, then sideline him, and—in the final months of the race—try to pin the blame on him for the loss. But now Trump World staff worried that DeWit had misunderstood his mandate and was actually going to investigate all aspects of campaign spending—a swampy mess of potential misconduct that few of them actually wanted waded through.

———

One major change under Stepien was the campaign's relationship with the Republican National Committee. Friction remained from the 2016 race between Stepien and much of Ronna's senior leadership team. Ronna was running the Michigan Republican Party during that race, but Stepien disapproved of her decision to keep many of those same players in her orbit. Katie Walsh had become one of Ronna's top advisers. Ronna elevated Richard Walters, who had been the party's top finance director the year before.

Walters had worked his way up inside at the RNC to become its top staffer. But that was part of the problem for Stepien. Not only had the RNC been a reluctant partner for Trump in 2016—and continued to be influenced by many of the same people in 2020—but he viewed the party as an organ of the presidency that should remain fluid and scrappy, staffed with young operatives devoted to the party's leader instead of their own bank accounts. Walters had obscured exactly how much he was being paid by the RNC, and the party was embarrassed by a February 2020 report from *ProPublica* showing that in addition to his salary of $238,200 Walters also earned $135,000 through his company Red Wave Strategies. But the RNC wasn't merely an extension of the Trump campaign. The deal with Brad had effectively turned them into a full partner, and Ronna had become one of the president's closest advisers. The RNC was paying for the field staff. They were covering costs for state directors who couldn't get calls returned from campaign headquarters. Even the lease for the campaign headquarters was being paid for by the RNC.

But that level of investment elevated the RNC's expectations for the relationship. Ronna and her team wanted their opinions to be considered. Jared had always tried to limit Ronna's influence with Trump in order to protect his own, but Brad viewed the RNC as a crucial partner. Under Stepien, however, Ronna was often left on the outside looking in—sometimes literally. In June, she had arrived at the White House for a political meeting, but waited in the lobby for more than an hour before she was brought into the Oval. When she walked in, the president asked why she was so late.

"They don't want me sitting in the meetings with you," Ronna told him.

Beyond the power struggle between Jared and Ronna and the philosophical differences between the new campaign manager and the head of the RNC, Stepien was correct to question the loyalty and dedication of Ronna's staff to Trump. The president's handling of Covid and the White House's treatment of Ronna had top staffers inside the RNC openly musing—for the first time in their lives—about not voting for the Republican nominee for president. Ultimately, some did not cast their Election Day ballot for Trump.

Stepien spent much of his first weeks on the job on a very un-Stepien pursuit: relationship building. He met with Ivanka to talk about the travel schedule she wanted to ramp up and her portfolio of promoting skills-based training and women's and working family issues. He praised Lara for how hard she was working, telling her how effective he thought she'd been.

"Every time I look up, you're on TV," he told her. "You're killing it."

He knew he had work to do with the Trump family, and he went out of his way to tell them how much he appreciated what Brad had done and how he'd built the campaign.

"I hope he knows I was never gunning for him," Stepien would tell Brad's allies.

Stepien also reached out to Brad's enemies. Brad had spent most of 2019 describing how wonderfully the reelection campaign was running, how much money had been raised, how much groundwork had been laid, and how gorgeous the new office was. All generally true. But Brad's only point of comparison was the 2016 race, which infuriated Kellyanne, Bossie, and Corey. They all had leadership roles steering that secondhand clunker down the street, siphoning gas from the neighbors just to get the old beater full of back-biters and gossipmongers over the finish line. But they had finished first—a fact Brad barely bothered to mention—and now they were determined to finish him. Stepien was not about to repeat that mistake. He praised Kellyanne to the president. He made sure to show Bossie respect. He was on the phone multiple times a day with Corey, who, just four short years earlier, had tried to keep the New Jersey operative out of the campaign.

Stepien gave stilted pep talks to the staff and dialed into a conference call with grassroots groups asking them to stay in the fight. He reluctantly engaged in a conference call with reporters, walking them through a battleground map state by state.

Trump would overcome polling deficits in Pennsylvania by running up margins in the smallest, most rural counties in the state, Stepien said on the call. Their Wisconsin team had spent the past year finding new Trump supporters and registering them to vote, he added. He noted that public polls—the same ones he had criticized to start the call—showed Trump exceeding his 2016 margins with certain key demographics. He identified Minnesota, Nevada, and New Hampshire as possible pickups.

"I would advise we not get stuck in that 2004 mindset of viewing Minnesota through an old, outdated political lens," Stepien said. "Look at the pathway exposed by the president in 2016, the playbook. There are enough votes in Minnesota to win. Now we have the resources to go get them."

Stepien opened the July 16 conference call for questions and scoffed when a reporter asked about Georgia, where polls showed that Biden was starting to break through.

"I invite Democrats to spend a lot of money in the expensive media market of Atlanta and keep thinking it's for real—because we had the same conversation in 2016," Stepien said.

Stepien felt good about Georgia, and several other states, too. But he was largely running on his gut at that point, because the various data he was getting at the campaign was starting to conflict with itself. And he didn't know what to believe.

13

The Trump TV Convention

"With a heart full of gratitude and boundless optimism, I profoundly accept this nomination for president of the United States."
—*Convention speech, South Lawn, August 27*

After Pence had explained to Trump that the smothering of Susie Wiles was a vicious opening salvo of the 2024 presidential race, Ronna had revealed that Wiles had been secretly helping the party with convention planning in Jacksonville. Wiles agreed to provide her help free of charge, which let the party keep the arrangement off the books and out of public campaign finance reports that DeSantis and his team might have seen.

In early July, Trump finally called the Florida governor.

"What's the deal with Susie?" Trump said on the call. "She won Florida for me."

"Well, that's just like saying the batboy won the World Series for you," DeSantis responded.

But Trump had had enough, and he decided to hire her back. On July 2, he dictated a tweet from inside the Oval Office that his team posted on the campaign's social media account. The tweet was unsigned but the author's voice was unmistakable.

"Susie Wiles (@susie57) was a very important part of how we Made Florida Great Again with @realDonaldTrump in 2016 and it's tremendous to welcome her back to the team. We will win Florida again going away!"

DeSantis was furious when he saw the news back in Florida and immediately phoned Trump, who ignored three consecutive calls and finally answered on the fourth. The conversation quickly grew heated.

"This isn't your fucking decision," Trump told DeSantis. "Stay out of it."

Amidst all the tumult inside the campaign and surrounding the convention, Trump finally wore a mask in public.

The moment came during a July 11 visit to the Walter Reed National Military Medical Center, where he met with wounded soldiers and health care workers caring for Covid patients. The virus had infected more than 3.2 million Americans and killed at least 134,000 by the time Trump slipped around his ears the bands of the navy blue face covering that matched his dark suit and was embossed with a gold presidential seal in the bottom left corner. He walked the halls of the hospital with his trademark squint, giving his best Clint Eastwood impression but with his mouth shielded for medical purposes instead of clenching a cigar.

Polling showed that as many as 80 percent of Americans supported wearing masks outdoors, and Trump's political team celebrated the victory over White House advisers who had repeatedly urged him not to cover his face. Few voters had blamed Trump when coronavirus started to spread. But his refusal to remain focused on the deadly pandemic had put his polling in free fall for two months—a 4.4 point deficit with Biden in May in the *RealClearPolitics* national poll average had nearly doubled to 8.6 points on the day Stepien was promoted in July.

Yet Trump was proud of how he looked in the mask and sought feedback from aides in the days that followed. About a week after his visit to the military hospital, Trump asked Tony Fabrizio, his chief pollster, if he'd seen the public images of the mask-clad president. Fabrizio had repeatedly pushed Trump to don a mask and support a national mask mandate that would demonstrate his seriousness when it came to stemming the contagion.

"A lot of people said maybe it looked weak," Trump said.

"It didn't make you look weak, it made you look strong," Fabrizio said.

Trump nodded and walked toward the White House briefing room for a news conference. But he paused and turned back to offer his pollster one more concession.

"I promise I won't call it the Kung Flu," Trump said. "Because I know you don't like that."

"It's not about my personal opinion," Fabrizio said. "When you call it the Kung Flu, you're demeaning people who take it seriously. And it makes it sound like you're not taking it seriously."

"Yeah, I'll just call it the China virus," Trump said.

"Well," Fabrizio said, "that's not good, either."

Jason Miller, Trump's communications strategist, asked Fabrizio how quickly Trump's polling would improve now that he'd publicly worn a mask. Fabrizio chortled at Miller's optimism.

"This is like a guy who smoked for twenty-five years, suddenly stopped, and then wants a lung X-ray and asks if it's all clear now," Fabrizio said. "It doesn't work that way."

"We're the fucking doctors," Miller shot back. "So we gotta prescribe something."

"The prescription stays the same: Stick with it," Fabrizio said.

But Trump wouldn't take his medicine. After a political meeting ended inside the Oval Office at the end of the month, Trump introduced his team to Dr. Scott Atlas, a radiologist who had been chief of neuroradiology at Stanford University Medical Center and had advised Giuliani during his 2008 presidential bid. Atlas had denounced lockdowns and embraced the idea of herd immunity, which would let the virus spread freely under the assumption that most of the population would quickly build resistance to the contagion. His persistent criticism of Dr. Anthony Fauci, the administration's top epidemiologist who had been a vocal advocate for masks and social distancing, earned him frequent appearances on Fox News.

Trump asked Atlas to share his Covid prediction with the campaign team.

"Coronavirus is going to be gone by September," Atlas said. "By the end of September, it will be a memory."

"See?" Trump said. "What did I tell you?"

"With all due respect, Mr. President, I don't think that's correct," Fabrizio said.

"This guy's an expert!" Trump said.

Trump hired Atlas as a coronavirus adviser in the White House a month later. Atlas's controversial theories and aggressive behavior quickly became one of the few things that could unite Trump World.

Fauci complained to colleagues that Atlas was a "total nutcase." Even Kayleigh McEnany, the White House press secretary, who had her own casual relationship with the truth, had been reluctant to cite him.

"I'm worried he's a little fast and loose with the facts," she told her team.

Inside the White House, much of Atlas's hostility was directed at Dr. Deborah Birx, a global health expert on immunology and vaccine research whom Trump had brought into the White House earlier in the year to help coordinate the administration's Covid response. Atlas attacked her suggestions on social distancing guidelines in emails he would blast across the administration, and shouted at her in private meetings.

In one meeting inside the West Wing in late August, Birx expressed concern about the upcoming Labor Day holiday weekend and suggested that the White House remind the American people to practice social distancing. She wanted to prevent a spike in Covid cases heading into the fall.

"You just want to shut down the country!" Atlas shouted. "I speak for the president, and we are not shutting down the country!"

Birx glared back at him. "That's fine, but just know that you are killing people," she said.

The rest of the room sat in stunned silence.

"Well," Jared said. "It's good to have a robust debate."

———

Despite Trump's battle with DeSantis over Wiles's return to the campaign, convention planning had been coasting along in Jacksonville. One of the biggest questions early on from the RNC was whether there would be enough lodging to accommodate all the visitors. The city had hosted a Super Bowl in

2005 and immediately suggested the same solution they had used that year: seven massive cruise ships docked along the St. Johns River.

But there had been too many headlines about cruise ships infected with Covid in 2020—and no one wanted to live through a rehashing of Trump's hostile refusal to care for sick passengers in a callous attempt to keep a lid on the number of Covid cases in the country.

"Absolutely not," said Walters, the RNC chief of staff. "It's a nonstarter."

Ultimately, the hotel issue had mostly solved itself as it became quickly apparent that a full convention would be impossible. The risks seemed to be growing, and Ronna was alarmed. There was no escaping the urgency of the situation when she traveled to Jacksonville in mid-July for a walk-through of venues the party wanted to use for the convention. When she and her team pulled into the parking lot of TIAA Bank Field, the 67,000-seat pro football stadium Republicans were considering for the convention, they were greeted by an hours-long line of cars waiting for drive-through Covid tests.

"Holy crap," Ronna said.

She felt responsibility for her party's activists. The average age of their convention delegates was over sixty-five, which increased the odds of severe illness from the virus. Some had told her they were nervous about traveling. But others were ready to risk it all to give Trump the show of support they knew he desperately wanted, and to make sure he wasn't embarrassed again like he had been in Tulsa. One delegate pledged his attendance despite a medical condition that made him susceptible to Covid's most dangerous symptoms, and told Ronna that he considered his participation to be on par with going to war.

"No!" Ronna said. "This is not going to war. And we don't want you to die going to the convention and fighting for our president."

Ronna had regretted not acting more forcefully with Trump about the Juneteenth rally. She could have taken her concerns about the date directly to him, but instead stayed in her lane and everyone got burned. The convention was clearly her jurisdiction and she wouldn't make the same mistake again.

Ronna called Trump. "We can give you the best speech—we can build the best stage," she said. "But if one person leaves and dies, it will overwhelm anything we do."

Trump paused. He'd been strident and unequivocal in public about reopening the country, but the surge of sickness in Florida had spooked him.

"It's not the right time," he said. "We should not be doing this."

Stepien, Meadows, and Jason Miller were patched into the call. The decision was made to cancel the in-person convention in Jacksonville. Trump said he'd make the announcement the next day at the Coronavirus Task Force news conference.

Still, there were doubts within Trump's inner circle about whether he'd go through with it. He'd been anticipating the convention for months and was known for making last-minute reversals.

The next day, about a half hour before the news conference, Stepien called his team with an update: "This is actually happening."

Trump stood behind the lectern in the White House briefing room and described his reluctant decision. His political team, he claimed, had practically begged him to hold the convention online.

"I have to protect the American people," he said. "That's what I've always done. That's what I always will do. That's what I'm about."

———

Trump's announcement that he was pulling the convention from Jacksonville—made at the top of a White House press briefing—was news to the rest of the convention team and just about everyone else involved in the planning in Jacksonville.

As attention moved to where they would hold the now virtual convention—now just weeks away—Trump floated the possibility of giving his speech at Gettysburg, and privately inquired about other national monuments. But there was no time for the kind of prep work and security measures that would be needed for those locations.

By the end of July, less than four weeks from the convention, the Trump campaign still had no program for four nights of a prime-time, made-for-TV convention featuring the nation's first reality TV star turned president. No pressure.

The campaign needed to slot in people who were up for the job, but the president was also a prickly pear, and they knew they needed people who made Trump feel comfortable, knew his voice, and understood his politics. The answer, as it almost always was for personnel decisions in Trump World, was to hire people with previous experience—good or bad—working for Trump. That meant bringing in Sadoux Kim, a former co–executive producer of *The Celebrity Apprentice*, to oversee production and logistics from a war room/control room set up inside Trump International Hotel, but also Cliff Sims, the former White House director of message strategy—whom Trump had sued the year before—to handle speechwriting duties for almost all of the ten-plus hours of programming.

To assemble the programming, Jared tapped forty-four-year-old Tony Sayegh. The son of politically attuned Lebanese immigrants, he had long ears, brown eyes, and dark black hair turning gray at the temples. Sayegh was a vice president at Jamestown Associates when the Trump campaign landed in his portfolio in 2016. After a good word from Judge Jeanine, who had once employed him on her Fox News show, he joined the Treasury Department as an assistant secretary and returned to the White House in 2019—taking a brief absence from a consulting gig at Teneo—to assist the White House during impeachment proceedings. Sayegh earned high marks from both Bannon and Jared, which was no easy task, and was generally well liked by the people who worked under him. He was also extremely competitive with his peers. The race to replace Hope as White House communications director in 2018 grew so vicious that Sayegh and the other contender were both eventually disqualified and the job went to Stephanie Grisham, whom he then tussled with during impeachment proceedings. The Sayegh-Grisham rivalry played itself out again during convention planning as events in the East Wing, controlled by the first lady's office, where Grisham had returned, were canceled and rescheduled without any explanation. No one bothered to ask for one, either.

Sayegh assembled a convention team of some of the most capable hands to find their way into the Trump White House. Despite well-earned headlines about record West Wing turnover and woefully miscast roles—six national security advisers in three years, an explosive eleven-day run as White House communications director for Anthony Scaramucci—some corners of the West Wing had been quietly populated by steady hands, who, behind the scenes, worked to keep the trains running. One of those was Adam Kennedy.

Kennedy joined the White House as a deputy research director and left in the spring of 2020, just before coronavirus lockdowns set in, as the No. 2 official in the communications office. He avoided the TV cameras while supervising a rapid response team of thirteen people he'd assembled during the Mueller hearings, and put back together for the Senate impeachment trial. His work earned high marks from Republicans in Congress, who were constantly frustrated by their struggle to extract any guidance or game plan from the White House. Sayegh took notice and reached out to Kennedy, who had joined an outside conservative firm.

Sayegh also brought in Steven Cheung, who had worked in PR for the Ultimate Fighting Championship before finding his way to the Trump campaign in 2016. Cheung followed Trump to Washington, where he kept a low profile in the communications shop, while playing a key role in some of Trump's most notable successes, including the confirmation of Supreme Court justice Neil Gorsuch and the overhaul of the tax code, where he worked closely with Sayegh.

And then there was Cliff Sims, whose return to Trump World was surprising, but not shocking. One of the few aides with access to Trump both during the campaign and at the White House, Sims left the administration in 2018 after John Kelly, then the chief of staff, accused him of secretly recording the president. Sims denied it, then wrote a tell-all memoir of his time with Trump that brought a seven-figure payday—and a lawsuit from the Trump campaign. Trump accused him of violating a nondisclosure agreement and Sims sued Trump, accusing him of improperly blocking former employees from invoking their First Amendment rights. The two sides eventually settled.

A teetotaling Southerner who used expressions like "Oh my gosh" and "Golly," Sims remained in contact with Jared and Hope. They told Trump that Sims's book wasn't an attack on him; it was a critique of the infighting around him. When Kellyanne learned Sims was back in the fold, she asked Trump if that was such a good idea after what had happened the first time.

"I heard it wasn't so bad for me as it was for you," Trump shot back.

With a convention team in place, Sayegh's first task was a meeting with Vince Haley and Ross Worthington, the two main White House speechwriters. Much

of Washington associated Stephen Miller, the steely-eyed anti-immigration provocateur, with the wordcraft behind the president's teleprompter. White House
flacks like Hogan Gidley insisted that every speech was 100 percent Trump's
own words. But the truth was that Trump rarely wrote anything longer than
a few words scribbled with a black Sharpie on a printout of a news article he
would then sign and send to whichever aide, Cabinet member, or journalist he
was either praising or blaming for the story. In reality, from the very start of the
administration, Trump's speeches were being written by two Newt Gingrich
acolytes: the fifty-three-year-old Vince Haley, who had managed the former
House Speaker's 2012 presidential campaign, and Ross Worthington, who was
deputy communications director on that presidential bid and, two years later,
coauthored the former speaker's book *Breakout: Pioneers of the Future, Prison
Guards of the Past, and the Epic Battle That Will Decide America's Fate.*

It wasn't just the Washington press corps that missed the rise of Haley
and Worthington. It was a well-guarded secret inside the West Wing and,
for months, kept even from the president himself. Miller had indeed penned
Trump's speeches during the final months of the 2016 campaign, and the two
spent so much time together that Miller knew the president would throw a fit if
he tried to phase himself out of the speechwriting. Trump viewed himself as a
complex personality and intricate thinker whose worldview couldn't be easily
shoehorned into traditional definitions of conservative and liberal. But Trump
was a creature of comfort, immensely more at ease with the devils he knew.
Nothing tasted as good as dinner at a Trump hotel restaurant. No bed was as
restful as his own. And he didn't know Haley, and he didn't know Worthington. So even though the two men were clearly identified as the highest-paid
speechwriters on the White House payroll from Day One, Miller kept the
arrangement from Trump so he could continue to free himself up to focus on
his true passion—immigration policy. The plan was to slowly introduce Trump
to Haley and Worthington. They started attending meetings, then started
traveling, and eventually, Trump got to know them and trust them.

The week before the Republican convention was set to start, Trump paid close
attention to the Democratic show. He was not a fan of what he saw. He was

bored by the pace of the evening and the speeches he watched, and on the third night—just five nights before the opening of his own convention—he ordered across-the-board cuts to the lengths of all the speeches. No one objected, except for Trump's own children. Don Junior had already finished his speech. Ivanka was not about to be treated like all the rest. Hope agreed to increase time for them both, under one condition: They couldn't tell anyone else in the family, or then everyone would want more time.

But most of the speechwriting hadn't been finished anyway. Many drafts weren't finalized until the day they were supposed to be delivered. While speeches for Trump, Melania, and Pence were left to their own teams, Sims and his team handled nearly all the rest. Jason Miller had given him specific but broad guidance.

"Ramp up the economic populism and the foreign policy nationalism in everything we've done," Miller said. "Throughout everything."

By the third day of the Democratic convention, and with five days until the start of Trump's convention, Mike Pompeo still hadn't been asked to be included as a speaker. That wasn't unusual. The sitting secretary of state rarely spoke at a party's political conventions, a decision rooted in a tradition of keeping the country's top diplomat out of domestic politics to maintain a semblance of nonpartisanship. Earlier in the year, the State Department had disseminated several legal memos that put limitations on the political activity for those working in the agency. "Senate-confirmed Presidential appointees may not even attend a political party convention or convention-related event," read one. Not only did that sentence seem to apply to Pompeo, but it was one of the few in the memo that was bolded.

But Pompeo had let it be known in Republican circles that he was interested in running for president someday, and he wasn't about to cede the stage to other potential 2024 contenders, like Mike Pence, Tim Scott, and Nikki Haley. Pompeo suggested taping his speech from Jerusalem. It wasn't public yet, but Pompeo was traveling to the Middle East on a five-day tour intended to discuss regional peace and security. In his estimation, that would give him a perfect backdrop to espouse the president's foreign policy accomplishments and maybe squeeze in a bit of back-patting for himself, too. Trump didn't give it a second thought, and by that Friday, Pompeo was locked in.

The success of a party's convention rests on the final speech from the nominee. Not only did Biden exceed the expectations set by Trump World—which were so low that no one would have been surprised if the former vice president stopped his speech to start eating the paper the words were written on—but was actually good enough that it worried the Trump campaign team.

"That son of a bitch cleared the bar," Stepien told his team. "Now our convention matters a lot more than it did before that speech."

Trump's team had convinced themselves that the Democratic convention would be so boring and such a disaster that it almost didn't matter what their own would look like. When they saw that Biden could in fact string more than three sentences together, there was sudden interest and concern about their own programming. Sayegh's phone started buzzing with messages from Hope and Scavino from inside the White House, and Stepien and Justin Clark at the campaign. Ronna wanted assurances. The messages ranged from gentle "Hey, what's going on with our convention?" texts to more aggressive demands that it better be good.

On Friday, the day after the Democrats wrapped, Sayegh called his team together. "We've got to put everybody at ease," he told them. Kennedy and Sims pulled an all-nighter preparing a memo, with details on all the speakers they'd lined up and key quotes from their remarks. Sadoux Kim focused his aides' efforts on assembling the opening video and highlight reel.

First thing Saturday morning, in an office on the fifteenth floor of the campaign headquarters, all the senior political aides sat around a table: Jared, Ivanka, Lara, Eric, Hope, Stepien, and Scavino. There was no talking. They all fixed their gaze on Tony. He cued up a video and pressed Play.

The video was narrated by Jon Voight, a Trump favorite and Mar-a-Lago member, and included snippets from Cardinal Timothy Dolan's opening prayer and speeches that were already in the hopper. The video was well produced, and the Mellon Auditorium in Washington, where speakers would address the nation beneath brass chandeliers and gold leaf bracket lamps, popped onto the screen. A sense of relief washed over the room. Heads nodded as they paged through the list of speakers and speech highlights. The campaign had initially demanded final approval over every speech. After that meeting, no one ever asked to see anything else.

───────

One of the prime-time speakers lined up for night three, "Land of Heroes," was Dan Crenshaw, the thirty-six-year-old former Navy SEAL, who'd lost his right eye in Afghanistan. Crenshaw, a Republican, was elected to the U.S. House in 2018 to represent a suburban Houston district that Trump had won by nine points. During the 2016 race, Crenshaw posted on social media that Trump was an idiot, insane, and ignorant. But in his first eighteen months in Washington, Crenshaw voted against both articles of impeachment against Trump, then after the coronavirus lockdowns were about a month old, Trump retweeted a video Crenshaw recorded blaming China for the contagion instead of the president.

"BRILLIANT," Trump wrote.

By the time the convention rolled around, Crenshaw's past criticisms of Trump were forgotten. But maybe they shouldn't have been.

This freaking guy, Sims thought to himself after reading Crenshaw's prepared remarks.

Sims had read thousands of words of convention speeches at that point, and written just as many. Surely his eyes must just be getting tired. He must have just missed it. Sims pressed Command+F on his iMac and searched for the word "Trump."

Nothing.

He erased that, and searched for the word "president."

Nothing.

Sims had had to Trumpify a handful of convention speeches—adding some of the president's accomplishments and additional superlatives. For Crenshaw, Sims added a few mentions of Trump to fit the military veteran's remarks, including one that would credit Trump for taking out ISIS and a final line that endorsed Trump: "And by voting for Donald Trump on November third, you can be sure it will continue to be protected by the president as well."

Sims attached the revised remarks to an email, noted that he'd made a few edits, and hit Send.

"Hey, Cliff," came a reply from Justin Discigil, Crenshaw's communications director, a few hours later. "Just spoke with my boss. He feels very strongly about the speech. The speech is written in his words, and he drafted it completely himself."

Sims called Discigil.

"Dude. What is going on?" Sims asked as soon as the aide answered. "If you think your guy is going to speak at the president's convention without mentioning him and no one is going to notice, you're crazy."

The speech was in the middle of a political convention, but Crenshaw wanted to keep his remarks free from partisanship. The campaign had asked him to speak about military heroes. He'd had friends killed in action and didn't view their valor at the province of Republicans or Democrats. Crenshaw was ready to walk if Trump World tried to take over his speech.

But there was also a political calculation on the part of the Texas Republican.

"The president is the biggest liability to our reelection," Discigil said.

Sims lost his mind. Why would Crenshaw agree to speak at the convention? Why would he think he could have it both ways?

Crenshaw eventually agreed to credit "the president" for supporting the military but never mentioned Trump by name. Inside the campaign, Miller and Clark decided not to elevate the issue to Trump, and instead bumped Crenshaw out of a prime-time slot without informing the congressman about the change.

After the speech aired, Sims texted Discigil the links to every tweet he saw mentioning the conspicuous lack of Trump mentions in the congressman's speech.

Discigil never responded.

Trump focused on his speech to close out the final night with unusual attention. During the week, he repeatedly practiced the address in the Map Room of the White House with Jared, Hope, Jason Miller, and his two speechwriters, Haley and Worthington. Trump rarely reviewed speeches—let alone practiced them—before the words were fed into the teleprompter for him to read in front of the cameras. His investment of time into his own convention address explained to some aides why he remained largely glued to the script for the hour-long address.

Trump attacked Biden, promoted his baseless theory that the Obama administration had spied on his campaign, and portrayed himself as the defender of working Americans. He made little mention of the civil rights protests, other than to tick through a list of cities he said had been overrun by street violence. And he made exaggerated claims about coronavirus as he bragged about his handling of the pandemic to a large audience that was mostly unmasked—despite sitting shoulder-to-shoulder for the speech.

"Everything we've achieved is now in danger," Trump said. "This election will decide whether we will defend the American way of life or allow a radical movement to completely dismantle and destroy it."

Trump's speech was followed by a brilliant fireworks display. He'd asked for it only after seeing what the Democrats had done for Biden on the last night of his convention.

———

At the first light on the last Friday in August, temperatures in the capital were in the low 80s, humidity was rising but not yet uncomfortable, and a bed of cottonlike clouds had for the moment blocked out the oppressive heat beating down from the midsummer sun. A punishing downpour was in the forecast, but the morning was gorgeous and Trump woke up feeling better than he had in months.

He had just wrapped up the Republican National Convention by accepting his party's presidential nomination for the second consecutive election in a beautiful setting on the South Lawn of the White House. He didn't even tweet until almost 10:00 a.m. that morning, and even then it was only to say thank you for the great ratings and reviews from the night before. Sure, ratings were lower than they were for Biden's speech the week before, but from where Trump stood that evening, it had been a pretty spectacular event.

Waiting in the Rose Garden the morning after his speech was the merry and buoyant band of Trumpsters largely responsible for the convention success: a group of little-known outcasts, misfits, and retreads who had all traveled different paths into Trump World.

Sadoux Kim, Adam Kennedy, and Sayegh were there, as was Jason Miller, and of course, Sims. This motley crew—their nasal passages freshly swabbed for Covid—stood outside making awkward small talk, hands in their pockets or otherwise picking at their fingernails with an energy that seesawed between nervousness and excitement.

Finally, the Oval Office doors swung open.

"My team!" Trump bellowed, smiling as he descended down six steps from the colonnade, over the newly laid limestone paving that framed the lawn— another Melania-approved update!—and into the garden. "These are the people!"

Trump had gathered them to toast their success, reveling in the moment the only way he knew how: reserving credit for himself, and roasting his guests.

"We should do those South Lawn events every single week," Trump said. Nervous laughter rippled from his brigade. He was kidding, right? No one really ever knew for sure. Trump barreled on. He talked for a few more minutes about his convention address, made sure everyone had loved it as much as he had. Everyone would remember later how much time he spent talking about the testimonial from Herschel Walker, the former football star who asserted that his love for Trump was greater than all the friendships he'd lost over it.

Then Trump spotted Sims.

It had been two years since Trump had laid eyes on the thirty-six-year-old Alabamian.

"There he is—we always loved him," Trump said, pointing at Sims and suddenly speaking as if he were the narrator reminding viewers about scenes from last season.

The peanut gallery in the Rose Garden had been anticipating this moment and they were eating it up.

"Then I had to sue his ass off," Trump continued. "But I won, and now I've brought him back, because I'm such a nice guy."

Inside, Trump wanted to hand out small souvenirs, mostly little tchotchkes with the White House seal. Trump had turned the private dining room just off the Oval Office into a gift shop where he kept tote bags, mugs, cheesy faux crystal plates, and red MAGA hats—tons of them—to hand out to visitors. Everyone who crossed the threshold also heard the only historical fact about the White House that Trump ever consistently repeated: This was a room where President Clinton would bring Monica Lewinsky and, well, you know.

Trump tried to make these Oval Office moments for visitors feel larger than life, because what he really wanted was to be talked about: He wanted his guests to tell their friends how gracious he'd been, remember how much fun they'd had, and reaffirm that, yes, he definitely deserved the job. There was something touching about Trump's little room of cheap knickknacks, but also kind of tragic. The harder Trump tried to make the experience feel majestic, the more he made it feel smaller. The gifts he was so excited to hand out weren't all that different from Washington Monument snow globes or the "Trump-Pence 2020" coffee mugs at the gift shops trying to snag tourists walking through Reagan National Airport. His jokes were crude but, to be fair, often memorable—and no one in the Oval Office that Friday morning would forget anytime soon the show he was putting on for them.

Trump turned to Sayegh and motioned to the elementary-school-age son he'd brought with him to the White House.

"Give him one of the ashtrays," Trump instructed, then told the boy, "You can put it on eBay tonight."

Trump next called Jason Miller up for a photo.

"You must have the most patient wife in the world," Trump said.

It was a dig at Miller's well-publicized extramarital affairs. Cheung felt tears welling in his eyes and turned his back and walked to the other side of the office to keep from bursting into laughter. Others couldn't look away as Trump needled Miller.

"What she puts up with I don't understand. She puts up with a lot, doesn't she?" Trump said. "I don't know how he keeps her. That's why he's good at his job, I guess."

If Miller was tempted to return fire on the thrice-married Trump, he kept it to himself.

"You're very right sir," Miller said through a half smile. "She's fantastic. She's very patient."

"Why don't you take one of the ashtrays for her," Trump told him.

14

Hell Week and a Half

"This was a blessing from God that I caught it."
—*Recorded video, Rose Garden, October 7, 2020*

The main entrance from the south side of the White House is a set of doors that open into the Diplomatic Reception Room—one of four similarly sized oval-shaped suites in the building. But the Dip Room, as the locals call it, holds its own unique history. In the 1830s, slaves used the space to polish silver. In the 1930s, FDR sat near the open hearth and delivered his popular fireside radio chats. In 1961, First Lady Jackie Kennedy redecorated and hung striking hand-painted wallpaper depicting panoramic views of American landscapes and entertained ambassadors and visiting diplomats who were welcomed there for much of the twentieth century.

On September 26, 2020, President Trump used the room to host a Covid-19 superspreader.

Just like so many other key moments in the Trump White House, the superspreader was a spur-of-the-moment thing. And just like a long list of Trump's self-inflicted troubles, this one arose from a willful disregard for traditional protocols.

The moment, from a legacy perspective, was monumental. No president since Reagan had more than two Supreme Court nominees confirmed. No one had three in their first four years since Nixon, who had four. But more important, Trump's third pick would tip the political balance of the court toward conservatives. For all those reasons, he wanted to play up the drama of the unveiling of his chosen justice as much as he had for his first two nominees.

In 2017, the White House counsel's office had Neil Gorsuch wait at a friend's house in Denver in order to avoid reporters who might have been staking out his own home for signs ahead of Trump's announcement. In 2018, Trump was so pleased that his selection hadn't leaked that he teased the audience in the East Room for nearly five minutes before introducing Brett Kavanaugh, who then emerged from behind a closed door with his family.

For Amy Coney Barrett, the White House sent one of the Air Force's newest purchases—a $64 million Gulfstream business jet designed to chauffeur government VIPs around the globe—to pick her up in South Bend, Indiana. The day of Barrett's announcement was scripted down to the last minute. Republican senators and Cabinet members would be tested for coronavirus in the Eisenhower Executive Office Building next door to the White House, and then escorted to the Cabinet Room in the West Wing to wait until it was time to take their seats. At 4:45 p.m., the gates would close at the visitor's entrance at 15th Street and E Street NW, and reporters would be directed to a patch of grass roped off behind a couple hundred seats on the Rose Garden lawn.

Guests would be seated by 4:50 p.m. Five minutes later, Pence and his wife, Karen, would take their seats, front row and center. Then, at 5:00 p.m., the president's military aide would announce the start of the event with the big reveal:* "Ladies and gentlemen, the president of the United States and Mrs. Trump, accompanied by Judge Amy Coney Barrett and family."

The Trump and Barrett families, who would be mingling inside the Oval Office, would emerge from the West Wing. Melania would walk the judge's family to their seats. The president would take his place behind the lectern, deliver his remarks, and then step stage right as soon as he finished. That

---

* Trump had been scooped the day before by the *New York Times*, but the White House had still refused to confirm Barrett's selection.

would be Barrett's signal to deliver a few brief words. The speeches would wrap by 5:20 p.m.

Most of the afternoon seemed to stay on script. Even Trump's ad-libbing at the end, when he took the lectern back after Barrett had finished and thanked his guests for coming, had barely taken any time.

"All of the senators—please, we really appreciate it," Trump said. "I know you're going to have a busy couple of weeks, but I think it's going to be easier than you might think."

Just as planned, after the speeches, the Trumps and the Barretts exited the Rose Garden the same way they'd entered, but then turned away from the Oval Office and instead walked along the West Colonnade toward the Diplomatic Reception Room for a few clicks to commemorate the moment.

When the Dip Room's doors closed behind them, the press team was to escort reporters out of the Rose Garden, through the Palm Room, and back into the White House briefing room. The other 200 guests—lawmakers, conservative activists, Fox News personalities—would then be directed away from the White House, along the curved driveway past the South Lawn putting green, and down to the southwest gate at 17th Street and State Place NW.

By 5:40 p.m., the event would conclude.

But in the Trump White House, it was never quite that simple.

Trump—always the maître d' in chief—asked aides to invite in his Rose Garden guests for an impromptu after party as soon as he had entered the Dip Room. The past six months had been a parade of horribles—the nationwide death toll from Covid had just eclipsed 200,000 just a few days earlier—and this was a rare, big moment to enjoy.

"Bring in the senators," Trump said.

Within minutes, a procession of conservative senators filed into the room. Mike Lee. Thom Tillis. Josh Hawley. Ben Sasse. Kelly Loeffler.

Sasse and Tillis, who had worn masks in the Rose Garden, removed them inside.

Attorney General Bill Barr invited himself in, as did Health and Human Services secretary Alex Azar, a key member of the White House Coronavirus Task Force. Trump's Cabinet secretaries knew they didn't need a special invitation in the White House—Trump always wanted things loose and doors open.

Meadows brought in a few guests. Pat Cipollone walked in with his wife, Becky, and longtime family friend Laura Ingraham, the Fox News personality. Labor Secretary Eugene Scalia brought in his wife, Trish, and mother, Maureen, the widow of former Supreme Court justice Antonin Scalia.

Former New Jersey governor Chris Christie had been at the White House that morning to help Trump prepare for his first debate with Biden—now three days away in Cleveland—and then stayed for the Rose Garden event. When he walked inside to retrieve the briefcase he'd left in the Map Room, Kellyanne, who had been helping with debate prep, too, flagged him down.

"There's a reception," she told him. "You should at least stop by."

Christie stuck around.

He spent a few minutes talking to Barrett and her family. He chatted with Melania, and he eventually said goodbye to Trump.

The day after the Rose Garden event, Christie returned to the White House to continue preparations for the debate. It was a Sunday, but the first debate was now just two days away. It was a famously tricky moment for incumbents, who often assumed their day job over the past four years was preparation enough, but then found themselves to be rustier than their rivals, who had spent months honing their skills during the primary season.

Trump had started his prep in mid-August, at his Bedminster golf club, and eventually endured a total of eleven practice sessions, with most of the meetings occurring in the White House. But Trump defined debate prep differently than any other major party's presidential nominee.

Even in 2016, when prep was mostly overseen by Stephen Miller, Trump's debate meetings usually resembled bull sessions. Other presidential candidates often prepared by combing through a 300-page binder, reading and memorizing as much as possible. Then a typical candidate would find a political ally to play the role of the opponent to sharpen their verbal sparring and get a feel for how the evening might unfold. But that was too formal for Trump. He gave some of his advisers the impression that he was afraid to acknowledge he needed practice, and that it would make him look weak even inside his inner circle. Debate prep in 2016 was mostly an attempt to make Trump feel comfortable.

That's mostly how debate prep happened in 2020, too.

His team prepared him a three-page packet of material, which included reminders of his accomplishments in office and what he planned to do with a second term.

He didn't want to stand behind a podium to familiarize himself with the setup and didn't need anyone to play the part of Biden. Instead, he mostly wanted to talk through strategy and refresh himself on the issues. But sometimes he could barely be bothered to do that much.

Trump took phone calls during some practice sessions, while Christie, Kellyanne, Stepien, and Jason Miller sat and waited. He ended one debate session by saying he wanted to save his voice for a rally that night. Another time he cut it short to prepare for the Barrett announcement.

The prep team was constantly changing, too. Kellyanne, Christie, Stepien, and Miller formed the core, but Hope sat in on most sessions. Stephen Miller attended at least one, where he reminded everyone that Biden was willing to give illegal immigrants health care. Rush Limbaugh, the conservative radio shock jock, phoned Trump to offer pointers. Reince Priebus, the former Republican National Committee chairman and Trump's first White House chief of staff, repeatedly lobbied to be a part of debate prep, but was shut out. For the final two debate prep sessions, Trump demanded Rudy Giuliani's addition to the team.

Others just happened to walk into the room. Kayleigh McEnany came in during one session and Trump engaged with her for so long that others assumed debate prep was over.

The day after Barrett's Rose Garden announcement, Trump had been in his 4:00 p.m. debate prep for less than an hour—after spending five hours at his Virginia golf course—when Derek Lyons, the White House staff secretary, interrupted to remind the president about a news conference at 5:00 p.m. Kellyanne and Jason Miller were furious with Lyons, and tried to convince Trump to skip the news conference. It was a Sunday evening, and few people would be watching. Plus, he could hold one the next day. Christie discouraged him, too. But Trump insisted.

Trump wanted to avoid debate prep partly because he knew Christie was going to hammer him. Trump had a quick temper, but mostly preferred to avoid confrontation. And tussling with Christie felt like a chore. For Trump, it was another homework assignment to be avoided.

But Trump was right in at least one sense: Christie absolutely blasted him behind closed doors. To others in the room, the heated exchanges seemed to trigger something interpersonal between the two of them. There were moments when Trump enjoyed the back-and-forth, but Christie was determined to rattle Trump, especially over his handling of coronavirus.

"You messed up Covid—you killed people!" Christie shouted at Trump, trying to push him off balance. "All you think about is politics!"

The gambit was to hurl tough questions at Trump, see how he would respond, and figure out where improvements were needed. While there were no formal roles, Christie had taken on the job of channeling Biden, while Kellyanne assumed the role of moderator, Fox News Sunday anchor Chris Wallace. And like Christie, Kellyanne charged at Trump with every bit of fire and fury she could muster.

She fashioned a question by telling Trump that the audience included the mother of Heather Heyer. That was the woman, she told him, who was killed that Saturday afternoon in Charlottesville, where protesters were carrying Tiki torches, chanting racist mantras, and wearing MAGA hats.

"And yet you say they're fine people?" she asked him.

"I didn't see any MAGA hats!" Trump shot back. He had burrowed in on the minutiae and the team urged him to focus instead on the broader question.

She hammered him over his claim that he hired only the best people. Then why, she asked, had so many of his campaign and White House advisers been indicted or jailed? Why were the four-star generals who had worked for him now supporting Biden?

"Well, they didn't give such good advice," Trump responded.

Kellyanne stared at him.

"You're not listening," she said.

She peppered him with abortion questions and attacked him over his struggle to address race relations. She told him to think thematically so that he'd have a three- or four-point answer waiting in the wings whenever race or abortion came up—regardless of what specific question had been asked.

Kellyanne went after him on health care, too. She had sided with Attorney

General Barr over the summer and urged Trump not to ask the Supreme Court to overturn Obamacare, which would have wiped out medical coverage for some 23 million Americans in an election year.

"You're taking away people's health care in the middle of a pandemic," Kellyanne told Trump.

"No," he argued. "I'm giving them better health care."

"Well, where is it?" she asked him.

Her aggressiveness and sharply worded questions both inspired and deflated some of her colleagues.

"When I hear the way you phrase things, I want to quit my job," one staffer later told Kellyanne.

Jason Miller and Giuliani warned Trump that Biden was going to interrupt him, as he had Paul Ryan in the 2012 vice presidential debate. They told him that was how Biden won the debate, and Trump shouldn't let him do the same to him.

But Kellyanne disagreed. She said Biden had won that debate by looking like the elder statesman schooling a young pupil—a dynamic that Biden wouldn't be able to replicate against Trump. She also didn't think Biden was as sharp or as witty as he had been during that race. She urged Trump to consider Biden's 2008 vice presidential debate against Sarah Palin, who, like Trump, brought a unique approach to the debate stage and seemed to fluster Biden at times.

On topics Trump was most passionate about, he would argue back angrily with his sparring partners. On subjects he cared less about, he would just shake his head and mutter retorts.

"Wrong," he would say.

"Untrue," he'd offer with a shrug.

Trump also repeatedly turned questions back to the subject of Hunter Biden. But the attack was convoluted and hard to follow. Kellyanne urged him to keep it simple, and offered a pared-down rejoinder. "Joe Biden gives us Hunter Biden—Donald Trump gives us Amy Coney Barrett," she said.

They urged him to challenge each and every time Biden used a number, because the odds were that Biden had mixed it up. Kellyanne and Jason Miller both told Trump that Biden almost always confused thousands, millions, and billions. Christie, Kellyanne, and Miller also told Trump to be aggressive—but not to the point that it would overshadow Biden.

"Let him speak, because that's going to wear him down," Kellyanne advised Trump. "Biden doesn't do well when he has to speak at length."

Christie urged Trump to let Biden speak first. "When your adversaries are in the midst of committing suicide, there's no reason to commit murder," he said.

Giuliani suggested he open the debate aggressively, believing it would rattle Biden. "We can live with a headline that you were too tough on him," he told Trump. "We can't live with a headline that he dominated the debate."

After one final practice on the morning of September 29—the day of the debate—Christie had some lunch, got into his car, and drove home to New Jersey feeling confident that Trump was in a good place.

"He's really ready," Christie told a friend who called during the drive home. "He's going to have a good night tonight."

When the debate commenced that evening, held in an auditorium at the Cleveland Clinic, strict health precautions meant that only about 100 people were in the audience, instead of the thousands that typically attend a presidential debate. Only one reserved seat went unused. Ronna had canceled at the last minute. She had flown home from Washington on Friday—a day before the Rose Garden event—when she learned that her teenage son was sick with coronavirus. Now she felt ill, too, and skipped the debate out of an abundance of caution.

Trump's side of the hall was filled with family, staff, and other guests—including local pastor Darrell Scott, U.S. Representative Jim Jordan, and UFC fighter Colby Covington in his red MAGA hat. Almost all of them had taken their seats in the hall without their masks on, which was against the Cleveland Clinic's policy, including Trump's family and White House staff who viewed wearing a mask as a sign of weakness.

Because of Covid, the two candidates agreed not to shake hands at the start of the debate and to keep their distance. It was just as well. Any degree of decorum was out the window almost from the moderator's introductions.

The first question from Chris Wallace was about Trump's decision to nominate a Supreme Court justice so close to an election. The president defended his right to make the pick—elections had consequences and Democrats would have done the same, he said, using only ninety seconds of the two minutes he was given.

Biden used his entire time to argue that while elections had consequences, the 2020 decision was already under way—tens of thousands of people had already cast their ballots, and the nomination should wait until everyone had their say. Biden then pivoted and said that Barrett's confirmation would almost surely mean the end of Obamacare since Trump had tried to have the health care policy repealed in the middle of a pandemic.

Trump shot back that Biden had misstated the number of Americans with preexisting conditions—but Biden had the number right. Trump accused his rival of supporting a health plan that had been pushed by his Democratic primary rivals that would end the private health insurance market.

"You're going to socialist medicine," Trump said.

"He knows what I proposed," Biden said. "What I proposed is that we expand Obamacare and we increase it."

"It's not what your party is saying," Trump shot back.

"That is simply a lie," Biden said.

"Your party wants to go socialist medicine and socialist health care," Trump continued.

"The party is me," Biden interjected. "Right now, I am the Democratic Party."

"And they're going to dominate you, Joe. You know that."

Biden pointed out 200,000 Americans had died of Covid since Trump had been president—"On his watch," he said—and again questioned the wisdom of repealing Obamacare during a pandemic.

Trump said two million people would have been dead from Covid had Biden been president.

Wallace tried to get control, but Trump—who scowled, sneered, and wagged his finger for most of the debate—talked over him.

"You're not going to be able to shut him up," Biden told Wallace. The jab triggered another back-and-forth between Trump and Biden.

Biden insisted that *Roe v. Wade* "was on the ballot" in the race. It was a simple turn of phrase that both sides of the abortion debate tended to agree with every election year. But Trump argued even that point. Biden tried to explain what he meant, but Trump seemed to sense this was an opportunity to land a knockout punch. He wouldn't relent.

"You don't know what's on the ballot," Trump said. "Why is it on the ballot? Why is it on the ballot? It's not on the ballot. I don't think so. There's nothing happening there."

"Donald, would you just be quiet for a minute," Biden said.

"You don't know her view on *Roe v. Wade*," Trump said about Barrett. "You don't know her view."

Wallace tried to ask his second question, which was about what Trump planned to do if the Supreme Court struck down Obamacare. But Trump interrupted before he could get the words out. Wallace admonished him, but then Biden interjected.

Wallace reset himself and tried to ask his question again as Trump started to talk over him once more. Now it was an argument between Trump and Wallace.

"Sir," Wallace said. "You're debating him, not me. Let me ask my question."

"Well, I'll ask Joe," Trump said.

"No!" Wallace said.

"The individual mandate was the most unpopular aspect of Obamacare..." Trump said to Biden.

"Mr. President, I'd like you to..." Wallace said. "Mr. President!"

"I got rid of it, and we will protect people with preexisting conditions," Trump said.

"Mr. President!" Wallace said again, a noticeable quiver in his voice. He was losing his patience. "I'm the moderator of this debate, and I would like you to let me ask my question and then you can answer."

Trump paused.

"Go ahead, Chris," he said.

"You, in the course of these four years, have never come up with a comprehensive plan to replace Obamacare," Wallace said. "And just this last Thursday you signed a largely symbolic executive order to protect people with preexisting conditions five days before this debate. So my question, sir, is what is the Trump health care plan?"

"Well, first of all, I guess I'm debating you," Trump said. "But that's okay, I'm not surprised."

From there, the sniping only intensified.

━━━

On the next question, Biden interrupted Wallace. The subject was still the Supreme Court and health care, but somehow Trump and Biden were bickering over the margin of victory in the Democratic presidential primary.

"Everybody knows he's a liar," Biden said.

"You're the liar," Trump shot back.

When Trump accused Biden of supporting a liberal "manifesto," Biden sighed. "Folks, do you have any idea what this clown is doing?" he said into the camera.

Wallace appealed to Trump, and asked him to stop interrupting so both candidates could receive equal time.

But Trump couldn't help himself. When Biden refused to answer a question from Wallace about whether he'd support expanding the number of Supreme Court justices—an issue favored by liberals but condemned by conservatives as court packing—Trump pounced.

"Are you going to pack the court? Are you going to pack the court?" Trump said, just ten seconds into Biden's answer. "He doesn't want to answer the question!"

"I'm not going to answer the question, because..." Biden attempted.

"Why wouldn't you answer that question?" Trump said.

"Because the question is..." Biden said.

"You want to put a lot of new Supreme Court justices, radical left..."

Biden closed his eyes tight, like he was trying—and failing—to block out the aggressiveness of the fellow septuagenarian to his right.

"Will you shut up, man!" he pleaded.

And that was just the first fifteen minutes.

━━━

After about an hour, Wallace asked Trump if he was willing to specifically condemn white supremacists and militia groups. He asked Trump if he would say those groups "need to stand down and not add to the violence" in places like Kenosha, Wisconsin, and Portland, Oregon.

Trump said he was "willing to do anything." But it took Wallace three more tries before Trump agreed—and during the back-and-forth with Wallace and Trump, Biden repeatedly chimed in from the other side of the stage.

"Say it!" Biden said. "Do it! Say it!"

"Well," Wallace said to Trump. "Do it."

Trump paused. He looked at Biden from the side of his eye, and then back at Wallace.

"What do you want to call them?" Trump asked. "Give me a name. Go ahead. Who would you like me to condemn?"

"Proud Boys!" Biden interjected, naming the far-right group that had endorsed violence and agitated some of the civil rights protests in the Pacific Northwest.

"White supremacists and right-wing militia," Wallace said.

Trump decided to answer Biden.

"Proud Boys—stand back, and stand by," Trump said, as much a call to action as a condemnation.

Once again, Trump had flubbed a seemingly simple request to condemn white supremacy. He said the next day that he'd meant it as a condemnation, but the phrasing was imprecise and cryptic. Just like the violent white supremacists in Charlottesville, the conspiratorial wingnuts of QAnon, and the dictators and global strongmen he'd befriended, Trump couldn't bring himself to renounce someone's support no matter what they believed, or said, or did—regardless of the danger their words or actions presented to others. By the end of the debate, the leaders of the Proud Boys had interpreted Trump's comment as an attestation and adopted the slogan as a rallying cry.*

---

* Trump claimed the next morning that he didn't know who the Proud Boys were, but it was impossible to know the truth. He denied hearing of David Duke in 2017, which was ridiculously false. But instead of correcting himself, he doubled down. And after four years of this, the media's instinct wasn't to give him the benefit of the doubt.

One of the most cringeworthy exchanges was still to come when, a few minutes later, Wallace asked a fairly simple question about how each of them viewed their own record in the White House, and why that made them the better candidate.

Biden pointed out that he and Obama had taken office in 2008 amid an economic collapse. Since that Democratic ticket left office with the country in recovery, Biden said, that showed he could repair a country that Trump had made "weaker, sicker, poorer, more divided, and more violent."

Trump quickly interrupted.

"Your son got three and a half million dollars!" he said.

The jab seemed to come out of nowhere and was devoid of any context for the casual viewer.

Trump was attempting to take aim at Hunter, and the consulting work he had done both domestically and overseas for years—including while his father was vice president. But it was unclear what point Trump was trying to make, other than to interrupt Biden.

"Wait a minute, Mr. President," Wallace said. "Your campaign agreed both sides would get two-minute answers, uninterrupted. Your side agreed to it and why don't you observe what your campaign agreed to as a ground rule. Okay, sir?"

"Because..." Trump started to say.

"No, no, no!" Wallace shot back. "I'm not asking! That was a rhetorical question."

Biden concluded with a pledge of support to the military, which he underscored by mentioning his firstborn son, Beau, who had been awarded the Bronze Star for his service in Iraq before dying of cancer.

Trump mystified members of his own team by turning the moment into another attack on Hunter.

"I don't know Beau—I know Hunter," Trump said. "Hunter got thrown out of the military. He was thrown out—dishonorably discharged for cocaine use. And he didn't have a job until you became vice president."

Hunter Biden was never dishonorably discharged, which is a punitive designation the military reserves for the most egregious conduct from its soldiers.

But Hunter Biden had received an administrative discharge from the Naval Reserve after a positive drug test in 2014, for which he'd publicly apologized.

Trump also accused Hunter Biden of making "a fortune" from jobs in Ukraine, China, and Moscow while Biden was in the White House. Biden, meanwhile, stole the moment back when he framed it in a way that plenty of Americans could understand.

"My son, like a lot of people—like a lot of people you know at home—had a drug problem," Biden said, looking directly into the camera. "He's overtaking it. He's fixed it. He's worked on it. And I'm proud of him, I'm proud of my son."

"But why was he given tens of millions of dollars?" Trump interrupted.

"He wasn't given tens of millions of dollars," Biden said. "That's been totally discredited."

"All right! All right!" Wallace shouted. "We've already been through this. I think the American people would rather hear about more substantial subjects."

=====

Inside the hall, the crowd sat in stunned silence. Guests for the two candidates were divided between two sections, like a church halved between the families of the bride and groom, but there was little difference in their reactions. Fear and loathing permeated both parties. Men and women in their seats exchanged quick glances and short whispers. At the very moment the bickering seemed to subside—just past the hour mark of the debate—the melee onstage suddenly and furiously whipped back up again.

Trump roared at Biden.

Biden yelled at Wallace for more time.

Wallace shouted at Trump as he tried to impose some measure of order.

"That was a shitshow," Dana Bash, CNN's chief political correspondent, said live on air moments after the debate ended.

But no one was more distressed inside the hall than the man seated just to my right: Steve Scully, the veteran journalist from C-SPAN who was lined up to host the second debate scheduled for two weeks later.

The sixty-year-old Scully was best known for his role as host of *Washington Journal*, a town-hall-style call-in show that provided separate phone numbers for Republicans, Democrats, and independents. The show was like a cross between

a 1980s telephone party line and the Internet comments section on Breitbart
.com. But what was unfolding onstage in front of us was far more than anyone
would have bargained for. Scully's eyes were like saucers after the first few minutes. If only he could have that trusty mute button from his call-in show…

"How would you like to be the next debate moderator?" he asked me.

I wasn't sure how to respond.

"Sure!" I said.

Scully cycled through all the stages of grief, and seemed to have found
some measure of acceptance about halfway through. He laughed and showed
me a meme on Twitter, which was a gif of NBC *Late Night* host Seth Myers
scribbling furiously with the caption *Steve Scully watching the debate right now.*

When the debate ended and the lights came on, I tried to offer Scully
some encouragement. Trump's strategy must have been to go after Wallace,
who was a fighter himself, I told Scully. The format for Scully's debate was
supposed to be a town hall, and I suggested that Biden and Trump couldn't
possibly bicker like that in such a setting. But Scully wasn't interested in chatting. He quickly packed up, forced a head nod in my direction as I talked, and
scurried off the riser and out of the auditorium.*

It was impossible to blame Scully for his reaction. I'd been covering Trump
for five years, and even I struggled to square in my own mind what I had just
witnessed.

"That was the singular worst I've ever seen him—even privately," one close
adviser said after the debate. "I've been with him when he's been pissed off
privately—and he's never been that big of a cocksucker."

To me, the most surprising aspect of Trump's performance wasn't what
he'd done onstage—it was what he'd left out. Trump always escalated political
fights. But he'd always battled his opponents with some measure of humor and
wit—and that was a big part of his appeal.

---

* Scully's debate story didn't end well. The president attacked him as a "Never Trumper,"
and Scully panicked and sought advice from Anthony Scaramucci, a Trump ally turned
critic. But Scully accidentally publicly posted his private message to the Mooch on Twitter. He claimed he'd been hacked, then fessed up, and was suspended by the network.

Whether Trump's jocularity was more appropriate for a middle school playground than a presidential debate stage was a fair topic for discussion. But Trump was funny.* Trump ran golf courses and hotels—he knew how to be charming. Trump, in his own unusual way, was likable. But none of that was on display in Cleveland.

Trump's prep team had urged him to be aggressive, but there had been little talk about what happened if that initial attack failed to flatten Biden. Trump had no second move. He'd spent months insisting that Biden was too old and feeble for the presidency, and now it became clear that Trump and his team believed their own spin. They thought Biden actually did have dementia. But Biden hadn't just withstood the initial landfall of Hurricane Trump; he'd remained behind the lectern, unscathed.

Trump's style had changed from four years earlier, but so had he. This time, Trump had something to lose, and it rattled him.

"No one wants to vote for somebody acting like an angry asshole," one of Trump's closest advisers said afterward.

"One of the most incredible self-inflicted wounds of all time," another said.

"He shit the bed," offered a third.

Everyone seemed to understand how much damage Trump had just done to himself.

But no one wanted to tell the one man who needed to hear it.

<hr>

Backstage after the debate in Cleveland, Don Junior looked around as his family and his father's closest advisers high-fived, slapped each other's backs, and told his father what a wonderful job he'd just done. Don Junior wondered if he had just dreamed the last ninety minutes.

Don Junior had attended one of the country's elite boarding schools, enrolled at the same Ivy League college as his father, and, after graduation, accepted an executive-level job waiting for him in his father's company. He was in every way a child of privilege, but he was also deeply in touch with his

---

* When I started covering Trump during his first race, I was appalled by his over-the-top attacks. Or I thought I was, at least. But then I turned on my recorder after a rally to check quotes and heard my own barely stifled laughter in the background.

own animal spirits—certainly more so than anyone traveling with his father to Cleveland that night.

Don Junior spent many of his childhood summers living in rural Czechoslovakia with his maternal grandparents, where he learned to hunt and fish. It had instilled in him a different set of values than what he was used to in Manhattan. He often was more dialed into Trump World voters than even the president. He was also more like his father than any of his siblings, which was a complicating factor in their relationship. Trump's own self-loathing could manifest itself into contempt for his firstborn son when it came to either politics or the family business. At times it seemed Trump would dismiss an idea from Don Junior based more on the source than the substance—a dynamic that distressed staff both on the campaign and in the company and limited the amount of input Don Junior could offer.

Still, it frustrated the eldest Trump scion to watch the fawning and flattery that followed the debate. No one wanted to level with Trump, but that included Don Junior, too. He had a campaign event the next morning in Ohio, and didn't speak to his father about the performance before he left or after. And the flight back to Washington looked more like a party cruise than a work trip. Some of the president's children had seats on the plane, along with their spouses. Meadows brought his son and daughter-in-law, Blake and Phoebe Meadows. Chris Liddell, a deputy chief of staff, brought his wife, Renee Harbers, and their son, Luc Harbers Liddell. Rudy Giuliani tagged along, as did Alice Johnson, the leader of a cocaine ring whom Trump had freed from prison.

As *Air Force One* departed from Burke Lakefront Airport that night, the president told his friends and family that he'd been perfect onstage. Everyone nodded. It wasn't until he turned on the TV in his cabin that he got his first glimpse of the public reaction. Trump brushed it off and insisted that everything was fine.

It was Chris Wallace, he said, who was to blame for the constant interruptions.

Heading into the debate, Biden had maintained a decent lead over the incumbent in national polls. But Trump was still within striking distance, which was remarkable given all that had happened so far in 2020. For seven consecutive months, Biden's lead in the national *Wall Street Journal*/NBCNews poll barely budged: eight points, nine points, seven points, seven points, nine points, nine points, eight points. The day after the debate, the same media pollsters conducted a two-day survey to measure reaction to the matchup. Biden's lead had ballooned to fourteen points.

For the first time in the poll, Trump's support nationally fell below 40 percent. His twenty-point gap with women a month earlier widened to twenty-seven points. Support softened even among key voting blocs of his base, including working-class white men. For the first time since he'd taken office, more than 50 percent of the country said they had a negative view of Trump. Meanwhile, views of Biden were now net positive for the first time since 2018.

Back in 2016, Jared similarly had to scramble to find friendly media person-alities and other allies who would level with Trump about his troubling first debate with Clinton. When Jared called Christie and asked for his assessment, the former governor was blunt.

"We lost," Christie told him.

"I think so, too," Jared said. "But he thinks he won. You should call him and tell him that he lost."

Christie did, but Trump wouldn't listen. He instead pointed to a poll on the Drudge Report that showed he had won. Christie told him that poll meant nothing, especially since roughly 100 percent of Drudge Report readers were already going to vote for him.

Trump hung up on the former governor.

But then Trump called back a few days later and asked Christie to take over debate prep from Stephen Miller.

In 2020, Christie didn't wait for a call from Jared. He phoned Trump after lunch on the day following the debate.

"I won, right? I did great," Trump told Christie.

"No," Christie said. "You did terribly. You interrupted him seventy-three times in ninety minutes. I didn't think that was possible. We have to totally change our approach."

"You're being too harsh," Trump said. "You always say I don't do well."

But privately, Jared was concerned that Christie and Kellyanne were at fault. The pair had come of age in New Jersey's aggressive and pugilistic style of politics, and he worried that Trump's pettiness and anger had been a result of their prep.

He phoned Nick Ayers in Georgia and implored him to come back to Washington to talk sense into Trump and help with the next debate. Jared considered making changes to the debate prep team and asked colleagues about bringing in Pence or maybe some of Pence's debate team.

Others in Trump's orbit reached out to Tucker Carlson to talk to Trump. Carlson had been blunt in his assessment of Trump's performance—he thought the president came off as unappealing and rude.

"When Biden told him to shut up, I agreed with him!" Carlson said.

But Carlson declined the request to consult with Trump. He had crossed that line one time—to urge the president to take coronavirus more seriously—and didn't want to do it again.

But Trump decided to call Carlson himself. With several aides sitting with him in the Oval Office, the president called Carlson's cell phone. Carlson sent it to voicemail. Trump called again. One ring, right to voicemail. Eventually, one of Trump's aides called Carlson's producer, who patched the Oval Office in with the prime-time Fox News personality.

"Everyone says I did a good job," Trump told Carlson when the two were finally connected.

"I don't know who told you that was good," Carlson said. "It was not good."

Trump was taken aback. Carlson told Trump it had been a mistake to spend so much time ahead of the debate describing Biden as senile. The Democratic nominee had easily cleared that bar in Cleveland.

Meanwhile, Ronna had been trying to reach the president that morning. She'd been rattled by Trump's performance and knew it would be problematic when even her brother, one of Trump's biggest fans, had been unnerved by the president's answer about the Proud Boys. But she wasn't calling about his debate performance. She'd tested positive for coronavirus. When she couldn't get through, she left a message with the White House physician.

Ronna had been with Trump five days earlier in Washington at a campaign fundraiser. She had been told by her doctors that she probably wasn't infected until she got home that night to care for her son, who had contracted the virus in the three weeks she'd been away for work.

Trump didn't mention anything about Ronna's positive test when he met with Giuliani that afternoon for forty-five minutes in the Oval Office. The two had planned to meet to review Trump's debate performance, and Giuliani urged the president to give Biden more room to speak next time.

"There were a couple of occasions I felt Joe was going off the cliff, and you saved him," Giuliani told Trump.

Trump didn't react. Giuliani could never tell whether the president agreed.

Their meeting ended, and fifteen minutes later, Trump was walking across the South Lawn headed out for a two-stop swing through Minnesota.

At the airport in Minneapolis, Trump was greeted by a group that included U.S. Senate candidate Jason Lewis, state senate Republican leader Paul Gazelka, and state house Republican leader Kurt Daudt. They'd all been tested for coronavirus and told not to shake hands with Trump or get close to him, in order to comply with pandemic protocols.

Trump descended the stairs from the plane, and immediately offered to take photos with the group. The greeters stood less than a foot from Trump. None wore a mask.

"You've been tested, right?" Trump asked.

After the fundraiser, on the flight from Minneapolis to Duluth, Hope fell ill. She'd been fine on the flight from Washington, sitting with other aides and typing on her laptop. But she sought out Conley, who recognized the symptoms of Covid. He recommended she put on a mask, isolate herself on the flight, and rest.

Trump spoke for just forty-five minutes that night in Duluth, about half as long as one of his typical rally speeches. Some White House officials thought he seemed unusually tired. Others chalked up the brief speech to the chilly temperatures and the icy gusts that swept over the event that night. Trump noted within the first two minutes of his speech that "Minnesota is a little on the windy side." He blamed the cold for his refusal to introduce a handful of Democratic mayors from the state's Iron Range who had endorsed him.

"I'm not introducing you," Trump said. "It's freezing out here."

On the flight back to Washington, Meadows walked back to the press cabin to brief reporters on Trump's plans to sign the temporary spending measure from Congress that had arrived at the White House earlier that day.

Meadows was aware that Hope had been sick enough to have self-isolated inside the plane for the past three hours. But he spoke to reporters without a mask, and gave no indication that one of Trump's closest aides had quarantined just a couple of cabins away on the plane.

***

Hope usually arrived at the White House every day around 7:30 a.m., but the morning after Minnesota she still felt like hell. She canceled her early meeting, skipped Meadows's senior staff meeting, and instead stayed home to rest. When she didn't feel any better around 11:00 a.m., she dragged herself to the medical office in the White House where Covid tests were administered.

Under White House protocols, staffers were first administered a rapid test, which provided results in ten to fifteen minutes. The rapid test was faster and less intrusive than the "PCR" test, which collected a genetic sample from deeper in the nasal passage and generally took about an hour to get back. But the rapid test was also much less reliable. It occasionally produced false positive tests and, at a much higher rate, false negatives.

To account for some of that volatility, staffers who received a positive result from a rapid test were given a second rapid test. Two positive rapid tests required a more extensive—but much more reliable—PCR test.

Hope returned home, and received the finals results after noon.

Positive.

She told almost no one. The White House tried to keep a lid on the news.

Trump was scheduled to depart from the White House at 12:45 p.m. to attend a campaign fundraiser at his Bedminster golf club, and the White House scrambled to quietly remove Hope's close contacts from the trip. Last-minute changes were made to the flight manifest but no one was told why they had been pulled or why they were added. One clue something was up: Staffers in Meadows's office and outside the Oval Office were suddenly wearing face masks.

But there were few aides who spent more time in closer contact with Hope than Trump—and vice versa. Trump went to Bedminster anyway.

═══

Trump had stopped taking daily Covid tests sometime in the summer based on the belief that it was enough that everyone around him was being tested. But the rapid tests were only about 80 percent accurate—and Trump's doctor and his chief of staff were both aware the night before that Hope almost certainly had coronavirus. Given Hope's status as one of the president's closest aides, senior aides in the White House assumed her test results had been passed on to Trump. That information should have prompted the president to take a coronavirus test by the next morning.

According to some aides, Trump did take a rapid test on the morning of October 1—and tested positive. But that scenario would make his decision to travel to Bedminster incomprehensible. Trump would have jeopardized the lives of staff traveling with him and just about everyone at Bedminster, as well as his own. Meadows and Tony Ornato, the deputy chief of staff for operations, didn't weigh-in on contract-tracing or quarantine decisions and deferred to the medical team on when Trump could or couldn't travel because of Covid, a spokesman for the two men said.

One White House official with knowledge of the positive test said Trump believed it was a false positive, a result he had received before on the rapid test. As he had before, Trump took a second rapid test that morning, which came back negative.

I asked why even a single positive rapid test for the president wouldn't have prompted a more reliable PCR test. The official said there was no good answer.

"What can I say? It's just the way we operated," the official told me. "It wasn't dealt with in the appropriate way it should have been."

Trump told me later in an interview that he wasn't sure what had happened.

"I don't know the exact timing," he said. "At some point I was told I tested positive."

Trump would have discussed the trip with a White House doctor, who would have asked the president to describe his proximity to Hope, considered her test and the incubation period of the virus, and made a recommendation.

Other White House officials who should have been notified about a positive test—and discussed the wisdom of traveling knowing Hope was sick—included Meadows, and Tony Ornato, the deputy chief of staff of operations who had been detailed to the White House from the U.S. Secret Service, where he'd been one of the agency's top officials. There was no indication that either Meadows or Ornato objected to Trump's trip to Bedminster.

Meadows hadn't spoken to Hope before Trump left the White House. He called after *Marine One* had lifted off.

Inside *Marine One*, Trump sat in his usual captain's chair behind the helicopter's pilot as a skeleton White House crew piled into the seats around him. The others included Ornato, press secretary Judd Deere, personnel director Johnny McEntee, and political director Brian Jack.

It wasn't until *Marine One* had landed at Joint Base Andrews, Trump and his staff had boarded *Air Force One*, and the plane was on its way to New Jersey that lower-level staffers—including some who had been last-minute adds to the manifest—started to be notified about Hope's positive test.

Deere was among those who saw the note on his phone but never considered the possibility that Trump might be positive, too, and that now he might have been exposed.

Air Force One landed at the Morristown, New Jersey, airport, and Tommy Hicks, a Dallas-based investor who was cochairman of the Republican National Committee, joined Trump on the second helicopter ride, this one from the airport to the golf club.

Inside the second leg of *Marine One*, Brian Jack gave the president the usual briefing materials before a fundraiser—a rundown of the schedule, who was in attendance, some of the issues they'd want to talk about. But Trump barely bothered to look at it. It was unlike Trump. He would always at least flip through the packet.

At the club, Trump was scheduled for forty pictures with donors, all of whom were required to stand at least six feet away from the president to comply with guidelines aimed at stemming the spread of coronavirus.

After the clicks, Trump held a private meeting with a dozen donors. He raised some eyebrows that afternoon when he repeatedly called on Jack to answer questions. It was unusual for Trump to cede the floor to any staffer during a roundtable. But Trump asked Jack to spell him on several questions about polling and the presidential battleground map.

Trump then delivered remarks outside to the rest of his supporters, and cut the event short. He had been scheduled to spend more than two and a half hours at his property, but ended it more than forty-five minutes early. He seemed tired, but staff chalked it up to a travel schedule that had started to ramp up ahead of the election.

Back at the White House, Trump sat for three "tele-rallies." Trump and his team said little during the campaign about his tele-rallies. They were phone calls, typically about five minutes long, between the president and a Republican congressional candidate that were blasted out to landlines in a House district or Senate candidate's state so that people could listen in. They were essentially spam calls, but instead of getting sold an exotic vacation, the pitch was about the Republican vision for a brighter future.

"The president of the United States will soon be on the phone," the operator would say.

Regardless of how many voters picked up the phone, or bothered to hold the line, the real value was the recording of Trump's endorsement for his fellow Republican. The candidate's campaign would turn the president's words into a short clip to use for advertisements and their own round of recorded robocalls later.

That night, starting at 7:30 p.m., Trump dialed into a tele-rally with Burgess Owens of Utah, Scott Perry of Pennsylvania, and Jeff Van Drew of New Jersey.*

He had finished by 8:09 p.m. when Jennifer Jacobs of Bloomberg News reported what he'd wanted to keep secret: Hope had tested positive.

Sean Hannity, the prime-time Fox News host, immediately reached out and booked Trump for a last-minute interview on his show that night at 9:00 p.m.

---

* In all, Trump participated in fifty-eight tele-rallies for fifty-four House candidates and four Senate candidates: Steve Daines in Montana, Bill Haggerty in Tennessee, Mitch McConnell in Kentucky, and Dan Sullivan in Alaska. Republicans won every race, including toss-up House races in California, Iowa, Minnesota, and New York.

On the program, Trump said that he'd just learned of Hope's positive test and was awaiting his own results.

At 12:54 a.m., Trump tweeted that he and the first lady had tested positive.

"Tonight, @FLOTUS and I tested positive for COVID-19. We will begin our quarantine and recovery process immediately. We will get through this TOGETHER!"

Trump's positive test triggered some of the most chaotic days of his four years as president, and on either of his two campaigns. West Wing officials were certain that no single location in the world performed more regular coronavirus tests than the Trump White House. Few places would have had similar access to that scale of testing. But even with that advantage, Trump had been unable to keep himself from getting infected. It was a devastating development barely forty-eight hours after his disastrous debate performance and just thirty-three days until the election.

"There was definitely a sense that morning that it was all over," one senior administration official said.

No one had reached out to Stepien or the campaign to say Hope had tested positive the day before. On Friday morning, just hours after Trump tweeted about his own infection, Stepien canceled his regular campaign staff meeting so he and his colleagues could get tested. Within the next twenty-four hours, three members of the president's debate prep team—Christie, Stepien, and Kellyanne—announced that they, too, had tested positive.

Christie had to find out about Hope and Trump from the news, and he was livid.

Giuliani woke up that morning to find several missed calls from the White House, including Meadows, to alert him about Trump's positive test. But the former mayor had already scheduled a Covid test after reading on Twitter that Hope had tested positive.

At the White House, any remaining credibility on the Covid issue was quickly evaporating. No one would say when Trump had last tested negative. There were conflicting internal briefings about what had happened. Meadows barked that it wasn't his job to keep track of White House testing protocol. He told others that the White House had a rigorous contact tracing program that had been activated after Hope tested positive—a claim that was demonstrably false. Some officials who should have been notified said they received clandestine calls from an internal tipster who urged them to get tested. Anxiety was rising within the West Wing.

"I'm glued to Twitter and TV because I have no official communication from anyone in the West Wing," one administration official said.

Ronna asked her staff, which had helped put on the New Jersey fundraiser, why the event hadn't been canceled. But the White House hadn't looped in the RNC.

Meanwhile, Trump's health had taken a turn for the worse. He called Ronna, who was just starting to feel better from her own Covid infection. She was alarmed to hear how congested he sounded. White House officials were alarmed, too.

Trump was bedridden for hours on Friday in the White House residence. While he and Melania had both tested positive, they were instructed to remain away from each other since Trump was so much sicker than his wife. Meadows told reporters that morning that Trump had mild symptoms. Inside the White House, however, he was worried enough to suggest that other staffers say a prayer for the president.

Ornato and Conley urged Trump to let them transport him to Walter Reed, where he would have access to better care than could be provided from inside the White House. Trump relented only after he was presented with the choice of walking out while he still could—or risk being wheeled out if he became too sick to decide for himself.

———

Trump's helicopter ride from the White House on the evening of Friday, October 2, may be remembered as the second most famous *Marine One* flight. It's hard to think of any other that could compete, other than President Nixon's final exit from the White House on August 9, 1974, when he flashed the victory sign with both hands just before ducking into the chopper.

But even after being forced to resign or face impeachment, Nixon wore a wide smile as he walked across the South Lawn that sunny summer afternoon.

Trump was in no mood to smile by the time he exited the Diplomatic Room doors.

Waiting for him outside was a gaggle of White House reporters nervous about what was about to happen. The severity of Trump's condition was still being concealed—a statement from McEnany announcing the departure repeated the fib that Trump had only "mild symptoms." But Trump was clearly infected, probably contagious, and the White House's record on health protocols was getting worse instead of better.

Trump often addressed reporters before boarding *Marine One*, and if he was experiencing only mild symptoms, there was a chance he'd try to speak to them before leaving for the hospital. Plus, he'd been reluctant to wear a mask. Meadows, who had been with him all week, hadn't worn a mask that morning while addressing reporters, and neither did Larry Kudlow, Trump's economic adviser, when he spoke to the press.

The group of reporters made a pact that if Trump did approach them, they would insist he maintain his distance from them. But at 6:16 p.m., Trump walked through the Dip Room doors in a dark suit, a light blue tie, and a black cloth mask over his face. He flashed a thumbs-up to reporters, walked past, and boarded *Marine One*. Meadows climbed in behind him. He arrived thirteen minutes later at the hospital's landing zone, where a black SUV drove him to the hospital.

At the hospital, Trump grabbed his small overnight bag and carried it inside. But he had been so weakened, the president dropped the bag after a few feet.

When it fell to the floor, the doctors, aides, and law enforcement officers around Trump all seemed to take a step back. It appeared to Trump as if they were nervous about his infection and didn't want to touch his belongings.

But at that moment, Meadows stepped forward, picked it up, and carried it to his room.

"That's when I knew you're my guy," Trump would tell him later.

———

Trump's condition was being shrouded from the campaign, too. Amid the confusion, a decision had been quietly made inside campaign headquarters on Friday to play it safe until they had more information on the president's health. The campaign paused parts of its surrogate operation—the team that makes sure the president's allies are equipped with talking points and booked for interviews on national TV, local radio, and with regional newspapers. The campaign also held off on scheduling surrogates on TV that weekend over uncertainty about what to say regarding the president's illness.

Meanwhile, Trump's communications team saw, however briefly, a possible opportunity to seize the moment. At the campaign, Jason Miller told Stepien that the infection might be a chance to reset Trump's message on the virus. Inside the White House, Alyssa Farah told Jared that this might be a potential turning point. Trump could speak about his firsthand experience with the tough and challenging virus, and urge the country to pull together to defeat it. The whole world was watching—and even rooting for Trump's recovery— which presented the White House with the opportunity to get a new message quickly in front of Americans.

"If we keep this tight and do it right, this could be a turning point for us," Farah said.

Jared asked her to start working up some language.

———

On Saturday, Jared called his wife and her siblings, who hadn't spoken to their father since he'd gotten sick Thursday night, and told them Trump was going to be fine.

Conley delivered a similar message at a news conference outside the hospital, where he told reporters that Trump's symptoms were improving. But since the president had tested positive, Conley had been directed by both Trump and Meadows to reveal nothing—about Trump's condition or his testing regiment. The doctor, who had little experience speaking to reporters, came off as evasive and overly optimistic.

But Meadows, who had slept overnight in the hospital, was flustered. He was concerned that the doctor had set expectations too high. Trump had improved, but doctors told them inside that they needed more time to monitor the president.

As Conley and his medical team walked back inside the hospital, Meadows walked over to reporters. He asked to speak to them off the record, told them that Trump's symptoms had been "very concerning" just twenty-four hours earlier and that the president wasn't out of the woods yet.

Media outlets sent news alerts based off Meadows's update, and sourced the information to a person familiar with the situation. When Trump saw the headline flash on the TV inside the hospital, he was furious and immediately started calling aides.

"Who the fuck said that?" he shouted at one adviser.

Some TV cameras—including an Associated Press cameraman—were still recording when Meadows walked over to the journalists and asked to go off the record. The AP was suddenly in the uncomfortable position of having a story on the wire citing an anonymous source, with its own video footage strongly suggesting that the source was Meadows. He realized his flub and let the wire service identify him on the record.

Meanwhile, Trump connected with Ronna in Michigan to compare notes about their coronavirus infections. Like Farah and Jason Miller, she had a similar thought that Trump might be able to make up some lost ground with voters who had disapproved of his response to Covid. She urged him to commiserate with people who had to battle the infection without the same resources afforded to the president, and to acknowledge how scared he felt when he was at his sickest point.

"Tell people we'll get through this together," Ronna said.

"I love it," Trump told her. "I think that's great."

━━━━━

Trump was eager to clarify the conflicting reports, and noticed that afternoon that there had been a long gap on Fox News when none of his usual supporters were on the air. He closely tracked who defended him on television and seemed to have an internal radar for his surrogate operation's activity.

He was told that Jason Miller had effectively shut down the comms shop when the president and his campaign manager fell ill. Miller couldn't get straight answers from the White House about Trump's condition, and played it safe.

Trump erupted when he learned one of his campaign's biggest weapons had been holstered during his hospital stay. He was always concerned about whether he had enough air cover on TV, and was rarely satisfied with the support he received. Now confined to the hospital, almost literally unable to fight for himself, he viewed the surrogate operation as even more important. He wanted to see his killers on television.

"I want my fucking surrogates out there," Trump said. "Get everybody on the Sunday shows, and push back on this narrative that I'm not doing well."

Trump mouthpieces raced back to the airwaves. Losing patience over conflicting reports on his health—a discord that had been struck by his own team—Trump called Giuliani from the hospital and dictated a statement, declaring himself well enough to leave the hospital.

"I'm going to beat this," Trump told Giuliani to say.

But the truth was, Trump also felt vulnerable. He tried to puzzle together Covid timelines with other staffers to figure out when different members of Trump World had gotten infected. On Saturday night from his hospital room, Trump called Christie, who was hospitalized with coronavirus in New Jersey.

"Do you think I gave it to you?" Trump asked him.

"I don't know," Christie told him. "At this point, who cares?"

═══════

Trump's doctors acknowledged on Sunday that he'd started a steroid treatment, which caught Ronna's attention. She'd had a similar treatment for her case of coronavirus and didn't like how agitated and aggressive it made her feel.

But Trump continued to recover, and that evening he coordinated his own drive-by for supporters who had spent much of the weekend gathered outside the hospital. He waved and gave a thumbs-up as he drove past them wearing a mask with the windows up. His fans loved it, and his critics went crazy, insisting that for nothing more than his own narcissism he had jeopardized the health of the two Secret Service agents who wore head-to-toe personal protective equipment as they went along for the ride with him in the hermetically sealed presidential limo. (What no one knew at the time was that the Secret Service only sent agents with Trump that weekend who had already contracted coronavirus.)

Trump's doctors signed off on a plan to release him on Monday evening despite signs of pneumonia. An excited Trump phoned friends and planned a grand entrance at the White House, where he'd pretend to have been weakened—and then rip off his dress shirt to reveal a Superman T-shirt underneath. Aides hoped Trump was joking, but the message was clear: There would be no pivot to empathy.

Instead, Trump arrived at the White House and climbed two flights of stairs to the balcony—gasping for breath as he went—before he gave a salute and disappeared inside. He returned with a camera crew to shoot the scene again, and released a video of his triumphant return. There was none of the compassion or sensitivity that Ronna, Stepien, and Jason Miller had urged him to demonstrate. Trump instead framed his illness as a result of his heroic leadership in a pandemic instead of the willful neglect of health protocols intended to keep people safe.

"Don't be afraid of it," he said.

Ronna called Jared and told him she was nervous the steroids were fueling Trump's aggressiveness. "I'm worried about what these medicines are doing," she said.

———

The ten days that started with the Rose Garden superspreader event, included his hurricane of hectoring on the Cleveland debate stage, and ended with his self-satisfied discharge from the hospital presented Trump with the most politically devastating stretch of the election year—if not his entire presidency.

When Trump's week and a half of hell was filtered through the past four years of *Wall Street Journal*/NBC News polls, the result showed that each of the president's missteps underscored—if not exacerbated—what voters had long identified as his chief vulnerabilities. When it came to his handling of coronavirus, a majority of voters from the start of the pandemic said Trump had not taken the contagion seriously enough. At least thirty-five cases of coronavirus were eventually linked back to the Rose Garden event, a significant enough spread that Fauci's colleague on the White House coronavirus task force, Dr. Deborah Birx, told other senior officials there were probably multiple infected and contagious people at the event, instead of a single Patient Zero.

Then, Trump's debate performance—criticized by his own advisers as too angry and mean—went directly to the question of temperament. Just 21 percent of voters said Trump had the right temperament to be president on the eve of his inauguration in 2017. Almost four years later, when asked which candidate had the right temperament for the job, the president's numbers had barely improved—just 26 percent of voters picked Trump.

Finally, the contradictory accounts of both Trump's Covid diagnosis and his treatment highlighted a concern voters long had about the president's reliability that had never been adequately addressed. In January 2018, 29 percent of voters gave Mr. Trump a good or very good rating for honesty and trustworthiness. When asked in September which candidate was better at being honest and trustworthy, 30 percent said Mr. Trump while 47 percent said Mr. Biden.

Inside the White House, Fauci told colleagues that a Covid outbreak in the West Wing had been inevitable since the spring, when Trump began pushing a message that the pandemic was almost over.

"There was definitely a false sense of security about the testing," Fauci said.

The silver lining for Trump was that there was still a month left in the race. It would take a few more days until he would be cleared to travel, but several senior campaign aides thought it would be possible to close the gap. The voters who had drifted from him in the final days of September and early days of October were the kind of people who were still open to Trump's candidacy after three and a half years in office. If they were able to withstand the onslaught of controversies and chaos over that period, it stood to reason that he could win them back in the final days.

"I'm strong again," Trump told an aide after arriving back at the White House.

15

Where's Hunter?

"The *Wall Street Journal* is working on a very, very important piece."
—*Call with campaign staff, October 19, 2020*

L ess than three weeks until Election Day, Covid cases were again on the rise, the economy had flatlined, and Donald Trump's odds of winning a second term were plummeting.

He was falling farther behind Joe Biden in public polls, and the internal campaign metrics were worse. The campaign's most recent poll—an exhaustive survey in seventeen states that Trump's brain trust viewed as the most competitive battlegrounds—showed that the self-described King of Ventilators was, politically speaking, gasping for air. The last few persuadable voters in America—a paltry but still pivotal cross-section of the country—overwhelmingly preferred Biden to handle the coronavirus pandemic. And Trump's campaign, in the parlance of the pandemic, was riddled with comorbidities.

He was shedding support from white suburban women, an indispensable bloc of voters, who were horrified by his leadership on law-and-order issues, which had been the organizing principle of both his 2016 and 2020 campaigns. His years-long advantage over Democrats on economic policy had evaporated. Eight months earlier, his team had shown Trump a map with him on the way to 330 electoral votes. Now he was losing to a man he'd described publicly as the worst presidential candidate in American political history. Privately, he was even more crude.

"How am I losing in the polls to a mental retard?" Trump had said in June, interrupting a policy meeting in his office to vent about the race just weeks before his campaign staff shakeup.

But that reset hadn't worked. The Republican convention that had left the president feeling positive and confident was now just a distant memory. His first debate with Biden wasn't just a letdown; it was an unmitigated disaster.

Still, Trump thought he had one last play.

The only rub: It had never worked before, he'd gotten himself impeached when he tried, and no one around him had any idea how to pull it off.

═══

It was a warm, early October evening in Washington. I was excited about a long Vespa ride across town but wary of my final destination: an off-the-books rendezvous in McLean, Virginia—a leafy suburb tucked along the southern banks of the Potomac River—with a handful of Trump World lawyers, fixers, and backroom operators.

And I was already late.

Time, however, was notional in Trump World. As a White House reporter, I felt like I was aging in dog years covering Trump, as he somehow managed to pack seven days' worth of news into each one. But on this particular day— Friday, October 9—the pace was especially nuts. Trump was still confined to the White House with a Covid infection, but the news was metastasizing.

On the Rush Limbaugh radio show that morning, for two whole hours, Trump had warned Iran not to "fuck around with us." He'd designated Black Lives Matter to be "such a racist term." He'd criticized Fox News for failing to be wholly and abjectly submissive. He'd attacked Barr and Pompeo, two of his top Cabinet secretaries.

And that was all before lunch.

By midday, the White House announced Trump would resume public events with a rally on the South Lawn in less than twenty-four hours. The Commission on Presidential Debates had canceled the second of the three Trump-Biden encounters, after Trump, the day before, had said he wouldn't go. Mitch McConnell, the leader of the Senate Republican majority, said Congress had run out of time to pass the economic stimulus plan Trump wanted before Election Day.

Senator Lindsey Graham refused to take a Covid test before a Senate debate in South Carolina, afraid that a positive result would force him to quarantine and jeopardize the confirmation process for Trump's Supreme Court nominee. Dr. Anthony Fauci, the nation's top infectious disease expert, told CBS Radio during an interview that day that the ceremony where Trump had unveiled his Supreme Court pick turned out to be "a superspreader event at the White House."

I hurried to leave my house before Trump's medical evaluation that night live on Fox News, which was precisely how the network was promoting Trump's first on-camera interview since his coronavirus diagnosis.

My phone buzzed with a text from one of my Trump World hosts: "ETA?"

The siren song of a well-spun conspiracy is an alluring one, indeed. That night, the seductress crooning for me was a former captain of the Penn State wrestling team and ex-Navy lieutenant named Tony Bobulinski.

I didn't know Bobulinski's name yet. I'd been lured to McLean with the promise of getting a glimpse of the proverbial holy grail in Trump World: undeniable proof that Joe Biden was profiteering off the predilection of his troubled son, Hunter, for monetizing the family name. To Trump, just one sip from this sacred chalice would miraculously clear the infections and heal the wounds of his damaged reelection campaign while simultaneously poisoning Biden's bid to take him out.

I was intrigued, but skeptical. Biden the Elder had long said he wasn't involved in any of his son's foreign deals. Officials in Trump's own administration had testified, under oath, that Biden had been carrying out U.S. foreign policy when he threatened to withhold $1 billion in aid until Ukraine fired its top prosecutor. That threat, as Trump alleged, wasn't because the prosecutor, Viktor Shokin, was investigating Burisma, the Ukrainian energy company on whose board Hunter sat. Shokin's probe into Burisma had already been shelved. Instead, Biden's push was because Shokin hadn't seriously pursued political corruption in Ukraine, which the Obama administration viewed as key to Russia's outsized influence in the country. Biden had done nothing obviously unethical—but Trump, however, had been so obsessed with having

Biden investigated over the matter that he'd been impeached on a charge of abusing his power.

But impeachment hadn't chastened Trump, and failures had never slowed him down. Instead, the search for damaging information to hobble Biden's campaign devoured a tremendous amount of energy, attention, and time during Trump's last two years in office.

What was different this time, my sources told me, was that there were receipts.

Bobulinski had gone into business with Hunter Biden and kept all the text messages, emails, and signed corporate documents from an investment venture they'd created and had planned to seed with millions from Chinese investors. The documents, I was told, detailed specific payouts for Joe Biden. The text messages warned the other partners to keep quiet about his involvement.

"These are legitimate documents," Arthur Schwartz, a bare-knuckles public relations brawler who helped coordinate the meeting, had assured me.

Schwartz had trained as an attorney but instead found himself drawn to the emerging dark art of Internet trolling. Using the pen name "Cornholio Esquire,"* he helped start a message board in the 1990s that gained a fair amount of renown in New York legal circles and was later replicated in other cities. Schwartz was combative and cruel, but I also had a soft spot for him. While he expressed it in unusual ways, he had a deep appreciation for the press and its power. And in small groups when he'd sheath his sword and emerge from his defensive crouch, Schwartz could reveal a certain amount of charm, even hints of kindness. He was a thoughtful host who would offer a beer even though he himself didn't drink and fill bowls with various chocolates for his guests until he was completely out.

"Going to order food," he texted me earlier that Friday afternoon. "Burger okay with you?"

=====

---

* The Great Cornholio, of course, was the hyperactive alter ego of Beavis from the 1990s animated television show *Beavis and Butt-Head*. When Beavis turned into Cornholio, he would pull his shirt over his head and run around in spastic convulsions—and then afterward have no memory of the episode.

The burgers were long gone by the time I arrived in McLean, but I wasn't thinking about food. I was suspicious and excited to find what awaited me behind the heavy front door of Schwartz's home, which was surrounded by tall, skinny pine trees and a lush, manicured lawn. I hadn't foreclosed on any possibilities, particularly since Bobulinski had sent a pair of lawyers on his behalf.

Sitting next to Schwartz at a circular dining room table was Eric Herschmann, the attorney on Trump's impeachment team who had recently joined the West Wing formally as an adviser to the president; and Stefan Passantino, a former White House attorney who was business partners with Trump's deputy campaign manager Justin Clark and represented Bobulinski from his perch as a partner at Michael Best & Friedrich, a Washington firm with extensive links to the Trump White House.* No one would tell me who had referred Bobulinski to Passantino. From what I could gather, Bobulinski had been complaining to an associate that the Hunter story wasn't being fully told. When the Senate Homeland Security Committee released the findings from its investigation into Hunter Biden in September, Bobulinski was furious to learn that a Chinese investor who had stiffed their startup out of $10 million had given $5 million to another of Hunter's companies—one that Bobulinski didn't know existed. Bobulinski was convinced that cash infusion was supposed to be money for their company, that he had been double-crossed, and that the Bidens were corrupt. The person to whom Bobulinski kept complaining about Hunter had ties to Trump World and had put him in touch with Passantino.

Seated in Schwartz's house with half-finished glasses of red wine in front of them, Herschmann—who had taken on the Hunter portfolio during impeachment—and Passantino spent the next several hours telling a hair-raising tale of high-stakes international deal-making and influence-peddling in places like Kazakhstan, Luxembourg, and Oman. Toward the end, Bobulinski called in to the meeting, and we talked on speakerphone.

---

* Best was also one of the Trumpiest firms: Former Trump White House chief of staff Reince Priebus was president and chief strategist. Tory Maguire Sendek, a former White House director of scheduling, was managing director. Katie Hrkman, who oversaw White House fellows, was director of operations. Michael Ambrosini, a former chief's office director, was a principal, as was Alex Angelson, a former White House legislative liaison. Olivia Imhoff, a former intergovernmental affairs deputy in the White House, was a legislative assistant.

The scenes they described were something out of an international thriller.

There was Hunter, texting from a Ukrainian oligarch's yacht that had been anchored along the coast of the Mediterranean Sea during the Monaco Grand Prix. Emails outlined how the unlikely quintet of business partners—including two Bidens, a former Clinton administration official, the retired Oman station chief for British intelligence, and, of course, Bobulinski—consecrated their partnership with a round of handshakes in Bucharest, Romania. A Chinese billionaire named Ye Jianming, who, like the younger Biden, was a Gen-Xer with family connections and an appetite for risk, went missing in Beijing just as he was supposed to provide the new company its initial $5 million investment.

To an extraordinary new degree, the documents detailed Hunter's involvement at a stratospheric level of Chinese politics and business. He shopped for apartments in New York with Zang Jian Jun, the former executive director of CEFC China, one of the world's largest energy companies. Emails and texts referred to Hunter's previously unreported deals with Chinese investors in Kazakhstan and Oman. He and his uncle pulled strings to enroll Ye's daughter at The Spence School, a private, all-girls K–12 school in New York with a famously long wait list of applicants.

Those details, along with drafts of corporate documents, offered rare visibility into the creation of a closely held, multinational investment venture driven by a pair of ambitious risk-takers. One was the grandson of a former high-ranking Chinese Communist Party officer and long rumored to be a princeling of the People's Liberation Army. The other, an American who had spent much of his adult life drafting behind the last name of his famous father and wrestling with the demons from the middle name he went by, the one he shared with his mother. Neilia Hunter Biden and his baby sister were killed in a 1972 car accident that the two-year-old Hunter survived. The tale of Hunter's pursuits in China was intriguing and offered a glimpse into the embryonic stages of high-stakes deal-making between business executives from the world's two largest economic powers. But that wasn't the story they were pitching. These conservative operatives wanted a tale showing that Joe Biden himself knew more about his son's dealings than he let on and was taking a cut of the action.

Their best evidence was a document drafted by James Gilliar, a former MI6 officer, that suggested a 10 percent cut of the business should be held by

Hunter for "the big guy." It was clear after reading all the messages that Gilliar was referring to Joe Biden, who had long denied any knowledge of Hunter's international deals. It was intriguing. But it wasn't proof that Biden was lying. The document hadn't come from either Hunter or his uncle, nor was there any mention of "the big guy" in the final agreement. That document was worth a question to the Biden campaign, but their denial was easy to predict.

Hunter's messages to the investment group showed how he repeatedly asserted his importance to the group and referred to the family legacy he was putting on the line. But that reflected more on him, not his father. Hunter argued with his business partners for terms that would allow him to withdraw cash from the new company in one text exchange.

"My chairman gave an emphatic no," Hunter wrote.

Another partner, Rob Walker, then texted Bobulinski to explain that Hunter often referred to Joe Biden as his "chairman." Interesting, yes. But far from a smoking gun.

Bobulinski then recalled a dinner with Joe Biden at the Beverly Hilton that left him with the clear impression the former vice president was aware of the deal. But Bobulinski couldn't recall anything specific, other than Joe Biden asking about his family and thanking him for his military service. Bobulinski had been told by the other family member involved in the deal—Joe's brother, James Biden—not to talk business during dinner. Bobulinski believed that was proof—but of what, it was never clear.

After hearing all of this, my first instinct was that Bobulinski was probably a legitimate businessman who wasn't lying. And if he and his records checked out, then I could pitch a Hunter-in-China story. I told my hosts that it could take weeks to vet the documents, report the story, and then put it through the *Journal's* rigorous editing process. I warned them that if it was a hit on Joe Biden they were looking for, these documents didn't show that. If they disagreed, they should pitch it to another news outlet.

To my surprise, they agreed. My newspaper's rigorous editing process was exactly what they wanted.

My sources wanted the imprimatur of the *Journal* on any story about Hunter Biden's dealings. For the past two years, mainstream media outlets, including the *Journal*, had found little more than innuendo when it came to

Joe Biden's involvement in Hunter's pursuits. My informants feared that providing these documents to a friendly publication like Breitbart News or the *New York Post* would only create the same doubts about the story's legitimacy.

We finished the meeting with a passionate discussion that the documents and conversations would remain off the record unless the *Journal* decided to pursue and publish a story. I was wary of the deal, fearful they would publicly blame me if we agreed to pursue a story and then, for any number of legitimate reasons, instead decided not to proceed. My one stipulation was that these men also had to agree to the same off-the-record deal—and that it would be null and void if anyone in the room talked about our meeting or the fact that the *Journal* was looking into this story. I knew the *Journal* would want to do its own reporting and fact-checking before deciding what sort of story, if any, it had. And I didn't want to be constrained by an off-the-record agreement if anyone in Trump World found out about the meeting and tried to use it against me.

Everyone unequivocally agreed.

But those professional niceties would all blow up in a matter of days.

———

I brought the tip back to the paper's editors and made them the same pitch I had promised Bobulinski's crew. I advised that the reporting was unlikely to result in a quick, direct hit on Joe Biden. And if we were interested in a story on Hunter's dealings in China, that tale might be better suited for our reporters who had already been focused on that issue. By Monday, the editors had tapped James Areddy, who had written extensively on U.S.-China business, including Hunter's previous pursuits; and Andy Duehren, who had reported on the recent Senate Homeland Security Committee report and was pursuing some loose ends in that investigation.

But two days later, well after 10:00 p.m. on a Wednesday, my cell phone buzzed with a call from Steve Bannon. Darth Bannon. The nation's arsonist in chief. The Great Manipulator, according to an iconic *Time* magazine cover early in the administration.

Of course I answered.

"Steve!"

"What the fuck are you up to?" he responded, dispensing with any salutations or small talk. His voice was aggressive but also a little shaky. He was clearly under pressure.

"Your name is being bandied about by some crazy guy at the White House who says you're leading a thirty-man team at the *Wall Street Journal*, and you have some massive article about Hunter that's going to be on the front page on Monday," Bannon continued.

"Goddamn it," I responded.

While I had been receiving Biden family business records from one of Trump's White House attorneys and another lawyer working with Trump's campaign, there was an almost identical operation underway from the president's attorney, Rudy Giuliani, and Bannon. Giuliani and Bannon were pushing many of the same documents—and as it turned out, all the records on Hunter's entire laptop—to the *New York Post*, which, like the *Journal*, happened to be another newspaper asset of News Corp.

When the *Post* published its story on October 14, both sides were stunned to find out about the other.

"That was a bit of a surprise, even though Rudy had been working on it for a month," one senior campaign official said.

Two parallel, covert operations within the same campaign revealed in tragic detail how little coordination existed within Trump World. Top White House aides were barely talking to the campaign. Campaign officials ignored the Republican National Committee. The president seemed to be talking to everyone and agreeing with each side along the way. It was chaos as an operating principle. Trump encouraged rivalries all around him, and this was the result. Bannon had so many enemies in the White House, there was no way he was making sure they were aware of what he was up to. Rudy thought the campaign's attorneys were fools. Stepien, who had told friends that running the campaign was like trying to land a plane without wings, now described it as an aircraft with its engines on fire.

The competing Hunter psyops teams also reflected a broader rift in the conservative world about weaponizing the media to win elections. It was an argument happening inside Trump World, inside the conservative wing of the

House Republicans, and in other corners of conservatism across the country: how much to talk to just their own voters versus how much to try to win over a more even-minded middle.

For Schwartz and Passantino, another headline about Hunter in the conservative press was another drop in the bucket at a time when Trump needed a game-changer. They didn't care if the *Journal* wrote the exact story they wanted—and to be clear, sources never dictate the stories we write. They wanted the *Journal*'s trustworthy brand to signal there was something here worth reading and hoped it would force the rest of the media ecosphere to pay attention.

Bannon, meanwhile, believed in pumping as much electricity as possible into the conservative base to activate an army of talk-radio-listening zealots who would walk through a brick wall on Election Day to vote for the president. The former chairman of Breitbart News, Bannon had never considered pitching the Hunter story to the *Journal*; he knew he could never get the story he wanted there.

He almost couldn't convince the *Post*.

The first whispers of Hunter's laptop came in late 2019, during the impeachment hearing in the House. In the hearing's anteroom, Republican lawmakers and their aides passed around an email written in a bizarre font from someone claiming that Hunter's laptop had been left at a repair shop in Delaware. The FBI confiscated the computer, but the shop owner had copied the hard drive, according to the email. The most visible pro-Trump Republicans during impeachment—John Ratcliffe, Jim Jordan, Devin Nunes, and others breathlessly defending Trump on Fox News and the conservative One America News Network—were already receiving hundreds of wild-eyed emails from viewers every day who were seeing secret messages in their Cheerios. The Hunter laptop email raised eyebrows, but that was it. It was dismissed as an outlandish idea and given little thought.

"No one was excited about it," said one aide who was part of those discussions.

The story went like this: In April 2019, a man who identified himself as Hunter Biden walked into a computer repair shop in Wilmington, Delaware—the Biden family hometown—with three laptops, all with various degrees of liquid damage. The store owner, J. P. Mac Isaac, was never sure it was, in fact, Hunter Biden: Mac Isaac was legally blind. But the person who identified himself as Hunter told Mac Isaac which was the most critical laptop out of the set. And after assessing all three machines, Mac Isaac determined that the most important MacBook was the one that required the most attention. The person filled out a work order, left, and never returned to pick up the machine.

When Hunter Biden's name emerged a few months later as part of Trump's impeachment inquiry, Mac Isaac turned to his father, Steve Mac Isaac, a former Air Force colonel who was living in retirement in New Mexico. Mac Isaac consulted with his friends from the Air Force and eventually notified the FBI about the laptop. According to the Mac Isaac timeline, the FBI showed up at the computer store in December 2019 and confiscated the computer. But J. P. Mac Isaac had made a backup copy just in case he needed it. And when the laptop never surfaced during the impeachment proceedings, the Mac Isaac bunch grew concerned that perhaps the FBI had kept it from the president.

"J.P. fears for his life," Dennis Haugh, a 1973 graduate of the U.S. Air Force Academy, told congressional staffers in June.

They emailed Republicans again in the summer of 2020, and again the email was flagged by Republican aides, but lawmakers only shook their heads.

But this time they also emailed Giuliani, who had sharpened the president's focus on Hunter's foreign dealings in the first place.

Giuliani, whom Trump once referred to as "probably the greatest crime fighter over the last fifty years," only happened upon the laptop by chance, according to Giuliani's attorney, Robert Costello. A longtime friend of Giuliani's, Costello was hired in November 2019 to represent Giuliani amid congressional investigations into his friend's business dealings and interactions in Ukraine, which led to Trump's impeachment. In August 2020—on a whim, as Costello described it to me—he asked Giuliani's assistant to keep an eye out for any strange political tips coming into the email boxes for Giuliani's various companies. Costello had a couple of dozen emails within a few days, including one from J. P. Mac Isaac.

Costello said he received a copy of the files and contacted Fox News, which declined the story. Giuliani then brought in Bannon, who took it to the *Daily Mail*. They passed, too, but promised to be the first to match whatever outlet broke the news. The *New York Post* showed some interest, but it took two weeks to convince them, infuriating Costello in the process.

"We went to a lot of places," Costello told me. "Everybody was afraid to touch it."

A *Post* reporter visited Costello's home on October 4, spending the day going through all the documents. When the newspaper agreed to write a story, Giuliani handed over a copy of the drive on October 11, two days after I had met with Passantino and Schwartz and spoke on the phone with Bobulinski.

On October 14, the *New York Post* splashed a screaming headline across the front page: BIDEN SECRET E-MAILS.

Giuliani and Bannon thought they'd scored.

But the story about Hunter's water-damaged MacBook not only failed to catch on with the mainstream press, the world's biggest social media companies actively warned readers that the details hadn't been verified and limited the article's distribution on their platforms. The *New York Post*'s mishandling of the story—the reporters hadn't reached out to the Biden campaign for comment on some of the most salacious aspects—allowed Democrats to play the victim card, including Adam Schiff, the Democratic chairman of the House Intelligence Committee, who said it was all part of a years-long disinformation campaign from the Kremlin.

On Monday, October 12, a post-Covid Trump returned to the trail. He would hold at least one of his signature political rallies on twenty-one of the final twenty-two days of the campaign.

From the stage, Trump immediately developed a new bit. He portrayed himself as possessed with a sort of pandemic superpower: He'd battled the disease and beat back coronavirus—and now he was immune!

"I feel so powerful," Trump told thousands of people at Orlando Sanford International Airport.

Trump had his health, yes. But the campaign was falling apart as the president continued to make the race about himself instead of Biden. At each rally, he'd air out all the problems plaguing his campaign, drawing attention to the white suburban women fleeing his side and the scores of seniors scared off by his refusal to take the pandemic seriously. Instead of working to win these voters back, Trump played the role of political prognosticator, verbalizing his worst nightmare about the abject embarrassment that would overwhelm him if he lost to Biden.

Trump would never let on how sick he'd become from coronavirus.

"I didn't love it," was as much as he'd concede.

Instead, he continued to minimize the pandemic from the rally stage.

"It's going to peter out," he said at a North Carolina campaign rally on October 15, just a day before the number of Covid cases in the United States topped 8 million.

He was infuriated to find out that the nation's most prominent newspapers had refused to travel with him on *Air Force One* for most of that first week because the president, and his staff, continued flagrantly flouting safety protocols and shunned face masks, even amid the ongoing outbreak inside the White House.

Trump was so frustrated by his team's handling of his coronavirus diagnosis that he started pestering advisers and donors about what they thought about Stepien and Jason Miller. Top Republicans were petrified that Trump was considering firing his campaign manager and communications strategist in the race's final days.

With that mindset, Trump awoke in his Las Vegas hotel on Monday, October 19—just fifteen days before the election—and decided to deliver an impromptu pep talk to his team. But the actual intent was to push his message into the media. He told Stepien to make sure the call-in number was leaked to the press.

At 10:50 a.m. in Washington, Tim Murtaugh, the campaign's communications director, quickly texted a couple of dozen other reporters and me.

"Having an all-staff call at 11:00 AM. POTUS will speak to the entire staff."

Stepien introduced Trump with his best attempt at positivity and assuredness. Yet his voice was shaky as he stumbled over his words.

"I've never been more confident than we, every single one of us, is right now that we're going to win this campaign in fifteen days—we are going to win this race," Stepien said.

Stepien sounded like he was trying to talk himself into his prediction. He handed the call over to Trump, who was off and running for the next twenty-five minutes.

Trump immediately complained about a "false narrative" in the media. He denied any dissension in the ranks. He reaffirmed his support for Stepien, Miller, and Ronna. He denied a report that morning that he might fire Meadows after the campaign.

And, oh yes, the campaign. Trump grumbled twice about the *New York Times* not calling him more often before finally getting to the supposed point of this meeting.

"They said, 'Would you like to be on the call?' " Trump said. "I said, 'Yeah, I'd like to be on the call.' And this is all I'm telling you: We're gonna win. I wouldn't have said that three weeks ago. Three weeks ago, two weeks ago. I don't know. I wouldn't have said it. It was tougher for me."

Trump's enthusiasm was jarring. But he was just getting warmed up. He complained about a story from the *Atlantic* that at that point was forty-six days old. He said he had been losing the 2016 race until the very last day.

Trump had mentioned earlier in the call that Hunter's laptop was "a criminal enterprise" and complained that only the *New York Post* had written about it. He suggested that everyone in the media was pulling for the Democratic nominee, whom Trump compared to "a piece of wood." And then he was off on another tangent.

But when he returned to his obsession with the Biden family corruption, Trump seemed to remember something he'd been told.

"Joe Biden has a scandal coming up that's going to make him almost an impotent candidate," he teased. "This scandal is so big."

Trump said he'd known about the *Post*'s Hunter story ahead of time and claimed responsibility for providing the information to the newspaper. He again complained that more news outlets hadn't picked up the story. He complained again about the *New York Times* and said the corruption at that newspaper was rivaled only by that at the *Washington Post*—then recalled reading a *Washington Post* story that morning about Democrats "getting a little bit scared."

"And the *Wall Street Journal*," Trump continued—my eyes widened at the mention of my employer—"is working on a very, very important piece, which should be very good, actually. But the *Wall Street Journal*, I never thought they treat us good. But the economy is good. We have built up our economy again. And it's the biggest thing for us to discuss is the economy."

Then Trump was off on another stream-of-consciousness. Before the call was over, he would declare that Americans were tired of hearing about Covid, that Fauci was a disaster and an idiot, and that the only thing keeping him from raising more campaign cash was his reluctance to sell out the American people.

To Trump, it was a casual, off-the-cuff mention about a story he'd heard we were reporting. And as I scrambled to track down what had happened, the answer seemed like a bad game of telephone: just about all of my sources blamed someone else for telling at least one fellow Trump World ally, who had then told at least one more person, until the breach finally reached the president himself.

Later, the people who were in a position to tell Trump about our reporting would claim that someone, seeking to feed good news to the president at the moment with little consideration of the consequences, simply told Trump that the *Wall Street Journal* had something big on the Bidens almost ready for publication. Someone on his campaign had teased Trump, and now he was doing the same thing to the campaign staff and political reporters at every major news outlet in the country. In short, Trump had merely repeated out loud everything he knew.

But Trump's passing mention of the story was about to cause an enormous amount of trouble in my world. I had emailed our team as the words fell from Trump's mouth, and editors phoned me before the campaign call was over. Senior officials from the White House blew up my phone, trying to connect the dots.

But at the moment, I was less concerned about how it had leaked out than about what it meant: We were screwed.

An already tricky story about the son of the Democratic presidential nominee just days before the election had suddenly become even more challenging. We'd be accused of carrying Trump's water if we wrote it. We'd be accused of burying a kill shot on Biden if we spiked it. And neither accusation would be correct. The editors, to their credit, told the reporters to put the politics aside, continue reporting the story, and let the journalism stand on its own.

———

The president blurting out the storyline had also increased pressure on Schwartz, Passantino, and Herschmann to deliver. My earlier warning about the *Journal's* rigorous editing process no longer meant anything. By Tuesday, Herschmann was back digging through Bobulinski's documents in search of a silver bullet. Passantino tried to calm Bobulinski, who was sure his life was in danger and had retreated to a safe house.

On Wednesday, Trump's team coordinated with Senate Republicans, who wrote emails to Bobulinski and the other business partners involved in Hunter's project, referencing documents that had been released as part of the *New York Post's* now ongoing series on Hunter's laptop, and asking for copies of all records related to the business venture. Bobulinski was the only investor who responded.

On Thursday, the morning of the second and final presidential debate in Nashville, Homeland Security Committee chairman Ron Johnson and Finance Committee chairman Chuck Grassley announced that they had received Bobulinski's records and would speak with him for an informal interview on Friday.

After all, Bobulinski couldn't speak to them any sooner. He had an important date on Thursday.

———

Trump arrived in Nashville more than six hours before his final debate with Joe Biden. But not for debate prep. Trump hadn't bothered with much debate prep this time. Instead, it was for a fundraiser at the JW Marriott Nashville. The event attracted Kid Rock, country music singer Lee Greenwood, and former PGA champ John Daly, wearing jeans, a white golf shirt, and a blazer designed to look like an American flag. But after the fundraiser, Trump's team planned a surprise press conference, featuring none other than Tony Bobulinski.*

Ivanka and other family members wandered in and out of the fundraiser but mostly waited in a penthouse room with other White House and campaign staff, as well as Passantino and Herschmann.

---

* When Jason Miller told Trump about Bobulinski's surprise appearance, the president immediately thought of the 2016 debate when he invited me and a few other reporters to watch a few minutes of debate prep—only to spring on us several women who had accused his opponent's spouse, Bill Clinton, of sexual misconduct. "This is kinda like when you guys brought the women to debate in 2016?" Trump asked Miller in Nashville. "Kinda," Miller told him. "Okay," Trump said. "Go for it."

"This Hunter stuff we've got," Passantino told some of the others in the room. "It's a bombshell!"

Bobulinski was still on his way in from California, and Trump aides found themselves troubleshooting a pair of only-in-Trump-World problems. The first was that Bobulinski had boarded the plane with a suit but no dress shirt.

"What's he wearing?" Jason Miller asked Passantino.

"Well, he's wearing his suit," Passantino said.

"Who the fuck puts on a suit but not a dress shirt?" Miller said.

Miller was annoyed to be stuck with the supremely stupid task of figuring out Bobulinski's neck size and sleeve length and then finding a field staffer to hustle to the department store to buy a button-down shirt. But that irritation was quickly eclipsed by a much more urgent issue as Meadows sauntered up to Miller.

"Hey, so, um, do you know about a private plane flying in?" Meadows asked.

The White House chief explained that Nashville was effectively a no-fly zone while Trump was on the ground. The military threatened to blast Bobulinski out of the sky if his plane didn't immediately turn around.

"So these guys are telling the truth?" Meadows asked. "They're coming to see you?"

"Yes, it's Bobulinski," Miller said.

"Uuuuugghhh," Meadows said, rubbing his temples. "Let me go see what I can do."

The White House cleared the air restrictions. Bobulinski landed in Nashville and found two black Suburbans waiting to drive him and his entourage—including bodyguards and attorneys—back to the Marriott where a selection of dress shirts awaited Trump World's hero of the moment. He picked a white shirt, which fit nicely. But the suit jacket he brought was too tight to button.

Miller had pushed to have Trump join Bobulinski at the news conference, but no one could agree. Farah suggested a guerrilla-style news conference where Trump and Bobulinski would cross paths in front of the hotel, and the president could spend a few minutes with him before continuing on his way. No one knew what Bobulinski would say, so they decided not to put any campaign banners behind him for the news conference. The internal debate continued until thirty minutes before it was set to start. In the end, Bobulinski was sent into the media room mostly on his own.

"Ladies and gentlemen, Tony Bobulinski!" Miller announced.

Bobulinski walked into a conference room that looked like every other Marriott conference room across the country: beige walls, nylon carpet with a geometric pattern, and shades of blue and gray. What followed was equally lackluster. Bobulinski wore a confused look for much of it, his right eyebrow almost constantly raised, and his nose and mouth puckered like he'd just eaten something sour. He had three mobile phones, which contained all of the Hunter Biden messages and that he had carried into the hotel in a toiletry bag. Bobulinski had a statement to read, but with no lectern set up, he asked the media for a chair, which he used as a table on which to set down the iPhones and read his statement. Miller slid the chair into the shot, then retreated again to his seat in the corner.

Bobulinski's short statement was the Wikipedia version of his dealings with Hunter Biden. He said he'd had a dispute over money with Hunter, that Joe Biden knew more about his son's business pursuits than he had admitted, and that he planned to tell everything he knew to a Senate committee the next day. Bobulinski answered two questions and then decided that was enough and left the room. CNN and MSNBC didn't carry him live, and when Miller returned to the team's penthouse suite, not one network was discussing the spectacle.

"That was amazing," Miller told the group.

———

In 2008, by the time Barack Obama and John McCain met onstage for their second debate in the Curb Event Center at Belmont University, the economy was in free fall as bankruptcies threatened or had already taken down the nation's largest banks and markets collapsed. Congress forked over $700 billion to let the Treasury bail out AIG and auto companies and restore credit markets. NBC's Tom Brokaw opened the event by taking stock of what had happened since the previous debate.

"Since you last met at Ole Miss twelve days ago, the world has changed a great deal, and not for the better," Brokaw said. "We still don't know where the bottom is at this time."

Twelve years later, Trump and Biden took the stage in the same arena at the same university for a debate hosted by the same network. A historic crisis was once again unfolding, and, just like back in 2008, it had escalated since the first debate. A few days before Nashville, on October 15, there were 60,000 new Covid cases reported in a single day in the United States.

"The country is heading into a dangerous new phase," NBC's Kristen Welker said to open the debate. "And since the two of you last shared a stage, sixteen thousand Americans have died from Covid."

Trump didn't want to talk about Covid. He was eager to go on the attack with the Bobulinski bombshell in his pocket, a pivot he was able to make before the two men had been onstage for twenty minutes. But Trump couldn't quite land it. For one, he couldn't remember Bobulinski's name—he'd referred to him as "Bo" backstage. He hadn't taken the time to understand the details, so his accusations ended up wildly off base and challenging for an average viewer to follow. Running against Hillary Clinton four years earlier had masked that shortcoming of Trump's propensity to attack in tabloid headlines. She and Biden had spent about the same amount of time in public service, but Clinton's controversies had been amplified and looped on repeat. Voters could follow Trump's jumbled word association with Clinton much more readily.

"You were getting a lot of money from Russia—they were paying you a lot of money, and they probably still are—but now, with what came out today, it's even worse," Trump said on the debate stage that night. "All of the emails—the emails, the horrible emails—and the kind of money that you were raking in, you and your family. And Joe, you were vice president when some of this was happening, and it should have never happened. And I think you owe an explanation to the American people. Why is it somebody just had a news conference a little while ago? Who was essentially supposed to work with you and your family? But what he said was damning. And regardless of me, I think you have to clean it up and talk to the American people."

The attack was muddled, at best, and still Trump wouldn't let it go. He leveled another round of accusations against Biden over his son's business dealings in Ukraine but missed the target again.

In a holding room with other staffers watching the debate, Bossie stomped across the floor.

"Fucking Jesus Christ!" he shouted.

Time was ticking away.

Back onstage, Biden insisted that he'd done nothing wrong concerning Ukraine.

"The guy who got in trouble in Ukraine was this guy," he said, extending his right index finger toward Trump without breaking eye contact with Welker. "Trying to bribe the Ukrainian government to say something negative about me, which they would not do, and did not do because it never ever, ever happened."

Trump opened his mouth to laugh but seemed to gasp for air instead. He slowly shook his head and gazed at the lectern in front of him. His mouth fell open. But he quickly closed it, then lifted his head and peered into the distance with an unfocused gaze.

The next day, the *Journal* published its story on Bobulinski and the Bidens. Andy Duehren and James Areddy, a fellow reporter, had combed through all the text messages and documents. They reported that the venture—set up in 2017 after Joe Biden had left the vice presidency and before his presidential campaign—never received proposed funds from the Chinese company or completed any deals, according to people familiar with the matter.

"Corporate records reviewed by the *Wall Street Journal*," they wrote, "show no role for Joe Biden."

But Trump remained undeterred. After the Nashville debate—during the final eleven days of the campaign—Trump referenced Hunter Biden sixty-eight times at rallies, while giving interviews, and on Twitter.

"Where's Hunter?" Trump asked again and again. He posed that exact question to voters in nineteen cities across eight battleground states during that time.

"It's treason, or whatever you want to call it," Trump said on the last day of the race. "We caught the whole thing. The son—where's Hunter? Where's Hunter?"

16

Final Stretch

"Are we going to win, Corey?... I'll never speak to you again."
—*Campaign rally, Londonderry, New Hampshire, October 25, 2020*

Days until Election: 37

At the height of his twenty-nine-month run as campaign manager, Brad thought his unlikely ascendancy onto the mainstage of national politics would end with immortality in history books, or maybe at least a feature-length documentary. Instead, it was more like an episode of *Cops* when Brad—shirtless, shoeless, and hapless, with a beer in his hand—was tackled to the ground by police outside his Fort Lauderdale home and detained for a psychiatric evaluation.

News accounts at the time reported that Brad's wife, Candice, had called 911 in the midst of a days-long fight. They'd both been drinking, there were guns in the house, and the arguing had continued to escalate. Candice told dispatchers she thought Brad might hurt himself.

What wasn't known at the time was the source of the argument: Trump. Brad had been devastated by his demotion, and Candice thought her husband had been scapegoated. She was already furious at the Trumps for her husband's sake. But the final straw came that last weekend in September, when Brad shared something even more stunning: Jared wanted to bring him back inside, and Brad was going to fly to Washington the next day.

By that point, Jared had decided that Stepien's attempt to rebuild the campaign's polling and data operation had backfired. Jared thought the strategy Stepien and Jason Miller implemented to purchase TV ads wasn't precise enough in its targets, and he was concerned about the corrosiveness between the campaign and the Republican National Committee. Those were all areas on which he and Brad had been aligned for years.

In his diminished role, Brad had started to engage with the campaign again and sent an email to Jared, Stepien, and Miller at the end of August that analyzed the Biden campaign's TV buys for September and October, compared them to the Trump campaign's plans, and determined that Biden was acting more like the 2016 Trump campaign, while Trump's reelection bid more closely resembled Hillary Clinton's four years prior. Brad also sent his memo to Eric and Lara Trump, Don Junior, and Ken Kurson, the New Jersey strategist and Kushner family friend—and separately forwarded it to Ronna later.

Brad praised Biden's team for "buying deep." The Democrat would have ads in seventy-five media markets by the fall, and those buys would be complemented with spots on national networks that skewed toward female and Black viewers. Brad complimented the Biden team for running spots—thirty-six unique ads by his count—that focused on the same theme but varied in length and imagery based on which voters they were targeting.

Brad noted that Biden had been uncontested on local radio for weeks, except for a small buy the Trump campaign had made in New Mexico. The Biden team was also targeting addressable television, which was one of the under-the-radar Trump campaign tactics in 2016. The emergence of televisions and cable boxes with their own IP addresses had enabled campaigns and other advertisers to direct specific messages to specific types of viewers, and that kind of surgical marketing was still developing ahead of the 2020 campaign; in 2019, Gary Coby, Trump's digital director, had met with executives from some cable providers to help build their advertising tools—but the campaign halted those purchases once Brad was demoted.

"Biden's buying team is significantly ahead of Clinton's at this point in 2016 in terms of TV buying execution," Brad wrote in his email. "It actually looks a lot like what we did in Sept/Oct of 2016, and they seem to be executing many of the ideas that we had been working on for the last 18+ months."

Brad suggested changes that would make Trump's advertising more efficient by targeting individual voters instead of broader media markets, and he strongly recommended starting a radio advertising campaign focused on Black and Hispanic stations.

A few weeks later, Jared brought him to Washington for a campaign-wide media summit.

Everyone seated around the conference table on September 22 inside campaign headquarters theoretically played for the same team. But there was no denying the competitive atmosphere as tension rippled through the room.

Jared and Hope were there from the White House. Larry Weitzner, the campaign's lead ad maker, was at the table, along with representatives from National Media, a Virginia-based media-buying company that helped the campaign place its ads. Gary Coby was in attendance, as was Stepien, who left partway through the meeting.

Brad brought a high level of energy. He'd stayed up late the night before with his team focusing on things that excited him: integrated marketing strategies, and incorporating connected TV and video-on-demand. He and Coby geeked out like they had in the good old days. His pitch was high-level, with lots of the corporate jargon that Jared liked. Jason Miller's presentation was detailed, but focused on how many gross ratings points he would buy on specific days. Brad talked about being more efficient by targeting audiences instead of media markets and about increasing flexibility by setting aside pots of money for last-minute openings that networks often tried to unload at discounted rates. After the meeting, Jared asked Brad to come back and oversee the campaign's digital and TV advertising operation. Brad didn't know whether to punch him or hug him. He felt vindicated, but also like he was being asked to do the exact job he'd had taken away from him—but without the campaign manager title.

Candice's reaction wasn't quite as nuanced when Brad returned home and told her the news.

"Why the fuck would you go do this after they did this to you?" she shouted at him. "They're going to use you, throw you out again, you're gonna be more depressed."

They argued and drank and shouted until police arrived at their Fort Lauderdale home on September 27, a Sunday evening. The next day, Brad sat in the psychiatric ward of Broward Health Medical Center—an involuntary three-night stay and evaluation required under Florida law. He watched the video of himself getting leveled by the cop playing on a loop on national television. He had an iced tea, an antidepressant pill, and no telephone. Some of the other patients recognized him.

In some ways, it felt like a nice and needed vacation.

═══

Days until Election: 19

With Brad out of commission, the campaign had made some adjustments to the ad-buying operation, but gaping holes still existed. Stepien could barely bring himself to speak with Ronna, who was openly resented by campaign aides and White House staffers jealous of her access to Trump. The campaign's data operation was still having problems, and Gary Coby complained to other senior members of the team that he couldn't get a clear direction on where to spend tens of millions in digital advertising.

"I've got $65 million to spend on digital, and I don't know whether to put it in Pennsylvania, Michigan, Wisconsin, and at what levels," Coby said. "What's our first path, what's our second path, what's our third path?"

The campaign was complaining about money problems, but declined $55 million from the RNC to spend on television. The cash was the maximum amount the party could spend directly on behalf of Trump. Ronna thought the campaign's advertising was overly aggressive and too loud to win the kind of suburban moms and senior citizens whom Trump needed to bring back into the fold. If they were going to hand over that kind of money, she wanted to help shape the new spot. When the campaign said no thanks, she called Trump and told him she was going to do it herself.

The next day, Jared called Katie Walsh and asked her to take over the role he'd wanted for Brad.

"Bill is locked in decision paralysis," Jared told her.

One of Jared's go-to moves for moments of high stress was often to throw bodies at the problem, but choosing Walsh showed just how limited his options were. Walsh was a veteran and well-connected Republican operative, but her relationship with Trump had corroded so badly that she was forbidden from ever being in the same room with him. She and Stepien had been rivals since their blowout fights during the 2016 campaign.

But in the Reagan Room of the party headquarters, Jared ordered Stepien to start working with her.

Walsh's first move was to bring in Deep Root, a Virginia analytics company that had been crossing the RNC's voter scores with their own audience files to create a path for the campaign to reach the voters they were seeking. But Stepien had no faith in the RNC voter scores or in Deep Root, which the campaign had previously stopped using.

He didn't trust Ronna. And he didn't trust much of anything Brad had built before he left. The skepticism was warranted, but the RNC complained that none of the new regime ever asked for help. Instead, Stepien, Clark, and Jason Miller mostly kept their own counsel. The result was blunt-force advertising. Instead of targeting spots where they could find persuadable voters—Latino men thirty-five and older, for instance, or rural white men who rarely voted but liked Trump's message—ads were aimed at all voters, eighteen years and older, across entire media markets. Several Trump ads ended up airing on *Gunsmoke* and *Bonanza*.

"We needed to call time out to figure out how we were going to target people," one campaign official said. "Targeting them with bad data is worse than targeting them in a more old-school way."

The result was that the campaign started buying a certain number of ads per week—requesting, for example, forty-nine spots on Fox News in a single week with no explanation. The amount of money spent on Washington, D.C. cable increased, which seemed to others on the team an obvious attempt to catch Trump's attention instead of the district's voters, who in 2016 had overwhelmingly supported Clinton.

Other ad buys were influenced by media coverage. The campaign wanted to avoid any stories that they were pulling ads from states.

The RNC's spot, aimed at winning back seniors, struck a soft tone more akin to a pharmaceutical commercial than the campaign's more aggressive ads, and targeted Arizona, Michigan, and three other states. The party also put up another ad in the final days of the campaign that highlighted the pandemic, and featured a woman wearing a face mask standing at a voting machine as she mulled her ballot.

Days until Election: 15

In the summer of 2016, Randal Thom went into cardiac arrest at his home in southwestern Minnesota. The prostitute who was with him at the time seized the opportunity to steal his van. But whenever Randal would retell the story, he'd always smile wide and make sure to emphasize that at least she called 911 before she snatched his keys.

Trouble always seemed to follow Randal, but that was also part of his charm. In high school, he was student council president, a star on the football team, homecoming king—and arguably the biggest pot dealer in Windom, Minnesota. His beloved Alaskan malamute, whom he'd named after the president, was shot dead by a neighbor. The gunman claimed self-defense, having reached his limit from the terror campaign Randal's dogs had unleashed on the neighborhood—killing a local goat, disappearing multiple chickens, and once biting a passerby badly enough to require medical attention. Randal remained convinced his malamute's death was an assassination.

He'd also paid steep prices for his decisions. Randal had survived a plane crash about twenty years earlier that had killed one of his brothers, who had been piloting the aircraft. The accident had landed him an insurance payout—but he then spent much of the money on drugs, increasingly neglecting his family. His wife and two small children left him. Except for a few instances, they never spoke to Randal again. He was repeatedly arrested for theft and drug possession. He spent time behind bars.

Randal seemed to turn a corner in 2015 when he moved out to the country. He raised his dogs in peace and picked up some odd jobs from older siblings and their spouses. When he came home from his first Trump event that year, he seemed to find a new purpose.

"He had never really been politically active, so I remember him coming home very excited about Trump and telling everyone he's going to be the next president," said Randal's older brother Stan.

Randal started bumping into the same crew in line at Trump's campaign events in Iowa, and it was Randal who dubbed them the Front Row Joes. The rallies became the organizing principle in his life, and Trump fans loved him for it. Like Trump himself, all of Randal's past mistakes didn't matter to them. He hadn't impaired their lives with his bad decisions, and everyone liked his optimism. Randal's bedside manner wouldn't fit any typical definition of Midwestern Nice. He was loud. He was gruff. He had stories that never seemed to end. If female friends were annoyed with him, he'd ask if they were "on the rag" and erupt in a savage laugh at his joke. But he also instinctively welcomed newcomers like they were long-lost friends and was always the first to offer a warm smile and a cold beer. He took to social media like a Millennial, regularly sending links to Trump friends, posting updates on the Front Row Joes Facebook page, and checking in with people if he hadn't heard from them for too long. When Cindy Hoffman's mother died in 2017, she arrived at the gravesite to find Randal's red, white, and blue cowboy hat and a note: *In memory of your sweet mama. Love you Cindy, love the Front Row Joes.*

Cindy turned around, and—even though few people had attended the funeral—there was Randal, waiting for her at the burial. She started crying. And then she started laughing when Randal told her the first note he'd written before anyone had arrived had blown off the grass, under the casket, and into the six-foot hole below.

By 2020, family and friends were so encouraged by Randal's turnaround that they started helping finance his travel to Trump events. When the pandemic halted the campaign rallies, he went instead to the Trump boat parades that formed along the coast of Florida. The parades invigorated Randal, and the president. As Trump struggled to respond to the pandemic and close the gap with Biden, his aides made sure to route the president's Mar-a-Lago motorcade past the Trumpian armadas terrorizing the libs with loud country music and oversized Trump flags. Behind closed doors, too, Trump asked advisers if they had seen his followers' flotillas crowding waterways from the Great Lakes to the Gulf of Mexico. The president planned to attend a boat parade in southeastern Florida the second-to-last weekend of October with an elaborate display of showmanship even by Trump's standards. His campaign had drawn up plans for a floating landing pad for *Marine One*, but ultimately pulled the plug over Palm Beach County permitting issues.

The boat parade floated on. But it was the last Trump event Randal would attend.

On the afternoon of October 19, Randal had flown back to Minneapolis from Florida and was driving his Toyota minivan south on Highway 169. He was going too fast and started to swerve in and out of traffic. He clipped the back end of a 1994 Ford pickup, which then spun off the left side of the road, rolled over the guardrail, and landed on its roof. The sixty-seven-year-old driver was taken to the hospital, but he'd been wearing a seat belt and was released the next day. However, Randal refused to wear a seat belt, just like he had refused to wear a mask. The collision ejected him from the driver's seat and onto the highway, where he was crushed to death under his own minivan.

Alcohol was suspected, based on a witness's account of Randal's driving and the beer cans collected from the accident scene. But after an autopsy report didn't mention any alcohol in his blood, friends said the cans were probably from the cooler of beer he always kept in the van. Randal had also been in crippling back pain, long overdue for surgery related to a lingering injury from the plane crash, and he'd been given intravenous painkillers the previous day in Florida when the torment sent him to the hospital. But a friend didn't think he'd been given a prescription, and no pills were recovered on the scene. Some friends and family wondered if Randal had been texting and driving.

When police arrived on the scene, the battery-operated megaphone Randal used for his cheerleading routines for Trump crowds outside rallies had been powered on from the impact of the crash. It was blaring Lee Greenwood's patriotic country anthem "God Bless the USA," a staple of Trump rallies.

Hundreds of Trump flags had also burst from the minivan and fluttered down like confetti—shiny shades of red and white and blue—that now lay strewn across the highway. A patrolman picked up one of the flags and draped it over Randal.

Days until Election: 10

On October 24, Trump cast an early ballot at the Palm Beach County Library.

Trump had mailed in his primary ballot in August, but that wasn't an option after he'd spent the entire year warning about the dangers of voting by mail.

In May, he accused the "rogue" Michigan secretary of state of illegally sending millions of voters mail-in ballots for which they hadn't asked, but he was completely wrong. In June, he claimed that unnamed foreign countries would print millions of fraudulent mail ballots, without any evidence. In July, he promised that voting by mail would result in the "most inaccurate and fraudulent election in history"—and he called for the country to delay the election.

In August, he said on Fox News that Democrats were already "trying to steal the election" and that he planned to dispatch sheriffs, U.S. attorneys, and attorneys general to polling places—despite not possessing those powers. At his debate with Biden in September, Trump launched an extensive attack on mail-in voting that was teeming with falsehoods and misrepresentations.

From the debate stage in Cleveland, he accused Philadelphia election officials of improperly blocking his team from monitoring voters filling out mail ballots, even though state law gave his team no legal right to do so. He said a West Virginia mailman was selling ballots, without explaining that the case involved a postal worker—who pleaded guilty in July—switching several absentee ballot requests from Democrat to Republican.

"This is going to be a fraud like you've never seen," Trump said that night.

His team had begged him to stop. All of the claims were either baseless or wildly inaccurate. Plus, Republican state parties had spent years honing their vote-by-mail programs—including in Florida in 2016 when Wiles's hard-fought personal check from Trump paid for a program to remind vot-ers to return their mail-in ballots. But Trump wouldn't budge on his plan to demonize mail voting, so instead the campaign hoped a very public trip to an early voting location would help convince Republicans who had abandoned their mail ballots to start showing up at the polls.

The TV cameras captured Trump heading into the library but weren't allowed to follow him into the voting booth. Only his team and a few poll workers were inside when Trump arrived.

The president showed identification, received a ballot, and walked over to a plastic, pop-up voting booth. In the tiny booth, he spread his legs wide, hunched over with his elbows on the booth, and slipped a cheat sheet out from the inside pocket of his suit jacket to help him vote. The Palm Beach County ballot was multiple pages. Trump didn't want to be accused of tak-ing too long to vote, but he also didn't want to leave any questions blank. As Meadows circled the room and Stepien hovered nearby, Trump made his pick in each race, from president to sheriff to the Palm Beach Soil and Water Con-servation District Board of Supervisors.

Trump finally finished, slid his ballot into the privacy sleeve, and walked over to the voting machine. He fed the first page into the machine—the pres-ident who had very seriously and carefully filled out his ballot now wore a proud look on his face. He fed the second page into the machine.

But the third page wouldn't work. Trump glared at the machine and tried again. Nothing.

Wendy Sartory Link, the Palm Beach County elections supervisor, told the president there might be something wrong with the third page and offered him another ballot. Trump looked to his team and saw them nodding their heads. So he showed his identification again, received another ballot, and walked back to the voting booth to repeat his process.

He finished, slid the ballot into the sleeve, walked it back to the machine—and, once again the machine wouldn't accept it.

Link suggested trying a different machine, and Trump cast the final page of his ballot.

"Ha! I thought it was me for a minute!" he said to the poll workers, and then turned to his team. "I guess we're done here."

Days until Election: 9

As a young woman long before joining the Front Row Joes, Libby DePiero followed Trump more closely than she did politics. In the 1980s, her mother was especially fascinated with the dashing New York tabloid denizen. The mother-daughter duo spent one New Year's Eve at the Plaza Hotel when Trump owned it. They visited other Trump landmarks on their frequent trips to the city and daydreamed about moving into Trump Tower.

Libby became more interested in politics after the September 11 terrorist attacks and reconnected with her Christian faith. She married a Fox News fanatic, and she, too, was quickly hooked on conservative infotainment. By the time Trump announced his campaign, there was little doubt whom Libby would support. From her first chitchat with Trump at the Nashua Radisson to the 2020 primary night rally in Manchester, she'd attended fifty-eight Trump events in four years. She hoped to hit the century mark before November 3, but that goal vanished with the pandemic.

Libby hadn't been to a single Trump event in eight months when, with just nine days until Election Day, Trump returned to Manchester. It had been an agonizing dry spell. Her fellow Front Row Joes pressured her to travel to Tulsa and come float in the boat parades. But the pandemic had changed her calculus.

"It's like I'm a bad patriot because I'm wearing a mask," Libby said.

By October, the pressure got to her, and so Libby ventured out. The Trump rally was just a short drive from her Connecticut home, and she'd been so diligent about pandemic precautions that she made a plan. She started taking hydroxychloroquine, based on the president's touting of it as preventative medicine despite no proof. She would quarantine from her husband for two weeks after the rally, or at least until she could get a Covid test. And if her trial run panned out, maybe she could go to more rallies and partake in the final week of the campaign.

But as soon as she arrived at the rally at the Manchester airport, Libby realized she had made a mistake.

From the parking lot, she was crammed onto a bus that would shuttle her to the hangar for the event. After avoiding crowds for nearly the entire year, she felt uncomfortable packed in so closely with other people. About one-third of them weren't wearing masks.

Libby's friends had saved a seat for her up front, but the dense crowd was difficult to penetrate. In the commotion, Libby stepped on her shoelace and fell hard on the cement. Secret Service agents helped her to her feet. Her hip and tailbone were throbbing, but she refused medical attention. If she could walk, she thought, she could get to the front.

But the crowd was shoulder to shoulder across the hangar. Libby decided she was acting crazy. She wasn't going to get to the front, and it seemed silly to risk catching the virus in the middle of the crowd. So she walked to the opposite end of the hangar, where Trump supporters with service dogs or in wheelchairs were all in masks and socially distanced.

After watching nearly sixty rallies over four years from the front row, Libby spent her last one in the very back.

<hr>

Days until Election: 7

The weekly internal conference call run by Stepien, Clark, and Nick Trainer, the battleground strategy director, had just ended. And the flurry of text messages and sidebar calls immediately started:

Did that just happen?

The campaign's leadership used the call on October 27 to run through six different paths to victory on Election Day. The scenarios ranged from hitting exactly 270 electoral votes on one map, to a landslide victory with a total of 363 electoral votes. But it was the final scenario that drove the rest of the team crazy, which was a path that included winning the White House while losing Florida and North Carolina.

"What are these people smoking?" one campaign adviser fumed.

"The level of delusion is magnificent!" said another.

Trainer made clear that they believed Trump would win Florida. But what seemed inconceivable to others on the call was any scenario in which Trump could lose those Southern battleground states yet somehow win a slew of Midwestern states where Democrats traditionally had the advantage.

There were open questions about whether there was any strategy at all.

Ten days out, Trump had held a rally in Ohio, which had been a battleground for years but few believed Biden could win this cycle. In three days, Trump had another rally in Minnesota, which few outside of Trump, Jared, and Stepien thought Trump had a chance to win. Yet winning Minnesota was on three of their six scenarios. The team in Georgia was begging for more resources: more mail pieces to help persuade voters on the fence, a visit from Pence, a visit from a Trump kid—any Trump kid! All the requests had been denied, but maybe here was their answer: There was no scenario in the six in which Georgia was ever in doubt.

Inside the campaign, everyone seemed to have their own theory as to what the plan really was. One was that since the consulting firm owned by Stepien and Clark also had been working for the Minnesota Republican Senate candidate, Jason Lewis, maybe they were trying to bring Trump there in order to generate excitement for their other guy—a charge the two men disputed. But others countered that Trump himself had long believed that he would have won Minnesota in 2016 if he'd just done one more rally there. Some felt the campaign was just throwing darts at the board. Others believed it was a final, frantic Hail Mary pass in the final minutes of the game.

But after more than two years of chaos and in-fighting, the mistrust ran deep, and no one was willing to give anyone else the benefit of the doubt. At the RNC, Richard Walters suspected that Stepien and Clark were trying to undermine Ronna with a secretive process to rewrite the party rules. Stepien thought Brad had built the campaign almost exactly wrong. Everyone assumed Brad was taking an extra cut of campaign cash for himself, even though the president—and his family—could have investigated the issue to figure it out.

Stepien took input from all directions, one person after the next—Jared, Hope, Bossie—all claiming only they knew what the campaign should be doing. By the end, Stepien barely reacted anymore. Some wondered if he'd just checked out. But Trump's insistence on multiple mega-rallies a day—and his capacity to perform at each one—meant even more opportunities for debates over the schedule.

"Who the fuck made the decision to go to Nevada?" Corey had shouted on *Air Force One* a week prior.

And at the end of the day, no one in Trump World wanted to narrow the map. Trump wasn't dissimilar from other presidential candidates who thought they could win any state with enough time to persuade the voters. The difference was how firmly Trump insisted.

"Stepien had well-laid plans, and then the president goes and does something else," said one of Trump's outside advisers. "I'm not defending one or the other. But he had a principal who moves around the map and moves around the day just like he moves around a tweet button."

Two years earlier, when Trump political director Chris Carr was carving up the country into political regions and deciding where he should suggest placing battleground state directors and staff, it occurred to him that he should be prepared for these offices to remain open for the duration of the race. In 2016, Trump erupted when stories surfaced about the campaign pulling out of Virginia to reallocate those resources elsewhere. For Carr, there was something reassuring about that. He'd spent years building a field program based on the idea that Republican staff needed to be in key communities year-round to build the kind of relationships with volunteers that would pay dividends come Election Day.

In fact, Trump's final ten days of rallies in 2016 had been just as frantic as they were in 2020 and included stops in states such as Colorado, New Mexico, and Virginia—all places where Clinton would eventually clobber him.

So while the president may not have spent as much time as Carr did thinking about the Republican ground game, his campaign's political director had hit on a truism of Trumpism: Never, ever wave the white flag.

Days until Election: 2

In the final ten days of the race, Trump hosted thirty-three campaign rallies. Those events were spread across thirteen states, but mostly targeted in Pennsylvania (eight), Michigan (four), Wisconsin (four), and North Carolina (three). The campaign had gone back and forth for weeks over whether Pennsylvania or Michigan was most important. The original seventeen battleground states had been narrowed slightly to about a dozen and divided into three tiers in order to, ideally, guide decision-making on how to spend tens of millions of dollars in the final days and where to invest their most valuable resource—Trump's time.

But even after all the calculations, pondering, and tinkering, Trump stopped just once during those last ten days in Georgia, where his duel with Biden would be fought to a near draw and end in a defeat for the incumbent that ultimately would drive his Shakespearian descent into a postelection, voter-fraud delirium.

And even that lone visit almost never happened.

Trump's rally on November 1 in Rome, Georgia—an Appalachian mountain town nestled in the Republican-heavy corner of the state—wasn't added to the president's schedule until three days prior, and only after a barrage of phone calls to Trump from David Perdue, the Republican senator from Georgia. A former Dollar General chief executive and one of Trump's closest confidants in the Senate, Perdue was up for reelection and had grown increasingly concerned that both he and the president could lose. With less than a week left, early turnout was well below projections in Rome and the rest of northwest Georgia, where roughly four out of five voters consistently backed Republican candidates. Perdue's team didn't know exactly who or what to blame for the drag, but it didn't much matter in the moment. Perdue desperately needed Trump to inject some energy into that part of the state.

Perdue had long known that Georgia would be a slog for both candidates and had spent much of the year warning Trump World. But the pitch always fell flat. The predicament for Perdue—as well as Kelly Loeffler, Georgia's second Republican senator who was also on the November ballot—was that he needed to collect more than 50 percent of the vote to keep his seat and avoid a runoff in January. And the one certain way both Georgia senators could clear that threshold was if the president performed even better.* But Trump was too absorbed by his own race. Perdue's concern could never compete with that.

---

* The presidential candidates are usually the main driver of turnout in an election year, and 2020 was no different. In contested Senate races that year, Republican candidates who received more total votes than Trump almost all lost while those who underperformed him nearly all won.

The president knew that a simple plurality in his contest could capture the state's electoral votes, and he constantly reminded Perdue and other Georgia Republicans that he'd won the state comfortably in 2016. But Georgia was changing. The state had added more than 315,000 new inhabitants since 2016, a growth rate that was 60 percent faster than the national average. Perdue's team knew that the narrow, 1.4-point margin that had decided the Georgia governor's race in 2018 was a more accurate picture of the current political landscape than Trump's 5-point win just two years earlier. Georgia, in the course of a single presidential term, had become more politically competitive than even Florida—the predominant battleground in all five presidential elections in the twenty-first century, Georgia's southern neighbor, and the president's adopted home.

But even that stark point from Perdue hadn't landed. In the two years since the 2018 midterms, Perdue had watched as *Air Force One* flew over Georgia for nine campaign rallies in Florida, and then back north for ten rallies during that same time in North Carolina. Minnesota, where a Republican presidential candidate hadn't won since 1972, was targeted five times. Meanwhile, heading into the final weekend of the 2020 campaign, Georgia had hosted Trump for the same number of campaign rallies as Oklahoma: one.

The Perdue campaign had provided reams of polling and analytics to Trump World that were never disputed—just ignored. It was a confounding combination. The president's campaign never bothered to share any of its data with Perdue or his allies. Perdue's team worried that Trump viewed the need to compete in Georgia as a sign of his own electoral weakness instead of the state's changing political dynamics.

In fact, the Trump campaign had shelved most of its polling operation for the final months of the race. They were trying to cut costs, and had also started to focus more on analytics— tracking voters who had already returned their ballots and making inferences off of that. They didn't have projections to share until almost the end of the campaign, but even the campaign's modeling of Georgia was significantly off the mark.

It had taken more than six weeks, but Stepien's rebuilt data team was finally firing in the same direction during the first week of October. The shotgun marriage between Oczkowski and Skelly—whom Stepien had brought in to oversee the data operation—had surprisingly turned out to be a happy one. And the pair—with some assists from Fabrizio and the RNC—had delivered Trump World its first round of vote goals for each state. Using a mix of past election results, population changes, and consumer trends, vote goals were the total number of votes a campaign believed it would need to win each state. As Sasha Issenberg wrote in *The Victory Lab*, the 2012 book about the analytical revolution in modern politics, vote goals were a staple of any campaign plan—and usually among the initial documents that a general consultant or campaign manager drafted in the earliest days of the race.

For Trump, it had taken twenty-eight months into his twenty-nine-month reelection campaign, but he finally had his vote goals.

In the first meeting to go over the new numbers, Jason Miller pointed to the states with deficits, and the buckets of voters Skelly and Oczkowski had identified as most persuadable.

"This is great," Miller said. "But what do we say to them?"

"What do you mean, what do we say?" Skelly said. "It's literally the first week of October. What does our research say?"

Silence washed over the room.

Just like in July when Ronna had schooled Brad over how it was clearly and obviously the campaign's job to develop its own messaging for the convention program, the data team was stunned to hear Miller, the campaign's top communications strategist, ask how to define Trump's message to persuadable voters. Oczkowski argued he could point the campaign to which voters wanted to hear messages about jobs and the economy, or those who prioritized national defense. But his expertise wasn't setting broad, overarching message strategy—that was the campaign's job.

The data they did have only underscored the need for more messaging research: Some persuadable voters thought Trump had pushed too fast to reopen the country amid Covid, while others said the country wasn't opening fast enough. To address both issues required a level of nuance and subtlety that needed to be sharpened by focus groups and polling. There wasn't time for either.

Instead, the campaign turned to Chris Carr, the Republican field general in charge of thousands of ground troops spread across two-dozen states, who were already knocking on doors and organizing communities in order to push millions of conservative voters to the Election Day polls for Republican candidates up and down the ballot. But now, the campaign needed Carr to turn off that program and refashion it into a makeshift focus group. They asked Carr to grab his five best volunteers in each battleground state, arm them with a script the campaign was now scrambling to write, and send off the Republican foot soldiers with orders to return only after they'd each finished twenty-minute conversations with ten voters.

The advantages of incumbency should have prevented this kind of confusion so late in the race. But the silver lining was that the party's turnout operation had always planned to kick into high gear in the final weeks, and on the campaign trail there was a sense the race was tightening.

"It wasn't too late," one campaign official said. "Everyone thought it was possible."

<hr>

Carr's field program turned around its pseudo-focus group so efficiently and quickly that it surprised some inside campaign headquarters. But even as the campaign dug into the data, they were still at odds over how to puzzle together the electoral map to get Trump 270 votes.

The RNC's final round of voter scores on October 27 hadn't been much help. Those scores showed Trump losing in Florida, Iowa, and North Carolina—all states he'd comfortably win—and getting trounced by double-digits in Wisconsin and Nevada, both states he'd narrowly lose. In Georgia, the state Trump would lose by 0.24 percent, the RNC showed him trailing Biden by eight points. But it had been weeks since Stepien paid any attention to the RNC data—and it turned out he'd made the right decision. In the first months after the 2020 election, Ronna acknowledged significant problems with the party's data program and started implementing a round of personnel changes aimed at sorting out the issues.

Inside the campaign, the data situation wasn't much better. Fabrizio's last poll in Georgia showed Biden and Trump tied. There was just one problem—no one in Trump World saw those numbers. Fabrizio had been side-lined. Fabrizio's Georgia poll was paid for by the National Republican Senato-rial Committee—a group that was helping Perdue, who was relying, at least partly, on their polling to drag Trump back to Georgia.

The irony was that Stepien had always trusted Fabrizio's polling. In Stepi-en's first days as campaign manager, the veteran pollster had been one of few campaign hands he had asked for help. But then Stepien found out how much the campaign was paying for Fabrizio's expertise, and he couldn't get past the price. Fabrizio's rates were no secret—he was widely known as an expensive pollster. But Stepien had become obsessed with trying to watch every cent, even to the point of irritating campaign aides by putting a stop to catered lunch meetings.* Stepien exploded in a flurry of expletives over a monthly $25,000 fee Brad had approved to secure the services of Fabrizio's firm.

"Holy shit!" Stepien said when he learned about it. "I've never heard of a pollster having a monthly retainer!"

Stepien never asked Fabrizio about the retainer. He just mostly stopped speaking with him. During the first week of September, Fabrizio gave a lengthy state-by-state presentation that walked the campaign through a deep dive into which voters the campaign needed to target, what the messages should be, and which markets required the biggest investment of advertising dollars. Fab-rizio was hoarse by the end of the call. But Stepien hadn't said a word.

A few weeks later, Fabrizio sent around results from a "brushfire" survey that skimmed the battleground states to measure trends. The poll showed Trump's numbers had sharply fallen off a cliff. It was a confusing twist for an already angry campaign manager, and Stepien could barely conceal his frus-tration when he confronted Fabrizio over the data.

"You give me these numbers—what do they mean?" Stepien snapped. "Why did this happen?"

The poll was an average of the seventeen battleground states, Fabrizio told

---

* "It was like Bill didn't understand the size of this thing," one senior campaign official said. "We were close to being a multi-billion-dollar operation. Buy lunch for the team."

him. It was only a snapshot of the current landscape and was not intended to show why it looked that way. But Stepien wasn't satisfied, and the two men argued back and forth until Fabrizio was finally as angry as the campaign manager.

"You know what the problem is here? The problem is we can't control the White House message! And coronavirus cases keep going up!" Fabrizio shot back.

The campaign didn't ask Fabrizio for another in-depth poll for the final two months of the race. Instead, Stepien quietly brought in another pollster, Brock McCleary. McCleary was a former New Jersey Republican Party operative who had worked on several races with Stepien. Stepien explained the change around campaign headquarters by saying he had just as much confidence in McCleary, but at half the price of Fabrizio. McCleary's firm, Cygnal, billed the Trump campaign for $1.8 million in polling services over the final two months of the race. Fabrizio's firm had charged $4.5 million—over the previous two years.

In addition to McCleary and Skelly, the last addition to Stepien's rebuilt data team was also the most unusual: Kevin Hassett, a Penn-trained economist with ginger hair, a wide, boyish grin, and a long list of admirers in the White House. Hassett had been chairman of the White House Council of Economic Advisers for most of Trump's first three years in office and was known inside the West Wing for his sharp mind, endless optimism, and policy views that didn't fit neatly into political orthodoxy, including an openness to a carbon tax and reducing levies on corporate income.

Hassett had become close to Jared, who admired the economist's rosy outlook and brought him back into the White House at the start of the pandemic to assist with the administration's response to Covid. Hassett had no experience in public health or any background in infectious diseases, but neither did Jared. Hassett's optimism—he had authored a book in 1999 based on the argument that stocks were so undervalued that the Dow would soon surpass the 36,000 marker (it passed 27,000 on Election Day)—reigned supreme again. Back in the White House, he helped build a model that suggested the daily death count would peak in mid-April and then come to a halt by mid-May.

Even a year after that prediction—in May 2021—there were still about 700 Americans dying each day from Covid.*

To the surprise of some colleagues, including Stepien, who had worked for two years in the White House with Hassett, Hassett's interests also included partisan politics. He'd been an economic adviser to John McCain in 2008 and Mitt Romney in 2012, but Jared brought him into the Trump campaign to try his hand at modeling political data. During the final month of the race, Hassett was part of a weekly call with Jared, Stepien, and others, advising on where his models showed opportunities for Trump. By the final week, the call had become daily.

Inside the campaign, Hassett's sunny analysis was identified as the spark for a brief, internal battle over whether Trump should visit New Mexico in the final week of the race. The push came from Jared, who felt upbeat about Trump's surge at the end of the race—and his own decisions to replace Brad, elevate Katie Walsh inside Trump World, and build a reservoir of cash inside campaign coffers.

The campaign's key man in Ohio, Bob Paduchik, had told Jared the race was all but over there in mid-October. In Florida, Susie Wiles had been touting strong trends in unlikely demographics for Trump: Hispanic men and Black men. Meadows was confident North Carolina was done and dusted. The Midwest looked close—the surge of absentee ballots flipped the advantage in Pennsylvania back and forth every day—but Jared had seen the same show back in 2016.

Stepien and Oczkowski told Jared that Arizona looked close, but the margins from early voting were in their favor. And in Georgia, the campaign was predicting a victory with a 4 percent margin, surpassing Trump's victory there in 2016.

Jared pointed to that data when Trump asked about a final stop in Georgia.

"You'll be fine," Jared told the president.

But Trump wanted to go.

"If David is saying we need to go, then let's go," Trump said.

---

* Hassett shrugged off the criticism at the time and said his model wasn't meant to be predictive, but it was widely reported that White House aides had interpreted it that way and used it to influence their decision to quickly reopen the economy.

Trump World sent word to Perdue's campaign on October 29 that the president had agreed to a rally in Rome on November 1, just as the senator had requested. To fit the Georgia stop into the schedule, which already included five rallies on each of the final two days, the Trump campaign scratched one of two North Carolina events that day. But Trump had waited so long to commit to visiting Georgia that Perdue had to drop out of the final debate—which had already been scheduled for that night—with his Democratic opponent, Jon Ossoff, in order to attend the rally with the president.

At the rally, Trump donned a red campaign hat and repeatedly praised Perdue, talking about how wonderful and happy he felt to be on the campaign trail.

"I shouldn't even be here," Trump told the crowd at the start of the rally. "They say I have Georgia made, but you know what? I said, 'I promised we have to be here.' They said, 'Sir, you don't have to come to Georgia. We have it made. It's won, it's well.'

"But you've got to go vote," Trump added a few minutes later. "You never know. It's called politics. You never know. Got to be careful. Get out and vote."

Days until Election: 1

On November 2, Trump opened the final day of the campaign convinced that victory was his. He wasn't relying on his gut or his Twitter mentions. His campaign team had told him. Stepien's reconfigured data operation showed that Trump had been methodically closing the gap with Biden for weeks and that turnout would be abysmally low, which was a dynamic that had favored Trump in 2016 and would benefit him again in 2020. Trump heard from Stepien and Miller that he would win Arizona by a nose and capture Georgia by a comfortable four-point margin. Neither would happen.

But there was no denying the energy on the ground. Even public polls during the final stretch showed Trump closing in on Biden. With three weeks to go in the race, Trump trailed Biden by more than ten percentage points, according to the *RealClearPolitics* average of national polls, and that average dropped by about one point each week. Trump was in a good mood, mocking rivals and laughing out loud at a supercut of Biden's verbal stumbles that the campaign had spliced together and started playing at rallies. He finished each performance with a wide smile and an endearingly awful hip-twist and fist-shake—to call it a dance would only sully the word—to the 1978 disco anthem "Y.M.C.A.," from The Village People.

Trump, who had been sidelined with Covid until October 12, was competing with an energy that few even in his inner circle could believe. He would relax at night by watching a UFC fight on the flight home and flipping through the cable networks to find footage of the Biden rallies so he could laugh and make fun of the honking cars—a Biden campaign nod to Covid protocols. He'd walk through the plane to check on his team on the flight home—telling them to enjoy their meal and asking if they were tired yet. Ronna had campaigned with Trump for a few days and told him she was exhausted.

"I want Regeneron next time!" she told him.

The campaign team felt the gap closing, but the atmosphere inside *Air Force One* was beyond cautious optimism for a strong finish. There seemed to be a metaphysical certainty about a second term for Trump. Robert O'Brien, Trump's national security adviser who frequently traveled for campaign stops, told the president that he might win 340 electoral votes. Eric Trump carried a map with even more electoral votes. Jason Miller told reporters that the campaign felt more confident now than it had at the same point in 2016.

"We're going to win it, we're winning all over," Trump said in Traverse City, Michigan, on the last day of campaigning. "We see the real numbers."

But the reality was that it had been more than three decades since a Republican had won with the kinds of numbers Eric and O'Brien were touting. And the problems that the Stepien regime had been complaining about for months—too much superfluous spending under Brad, too many outside voices influencing decisions, and too many messages coming from the president—had never been fully addressed.

Instead, all three concerns were epitomized in a single campaign TV spot that aired in the last weeks of the race—including on the final day. "The one that Hannity wrote," as it was known inside the campaign.

In 2016, Hannity had appeared in a promotional video for Trump in which he touted the Republican nominee and pledged his personal support. And even though the Fox News star often described himself as a talk show host and not a reporter, the video crossed a line inside corporate headquarters, which billed the network as a journalistic outlet. Fox issued an unsigned statement at the time claiming that Hannity hadn't told anyone about the video in advance and that "he will not be doing anything along these lines for the remainder of the election season."

Now, four years later, Hannity told me that he had nothing do with the spot known inside the campaign as "the Hannity ad," and disputed that he wrote any commercials for Trump. He said he hadn't suggested ideas or offered any advice when it came to the president's campaign spots. Hannity said he had merely raised concerns with the campaign during the final months of the race about why they were being outspent by Biden on television in key swing states.

"The world knows that Sean Hannity supports Donald Trump. But my involvement specifically in the campaign—no. I was not involved that much," Hannity told me, when I asked him about the commercial. "Anybody who said that is full of shit."

If Hannity had written the ad—as campaign officials privately said he did and as Trump didn't dispute it—it would likely have set off similar alarms once again inside the network.

But even if Hannity had nothing to do with the spot, that would represent its own remarkable twist. The only reason the ad aired was because campaign officials were told Hannity wrote it with Trump's blessing; if Hannity had nothing to do with the commercial, that would raise significant questions about the decision-making process inside the campaign.

It was a memorable ad inside campaign headquarters. The Trump campaign aired more than 100 different TV spots in 2020, and this was one of just eight that were sixty-seconds long. Nearly all of the other commercials were thirty seconds.

Multiple internal campaign emails referred to the spot simply as "Hannity." Another referred to it as the "Hannity-written" spot.

"POTUS has not yet approved, but Hannity has," read one internal email.

"Hannity said this is our best spot yet," another campaign aide wrote.

But inside the campaign, the spot was mocked mercilessly—mostly because of the dramatic, over-the-top language and a message that seemed to value quantity over quality. The script that circulated in mid-September leveled almost two-dozen different attacks at Biden in a single minute—roughly one attack every two-and-a-half seconds.

"Everyone hated it," a Trump campaign official said. "It was so ridiculous."

The original script also included language that Hannity often used on his show during the final two months of the race. Biden was a "forty-seven-year swamp creature" who had "accomplished nothing" and supported a "radical, socialist Green New Deal." The Democratic nominee was partnering with "socialist Bernie Sanders," and Biden himself was "radical, socialist, extreme." It accused Biden of wanting to raise trillions in new taxes, supporting amnesty for undocumented immigrants, turning his back on law enforcement, and lacking the courage to denounce violence.

The campaign's legal team wouldn't allow the term "socialist" to be used so loosely, but the production team leaned into the absurdity. The spot was narrated with a deep, sinister male voice and included a series of outlandish images, including one with Biden rising out of a swamp.*

The final thirty seconds abruptly shifted to positive messages about how Trump was fighting for every American.

"Vote Donald Trump 2020 for you and your family's safety and security," the narrator said in the final line of the ad.

Campaign officials didn't think the spot would win Trump any new voters and deemed it so useless that they limited it to exactly one show: *Hannity*. The calculation was that running the spot in that hour of primetime on Fox News would ensure that both Trump and Hannity saw it. If the two men watched the spot on television—and were satisfied enough to stop asking about the commercial—that seemed to be the best result of the ad.

The total investment: $1.5 million to air on Hannity's show from October 12 to November 2. The spot aired on six of the sixteen primetime episodes of

---

* The Trump campaign already had an illustration of a Chuck Schumer swamp creature, and they simply clipped Biden's head and pasted it on the Senate Democratic leader's body for the spot.

Hannity during that time, and on three of the network's daytime programs on the final day of campaigning. For a campaign that had pulled down its ads in August and cut the size of its advertising buys in some Midwest battlegrounds in mid-September—both partly out of Stepien's concern they wouldn't have enough cash for the stretch run—it was a heavy price to pay.

———

Trump approved every TV spot before it aired, and "the one that Hannity wrote" was no different. But Trump's pollsters had showed him data that his own disjointed messaging—which the "Hannity" ad seemed to underscore— was hurting him against Biden.

One way the campaign tested messaging was an open-ended question that asked respondents to recall anything they could remember from the past week that Trump and Biden either said or did.

In late September, voters remembered ten different items about Biden. Several memories involed Supreme Court Justice Ruth Bader Ginsburg, who had just died. But the next five most frequent answers were centered around Biden's singular issue of the race: Covid. Some remembered that he'd said Trump had mishandled the pandemic. Others recalled Biden had said too many had died from the contagion. Still more remembered Biden saying that Trump's response showed he was unfit for office.

For Trump, voters remembered fifteen different topics—a list of issues that was as profuse as it was diffuse. Ginsburg's passing. Covid going away. Lies about Covid. He'd disparaged the military. The improving economy. Fighting with Fauci. Racist remarks. Something about the president being nominated for the Nobel Peace Prize. Voters recalled both of Trump's campaign slogans: Keep America Great and Make America Great.

Few things encapsulated Trump's mixed messaging in 2020 like his inability to decide between two different slogans. He had been vacillating between the two for much of 2019 and the first months of 2020, but hadn't used "Keep America Great" since the pandemic started. The switch back to his 2016 slogan seemed to just underscore a country—and a campaign—in regression.

Trump's campaign in 2016 was chaotic, crude, and reductive. But it was also consistent. His candidacy was defined by promises to build a wall, rewrite trade deals, and beat Crooked Hillary. He seemed to instinctively know where to needle opponents, and when he succeeded, he cruelly refused to let up. It was often elemental and painful to watch, but it was almost always effective.

In 2020, Trump's messaging strategy was less visceral and more accidental. In the summer, his campaign had aired TV ads with no less than a half dozen different messages. Depending on which spots were in rotation, Biden was too cozy with China, too eager to raise taxes, too liberal, or too cognitively impaired to be president. In some ads, Biden was too soft on crime. In others, he was too tough.

Trump had made derisive nicknames his hallmark but couldn't find the handle in 2020. He tried at least ten different times to rename the former vice president. "Sleepy Joe" was one of the first and most common, but that didn't sound like a villain so much as someone who needed to go to bed at 9:00 p.m. And, well, that sounded nice, especially after four years of Trump. He tried "China Joe," "Corrupt Joe," "Quid Pro Joe." At another point it was "O'Biden" when he tried to tie his challenger to Obama, which was another ill-advised strategy since the former president had remained widely popular across the country.

On his last day of campaigning, Trump hit the trail with the energy of a candidate who was about to pull off another improbable come-from-behind victory. But he spoke like one who didn't know what job he was seeking. With final-day rallies in North Carolina, Pennsylvania, Wisconsin, and two in Michigan, Trump criticized Fauci, Beyoncé and Jay-Z, Jon Bon Jovi, and Lady Gaga.

His crowd in Scranton started a "LeBron James sucks" chant. In Fayetteville, they reprised the 2016 anti-Clinton favorite, "Lock her up."

Just like 2016, the final rally in 2020 was in Grand Rapids, Michigan, and Trump was hoarse by the time he landed at Gerald R. Ford International Airport.

Trump was wrapped in a full-length black overcoat and a red campaign hat and black gloves as the temperature dipped into the 40s. His family joined him onstage. He and Pence tossed red hats into the crowd.

During his speech, he attacked Biden as "Sleepy Joe" and "One Percent Joe." He twice referred to "Barack Hussein Obama." He complained about witch hunts, fake news, the deep state, and Hunter Biden.

But in those final seventy-five minutes on a 2020 campaign rally stage, Trump mostly wanted to talk about what happened in 2016. He asked the crowd a dozen times to "remember four years ago." He reminded his fans what it had been like that night to win Michigan and Ohio. He reminisced about how they had watched news anchors crying over his victory. And he confidently predicted—no fewer than fifteen times—that he would repeat his success again the next day.

"We made history together four years ago," Trump said, "and tomorrow, we're going to make history once again."

17

Election Day

"Frankly, we did win this election."
—*Election night remarks, East Room, November 4, 2020*

Marine One touched down on the South Lawn of the White House just before 3:00 a.m. on Election Day. Trump gingerly walked down the six steps. He was an hour and a half late returning home, and exhausted. He'd hosted forty-five rallies in the twenty-one days since recovering from Covid. Four years earlier, he'd held fifty-one rallies over that same three-week span. Once again, Trump had run through the tape. His final seventeen hours of campaigning had included more than 3,000 miles of flights and motorcades, 367 minutes of rally speechifying, and five awkward and hilarious stage dances to "Y.M.C.A."

What was different this time was that he was confident he was going to win.

In 2016, Trump had told Melania—just days before the election—that his plan was to make sure his private jet was gassed up before the votes were counted.

"If I do lose, I'm coming out, we're going to leave everyone else behind, and fly right to Monte Carlo," Trump said.

He described a scene in which he'd arrive in Monaco like a high-roller dressed to kill—an older and heavier (but wealthier) James Bond.

Melania erupted in laughter.

"Donald," she said. "Nobody goes to Monte Carlo in November."

On his final day of campaigning in 2016, his tplane was about an hour from New York when Trump turned to Steve Bannon, his campaign's chief executive and one of the only other passengers still awake on the flight.

"Hey," Trump said, getting Bannon's attention. "How does this thing end?"

A tiny chortle escaped from Bannon. "How do you mean?" he asked. "We'll get the exit polls around four, and we'll have a data room where they watch all that shit. We'll be giving you updates on how people are turning out."

"No," Trump said. "The victory speech or the concession speech. Are those requirements? Like, legally?"

"No, no, there's no legal requirement," Bannon said.

"I don't want to give a concession," Trump said. "Fuck them."

Bannon laughed.

When Trump awoke later that morning, the first Election Day polls had already opened, and, once again, an unscalable fence had been installed around the White House out of concern for riots. He was running late for an interview with *Fox & Friends*, and his wife, Melania, was 1,000 miles away, absorbing the heavy ocean air surrounding the crown jewel in his series of sprawling South Florida holdings, Mar-a-Lago.

Melania, who preferred herbal remedies and natural healing over evidence-based medicine, was convinced of the therapeutic qualities of that salty South Florida sea breeze. She loved it at Mar-a-Lago, and made it obvious to everyone how much she preferred it to her life in Washington. She dreaded that return flight back to Andrews Air Force Base, and never more so than now, the long-awaited Judgment Day for her husband.

The source of her anxiety wasn't so much the result of the race. She wasn't sure how she'd react, win or lose. She'd feel excited and proud later that night at that tantalizing, but ultimately cruel, first taste of victory. A day before, she'd forcefully defended her husband at her own rally in Huntersville, North Carolina, a Charlotte suburb, where she took the stage to Tom Jones's swinging, sexist seventies tune "She's a Lady."

But the next night, election night, she seemed to betray the slightest signs of relief as the momentum shifted to Biden. The only thing she was sure of was that after four years, she mostly felt tired. No one would blame her for that. Plenty of White House aides felt the same.

In 2016, she and Trump voted together in New York. Four years later, the Trumps became the first president and first lady to cast ballots in Florida, albeit ten days apart. Trump had already voted early, but Melania wanted to vote on Election Day. It was sunny and in the mid-70s by the time she slipped on a $3,200 Gucci dress to cast her ballot at the Morton and Barbara Mandel Recreation Center. She pulled on a pair of tan Christian Louboutin stilettos, some square-framed sunglasses with a dark brown leopard print, and grabbed a $30,000 Hermès handbag.

If she had to go back to Washington after casting her vote, she was going to look sharp doing it.

What irritated her most about the trip back to the White House was what awaited her there. Hundreds of people were coming to the White House that night for an election party she'd tried to stop, but in the process had been trampled by Meadows, Jared, and ultimately her own husband. If it was up to her, there would be no White House parties during the pandemic. Technically, social events in the White House were the purview of the first lady's office. But it was a fight in which she was never successful. Even after her husband lost, she couldn't stop the holiday parties. Melania successfully cut the invite lists down from 1,000 or so to around 200. But that just seemed to make the invites all the more desirable. When South Dakota governor Kristi Noem wanted to attend multiple Christmas parties and refused to take no for an answer, Melania gave in to that, too.

"Fine," Melania said. "You know what? If she wants to get Covid that bad, that's up to her."

The constant use of the White House for blatantly political purposes also made her uncomfortable. She had tried to stop the campaign from using it for the convention, too. Her office had slow-walked several requests from the campaign ahead of the Republican National Convention, when she'd deliver her speech from the Rose Garden and the president would accept his party's nomination on the South Lawn.

Three times she'd rejected the request from Meadows to use the White House on election night. The campaign was supposed to use Trump International Hotel, just five blocks down the street, which had been sold out for the evening since January. Washington's regulations prohibited public gatherings of more than fifty people, but Trump didn't want to move his festivities. Nine days before the election, the campaign emailed supporters that they were still planning a party at the hotel. But Washington mayor Muriel Bowser, who had been a loud critic of the White House over the Rose Garden superspreader, signaled she was ready to play hardball.

"We'll be talking to our licensee, which is the hotel," Bowser said.

That day, Meadows called Melania to speak with her about holding the event at the White House. They really had no other choice, he told her. The hotel would face fines or other penalties that the White House, which was exempt from local regulations, would not. But still she said no.

"I'm not comfortable with it," she told him, and asked for more time to discuss it with her staff.

The regulations made sense to Melania. She didn't want all those people at the White House, and she wasn't sure how long the night would last. Timothy Harleth, who as the White House's chief usher was a de facto general manager of the residence, agreed with her. Stephanie Grisham, her chief of staff, warned about how long the party might last.

"Win or lose, there are going to be protests that night," Grisham told her. "Are we going to end up with a 300-person slumber party at the White House if these people can't get out?"

Melania sent word back to Meadows that they'd have to look elsewhere. Meadows brought the verdict to Jared, who raised it with the president. Four days from the election, Trump called his wife from *Air Force One* as he flew from a rally in Michigan to another in Wisconsin.

"This is your night—do what you're going to do," Melania told her husband. "You're going to do it anyway."

Melania would at least protect herself. She would stay in the residence with Barron and her parents, and only come if Trump needed her to stand next to him for a public speech.

———

The quick turnaround led to some tense negotiations between the campaign and the East Wing. Competing visions for the evening presented the main friction point. The campaign wanted to go Full Trump: big and loud, extravagant and celebratory. Winners. But the East Wing preferred something with the pandemic in mind.

"Let's not overdo it," Grisham said when the campaign presented plans for an elaborate and grand stage in the East Room.

But as always, there was a little more backstory. One corner of Trump World could never quite trust another. Adding to the heat of these talks was that the main point of contact for these discussions was Grisham and the campaign's chief advance man, Max Miller. The two had dated for much of Trump's presidency but were now broken up. Initial arguments in the negotiations over the party focused on Miller's plans for a giant stage with extensive lighting and televisions everywhere. Grisham argued that the White House was effectively a museum and should be treated as such. The East Wing initially declined requests to use the White House's caterers and social aides, then relented.

"It was a huge pissing match," said one White House official.

The campaign wanted to create a war room for their number crunchers in the Map Room, a small ground-floor room off the Diplomatic Room that earned its name during World War II when Franklin Roosevelt used it as a situation room. They wanted a smaller, more exclusive war room for Stepien, Clark, and Jason Miller in the Old Family Dining Room, an intimate space in the northwestern corner of the first floor, where they could meet in private with Trump. Presidents had taken meals with their families in the space for 130 years, until the Kennedys moved the family dining quarters into the private residence. For election night, the White House had extra couches brought in along with television sets. But the senior campaign team barely left the Map Room, and the dining room ended up being used mostly as an escape room for senior White House staff, like Hope and Scavino, to avoid the crowds, and for Katie Miller—the vice president's press secretary and wife of Stephen Miller, who would give birth two weeks later—to rest her feet.

Max Miller got his team into the White House to begin setting up with less than forty-eight hours before guests would start arriving. The next night, it was after midnight when the Secret Service told the advance staffers they needed to wrap up. But they still weren't finished. Miller called Grisham to have their time extended.

"They're kicking the team out, and we're still building the stage and finishing the lighting!" Miller said.

Miller and his team were just leaving the White House by the time the president landed at 3:00 a.m. They returned a few hours later for the final touches.

Trump's late night on his final day of campaigning caught up with him the next morning. He was forty-five minutes late calling in to a 7:00 a.m. interview on *Fox & Friends*, and just before he did, Hogan Gidley, the campaign's press secretary, posted a tweet asking if Biden had packed it in for the day.

Biden was, at that moment, at church. He'd started his day by visiting the grave of his older son.

But Biden's team wasn't relying on prayer to win. The campaigns for both candidates believed the race would end with either Biden in a landslide, or Trump by an even narrower margin than his 2016 victory. But Trump thought he was primed for a blowout, and predicted as much on *Fox & Friends* that morning. He sounded groggy and hoarse. Steve Doocy, the friendliest of the three hosts, speculated that Trump had had only a few minutes of sleep the previous night because he'd campaigned so long the day before. He asked the president if he was serious when he'd said at his last event that he might start crying when the crowd chanted, "We love you."

"Were you a little emotional right then because that could have been the last rally of your political life?" Doocy asked.

"Well," Trump said, "I was kidding, actually."

Ainsley Earhardt told Trump that she just liked that he said it. "When you love someone, that's always nice to hear back," she told him.

Brian Kilmeade stepped in and asked about a quote from Obama, who had accused Trump of caring more about drawing big crowds than keeping people safe during a pandemic. Trump answered by complaining about his coverage on Fox News, specifically the amount of time the network gave Democrats in 2020 compared to 2016.

"It's one of the biggest differences, this season compared to last," he said, the former *Apprentice* host slipping into TV lingo to refer to his two campaigns.

Trump started his day airing grievances about Fox on Fox. He'd end it in a fit of anger at the conservative network and a flurry of phone calls threatening to wipe them out.

═══

Boosting Trump's confidence that morning were gains in U.S. stock markets, which, paired with rally attendance, he believed was an even better indicator of his political fortunes than the polling his campaign had spent millions to produce. After he hung up with Fox News, he called a conservative radio show host in Pennsylvania.

"The ultimate poll is not some guy that makes a million dollars to go and talk to 213 people, which I've always felt was weak," Trump told R. J. Harris in Harrisburg. "The ultimate poll are these massive crowds that are showing up to rallies. Nobody's seen anything like it ever. There has never been anything like it."

"Tonight will be a landslide," White House press secretary Kayleigh McEnany told Fox News late Tuesday morning.

═══

By lunchtime, Trump was on his way to campaign headquarters in Virginia, just his second visit to the offices that now included two full floors and parts of a third in the Arlington office building. The event was designed for him to show some appreciation for the hundreds of people who'd been working for the campaign, a few minutes that would help get them through the rest of the day. Nearly all the staffers, standing at their cubicles and waiting in their office doorways, wore masks. When Trump entered the office, he wore a blue suit, a purple tie, and no mask, nor did much of his entourage. Meadows, who'd escaped a few close calls with Covid already, hugged several staffers. Kushner, in blue jeans and a black cashmere sweater, didn't bother with a mask. Nor did

Kayleigh, or Stepien, who shuffled awkwardly next to the president, his gray Patagonia fleece vest zipped all the way up to his Adam's apple.

The campaign staff welcomed Trump with a long ovation that brought a smile to the president's face, as if he was there to have his spirits lifted instead of the other way around.

Trump told the room that he thought he'd finished strong, and pointed to the rally and the debates, but then corrected himself.

"Certainly the second debate and the rallies, it was a good combination," he said. "I think we took off."

Asked if he thought there would be a result that night, Trump said he did, as Stepien nodded aggressively behind him. When another reporter asked if he'd written acceptance and concession speeches, Meadows repeatedly shook his head as he stood behind the president.

"Hopefully, we'll be only doing one of those two and, you know, winning is easy," Trump said. "Losing is never easy—not for me, it's not."

———

Trump returned to his motorcade, bringing several campaign staffers back to the White House complex with him. But on the way into the White House, Nick Trainer tested positive for Covid. At 3:00 p.m. that afternoon, the campaign had its first nightmare of the day.

Trainer was sent home and his close contacts were retested, including Clark, who had traveled from campaign offices to the White House with Trainer. Clark again tested negative, so Sean Conley, the White House physician, let him stay as long as he wore a mask and returned to the medical unit that evening to be tested again.

———

The campaign would keep Trainer's positive test under wraps for several days, and say nothing when he didn't show up for a scheduled call with reporters at 5:30 p.m. on Election Day. "Everybody on the Trump team, the president included, feels better and more confident about our positioning in 2020 than we did at this exact moment in 2016," Jason Miller told reporters on the call, only a couple hours after Trainer's test.

Stepien projected confidence about winning Arizona, Wisconsin, and Pennsylvania. To bolster his argument, he dove into county-by-county-level data in the crucial battleground states, sometimes precinct by precinct, showing the statistical recall of political data that had impressed the political newcomers in Trump World. But Stepien's data points that evening were mostly anecdotal, and he was still missing important pieces of the puzzle.

"We love what we see in places like the Upper Peninsula of Michigan," Stepien said that evening. Trump would go on to win those northern Michigan counties by 18.7 percentage points, but that was four points less than he did in 2016.

In Pennsylvania, Stepien pointed reporters to Dauphin County, which the campaign had targeted in September with a campaign rally. "We see Republican precincts matching and exceeding 2016 turnout," he said about Dauphin. "Democrat precincts are lagging behind, lagging behind greatly."

Biden would win the county by more than 12,000 votes.

In Wisconsin, Stepien was right that the central Wisconsin counties he was watching—Juneau, Green Lake, Waushara, Wood, and Waupacca—were all about to turn more votes in for Trump than they had in 2016.

"Turnout is very much matching our expectation of being, overwhelmingly, a Trump vote," he said.

But Biden won the state by more than 20,000 votes.

———

Stepien and Miller walked back to the Map Room. Gary Coby and data guru Matt Oczkowski were seated around a table centered in the room, and four TVs were showing live updates from cable networks or data they wanted everyone to keep an eye on, including one with a spreadsheet that showed live results coming in compared to Trump's performance in 2016.

Ronna was there, along with Justin Riemer, her chief counsel at the RNC. Jared and Ivanka wandered in and out, as did Eric and Lara and Don Junior and Kim Guilfoyle. Pence would come in for updates a few times that night.

As the networks started calling the first states—Vermont for Biden, Kentucky for Trump—the president breezed through the watch party. Trays of food were set out with sliders, chicken tenders, and pigs-in-a-blanket—all Trump favorites and each bite sealed under glass, one of the few acknowledgments that night of the pandemic raging through the rest of the country. Guests included Cabinet secretaries—Alex Azar, Bill Barr, David Bernhardt, Ben Carson—and senior White House staff, including Larry Kudlow, Avi Berkowitz, and Stephen Miller. Meadows, Scavino, Corey, and Bossie were there, as was Kellyanne, all of them coming in and out of the Map Room throughout the night.

There were a handful of media personalities, too, including author Raymond Arroyo, Laura Ingraham, and Jeanine Pirro. Diamond. Silk. But most of the other 250 guests had been chosen by Don Junior, Ivanka, and Eric. Some White House officials had thought the evening would include campaign staffers, but it was mostly a party for the kids. Still, Trump worked his way through the crowd, soaking up congratulations and telling guests about the turnout at his rallies for the past week.

By 7:30, West Virginia was in Trump's column, followed by South Carolina a half hour later. Alabama went to Trump a few minutes after that. Biden kept his home state of Delaware.

A swath of traditionally Democratic states in the Northeast fell into Biden's column: Connecticut, New Jersey, Rhode Island, Massachusetts, as well as Maryland and Illinois. Trump picked up Tennessee and Oklahoma. Indiana and Arkansas followed in short order.

The early results were no surprise, but the campaign was seeing data that helped feed their optimism. Some counties in northern Indiana were coming out strong for Trump, some by as much as 10 percent better than 2016. Obama had won Indiana in 2008, but there was never any doubt it was staying red in 2020. However, this kind of strong performance could mean good things in similar places across the upper Midwest.

Oczkowski pointed the numbers out to Coby. "We might pull this fucker off," Oczkowski told him.

By 8:30 p.m., excitement was building in the Map Room, where returns from Florida were exceeding internal expectations. Trump World started projecting some of those demographic trends onto other battleground states.

By 9:00 p.m., Trump returned to the residence, watching as Fox News called both Dakotas, Wyoming, Kansas, and Louisiana for him, while Biden picked up Colorado and New York.

None of the major battlegrounds had been called by 11:00 p.m., but anticipation was building in the Map Room. They were pushing the networks to call Ohio, and believed they'd won Florida and North Carolina, too. They extrapolated trends they were seeing in North Carolina and Florida, and started telling reporters they were confident they'd won Georgia as well.

At 11:04 p.m., the Associated Press moved a story that the biggest battlegrounds were still too close to call. At 11:07, the *New York Times* published a story that said the count could take days. Then, at 11:08 p.m., came the first major call of the night: Fox put Florida in Trump's column. A huge roar went up in the East Room and, one floor down, inside the Map Room.

In 2016, Florida had been called at about the same time. That was when a lot of staffers on that first campaign—including Stepien, Coby, and Clark—started to think Trump might actually beat Hillary. The same thing was happening again.

"We can win this thing," Clark muttered to Stepien.

Four years earlier, the Florida victory was quickly followed a few minutes later by North Carolina and Georgia. By 11:30 p.m., Trump was leading Wisconsin with 70 percent of the vote in.

But on November 3, 2020, at 11:29 p.m., the air rushed out of the room all at once as Fox called Arizona for Biden.

"That is a big get for the Biden campaign," Bret Baier told viewers.

Time seemed to freeze inside the Map Room.

Then, a sudden rush of people surged into the war room, and Stepien's phone rang. The president was calling.

"What the fuck?" Trump yelled into the phone.

As quickly as everyone had appeared in the war room, they were back out the door in a stampede to the president's private residence on the third floor.

———

By 2:00 a.m., Trump was still in shock he hadn't won. He still hadn't decided what to tell the crowd downstairs, and to Americans watching on television. Trump stood near the piano in the Center Hall of the residence with a confused, dejected look as a bevy of more than a dozen campaign advisers, White House officials, and family members shouted around him like berserk investors on a Wall Street trading floor.

Trump had been told for weeks that it looked like he could win. Stepien and McLaughlin had told him 66 million votes would probably be enough to win the second term. He was on his way to collecting more than 74 million, but now it looked like that still might not be enough.

Trump wanted to know how he lost this state, and that state. How could it be that the race wasn't over?

White House advisers including Meadows, Stephen Miller, and Pat Cipollone offered opinions. Top campaign officials including Stepien, Clark, Jason Miller, and Oczkowski told him the numbers still might turn. Family members including Jared, Ivanka, Don Junior, Eric, and Lara gave suggestions.

Giuliani went even further, and told Trump that he'd won. When campaign officials asked the former mayor how he knew that, Giuliani shrugged.

"Just say we won," Giuliani said.

Trump never allowed so many people in the residence, mostly because it drove Melania nuts. But it didn't matter now. No one could give Trump an answer he wanted to hear.

"It was a shitshow," one official said. "And the saddest thing I've ever seen."

Trump ordered the team to start calling Fox officials to figure out what had happened.

Jared told Trump he'd already spoken to Rupert Murdoch. Murdoch, Jared said, wasn't aware that Arizona had been called and would look into it. But Jared didn't expect anything to change. He thought Fox had called the state too early, but that wasn't on Murdoch. If the call turned out to be wrong, heads would roll at the cable network.

"My guys feel very confident," Murdoch told Jared a few minutes later.

As Trump was still trying to make sense of the situation, Biden had taken the stage in Delaware.

"We're on track to win this election," Biden said to supporters.

Several aides had been telling Trump he needed to decide what he was going to tell his supporters. While Biden was still speaking from a stage set up outside the Chase Center in Wilmington, Trump sent his first tweet of the night.

"We are up BIG," Trump wrote in his post, promising to make a statement soon.

═════

But Trump was in shock. Much of his team was, too, and it took another ninety minutes to get the president out of the residence and over to the East Room, where a stage was set up. Some aides encouraged Trump to get in front of the cameras soon—most East Coast viewers had gone to bed, and he was about to lose the West Coast audience. Trump ignored the advice.

"No, I'm not," he said. "They're going to watch me."

It was after 2:00 a.m. when Trump finally embarked with his team on a depressing parade toward the East Room.

Trump rode the elevator down from the White House residence and ambled through the deserted State Dining Room. A row of televisions—installed for guests to watch election night returns—remained tuned to cable news. Trump paused in front of each screen and watched, as if the race might have flipped in his favor since he last looked.

He eventually made it to the Green Room, which had been turned into a backstage operations center for the East Room event and where a dozen allies had gathered to give Trump some final words of advice.

"Go out there and tell them you're going to be president for the next four years!" shouted Boris Epshteyn, a friend of Eric's who had worked in the White House and advised both of Trump's campaigns.

Laura Ingraham, the Fox News personality, shot Epshteyn a disapproving look.

"You need to go out there and say it's not over," said Jeanine Pirro, host of the Fox show *Justice with Judge Jeanine*.

At 2:21 a.m., Trump finally entered the East Room.

From the stage, he falsely declared that he'd won Georgia. He asserted massive fraud without proof. He was still processing an emotional night in front of live network cameras: Results were looking phenomenal, he'd been preparing to celebrate something so beautiful, he was getting ready to win this election.

"Frankly, we did win this election," Trump said.

‗‗‗‗‗‗

In the Green Room after the speech, Trump asked his team how he did. Before anyone could answer, he asked for his election lawyers. He wanted to know where they could start fighting.

Melania quietly returned to her room upstairs. Trump walked back to the Map Room.

"What do we do tomorrow?" he asked his team.

Clark ticked through possible legal challenges, and Trump advised him to be as aggressive as possible. Clark agreed with some suggestions, and disagreed with others. Oczkowski fed Trump updates on vote totals from the states. The president finally returned to the residence after 4:00 a.m. that night.

He didn't come down to the Oval Office at all the next day.

‗‗‗‗‗‗

Trump remained behind closed doors for most of the first week after the election, emerging briefly on November 5 to give a seventeen-minute statement in which he described himself as the victim of a widespread conspiracy to steal the election. Plotting against him were enemies real and imagined: Poll workers and tech companies, Democrats and the news media. His story had clear villians and heros, but no actual details. He offered no evidence, and he took no questions.

"They're trying to steal an election," he said. "And we can't let that happen."

Trump's stream of falsehoods forced television networks to cut away from their live coverage of his statements. Chris Christie and former Senator Rick Santorum, two Trump allies, criticized his actions as dangerous and immoral. Even the *New York Post*, which had published the Hunter Biden laptop stories a few weeks earlier, ripped Trump's claims as baseless.

Trump's postelection legal-stategy was proving an embarrassment for his allies, too. Reputable Republican lawyers had started to quit rather than carry conspiracy theories into court and the campaign was forced to send Don Junior and Eric to Pennslyvania and Georgia, where they held news conferences to criticize the ongoing vote count. In Pennslyvania, Eric was joined by

Giuliani and Corey, who vowed to fight while ping ponging between unsubstantiated claims of wrongdoing and describing anecdotal disputes as evidence of widespread voter fraud.

Less than forty-eight hours after polls had closed, Trump's defense team was down to family members and his most devoted loyalists. Even Republican members of Congress had remained mostly mute—until Don Junior, Eric, and Brad launched a social media attack on the party for not quickly lining up behind the president's distorted version of reality.

"If you want to win in 2024 as a Republican, I would probably start saying something," Brad posted on Twitter.

The public shaming from Family Trump worked.

Senator Lindsey Graham, whom Don Junior had specifically attacked, went on Hannity's show that night, pledged a $500,000 donation to Trump's legal defense, and disparaged Philadelphia's election operation as "crooked as a snake."

Pence called for transparency in elections and for legal votes to be counted without addressing exactly how he believed the election was being stolen.

———

Trump left the White House for the first time after the election on Saturday, November 7, when he golfed at his club in Sterling, Virginia. He hadn't played for weeks.

He arrived at the club at about 10:30 a.m. and sat at his usual table in the dining room with a clear view of the course. After a breakfast of scrambled eggs, bacon, and toast, Trump took a few swings on the driving range, then climbed into his personal golf cart—complete with a presidential seal embossed in the leather seats—and drove to the first tee box of the thirty-six-hole course.

Trump was about to tee off at the seventh hole when Jared called to deliver the news: The Associated Press and major cable networks were about to call the election in Pennsylvania for Biden. The state's twenty electoral votes would push the Democrat past the 270-vote threshold. Trump had lost.

Trump took the call calmly. He nonchalantly strolled through the grass as he talked with his son-in-law for a few minutes, handed the phone back to an aide, and then finished the last twelve holes of the course as a motorcade of two dozen golf carts—filled with Secret Service agents, law enforcement, and White House aides—trailed behind him.

As Trump finished the back nine, club members playing on adjacent holes shouted their encouragement to the president, telling him he won the election and to keep up the fight. When he finished his round and pulled back up to the clubhouse for lunch, two dozen members were waiting for him on the back patio. They encouraged him to forge ahead and said that he had their support.

Trump loved the attention and spent a few moments chatting with the crowd under the clear blue skies of an otherwise perfectly pleasant fall afternoon.

"Don't worry," Trump told the club members. "It's not over yet."

18

Acquittal, Part Two: The Insurrection

"I don't do rallies for other people. I do them for me."
—*Senate campaign rally, Dalton, Georgia, January 4, 2021*

Trump returned to the White House on Saturday afternoon and found a stable of campaign advisers and lawyers waiting for him.

Trump was wearing the dark slacks and white cap he'd worn golfing and brought his team up to White House residence, where just a few nights before he'd disregarded everyone's advice—except for Giuliani—and declared himself the winner of the election. Trump sat in an armchair while Stepien, Clark, Jason Miller, Bossie, and Eric Herschmann—the White House attorney enamored with the Hunter Biden saga—pulled up seats around him. Their plan was not to tell Trump outright that he'd lost, as a round of major media outlets, including the Associated Press, CNN, and Fox News, had officially declared earlier that day. Instead, they focused on the improbability of his remaining path to victory.

"This has a 5 to 10 percent chance of success," Clark told Trump.

The others agreed.

Trump has a peculiarly imprecise way of speaking so that two people in the same room can walk away with two different impressions. But he also has a unique way of listening in that he hears what few others do. And the odds of success his team had given him would have sounded much different to Stepien's cautious, land-the-plane outlook than to Trump and his go-for-broke ethos. It had been almost exactly six years since Trump had sat in his New York office across from Corey, who told Trump he had a 5 percent shot of winning the 2016 presidential race—and Trump had countered that it was probably closer to 10 percent.

Corey, as it turned out, had underestimated Trump's chances. But the new "5 to 10 percent" plan from the 2020 campaign team seemed inflated from the start—a strategy in three acts that relied on lawsuits and recounts to reverse results in Arizona, Georgia, and Wisconsin. Trump—who had already lost—needed to hit the jackpot on each one to win. It was a nearly impossible task.

The first play was in Georgia. Votes were still being counted, but the trend clearly favored Biden. On election night—before absentee ballots had been counted—Trump had been ahead by more than 103,700 votes. But as the count continued, the margin dwindled and by the time Trump sat down with his team that afternoon, Biden was ahead by 900 votes. Trump's campaign had predicted a victory margin as wide as 290,000 votes in Georgia. He'd ultimately lose it by fewer than 11,800.

Trump would request a recount, but the odds of overturning that result were already lower than 5 to 10 percent. According to data compiled by Fair-Vote, a nonpartisan group that researches elections, there had been thirty-one recounts of statewide general election results in the previous twenty years. Of those, results had been overturned just three times. But in each of those instances, the race had been decided by the slimmest of margins: 0.009 percent, 0.014 percent, and 0.062 percent. Biden's margin in Georgia was 0.24 percent, or about four times wider than even the largest margin that had been overturned in two decades of recounts.*

The second target was Wisconsin, which had been called for Biden the day after Election Day. Trump's lawsuit there alleged ballots had been mishandled. The petition was ultimately rejected in the state supreme court, where it had arrived on December 1—the same day Attorney General Bill Barr announced that there was no evidence of widespread voter fraud in the election.

---

* The FairVote project showed that the biggest races were the least affected by recounts. In recounts of races with more than 2 million ballots cast, the average shift was 0.018 percent, which was nearly fourteen times smaller than Biden's margin. Almost 5 million Georgians voted in the state's presidential contest.

Their third state was Arizona, which had been correctly called for Biden on Election Day by the AP and Fox. The campaign sought to invalidate ballots in Phoenix that they alleged had been mishandled. The suit was dismissed, but the strategy never had a chance: The votes in question ultimately weren't enough to close Biden's margin of victory.

The team had walked through the plan for about an hour when Trump left the room to take a call. Stepien used the moment to gather the crew and again urged them to keep repeating the long odds.

"We want to be super clear," Stepien said. "We want to make sure there's no mistake he misheard something."

After the meeting, Stepien and Clark agreed that their message had been well received by Trump, and they left the White House feeling like they were all on the same page. But Jason Miller wasn't so sure. To Miller, Trump seemed more willing to keep fighting than he was to accept the low probability for success.

"I always thought we had much better odds," Trump told me during an interview after the election at Mar-a-Lago. "It was much higher than five or ten percent."

In many ways, it was a simple yet systematic failure of imagination in Trump World that prevented anyone from anticipating that the Oval Office was about to be overtaken by Rudy Giuliani; that the president would rush to install a band of sycophants across the administration; and that the repeated misuse and abuse of the bully pulpit from the world's most powerful political office would foment a revolution in the heart of the nation's capital.

Trump had spent four years insisting that anything negative about his brand was fake news. The media was lying, no other elected officials should be believed, and the courts weren't to be trusted. It was a lie that he repeated most consistently when it came to his standing among American voters. Positive polls were accurate, negative polls were wrong, and the only possible explanation for any electoral defeat—the 2020 presidential race, the 2016 Iowa caucuses, or even the 2004 Emmys—was the predictable, if false, claim of cheating and fraud. Each repetition of rigged elections was its own jackhammer to the foundation of the country's democratic principles.

But despite all the years and all the tweets and all the baseless claims of voter fraud, Trump World mostly assumed that the president, at the end of the day, would behave rationally—or at least reasonably. Ronna and Pence both had separately described that theory to others in Trump World—that Trump would find his own natural exit ramp from the fictional freeway down which he'd been barrelling for a month. Cipollone told other administration officials that Trump was in a good frame of mind. Ivanka told some White House officials she thought her father might invite Biden to the White House, as Obama had done for him. Even Mark Milley—the chairman of the Joint Chiefs of Staff who had battled with Trump all summer over the president's instinct to advance his own political goals by deploying uniformed soldiers on the streets of major American cities—conveyed some optimism inside the Pentagon after Trump had spoken about an agenda item in a meeting and momentarily acknowledged reality.

"We'll leave that for the next guy," Trump said.

During the first two weeks of November, the prevailing theory among campaign officials, political operatives, and White House aides was that Trump just needed the time and space to process the defeat, and that he would eventually come to terms with his grief and do the right thing. Few believed he had it in him to acknowledge defeat and concede the race—a troubling fact that everyone seemed to take for granted.

Let Trump be Trump, as Corey and Bossie liked to say. The focus instead was on the agreed upon belief that after a bit of pouting to protect his image, Trump would roll up his extra long ties, take down from the wall that bizarre painting of Trump himself sitting around a table with Lincoln, Nixon, and a half-dozen other Republican presidents, collect his supermodel wife and teenage son, and peacefully leave office.

One senior Republican official told the *Washington Post* less than a week after Election Day that there was little downside to "humoring" Trump for a little while.

"He went golfing this weekend. It's not like he's plotting how to prevent Joe Biden from taking power on January 20," the official said. "He's tweeting about filing some lawsuits, those lawsuits will fail, then he'll tweet some more about how the election was stolen, and then he'll leave."

Pence, Stepien, and Ronna told themselves that they were being respectful of the president and giving him the kind of space he required to blow off steam after an undoubtedly crushing defeat on the biggest stage in politics. But they were also unwittingly creating an opening for Giuliani and the most dangerous elements inside Trump World—a horrifying nexus of flunkeys and fawners who were willing to say and do anything to keep Trump in power, and their own feet in the door.

———

There was a corner of Trump World that had, however briefly, at least considered telling Trump he'd lost.

While Trump had been golfing that Saturday morning, a small circle of advisers had been sitting inside campaign headquarters around the table in a glass-encased conference room considering their options. They watched with alarm as Giuliani turned in a news conference performance so absurd that its location attained instant iconic status: Four Seasons Total Landscaping. Standing in a local landscaping company's parking lot, Giuliani had intended to highlight his allegations of voter fraud in Philadelphia, but the story out of the event was a flub over the location; Trump had initially tweeted out that the news conference would be held at the luxury Four Seasons hotel, only to have to clarify that the event was, in fact, at Four Seasons Total Landscaping. It was an embarrassing development for the campaign's skilled advance team that had been grounded in Washington because of budget concerns. As Giuliani stood in the northeast Philly parking lot of the cement block building—next to a sex shop and a crematorium—the Associated Press and all of the major cable news networks called the election. Even Corey was smart enough to stay out of that shot.

Giuliani mocked the news that the race was over, but back in Washington, the bungled news conference crystallized the finality of the moment for some of Trump World's most loyal lieutenants.

Hope articulated what several were thinking and suggested the team tell Trump that the election was over. If the president could find a way to begrudgingly concede, then he—and his team—could enjoy the final months of the presidency, she said. Trump could take one of the foreign trips he'd been planning for after the election. He could push through executive orders that he'd been told were too controversial to sign before the election.

"Let's do all the things we didn't get to do because of all of the distractions, and have fun," Hope said.

Bossie agreed. Herschmann endorsed the plan.

Then Eric and Don Junior shot it down.

Two days prior, Don Junior had posted encouragement on Twitter for his father to "go to total war over this election."

"Expose all of the fraud, cheating, dead/no longer in state voters," Don Junior wrote.

There was no easing up now.

"What you're talking about isn't even an option," he told Hope.

The two sons channeled their father's reaction. They warned he would never go for it and said it wasn't worth broaching.

"It's a nonstarter," Eric said.

The motion was tabled, and that was as close as Trump's family and some of his longest-serving aides would get to finding a way to tell the president the one thing they knew he couldn't handle: that he'd lost.

The group talked themselves into the 5 to 10 percent approach by saying that any president deserved to have his legal options pursued. Most believed that once those challenges were exhausted, Trump would downshift out of attack mode. Or, if not, certainly Trump would get himself there by December 14, when the Electoral College met in Washington to cast their votes in the presidential race.

Except that had never been Trump's plan. Stepien and Clark left their meeting with Trump on Saturday confident that the president would behave in a relatively realistic way when it came to his legal options. But they had barely made it off White House grounds when Trump signaled a very different approach on a phone call with Chris Christie.

Christie had lost his share of elections—he'd been voted out of the first office he ever held as a Morris County, New Jersey, freeholder and barely lasted two states in the 2016 Republican presidential primary. The pain of losing the White House, Christie understood, must be exponentially worse. Christie tried to empathize with Trump, and he told the president he should be proud of what he'd accomplished. Christie suggested a whirlwind domestic tour to take a final bow.

"But to do that, you have to say to people that you understand you lost," Christie said.

"Is that all you got?" Trump said.

"Yes," Christie told him. "Because that's all there is."

Trump didn't want to hear any of it.

"I can still win this thing," Trump said.

Trump wasn't untangling himself from the fraud accusations. He was pulling the knot tighter.

———

Most political campaigns end on election night with the team gathered in a hotel ballroom or campaign office with families and supporters. The moment of finality and closure provides candidates and their staff an opportunity to celebrate a hard-fought victory or, perhaps more importantly, grieve together over a loss. Trump's election night stretched over four days and much of Trump World had scattered by the time the race was called. One senior staffer was sipping coffee on her couch watching CNN when the news broke. Another had brought his son to a flag football game for the first time in months when Fox News alerted the result. Another was away at his sister's wedding.

Many of those who remained would be repulsed by Trump's actions over the days and weeks to come—an exodus that started when Trump fired his defense secretary, Mark Esper, by tweet.

The move broke a promise Trump and his team had made a few weeks earlier to David Urban, the Trump adviser who was friends with Esper. Urban was livid and immediately called Jared. Jared didn't want Esper fired, but he told Urban that Trump's promise was to keep him through the election. Urban already seemed to be teetering on the edge of Trump World—he was the campaign's top consultant for Pennsylvania, but he rarely left Florida during the pandemic and had become the top lobbyist at TikTok, the Chinese company that America-First Trumpians believed was a national security risk to the United States.

"I'm fucking done," Urban told Jared. "It's a dick move, and it looks like he's out of control."

But Trump was just getting started. Within days of firing Esper, Trump had replaced veteran defense and intelligence officials with inexperienced loyalists hungry to appease the new boss.

Administration officials like Pompeo and Milley believed some of Trump's new hires were conspiracy theorists and discussed whether others might have links to neo-Nazi groups. Senior administration officials weren't completely sure what Trump was up to, and they started hitting the panic button.

"The crazies have taken over," Pompeo warned a colleague about the White House.

Pompeo worried that foreign adversaries might view the domestic instability from the electoral uncertainty being fanned by Trump as an opportunity to exploit. Pompeo left one senior administration official with the impression that he was also concerned about the possibility that Trump might engage in a foreign conflict as a way to strengthen his political argument for remaining in office. Pompeo suggested a daily call with Meadows and Milley to all stay on the same page when it came to hot spots overseas.

But publicly, Pompeo played a cynical political hand and fed into the fraud conspiracy when, during a State Department news conference on November 10, he said he anticipated a second Trump term.

"There will be a smooth transition to a second Trump Administration," Pompeo said, adding that "there is a process—the Constitution lays it out pretty clearly."

Milley, meanwhile, took a more direct approach and started sending clear signals to the White House that, whatever Trump's plan, he should leave the military out of it.

"We do not take an oath to a king or a queen, a tyrant or a dictator," Milley said at the opening of the U.S. Army's museum on November 11 as Chris Miller, the acting defense secretary who had replaced Esper, sat nearby.

"We do not take an oath to an individual," Milley said.

Less than a week after Stepien and Clark had walked Trump through their legal plan, Giuliani was blowing it up—and pushing his way further into the Oval Office. On November 13, Trump summoned Clark into the Oval Office as Giuliani, on speakerphone, claimed the campaign had been too slow to contest election results in Georgia. Clark explained that state law required results to be certified before a recount could be requested, which hadn't yet happened.

"They're lying to you, sir!" Giuliani shouted.

Clark denied anyone was lying. Suddenly, the two men were shouting loud enough that it startled people waiting outside the Oval Office.

"You're a fucking asshole, Rudy!" Clark said.

Clark had been the campaign's top attorney for the past year. He'd spent most of 2019 in the weeds of state and national party rulebooks ensuring that it was virtually impossible for any Republican to challenge Trump in a primary. During Trump's first two years, he ground out long hours as a White House aide. Now, after one phone call from Giuliani, the president was entertaining nonsensical attacks on his ability to read Georgia election code and to give an honest answer to a simple question to the president he'd spent four years trying to reelect.

Clark stopped going to the White House.

Meanwhile, Bossie was sidelined with Covid—testing positive one day after he'd been put in charge of the campaign's legal team. Meadows had tested positive for Covid just before the election had been called, and he was out until mid-November. Hope had been consistently rebuffed when she pitched Trump on scheduling almost anything that didn't have to do with election fraud—and she had started to pare back her work schedule, as well.

Senior officials who remained in the West Wing avoided the Oval Office and engaged in gallows humor, coming up with titles for their tell-all memoirs about the final days in office, like *Series Finale: The Ugliest Transition*.

Jared considered stepping in to help Clark but saw only the downside. He knew his father-in-law had lost—he and Ivanka had started talking about moving to Miami before the race was even officially called. But he couldn't bring himself to tell the president to end the fight. Trump was the grandfather of his children. Jared didn't want to hear his father-in-law complain at every family gathering that a second term might have happened—if only Jared hadn't gone soft.

Instead, Jared wanted to avoid the Oval Office at all costs, too, and he left the country entirely. He saw an opportunity for more progress in the Middle East on peace deals, which he thought could potentially be among the lasting legacies of the administration. But Trump wanted him to skip the Gulf Coast Council summit in Saudi Arabia, stay in Washington, and fight alongside him.

Jared argued to make the trip.

"I'm probably going to disagree—you're going to be yelling at me," Jared said. "We've got to have a good relationship going forward. Let me go."

"Ok, fine," Trump said. "Go do it."

———

The same fight between Clark and Giuliani that was attracting eavesdroppers around the White House was also unfolding down in Georgia. Six hundred miles separated the two battles, but both were technically over Georgia election law, pitted Republicans against one another, and Trump was the provocateur at the center of each one.

In Georgia, the campaign had set up a team tasked with finding legal challenges that would improve Trump's margins. There had been barely any litigation filed during the first two weeks after the campaign's legal team gathered research and intelligence on what had happened as election officials continued to count ballots. But meanwhile, a parallel track was underway from the Oval Office where Giuliani and Meadows, who was just returning to work after being sidelined by Covid, started bringing in their own people.

Within days, the parallel teams, both launched at Trump's request, started converging in Georgia.

"We're from the White House," one attorney said after arriving in Georgia the day after the Giuliani-Clark fight.

"Well, if you were from the White House I'd know, because I'm from the White House," said another attorney who had been in Georgia for two weeks.

Meanwhile, panic was ripping through the Georgia Republican Party and the

Republican Senate majority in Washington. Both of the state's senators—David Perdue and Kelly Loeffler—had failed to win a majority on November 3 and were facing runoff elections on January 5. Republicans needed to win at least one of the two seats to maintain their advantage over Democrats in the Senate.

For several weeks, Republicans in Georgia—and Washington—had been giving Trump space to process the loss. Now Trump was tweeting about electronic bugs that were changing counts in voting machines. But Trump's Georgia Legal Team No. 1 had worked the angles in Atlanta to secure recounts that allowed them to trace individual votes to machines. Not a single machine had changed a single vote.

But when Trump's Georgia Legal Team No. 1 sent this information along, Trump's Legal Team No. 2 undermined them. Trump was told the first team wasn't working hard. They had been fooled by the Republican governor in Georgia. They cared more about winning the Senate runoffs than the presidential race.

Perdue, who had led the charge to bring a Trump rally to the state a few weeks earlier, mounted another attempt to talk sense into the president. Internal Republican data showed that Trump's constant attacks on mail voting ahead of the 2020 election had hurt their turnout efforts in Georgia. Now the president's constant attacks on the integrity of the Georgia election officials was depressing the Republican vote.

Perdue's chances of winning rested almost exclusively with Trump. He tried calling Trump. He asked other Republicans in the state to help. When none of them could reason with Trump, they appealed to Jared.

Jared didn't have good news for them either.

"Once Donald put Rudy in charge, it guaranteed this was going to be a clown show," Jared said. "I can't help you."

———

As Trump continued to move personnel inside the administration, one change he couldn't make was to install John Ratcliffe, his director of national intelligence, as attorney general.

Trump had offered Ratcliffe the job in mid-November, just as the chaos was underway in Georgia.

"I want you to be the attorney general," Trump said. "But only if you want to."

Ratcliffe asked for time to consider the offer but knew he couldn't accept.

As a former U.S. attorney who had been law partners with former Attorney General John Ashcroft, running the Justice Department was a dream job for Ratcliffe. He'd been a finalist for the nomination when Trump chose Barr, and the president gauged Ratcliffe's interest in replacing Barr nearly every time they spoke in 2020. It was an open secret inside the administration that Ratcliffe would replace Barr at the start of a second term.

But this wasn't the job they'd discussed before the election. Trump had become consumed by fighting ghosts in voting machines. He'd repeatedly asked Ratcliffe to seize voting machines that he thought foreign countries had corrupted. But Ratcliffe told Trump there was no intelligence to even suggest that might be true. Plus, his agency had no authority to seize voting machines from state election officials.

Trump was also furious that Barr and FBI Director Chris Wray weren't doing more to help him overturn the election results. Trump told Ratcliffe that he wanted him to replace Barr, then fire Wray.

Trump's offer meant that he wanted Ratcliffe to move over to the Justice Department and, as attorney general, validate the election fraud claims that would refute the very intelligence Ratcliffe had provided the president as national intelligence director.

Ratcliffe declined the job.

He told Trump he'd rather stay at DNI, where he was pushing to focus his agency on national security threats from China. He also told the president it would take months just to learn the agency.

"It will take me a week to find the bathroom," Ratcliffe said.

Ratcliffe stayed at DNI, but he couldn't avoid Trump's election fraud fetish. On almost a daily basis—and sometimes multiple times per day—Trump asked Ratcliffe to chase down the latest theory he'd heard from Sidney Powell, a former federal prosecutor with a history of propagating debunked QAnon conspiracies who had started advising Trump in mid-November.

Powell had convinced Trump he had been cheated out of votes by a computer bug buried deep inside Dominion Voting Systems machines. She repeatedly told Trump that DNI could seize the voting machines. Ratcliffe repeatedly told Trump that she was wrong.

"Remember, we've talked about this," Ratcliffe would remind Trump.

Trump dialed up administration officials to help him track down Powell's claims about a secret supercomputer changing votes. He repeatedly asked about another theory that China, Russia, and Iran had been working together to coordinate election fraud.

Trump's reluctance to believe his own spies vexed the intelligence community, particularly since the president had seen how wired they were into Iran when, in January, they'd pinpointed the location of Qassem Soleimani, the Iranian military leader, for a fatal missile strike. But now he repeatedly asked intelligence officials to double check Powell's accusation about Tehran's involvement.

While Ratcliffe worried about what Trump might have asked of him at the Justice Department, the irony was the president hadn't spoken to the actual attorney general for weeks after the election. Trump's relationship with Barr had been falling apart for months. The attorney general had blocked Trump's efforts to use troops to disrupt protests across the country. Meadows was constantly seeking information on an investigation into the origins of the FBI's 2016 Russia probe, and Trump was furious there hadn't been more prosecutions of his political enemies before the election.

Trump repeatedly made clear that he wanted the probe, led by federal prosecutor John Durham, to target both Obama and Biden and result in indictments for a set of former Obama Administration officials: FBI director James Comey, CIA director John Brennan, and James Clapper, the director of national intelligence.

"Don't talk to me about that!" Barr would yell. "You can't talk to me about that!"

Oddly, Barr's approach worked. It had been months since Trump had reached out to Barr with any frequency. Instead, Trump complained to everyone else about the attorney general—including to Fox News anchor Maria Bartiromo on November 29.

It was his first in-depth interview since the election and Trump ticked through a list of unfounded claims about widespread voter fraud, while seeming to create new ones in the moment—including an accusation that the FBI and Justice Department might have had a hand in rigging the election against him.

"This is total fraud," Trump said. "The FBI and Department of Justice, I don't know, maybe they're involved. But how are people allowed to get away with this stuff? It's unbelievable."

Trump said the Justice Department had been "missing in action" on voter fraud issues and suggested the agency was purposefully stalling the Durham investigation.

Barr was furious. He'd been considering opportunities to speak out about election fraud, and now he had his chance. Barr had heard Trump cranking about supposed election fraud for the entire year, and, contrary to Trump's accusations, he had pushed the department to look into allegations. But there hadn't been anything substantial.

Two days after Trump's Fox News interview, Barr went to lunch with Associated Press reporter Michael Balsamo and told him just that. The nation's top cop went on the record to say that the Justice Department had found no evidence of widespread voter fraud.

"We have not seen fraud on a scale that could have affected a different outcome in the election," Barr said.

Barr wondered if he'd last the day without being fired.

After lunch he went to the White House, where he had a previously scheduled meeting with Meadows and Cipollone in the chief of staff's office. Their meeting wrapped up and Barr had just walked into the counsel's office when a White House aide came in and said both Barr and Cipollone had been summoned to the Oval Office. The two attorneys briefly discussed whether Barr should make a run for it, and Cipollone would cover for him with the president. Instead, he went to meet his fate.

Trump was waiting in his private dining room off the Oval, and he erupted when Barr walked in. Trump sat at a rectangular table next to Meadows, who crossed his arms and scowled to signal exactly whose side he was on. On the other side of the table stood Barr and Will Levi, Barr's highly regarded chief of staff. Internally, Levi was viewed as one of the department's voices of restraint and reason, and had been agitating for weeks to get the department on the record contradicting the president's specious claims of a stolen election. The reward for the two Justice Department attorneys was a withering attack from Trump.

Barr pushed back, as he usually did, but Trump's volcanic eruption stunned the room, which included Cipollone and Herschmann. Trump ripped through a greatest hits reel of debunked claims of fraud—including a food truck that allegedly hauled thousands of ballots into Detroit in the middle of the night that had been dismissed just weeks earlier in court, and a video of Georgia poll workers stuffing ballots into suitcases, which turned out to be standard boxes used by local officials to transport and store ballots.

There had been so much obvious fraud, Trump said, that the only conclusion to draw from the AP story was proof that Barr hated him.

"I don't know if you've noticed but I've been leaving you alone," Trump said, a wicked suggestion that he'd been punishing Barr by withholding his attention. "You know we haven't spoken in months."

Barr told Trump his fraud allegations were "bullshit" and that the president didn't have a legal team—he had a "clown show."

Trump shifted away from the catalog of baseless claims to a more historical inventory of grievances with Barr. The Durham report should have been finished months ago. Barr should be embarrassed he'd never pinned criminal charges on Comey. Barr was protecting Hunter Biden and giving him far more consideration than any of Trump's children ever would have received.

"I can't believe you haven't done anything!" Trump shouted.

Barr had been certain that morning that there was a very likely chance he'd be fired before the end of the day. But he had withstood Trump's fury, and both men were still standing. Trump hadn't been able to pull the trigger. The president hated firing people and almost always outsourced the job to someone else—his chief of staff, sometimes his bodyguard, and once he had even tried to send a junior staffer over to the Justice Department to fire his first attorney general, Jeff Sessions.

But Trump hesitated. Perhaps it was the remaining good will from how Barr had scored for him on the media rollout of the Mueller report, which had limited the political fallout of the investigation. Perhaps it was his sense that Barr was among the few remaining adult voices in the administration.

But Barr wasn't going to prostrate himself before the president, either.

It was true that the two men hadn't met one-on-one for months. But Barr viewed that more as a blessing than a penance.

Standing in the dining room—a massive television on the wall to his right and the strange painting of Trump and his fellow Republicans on the wall directly facing him—Barr made clear that he wasn't going to subject himself or his agency to repeated insults and accusations from the president. Barr's harangue panicked White House officials that the attorney general was about to quit. Trump had just offered Barr's job to Ratcliffe two weeks earlier, but it was always a better look for Trump to push someone out than have them walk away.

Barr's car was about to pull out of the White House parking lot when Cipollone suddenly appeared and banged his hand on the window to stop the black sedan. The White House attorney climbed into the car, tried to calm Barr down, and urged his friend not to make any rash decisions. Barr agreed. No one wanted any definitive decision to be made that night. But Barr was shaken and unsure about what would happen next.

But the next morning, he was surprised by an early call from Meadows. The White House chief of staff asked Barr to stay until the end of the term. Barr agreed, and immediately regretted it. He'd been caught off guard by the unexpected call and even afterward didn't understand exactly why Trump wanted him to stay. But as Trump continued to amplify his increasingly outlandish claims of election fraud, Barr soon decided it was time to leave, and that he wanted to be finished before Christmas. Concerned that Trump might fire him before he could resign, Barr penned an obsequious and over-the-top resignation letter that he hoped would give Trump pause before firing him. It worked.

Barr hand-delivered the letter in the Oval Office on December 14, and Trump accepted it. That same day the Electoral College met to cast their votes, confirm Biden's victory, and ratify the election results in direct repudiation of Trump's refusal to concede. The total, 306 to 232, was the same margin Trump had won by four years earlier, when he bragged that he'd cleaned up in a landslide.

Barr had advised Trump to elevate Jeffrey Rosen, the deputy attorney general, into the acting attorney general role for the final month.

When Barr walked out of the Oval Office, Trump called Richard

Donoghue, who had been the U.S. attorney for the Eastern District of New York, and offered him the job. Trump didn't think Rosen was pliant enough for his liking. Donoghue declined, but agreed to be Rosen's acting deputy. Trump hung up and called Rosen.

"I'm really looking forward to working with you," Trump said to Rosen.

Before mid-November, Trump had never spoken publicly about Dominion Voting Systems. But in the final two weeks of November, he tweeted about the company two dozen times.

Trump had always sought opinions from a wide array of people. Even as a businessman in New York, he'd put the questions about big decisions to his top advisers—and then ask the waiter that night at dinner, giving each opinion equal weight. Suddenly inside the White House, Sidney Powell had as much credibility with Trump as the attorney general. Jenna Ellis, a legal adviser to the campaign with relatively little experience practicing law, had the same weight as the White House counsel.

Trump brought in Mike Lindell, the MyPillow executive, for briefings on voter fraud. Michael Flynn, Trump's former national security adviser who had pleaded guilty to lying to the FBI about his foreign contacts, also wandered in and out of the Oval Office and pushed Trump to impose martial law.

A turning point for others came after Giuliani's wild news conference on November 19 at RNC headquarters with Ellis and Powell, in which they continued to allege widespread voter fraud—arguments based on falsehoods and conspiracy theories and devoid of any evidence. Powell's arguments implicated billionaire George Soros and Venezuelan communists.

"President Trump won by a landslide, and we are going to prove it," Powell said.

After the election, Dominion filed a $1.3 billion defamation lawsuit against Powell, who defended herself by claiming that her allegations were too ridiculous to be believed.

"No reasonable person would conclude that the statements were truly statements of fact," Powell's attorneys told the federal judge presiding over the case.

Pence laughed out loud when he read the court filing.

Trump, meanwhile, cycled through all the feelings from his home in Palm Beach.

"I was very surprised at her statement. But that's Sidney Powell—she wants to get out. Maybe they're settling with her?" Trump told me during our second postelection interview at Mar-a-Lago. "All she had to say was 'upon information and belief.' I was shocked at her statement. Maybe it was a legal statement? I don't know. But I was very surprised. I was disappointed in her statement. I mean, I don't know. It can't be possible that she even made that statement. Maybe that's a legal statement that has to be made? I don't know. But I thought her statement was a very embarrassing one for her. You know, she doesn't represent me, by the way. You know that she never represented me? Do you know that?"

Giuliani said his claims were based on detailed allegations from specific individuals he said he couldn't reveal out of concern for their safety. By the end of the ninety-minute news conference, dark brown beads of sweat were dripping down the side of Giuliani's face. Inside the White House, Trump watched the news conference and asked aides if it was hair dye, or black mascara he'd used to touch up gray spots. Either way, it looked awful.

"This Giuliani strategy is not going to work," Herschmann told Trump afterward.

Ronna watched the news conference with alarm, too. She had been in and out of the White House after the election as she secured Trump's endorsement for a third term as RNC chairwoman. She warned allies that Trump had surrounded himself with people willing to tell him that he should keep fighting. But she thought at the time that Trump was processing the loss, that he would find a way to begrudgingly concede, and perhaps even use the fraud accusations to announce a 2024 reelection campaign before he left office. But she had new doubts after the news conference. RNC attorneys contacted her to raise their concerns about the party's legal liability if Giuliani and his team continued to use their building to spread dangerous and false accusations. She also started to push back on Trump.

Giuliani had been making several claims about voting fraud and irregularities in Michigan, and Trump asked for her help in her home state. Ronna agreed to check the allegations and made a round of calls. The attorneys dismissed them, and fellow Republicans in the state were even more pointed.

"This is fucking nuts," one top Republican in the Michigan House of Representatives told her.

Trump called Ronna for an update. The president put her on speaker with Pence in the room, and Ronna told the two men that the allegations were wrong.

"This is crazy, and I'm not doing it," Ronna said. "It's not true."

"Well, I think it is," Trump said.

"Nothing is going to happen with this—it's not going anywhere," Ronna said. "The RNC is not going to push this out."

Pence, as usual, kept his thoughts to himself.

The night the Electoral College met, four people were stabbed in Washington and more than thirty arrested as Proud Boys and other Trump supporters clashed with counter protesters.

"These Proud Boys are avowed white nationalists and have been called to stand up against a fair and legal election," D.C. mayor Muriel E. Bowser said in the aftermath of the violence. "This is a symptom of the hateful rhetoric, anti-science noise, and people who refuse to accept the result of a fair American election."

Most of Trump World thought the Electoral College vote casting would be when Trump moved on from the fraud allegations. But inside the Justice Department, officials said that Meadows had helped introduce Trump to DOJ attorney Jeffrey Clark, who was putting together a secret plan to oust Rosen, the acting attorney general, and force Georgia to overturn its results. Meadows disputed he had played any role.

Meadows also reportedly connected Trump with Mark Martin, a former North Carolina Supreme Court justice with a radical interpretation of the Constitution. Pence, Martin told Trump, had the power to stop the certification of the Electoral College results on January 6.

"Big protest in D.C. on January 6th. Be there, will be wild!" Trump tweeted on December 18.

The pandemic proved a blessing for Saundra's travel itinerary. She bought cheap airfare, repeatedly basked in the extravagance of an airplane aisle all to herself, and logged more flights in 2020 than at any point in her life—and certainly more than any other Front Row Joe. She attended twenty-five Trump rallies in 2020, which boosted her lifetime total to fifty-six.* She spent seventy-nine nights of the year away from her own bed. Saundra traveled so often during the pandemic that when a Delta flight attendant thanked her for being a Silver Medallion member and upgraded her to first class, she had to ask someone what that meant.

"It's nice because it's more comfortable and bigger seats up there," Saundra said about the perks of her frequent flyer status. "This whole year has just been so wild."

Saundra started 2021 the same way she'd spent most of 2020: on a flight. She flew from Detroit to Atlanta on Saturday, January 2, and slept that night in the airport. On Sunday, she met friends and drove ninety miles north to Dalton, where they spent a freezing night outside waiting in line for Trump's rally on Monday—ahead of the Georgia Senate runoffs. On Tuesday, as Republicans failed to turn out enough voters in both races and lost their majority in the U.S. Senate, she and her friends drove to Washington for the Save America rally on Wednesday, January 6.

Saundra was convinced beyond a doubt that Trump had been reelected on November 3, only to have it stolen in what she described as "a takeover by the communist devils."

"If someone put a gun to my head and said, 'Did Donald Trump win, yes or no? And if you're wrong, we're going to shoot your head off!' I would say yes," Saundra said. "I'm that confident that this stuff is not made up."

Part of her evidence was that Corey Lewandowski, a well-known high priest of Old Testament–style Trumpism, had foretold all that would happen way back in July when she'd come to Washington for the Republican National

---

* These totals double again if she counted Don Junior and Mike Pence rallies, but no proper Front Row Joe would ever try to pad numbers like that.

Convention, despite the fact she wasn't a delegate and there were no public events due to the pandemic. She didn't have much to do other than go to dinner at Trump International Hotel, the kind of temple where money changers and true believers were encouraged to interact. It was there that she ran into Corey.

"How's the election going to go?" Saundra asked him.

"It's going to be the most fraudulent election in the history of the country," Corey said. "You just watch the television. There's going to be a big red wave, and it's going to look like Donald Trump won. Then, in the middle of the night, the mail ballots are going to come in. You're going to wake up the next day, and you're not going to know the results of the election. We're going to have to settle this election in the court."

But her most significant data point was that Trump himself said he won. She hadn't seen a single correction, clarification, or retraction that Fox Business's Lou Dobbs, Newsmax's John Tabacco, and Fox News's Maria Bartiromo and Jeanine Pirro, among others, all had to issue after repeating those false allegations about Dominion Voting Systems machine cheating Trump out of votes.

"No, I'm getting all my news from Facebook," Saundra told me. "I turned all the news off after November 3."

When Saundra and her friends arrived in Washington on the evening of January 5, they checked into the Comfort Inn near the Washington Convention Center downtown and then went out for a walk. They strolled over to Harry's bar and the Hotel Harrington, where a memorial had been held a month earlier for Randal. Saundra bought a souvenir lanyard from a Washington street vendor.

They walked by the Ellipse on the National Mall, the site of Trump's Save America rally the next day. More than twenty people had already lined up by midnight. Saundra and her friends decided to join them and stayed out all night.

Earlier that day, Trump and Pence met to once again discuss the president's request to block the certification of Biden's victory. Pence had been a loyal lieutenant for Trump for four years—and was widely mocked for his subservience—but this was the ultimate test.

They had gone round and round in the Oval Office. Trump believed Pence had the legal right to reject the election results. Pence thought Trump was getting bad legal advice.

The president and vice president had labored through the same debate at least a dozen times since mid-November, when Pence allies said Trump first suggested blocking Congress from certifying the results. Earlier that week, John Eastman, an attorney who represented the president in some postelection legal battles, argued that election results had been rejected in 1801 and 1960. For the past several weeks, Giuliani and Peter Navarro, a top White House adviser, also supported that view. But Marc Short, Pence's chief of staff, told them that those examples had no comparison to what Trump wanted Pence to do.

The 1801 example was to correct a clerical error. And after the 1960 election, the vice president presiding over the vote was Richard Nixon, who had lost the presidential race that year to John F. Kennedy. Nixon had initially won the vote in Hawaii, but that state, too, after a recount, flipped to Kennedy. Nixon, acting against his own self-interest—and without objection from Congress—suggested awarding Hawaii's Electoral College votes to Kennedy.

But Pence wasn't practiced in confronting Trump. The most heated Pence had ever gotten with Trump was in May 2018, when news broke that Pence's super-PAC had hired Corey. Trump threw the article at Pence when they climbed into the presidential limousine on their way to the National Peace Officers' Memorial Service. Trump thought the story made it seem like his team was bailing on him in the middle of the Russia probe.

Trump gave Pence the silent treatment for the rest of the ride. He finally spoke to the vice president on the way back to the White House—just long enough to criticize his No. 2.

"So disloyal," Trump said.

Pence had enough. His fundraising committee had hired Corey as a favor to Jared, who, months earlier, had asked Pence for help. Jared was about to have Brad installed as head of the reelection bid, and he wanted to find something with which to pacify Corey. Pence had spent almost an entire lunch with Trump discussing the plan.

Pence picked up the article and threw it back at Trump. He leaned toward the president and pointed a finger a few inches from his chest.

"We walked you through every detail of this," Pence snarled. "We did this for you—as a favor. And this is how you respond? You need to get your facts straight."

Nearly three years later, the moment seemed to call for another get-your-facts-straight lesson from Pence. Some of Pence's advisers urged him to confront Trump like he had back in 2018. But this time, the vice president remained measured. His team claimed he'd been crystal clear with Trump for weeks.

"Anything you give us, we'll review," Pence told the president. "But I don't see how it's possible."

After Pence left, Trump heard commotion outside from the crowd already gathering at the Ellipse across the South Lawn for his Save America rally the next day. He summoned Scavino into the Oval Office, along with Judd Deere, the White House deputy press secretary. Trump had opened the door to the colonnade and wanted his aides to sit and listen to the celebration with him as he signed a stack of bills on his desk from Congress. Soon more staffers were pulled into the office. Trump was in a great mood as he bobbed his head to the beat of the classic rock blaring outside, exactly the kind of music he'd pick to play ahead of one of his own rallies.

The music was so loud that staffers could feel the vibrations—as well as the chilly January air—inside the Oval. Trump noticed the noise from the crowd, too, and noted how much energy his supporters had. He asked his aides if they thought the crowd would be even bigger than at one of his mega-rallies. His supporters were fired up, he said.

"They're coming here because they want Congress to do the right thing," he said. "Maybe Congress will do the right thing. Some members may not."

He asked if they thought the day would be peaceful.

"Everyone who comes to your rallies is peaceful," Deere told Trump. "Your supporters love law enforcement. Unless they interact with protesters, I wouldn't suspect any problems with our folks."

"Well," Trump ominously responded. "Don't forget these people are fired up."

Trump turned to Scavino and said he wanted to send a tweet that made sure the Pentagon, Justice Department, and the military was prepared for tomorrow.

"Antifa is a Terrorist Organization, stay out of Washington," Trump wrote in the tweet. "Law enforcement is watching you."

The next morning, the temporary gates set up for the rally opened at 7:00 a.m., and the first speakers took the stage several hours later. A little after 1:00 p.m., Saundra was on her way to the Capitol.

Mainstream media had reported for days that Pence planned to certify the election results. Trump called the reports fake news, but Pence never disputed them. Pence and his team viewed this as a show of respect for Trump—but some Trump supporters interpreted his silence as an indication that he might do Trump's bidding after all.

But as Trump was finishing his speech on the Ellipse, Pence released a formal statement that said he did not have the power to reject Electoral College votes.

When news articles started to post about Pence's plans to certify the election results in favor of Biden and Harris, Saundra's sister back home texted her the headlines. Saundra shouted the Pence headlines to the massive, slow-moving crowd around her.

"What do you mean?" someone yelled. "What's going on?"

"It's not looking good," Saundra said.

Similar alerts buzzed the mobile phones of other marchers, and Saundra noticed a surge of energy in the crowd. The crowd that had been on the march around her now felt like a stampede.

The anger turned palpable. Someone shouted about needing to find Pence at the Capitol. Someone else yelled that they should tear down the building. The crowd—many of whom had been chanting "Lock Her Up" just two days earlier at Trump's rally in Georgia—broke out into shouts of "Gotta Get Pence!" and "Hang Mike Pence!"

"If Mike Pence would have come out of that building, I guarantee he would have died," Saundra said. "And if it wasn't by gunfire, he would have been pummeled. They were going to kill him in the street."

The joint session of Congress had convened at 1:00 p.m. as the Trump crowd outside was clashing with police. Led by members of the Proud Boys who used earpieces and radios to communicate, they had broken through barriers and were marching through the Capitol grounds.

The police were overrun.

Trump had just finished his speech on the Ellipse. He'd urged his supporters to "fight like hell" and promised to walk with the crowd to the Capitol, but he returned to the White House instead.

Within the hour, just as the mob was pressing up against the Capitol doors, District police declared a riot. Soon afterward, at a few minutes past 2:00 p.m., a piece of lumber smashed through a window and rioters started climbing through. Another Proud Boy, later identified by police as Dominic Pezzola, used a Capitol Police shield he had seized to smash through another window a few minutes later. More rioters flooded into the historic building.

The initial intruders used pipes and flagpoles to shatter windows and break furniture. They broke into House Speaker Nancy Pelosi's office, where they rifled through her belongings, sat in her office chair, and put their feet on her desk. One man stole her lectern, the same one she had stood behind more than a year earlier to announce the impeachment investigation into Trump's dealings with Ukraine.

The mob streamed through Statuary Hall, where they largely stayed between the red velvet stanchions—as if they were awestruck citizens on a group tour instead of violent rioters engaging in an insurrection. They took out their mobile phones and took pictures of the artwork and smiled for selfies.

Pence was hustled off the Senate floor and into a nearby hideaway just one minute before a violent mob rushed up to the second floor, where the doors to the Senate chamber were. If the insurgents had arrived on the second-floor landing just seconds earlier, the man they had wanted to hang for treason would have been within eyesight—and reach.

Initially, Trump seemed to be enjoying the melee, heartened to see his supporters fighting so vigorously on his behalf. He watched more as a passive spectator than as the president of the United States, who had helped incite the violence unfolding little more than two miles away.

Trump also ignored the public and private pleas of his advisers, both current and former, who begged him to quell the riots. Terrified Republican lawmakers called White House aides and the president's children, pleading for help. Kellyanne Conway—who had received calls from D.C. Mayor Muriel Bowser's office asking for her help in convincing Trump to call in the National Guard—phoned a close personal aide to the president, relaying the mayor's request and adding that she, too, felt Trump needed to calm his supporters. The mayor twice personally implored Meadows for help.

Trump didn't call off the intruders until almost 4:30 p.m., about a half hour after Pence had called the Pentagon looking for support from the National Guard. Trump's video, which he posted on social media, told his supporters to go home, but didn't denounce the violence.

"Go home—we love you, you're very special," Trump said.

It would be hours before Capitol Police, with help from D.C. police officers, FBI SWAT team members, Secret Service officers, and National Guard soldiers were able to clear the Capitol of rioters and restore order.

The riots would leave five people dead, including a Capitol Police officer.

Pence, meanwhile, had repeatedly rejected Secret Service recommendations to evacuate him from the Capitol. He didn't want to appear cowed, or give the rioters the satisfaction of delaying the certification any longer than they already had. By 8:00 p.m., he was back in the Senate chamber. The vote was certified that night.

"Today was a dark day in the history of the United States Capitol," Pence said once he was back in the Senate. "To those who wreaked havoc in our Capitol today, you did not win. Violence never wins. Freedom wins. And this is still the People's House."

⎯⎯⎯

Outside, Saundra and her friends had made their way up the west side of the Capitol where the mob had pushed through police barricades and turned the steel bike racks on their sides, leaning them against stone walls like ladders. Some men helped Saundra climb up the rungs. People were everywhere, and it was difficult to move. Saundra and her friends scaled one more wall and were within about one hundred yards of the Capitol. But it had become so crowded—and they didn't want to lose each other—that they decided to stop on the west terrace, take some pictures, and soak up the atmosphere.

They paused in the same place where Trump and Pence were inaugurated in 2017 on a crisp, clear day amid a crowd of former presidents and against a Capitol decorated in red, white, and blue bunting. Four years later, Trump supporters swarmed marble terraces, walkways, and the steps of the west front of the same ornate building. Countless Trump flags flapped in the wind. Clouds of tear gas hung in the air against the purple twilight sky, and the orange light glowing from inside the Capitol's windows gave the scene a surreal, apocalyptic feel.

Saundra was inspired by a vista of Trumpian strength and patriotism: the Washington Monument off in the distance, the majestic Capitol in the foreground, and freedom-loving patriots fighting like hell to stop a stolen and fraudulent election, liberate their country, and save their president. She snapped pictures and recorded videos.

"It just looked so neat," she said. "We weren't there to steal things. We weren't there to do damage. We were just there to overthrow the government."

Saundra flew home to Michigan the next morning. In the twenty-four hours that had passed since the insurrection, she had become convinced that the violence around and inside the U.S. Capitol could never have come from fellow Trump supporters. She claimed to have watched a video that showed police escorting white vans full of Antifa into Washington. Another theory was that law enforcement was in on it the whole time—maybe they purposely didn't secure the building, she said, because they wanted to blame an insurrection on Trump and then throw him out of office.

Trump's own video posted during the violence, in which he urged his people to go home, had depressed her.

"We were supposed to be fighting until the end," she said.

But she reminded herself that he still hadn't technically conceded. As soon as she got back to Sault Ste. Marie, she packed for the next Trump trip. Saundra trusted that something was coming and wanted a rally go-bag ready if she needed to leave at a moment's notice.

"We're all on the edge of our seats waiting to hear about the next event," she said. "Now we're like an army, and it's like boots on the ground. Tell us where we need to go! Tell us where we need to be, and we just drop everything and we go. Nobody cares about if they have to work. Nobody cares about anything.

"The time is now," she continued, sounding at once urgent and wistful. "It's time to go."

———

The backlash against Trump was immediate. He was suspended from Twitter and Facebook the next day. A flood of White House officials resigned. Transportation Secretary Elaine Chao stepped down from Trump's Cabinet, and her husband, Senator McConnell, told colleagues that he hoped never to speak to Trump again.

"The mob was fed lies," McConnell said on January 19. "They were provoked by the president and other powerful people."

Trump was impeached in the House on January 13 for inciting an insurrection—the only president to be impeached twice—in a bipartisan vote that included support from ten Republicans. A week later, on January 20, he boarded *Air Force One* for the last time as president and flew home to Florida.

"We will be back in some form," Trump said before climbing into the plane.

———

One of the truisms in Trump World held that the constant chaos and plot twists were always surprising but never shocking. The absurdity of it all always seemed to make perfect sense. And Trump's insurrection was the ultimate coda—a horrifying but inevitable finale. He'd spent four years insisting that the media was lying, that elected officials weren't to be believed, and that the courts weren't to be trusted. He'd spent his entire presidency gaslighting the country with a version of reality in which he'd never lost, he'd never be convicted, and he'd never really go away.

And, true to form, the story continued to unfold back in Washington in ways that were surprising—but hardly shocking. Days after Trump left office, polls showed that he still maintained high levels of support from inside his party. House Republicans who had voted to impeach him suddenly found themselves the target of censure and primary challenges. Republican leaders made plans to visit him at Mar-a-Lago—a steady stream of supplicants bowing down before their exiled king.

And on February 13, 2021, the Senate—along with McConnell—voted to acquit Trump of the impeachment charges against him for a second time. In an interview on Fox News before the end of the month, McConnell was asked if he'd support Trump if he was the Republican presidential nominee in 2024.

"Absolutely," McConnell said.

Back in Mar-a-Lago, Trump celebrated the support from fellow Republicans who had, once again, protected him from impeachment, delivering yet another acquittal that would preserve his ability to run for president again. With his Twitter and Facebook accounts still suspended, he turned to his diminished staff to help him send out an email.

He vowed to keep fighting to deliver "American greatness" across the country. He described the MAGA movement as "historic, patriotic and beautiful."

"There has never been anything like it!" Trump said, offering a rare understatement.

Epilogue

"Things have happened that nobody can believe."
                    —*Interview with the author, Mar-a-Lago, March 11, 2021*

Donald Trump arrived at Mar-a-Lago unprepared for the post-presidency.
"What am I going to do all day?" he asked one aide after stepping off *Air Force One* in West Palm Beach on January 20.

Most of his inner circle had largely abandoned him after the insurrection, leaving many of the day-to-day duties in the final two weeks to Johnny McEntee, his thirty-year-old West Wing aide. McEntee spent those first few nights after the riots on a White House couch as Trump, barely able to sleep, roamed the halls into the early hours of the morning. But even McEntee needed some distance. After the government plane touched down in Florida, he jumped on one of the first flights back home to California.

Nothing was ready at Mar-a-Lago. Trump's office was embarrassingly cramped. His skeletal staff was brought to the resort's bridal suite, where random mattresses were strewn on the floor. Staffers had to drive over the intercoastal bridge to buy desks and chairs. Without Twitter, and with no White House press corps assembled outside, there was initially confusion about how to put out a statement.

Trump had grown so distrustful of everyone around him that he couldn't even take solace in the $80 million sitting in his leadership PAC, a combination of unspent campaign cash and postelection fundraising—as much as $50 million of which had been raised before Election Day. He wasn't even sure if it was really there. He wouldn't sign paychecks, refused to approve budgets, and ignored requests to send out fundraising emails until he could see the bank account statement with his own eyes.

He repeatedly asked friends if they blamed him for the riots at the Capitol. "You don't think I wanted them to do that, do you?" he asked.

He peppered club guests, friends, and political aides—those who started reemerging in February—if he should run for president again. He wanted to know which Republicans would run against him, and whom he should endorse in the 2022 midterms. But he seemed more interested in the idea of his political power than in actually putting together any plans to wield it in 2024. Few believed, in those first months after leaving the White House, that he would run again in four years.

There seemed to be a new melancholy to the former president's tone when he talked about the next phase of his life. Melania loved it at Mar-a-Lago, he told friends, and she looked more beautiful than ever. He acknowledged his own advanced age, mused about whether some of his health risks—he was overweight, adding "at least that's what they say"—might catch up with him, and even acknowledged a power higher than himself for lasting as long as he had.

"The Good Lord's given me good health up to now—but you never know," he said.

For Trump, it was a shocking amount of self-reflection.

But Trump slowly found relief in the new routine.

He golfed every day, sometimes playing as many as thirty-six holes at a time, and lost a noticeable amount of weight. A warm tone had reappeared in his face, and his hair was shaded with a color that was at least a bit closer to something found in the natural world.

His campaign aides had started to descend on Palm Beach again, along with other Republican leaders. The Republican National Committee spent hundreds of thousands on catering and rental fees for fundraisers.

And based on what I saw at Mar-a-Lago one evening in March, Trump replaced the adulation from his once roaring arena rally crowds with nightly standing ovations from his dues-paying members during the dinner service outside on the resort's terrace.

The ex-president sauntered across the stone patio, through the arched doorway of intricately woven iron grillwork, and into the Grand Salon of Mar-a-Lago, where I waited for our interview in mid-March.

His shoulders were slightly hunched and rolled forward inside his dark blue suit, and he walked with a slow, deep bend in his knees—the same fluid and carefree gait I had been struck by when I first interviewed him at his New York skyscraper early in the 2016 campaign cycle. Trump carried himself with the pace of a man who had somewhere to be, and assumed he'd get there soon enough—and on his own terms. He greeted me as if I'd spent the past six weeks of his post-presidency standing right there under the hundreds of gold-leaf sunburst squares carved across the forty-two-foot-ceiling in the main sitting room.

"Good to see you, Michael. Everything all right?" Trump asked me.

He motioned for me to sit on a gold-cushioned couch positioned beneath one of two massive imported crystal chandeliers. Each light fixture featured two tiers of candelabra bulbs snuggled in a tangled nest of twinkling crystal pendants that scattered the light across the Ming vases, marble tables, and centuries-old Venetian silk tapestries hung from the walls of the 1,800-square-foot room.

Trump poured his long, bulky frame across a curved-back chair about an arm's length away from me, and made himself comfortable. His shoulders tilted toward me and his excessively long, bright yellow tie slid off the side of his belly. He slung his right arm over the side of the chair at his armpit. The chair didn't recline, but Trump had found repose.

"We have Rick Scott coming tonight," he told me as soon as he sat down.* "We have a lot of people coming down, a lot of politicians coming here."

---

* Trump and Scott are a fascinating pair of Floridians—both controversial entrepreneurs and Republican outsiders whose initial victories shocked the political establishment. But Trump is a brash extrovert with a flair for tabloid drama, while Scott is a robotic introvert who has possibly never cursed. They first met in 2011 after Scott was elected Florida governor. After the meeting, Trump adviser Roger Stone called Scott strategist Tony Fabrizio. "Trump liked Scott but thought he was a little weird," Stone said. "That's funny," Fabrizio said. "Scott said the exact same thing."

It was less than two months since Trump had left office, and the seventy-four-year-old former president's disposition matched his relaxed surroundings. It was still 75 degrees in the evening. Just outside the fifty-eight-bedroom, thirty-three-bathroom mansion, a groundskeeper stood on the edge of the croquet greensward and casually sprayed touch-up paint on one of the game's six white wickets. The last bits of sunlight sparkled off the cresting Atlantic Ocean waves in the distance.

He'd just finished a round of golf with Ernie Els, the former pro golfer and two-time U.S. Open champion. Sean Hannity, the Fox News anchor, called midway through our interview—and Trump took the call and put it on speakerphone so I could listen to them banter. Club members had to walk past us as they arrived for dinner. They would say hello to Trump and offer encouragement.

"This is the *Wall Street Journal!*" he'd tell them.

Once the guests walked past, Trump would lean in to gossip with me about who was who—what company this person used to manage, how much money that person once had, who had battled cancer but made a miraculous recovery.

Trump was in transition. Weeks earlier he'd been leader of the free world. Now he was King of Mar-a-Lago.

Perhaps the biggest change, somewhat stunningly, was that Trump told me that he was glad to be off Twitter. He said his prewritten statements, now issued via news release, were "much more elegant."

"It's really better than Twitter because I don't do the stupid retweets that people don't like—the retweets are the ones that get you," Trump said. "And I saved a lot of time. I didn't realize you can spend a lot of time on this. Now I actually have time to make phone calls, and do other things and read papers that I wouldn't read. And with me, if I put a comma out of place or I accidentally misspelled a word, it was like the world coming down."*

But the adjustment wasn't complete. He maintained a list of grievances that was lengthy, personal, and bipartisan.

Senate Republican leader Mitch McConnell was "dumb as a rock" for not

---

* Trump's stable of seven campaign managers, chairman, and chief executives, as well as four White House staff chiefs, seven communications directors, and four press secretaries—along with half the country—had begged him for years to stop tweeting.

spending more money on Covid relief before the election. Representative Liz Cheney, the daughter of former vice president Dick Cheney who would be stripped of her House leadership position for contradicting Trump's false claims of a stolen election, was a "sleazebag" for voting to impeach him. He hadn't received enough credit for the strong performance House Republicans had in the November elections.

He remained fixated on his own reelection results. He still insisted the election had been stolen, and repeatedly mentioned disproven conspiracy theories about precincts in battleground states where the number of votes exceeded the number of voters. But he also added slightly more nuance to his argument, complaining that his chances to win had been diminished in the rush to change voting rules so close to the election. It was a stretch to describe that as stealing an election, but at least it was a point about policy that could prompt a legitimate debate.

Trump also remained conflicted about how to think about his former running mate.

The two had spoken a half dozen times by phone in the two months since they'd been out of office, and Trump told me he liked Pence "very much." But he continued to claim that the former vice president had made a mistake by not rejecting the election results. Trump said he was still disappointed in Pence about that. Pence had received bad advice—both legal and political— from his staff, and had shirked his constitutional duty to reject a fraudulent election, Trump said.

But maybe, I suggested, Pence didn't think the election had been stolen.

"Did Pence think the vote was correct?" I asked Trump.

"I didn't even ask him that question," he said.

Trump repeatedly told me how disappointed he was in Pence, but he also acknowledged that the two had spoken several times since leaving office. I asked Trump if Pence had apologized for not following his orders, given how unhappy Trump had been about the vice president's allegiance to the Constitution.

Trump paused.

"I don't talk to him about it," he said. "I don't care if he apologies or not. He made a mistake."

As the interview stretched into the evening, Trump's phone continued to ring, guests poured into the resort, and the former president said he wanted to watch his successor's first prime-time address that night—a short speech that Biden used to mark the one-year anniversary of coronavirus lockdowns, and pledge that the vaccine would be available for all adults starting in May.

Trump ended our interview, but he told his staff he wanted to continue our conversation over the phone at another time. Even though he'd replied to nearly every question I asked—no matter the topic—with an answer about election fraud, he told me he liked my questions, and he invited me to stay for dinner. He asked Margo Martin and Jason Miller, two members of his press team present for the interview, to sit with me on the terrace.

"He's not dating," Trump said about Miller. "He's got a wonderful wife at home, so what the hell?"

More than 200 guests sat at iron tables on the terrace, where they were serenaded by violins and cellos playing slow orchestral music. It was high season in South Florida. The guests who had been walking around earlier in yellow swimsuits and pants with turtle prints were now in evening jackets and long dresses. The men seemed to all be pushing their eighties, and many of the women were considerably younger. I sat down, and when a waiter wearing a face mask approached, I ordered a glass of Bordeaux, with a filet mignon, "Mr. Trump's Wedge" salad, and a side of glazed baby beets and roasted turnips. As I finished my meal, the waiter approached again to tell me dinner would be complimentary that night. This was welcome news for my dinner companions, but I tried to explain to the waiter that, as a journalist, I needed to pay my own bill. The waiter gave me a confused look.

"Mr. Trump insists," he told me, and after some back and forth, I let it drop.

A little past 8:00 p.m., Trump approached the terrace from the covered walkway, which I only realized when all of the guests stood up and cheered for the owner of their club, the former president of the United States. The applause was sustained and loud as Trump arrived at the hostess stand, where he met Senator Scott.

The two men were escorted to the president's table, set up in the middle of the terrace, but separated from the crowd with a burgundy velvet rope and stanchion. Guests craned their necks to see if they recognized whom Trump had invited to dinner.

Later, Trump sent the waiter to bring me over to his table. Scott, whom I had covered for the *Tampa Bay Times* when he was governor of Florida, seemed happy to see me and ran through a list of old staffers, wondering if I'd seen any lately and if I was still keeping up with his former team. Trump interrupted. He wanted to show me a poll that Scott, chairman of the Senate Republican campaign committee, had brought him. It wasn't a poll as much as it was a graphic—a bar chart showing that 83 percent of Republicans wanted him to run again for president.

Trump also told me that Republicans would have lost eight more Senate seats in 2020 had it not been for his help. It was only because of him that his party was tied, 50–50, with Democrats in the chamber. It was an interesting theory since most Republicans in Washington thought they'd have had a two-seat majority had Trump paid more attention to the Georgia runoffs instead of the election fraud conspiracies.

Scott interjected this time. The Florida Republican said Trump had saved ten seats, not eight.

"But do I get credit?" Trump said. "No."

Other guests finished their dinners, walked by Trump, and leaned into his roped-off area. They offered encouragement, and agreed that 2020 had been a sham. Trump, the unceasing host, welcomed the interruptions.

"Did you have the meat or the fish?" he asked. "Was it good?"

When he and Scott had finished and stood, the remaining crowd rose in their seats, too. Their numbers were smaller than earlier in the night, but their applause sounded just as loud, amplified by some boozy yelling and screaming for Trump.

The forty-fifth president of the United States smiled.

"Thank you," he mouthed melodramatically.

Trump acknowledged the applause with a wave of his hand, and then he disappeared into the suite of his club.

Acknowledgments

"I was the one to get it done, and even the fake news media knows."
—*News release, Mar-a-Lago, March 29, 2021*

The acknowledgments sections in books always struck me as a bit ridiculous. There's no other industry where you finish a job and immediately stand up and start thanking everyone you've ever met. But after writing my first book, I feel, well, a little different. Though not for the reasons I thought. Maybe it's my Midwestern Catholicism coming out here, but my instinct is to fill these next pages not with acknowledgments but with apologies.

I've never attempted anything remotely approaching the scale of this project, and it unfolded amid circumstances I wouldn't have believed even if Bill S. Preston, Esq. and Ted "Theodore" Logan would have snatched me from the streets of Washington in the summer of 2019, when I first considered writing this book, and brought me in their time-traveling telephone booth to the horrors that lay ahead in 2020. The pandemic wreaked havoc on all of our daily lives and routines, and I repeatedly considered abandoning this project in the face of the unexpected upheaval and chaos. Instead, I pushed ahead. I had thought about writing a book at different points in my career, and it seemed improbable that it would ever happen if I didn't try after five years of covering Trump, who has been the most fascinating political story of my lifetime. But I've struggled to come to terms with the fallout from my choice. I am so sorry that during this already troubled time I've been the source of additional stress to the humans I love most. Not a day passed that I wasn't filled with some combination of overwhelming guilt and humbling appreciation that my family believed in me enough to assume many of my responsibilities and help ease some of my burden at a time when they were already shouldering too much of their own. I hope my family has enjoyed these pages. This book exists because of them. And it's for them that every word here was written.

That dedication begins first and mostly with Ashley. The countless nights and weekends she cleared for me by buying groceries, cooking dinners, paying bills, potty training the baby, and making sure both girls were safe and fed and at running and soccer and gymnastics practices—and on time, too!—is a load I never should have put on her and a debt I will never fully be able to repay.* For that, I apologize. She did it while she worked two high-pressure jobs—and thrived at both—and while she pedaled a Peloton, finished a Shamrockin' Run, coordinated our summer, maintained all of her friendships, and found me nearby office space to rent so she could, as it turned out, kick me out of our bedroom/pandemic office/cycling studio. She read and reread chapters for me and improved them every time. Her handling of huge changes these past few years has been heroic and inspiring. I am exceptionally lucky and endlessly thankful to have her guidance, her support, and, most of all, her love.

The heaviest price I paid while writing this book has been time lost with my two daughters, who fill me with joy just by climbing through a bumblebee jungle gym or running across a softball diamond. Zoe, my ten-year-old peanut, handled the dual challenges of a distracted father and twelve months of online elementary school—sandwiched around two months of a lockeddown summer—with more generosity and grace than many adults. Nothing encouraged me to finish more than the little note she Scotch-taped to my desk lamp telling me that she knew I could do it. Mazarine bean, my two-year-old, updated me on everything I missed and asked only for tickles in return—and occasional visits to my "office house." The organizing principle of my life is that these two girls, someday, will be half as proud of me as I am of them.

I'm blessed to have the world's best mom. Elisa Bender drove halfway across the country in the middle of a pandemic when I needed her help, didn't blink when my chaos greeted her as soon as she stepped through the front

---

* But her habitual list-making makes me think she's got a few ideas for where I should start.

door, and did it all over again in my final scramble to meet my deadline. Both girls were always thrilled to find out about an upcoming weekend with my dad, Mike Bender, and his partner, Peg Drew, both of whom also pitched in during the crucial final days. I was lucky to have their help. My in-laws, Betty Parker and Justine Parker, constantly interrupted their own lives to find ways to provide support: making almond milk for Mazzy, reading her books, playing with Norman the gorilla, and putting her to bed. The unequivocal welcome Bruce Parker extended to me when I joined his family was a gift that continues to resonate today. Bruce unfortunately was unable to put a red pen to this manuscript, but he will be proud to know that his eldest daughter inherited his exacting editing skills.

My sisters and brothers-in-law kept me encouraged with constant texts, calls, and care packages: Courtney Bender, Sarah Bender, Monique and Romilly Taylor, Emily and Mike Iuzzolino, Alexandra and Freddy Hunt, and Jordan and Brandon Sandmann. Thank you all so very much. Thank you to Gigi and Papa—my endlessly clever grandmother and loving grandfather—for a lifetime of support.

A special thank-you to Marty Bacon and the entire Bacon family, who winterized the family river house so I could have a quiet place for reporting and writing, and to Norma for sharing her leftovers on the deck. Pop welcomed my family like we'd always been a part of his, and I'm forever grateful that the rest of the Bacons picked up that mantle.

Roberta Cummings isn't technically family, but a loving nanny feels like one in every sense of the word—and Roberta is the absolute greatest. We literally would not have survived without you, Roberta. Thanks to Henry Gelinas and Callum Czin for being such sweet little boys.

And while Bill and Ted never found me, Matt and Keith did. Javelin uber-agents Matt Latimer and Keith Urbahn provided advice, resources, and encouragement that finished this book. Sean Desmond, the publisher at Twelve, recognized potential in this project from the start and carried it to completion with savvy professionalism and sharp editorial guidance.

A very special thank you to Genevieve Smith, who provided invaluable edits along the way. This book was immeasurably improved by her attention to detail and organization. It's no surprise that she's one of the best editors at

New York magazine—and in publishing, generally. I learned so much about writing and reporting from her.

Thank you to Julie Tate for her careful read of the manuscript, and her support and encouragement along the way; Bob Castillo at Twelve for his round-the-clock work to get this book printed; Reagan Schmidt provided sharp and concise research assistance; Dylan Colligan and Khang Dang at Javelin for help with the source notes; Lissa Ryan Photography for the author shot for the book jacket; and Jarrod Taylor for the inspired cover design.

I spent the final months writing this book literally from inside a therapist's office, a space that was unironically provided by Melissa Kilbride after the pandemic suspended in-person consultations for her practice.

A posthumous note of gratitude to the great John Homans, the once-in-a-generation magazine editor who left a legion of admirers with indelible memories and writing lessons. I was lucky enough to work with John at Bloomberg News, and I could hear his encouragement and excitement whenever I scored a fun anecdote or managed to turn a phrase.

Thank you also to Sasha Issenberg for sharing invaluable and endless wisdom about the book industry and the joys and travails of the writing process. Thank you to everyone who read pages, offered consultations, or provided additional support to finish this book, including Rebecca Ballhaus, Nick Corasaniti, Sopan Deb, Reid Epstein, Carrie Frye, John Heilemann, John Kelly, Alex Leary, Jon Lemire, Ted Mann, Phil Mattingly, Mike Nizza, Andrew Restuccia, Andrew Rice, Phil Rucker, Michael Schmidt, and Eli Stokols.

This project wouldn't have been possible without the support and opportunities provided to me by the *Wall Street Journal*. A special thank-you to Matt Murray, Karen Miller Pensiero, Paul Beckett, and Ben Pershing for the time and space to finish this project. Thank you to my Trump World teammates, past and present, whose relentless reporting skills, graceful writing, and unmatched collegiality have made the past five years so memorable. Their wisdom and insights are reflected in this book from the first page to the last: Rebecca Ballhaus, Alex Leary, Catherine Lucey, Gordon Lubold, Andrew Restuccia, Vivian Salama, Louise Radnofsky, Ted Mann, Carol Lee, Peter Nicholas, Damian Paletta, Eli Stokols, Reid Epstein, Janet Hook, and Beth Reinhard. Additional thanks to my generous colleagues from the newspaper's

2020 campaign reporters and Congress team: Siobhan Hughes, Kristina Peterson, Byron Tau, Lindsay Wise, Julie Bykowicz, Dante Chinni, Eliza Collins, Alexa Corse, Chad Day, Emily Glazer, Josh Jamerson, Tim Hanrahan, John McCormick, Madeleine Ngo, Tarini Parti, Sabrina Siddiqui, Emily Stephenson, Ken Thomas, and Aaron Zitner. An individual thank-you-and-apology combo to Andy Duehren for getting dragged into the Hunter saga. And finally, my eternal gratitude to Jeanne Cummings and Jerry Seib, who adopted me into this strange and wonderful family in 2016.

Thank you to my White House press corps colleagues, whose relentless reporting, lively writing, and unmatched contributions to journalism I continue to strive to match, including Yamiche Alcindor, Peter Baker, Julie Davis, Josh Dawsey, Anne Gearan, Maggie Haberman, Steve Holland, Jennifer Jacobs, Weijia Jiang, Jonathan Karl, Annie Karni, Jon Lemire, Zeke Miller, Doug Mills, Sara Murray, Tolu Olorunnipa, Abby Phillip, Steven Portnoy, Maeve Reston, Katie Rogers, Phil Rucker, Justin Sink, Jonathan Swan, Katy Tur, and Cecilia Vega.

I'm proud to have had a newspaper career that started with a community paper that allowed me to write about people I'd have to face the next day in the grocery store, in the neighborhood, or inside the county commission building. Thank you to the journalists at the *Dayton Daily News*; the *Daily Sentinel* in Grand Junction, Colorado; the *Palm Beach Post*; the *Tampa Bay Times*; and Bloomberg News who gave me a chance to prove myself, put their faith in me when I needed a second chance, and made me a better reporter often in spite of myself: Bill Hershey, Vince McKelvey, Mike Wagner, Denny Herzog, Marc Masferrer, Rachel Sauer, Shannon Joyce Neal, Alex Taylor, Marija Vader, Tim Harty, Gary Harmon, Mike Wiggins, Bob Silbernagel, Zack Barnett, Bob Kretschman, Ted Taylor, Paul Blythe, Glenn Henderson, Brian Crowley, Dara Kam, Holly Baltz, S.V. Dáte, Amy Hollyfield, Steve Bousquet, Neil Brown, Adam Smith, Joni James, Stephanie Garry Garfunkel, Tia Mitchell, Janet Scherberger, Mary Ellen Klaus, Marc Caputo, Pati Mazzei, Joe Follick, Susan Goldberg, Steve Merelman, Josh Tyrangiel, Wes Kosova, Josh Green, Cesca Antonelli, Mike Tackett, Laura Litvan, Justin Blum, Josh Gallu, Julia Goldman, Nick Johnston, Lisa Lerer, David Lynch, Mark Niquette, Jim Rowley, Mike Shepard, Del Wilber, Craig Gordon, and Jon Allen.

Thank you to the families who formed a pandemic school pod that gave our girls a social outlet during online classes: Chuck and Renu Schmoyer, Matt Felix and Carrie Pugh, and especially Zoe's mom, Margot Susca, and her partner, Warren Stern, who graciously covered my pod shifts and have always provided Zoe with another loving home.

Special thanks to Whitman ballers Kat Bozarth and Catherine Kennedy; the Wednesday night Penn Zoom gang, including Nina Gribetz, Michelle Price, Emily Ruda, Alison Silber, and Karen Silverman; also Kasie Hunt, Matt Rivera, Rachel Streitfeld, Tim Runfola, Phil Rucker, the entire *Washington Post* family, and everyone else who extended their time and bottomless generosity to our family during this project.

To Saundra, Libby, Randal's family and friends, and all the other Front Row Joes who were inspired to become politically active for the first time in their lives: Thank you for entrusting me with your stories. My life is richer and my Trump reporting is fuller for knowing you all.

To all of the men and women inside Trump World who I cannot name here, thank you for sharing your accounts of the decision-making process for the past five years and especially the 2020 campaign. Your help and patience during long phone calls and multiple meetings—and constant follow-up questions—were invaluable contributions to tell the full story of this historic campaign.

Source Notes

This book emerged from five years of reporting on President Trump, his administration, and both of his campaigns for the *Wall Street Journal* and, previously, Bloomberg News. It draws most heavily from exclusive interviews, many recorded, with more than 150 White House officials, administration officials, campaign staff, outside advisers to the president, friends, and other firsthand witnesses to the events and conversations that have been re-created in these pages. Many were patient and kind enough to endure several hours of interviews in multiple sessions, and several shared emails, texts, pictures, calendar items, and internal campaign and White House documents that were relevant to the discussion. I also leaned heavily on numerous websites and Twitter feeds to track down times, dates, and quotes, including Factbase, Right Side Broadcasting, and the Trump Twitter Archive.

In addition, I drew from the following published and broadcast sources in each chapter:

Prologue

Michael C. Bender. "'It's Kind of Like an Addiction': On the Road with Trump's Rally Diehards." *Wall Street Journal*, 6 September 2019.

Chapter 1. Battle Creek

Natalie Andrews and Andrew Duehren. "Pelosi Announces Impeachment Inquiry of President Trump." *Wall Street Journal*, 25 September 2019.

Michael C. Bender. "Trump Team Bets Impeachment Will Backfire on Democrats." *Wall Street Journal*, 26 September 2019.

Will Steakin and Rachel Scott. "Trump Campaign Turns Impeachment Inquiry into Fundraising Bonanza." ABC News, 25 September 2019.

Max Greenwood. "Trump Campaign, RNC Raise $154M in Fourth Quarter of 2019." *The Hill*, 3 January 2020.

"Party Breakdown—117th Congress." U.S. House of Representatives Press Gallery.

"Casualty List—117th Congress." U.S. House of Representatives Press Gallery.

@realDonaldTrump (Donald J. Trump). "Well said, Brian!" Twitter, 18 December 2019, 7:11 a.m. Trump Twitter Archive.

@realDonaldTrump (Donald J. Trump). "Can you believe that I will be impeached today by the Radical Left, Do Nothing Democrats, AND I DID NOTHING WRONG!" Twitter, 18 December 2019, 7:34 a.m.

@realDonaldTrump (Donald J. Trump). "SUCH ATROCIOUS LIES BY THE RADICAL LEFT, DO NOTHING DEMOCRATS. THIS IS AN ASSAULT ON AMERICA, AND AN ASSAULT ON THE REPUBLICAN PARTY!!!!" Twitter, 18 December 2019, 12:44 p.m.

"The History Place—Great Speeches Collection: Bill Clinton Speech I Am Profoundly Sorry." *History Place*, 11 December 1998.

Chapter 2. The Forty-Year Itch

Arnold Braeske. "Backed by the Body, the Donald May Muscle His Way into the Ring." *Star-Ledger*, 14 September 1999.

Marylin Bender. "The Empire and Ego of Donald Trump." *New York Times*, 7 August 1983.

Callum Borchers. "The Amazing Story of Donald Trump's Old Spokesman, John Barron—Who Was Actually Donald Trump Himself." *Washington Post*, 13 May 2016.

William Geist. "The Expanding Empire of Donald Trump." *New York Times*, 8 April 1984.

David Segal. "Mover, Shaker, and Cranky Caller?" *Washington Post*, 25 August 2007.

Thomas Edsall. "The Lobbyist in the Gray Flannel Suit." *Campaign Stops*, 14 May 2012.

John Taylor. "Trump Princess: Inside Donald Trump's Lavish 86 Metre Superyacht." *Boat International*, 2 November 2020.

Lisa Gutierrez. "How Donald Trump Finally Decided to Run for President after Nearly 30 Years of Just Talk." *Kansas City*, 31 July 2015.

Michael Kruse. "The True Story of Donald Trump's First Campaign Speech—in 1987." *Politico Magazine*, 5 February 2016.

Bruce Bartlett. "Can Anyone Trump This Goofy Tax Plan?" *Wall Street Journal*, 16 November 1999.

Matt Lauer. "Interview: Donald Trump Discusses Possible Run for President." *Today Show*, 8 October 1999.

"Trump a Presidential Candidate? Don't Bet against It—Noted Developer Isn't Ruling It Out." *Charleston Gazette* via *New York Times*, 26 September 1999.

"Florida Affirmative Action." *Hannity & Colmes*, Fox News, 12 November 1999.

Adam Nagourney. "Reform Bid Said to Be a No-Go for Trump." *New York Times*, 14 February 2000.

Donald Trump. "Democracy in Action." CPAC 2011, 10 February 2011, Orlando, Florida.

Igor Bobic and Sam Stein. "How CPAC Helped Launch Donald Trump's Political Career." *HuffPost*, 22 February 2017.

Maggie Haberman. "CPAC to Trump: You're Hired!" *Politico*, 11 February 2011.

Goldman, Russell. "'Birthers' Mark President's Birthday by Claiming He Was Born in Kenya." ABC News, 4 August 2009.

trumprulezdotcom. "Donald Trump on the View 03/23/2011 Trump Wants to See Obama's Birth Certificate." YouTube, 25 March 2011.

"Talking Points Memo and Top Story." *The O'Reilly Factor*, Fox News, 24 March 2011.

"Great American Panel." *Hannity*, Fox News, 24 March 2011.

"Analysis With Jedediah Bila, Bob Beckel." *Hannity*, Fox News, 25 March 2011.

"Donald Trump Sits Down with Bill O'Reilly." Fox News, 30 March 2011.

Paul Steinhauser. "CNN Poll: Still No Front-Runner in the Battle for the GOP Nomination." CNN, 5 May 2011.

Andrew Wallenstein. "NBC Overhauls Sked with 12 New Skeins." *Variety*, 15 May 2011.

Karen Tumulty and Nia-Malika Henderson. "Donald Trump Says He Won't Run for President in 2012." *Washington Post*, 17 May 2011.

TreasuryDirect. "Monthly Statements, 2017." U.S. Department of the Treasury.

Ashley Parker and Steve Eder. "Inside the Six Weeks Donald Trump Was a Nonstop 'Birther.'" *New York Times*, 2 July 2016.

"Jeb Bush, R" OpenSecrets.org. Center for Responsive Politics.

Monica Langley. "Donald Trump Says Campaign Not in Crisis, and There Is 'Zero Chance I'll Quit.'" *Wall Street Journal*, 8 October 2016.

Michael C. Bender, Rebecca Ballhaus, and Alex Leary. "Never Mind Those Tweets, Trump's 2020 Re-Election Team Wants Order and Discipline." *Wall Street Journal*, 14 June 2019.

"Excerpts: Donald Trump's Interview with Wall Street Journal." *Wall Street Journal*, 25 July 2017.

Marc Tracy. "New York Times Tops 5 Million Subscriptions as Ads Decline." *New York Times*, 6 February 2020.

"#925 Richard LeFrak & Family." *Forbes*.

David Heath and Jennifer Agiesta. "How Voters Who Found Both Candidates Unfit Broke." CNN, 11 November 2016.

Sophia Rose Segarra. "Ranking the Most Insane Political Merch in Recent American History." *Document*, 31 July 2019.

Chapter 3. Momentum

Jacob Schlesinger. "Trump Forged His Ideas on Trade in the 1980s—and Never Deviated." *Wall Street Journal*, 15 November 2018.

Factbase Videos. "Speech: Donald Trump Announces His Candidacy in New York, NY—June 16, 2015." YouTube, 29 October 2017.

Paul Goldberger. "Architecture: Atrium of Trump Tower Is a Pleasant Surprise." *New York Times*, 4 April 1983.

"Donald Trump Transcript: 'Our Country Needs a Truly Great Leader.'" *Wall Street Journal*, 16 June 2015.

Katherine Tully-McManus. "House Approves Criminal Justice Overhaul, Sends to President." *Roll Call*, 13 December 2019.

Bridget Bowman. "Meet the Republicans Who Voted 'No' on the Tax Bill." *Roll Call*, 13 December 2019.

"H.R. 3450 (103rd): North American Free Trade Agreement Implementation Act—House Vote #575—Nov 17, 1993." *GovTrack.us*, 17 November 1991.

Roll Call 701, Bill Number H. R. 5430. 116th Congress, 1st Session, Dec 19, 2019.

@realDonaldTrump (Donald J. Trump). "The great USMCA Trade Deal (Mexico & Canada) has been sitting on Nancy Pelosi's desk for 8 months, she doesn't even know what it says, &amp, today, after passing by a wide margin in the House, Pelosi tried to take credit for it. Labor will vote for Trump. Trade deal is great for USA!" Twitter, 19 December 2019, 6:55 p.m. Trump Twitter Archive.

@realDonaldTrump (Donald J. Trump). "PRESIDENTIAL HARASSMENT!" Twitter, 9 July 2020, 8:40 a.m. Trump Twitter Archive.

Alex Isenstadt. "Top Trump Brass Launch Campaign Firm." *Politico*, 22 December 2020.

Chris Kleponis. "U.S. President Donald J. Trump and First Lady Melania Trump Depart the White House." UPI, 20 December 2019.

Sophie Germain. "Trump Golf Count." Trump Golf Count Blog.

"2017 Presidential Limousine Spotted Undergoing Secret Tests." Fox News, 28 January 2016.

Paul Eisenstein. "Trump's New Limo Cost $1.5M and Comes with a Fridge Full of His Blood Type." NBC, 25 September 2018.

"The Super Bowl Ad." Jamestown Associates, 3 February 2020.

@AliceMarieFree (Alice Marie Johnson). "Two Super Bowls Ago I Was Sitting in a Prison Cell. Today I Am a Free Woman and My Story Was Featured in a Super Bowl Ad. I Will Spend the Rest of My Life Fighting for the Wrongly and Unjustly Convicted! God Bless America! Pic.twitter.com/CGSyk54O37." Twitter, 3 February 2020, 7:07 p.m.

Julie Bykowicz and Chad Day. "Trump's Campaign Went into Debt but Raked in Postelection Cash." *Wall Street Journal*, 4 December 2020.

Alex Isenstadt. "Trump to Drop $10 Million on Super Bowl Ad." *Politico*, 8 January 2020.

Howie Carr. "Howie Carr: President Trump Ordered the Strike, and Came down to Dinner Cool, Collected." *Boston Herald*, 3 January 2020.

"Transcript: Defense Secretary Mark Esper on 'Face the Nation,' January 12, 2020." CBS News, 12 January 2020.

Kevin Liptak. "Trump Recounts Minute-by-Minute Details of Soleimani Strike to Donors at Mar-a-Lago." CNN, 18 January 2020.

Michael C. Bender and Gordon Lubold. "Trump Bucked National-Security Aides on Proposed Iran Attack." *Wall Street Journal*, 23 June 2019.

William Galston. "Trump Gets No Soleimani Bump." *Wall Street Journal*, 15 January 2020.

Arielle Pardes. "The Facebook Defectors Turning Trump's Strategy against Him." *Wired*, 16 September 2020.

"Don't Look Now." *Newsweek*, 18 November 1996.

Peter Baker, Ronen Bergman, David D. Kirkpatrick, Julian E. Barnes, and Alissa J. Rubin. "Seven Days in January: How Trump Pushed U.S. and Iran to the Brink of War." *New York Times*, 11 January 2020.

Sebastien Roblin. "Did the U.S. Use New Joint Air-to-Ground Missile to Kill Iran's General Soleimani?" *Forbes*, 4 January 2020.

Anthony Capaccio. "U.S. Reaper Drone Left Soleimani with Little Chance." Bloomberg, 6 January 2020.

"General Election: Trump vs. Biden." *RealClearPolitics*.

"President Trump Job Approval." *RealClearPolitics*.

Chapter 4. Acquittal, Part One: The Perfect Call

Chris Cillizza. "The 44 Weirdest Lines from Donald Trump's First 2020 Campaign Rally." CNN, 10 January 2020.

Wayne Barret. "Peas in a Pod: The Long and Twisted Relationship between Donald Trump and Rudy Giuliani." *New York Daily News*, 4 September 2016.

"Interview with Former New York Mayor Rudy Giuliani." *Your World w/ Neil Cavuto*, Fox News, 23 June 2015.

Julia Manchester. "Rudy Giuliani (Sort of) Endorses Donald Trump." CNN, 19 April 2016.

"Key People—Former Mayor Rudy Giuliani (R-NY)." P2008, Democracy in Action, 2 March 2009.

Rebecca Ballhaus, Sadie Gurman, Andrew Restuccia, and Michael C. Bender. "Tense Relationship between Barr and Giuliani Complicates Trump Impeachment Defense." *Wall Street Journal*, 1 October 2019.

Rebecca Ballhaus, Alan Cullison, Georgi Kantchev, and Brett Forrest. "Giuliani Sits at the Center of the Ukraine Controversy." *Wall Street Journal*, 27 September 2019.

Alex Isenstadt. "Trump Aides Cite Top Threats at White House Briefing: Harris, Biden, Warren." *Politico*, 25 July 2019.

@RepMattGaetz (Rep. Matt Gaetz). "We heard the death rattle for impeachment at the end of Mueller's testimony this week. @LouDobbs." Twitter, 26 July 2019, 5:09 p.m.

@SethAbramson (Seth Ambramson). "(THREAD) This open thread provides live updates on former special counsel Bob Mueller's Congressional testimony before the House Judiciary Committee and the House Permanent Select Committee on Intelligence. I hope you will retweet this thread for any you think may be interested." Twitter, 24 July 2019, 8:42 a.m.

"Articles of Impeachment against Donald John Trump." House Resolution 755, 116th Congress, 1st Session, 18 December 2019.

Michael C. Bender and Rebecca Ballhaus. "Trump Impeachment Team for Trial to Include Ken Starr, Alan Dershowitz." *Wall Street Journal*, 18 January 2020.

Nicholas Riccardi and Emily Swanson. "AP-NORC Poll: GOP More Fired Up for 2020, Democrats Anxious." Associated Press, 30 January 2020.

"Timeline: Every Big Move in the Mueller Investigation." *Axios*, 23 July 2019.

David Wallace. "David Foster Wallace on John McCain: 'The Weasel, Twelve Monkeys and the Shrub.'" *Rolling Stone*, 13 April 2000.

Michael C. Bender and Lindsay Wise. "GOP Senators Seek Quick Acquittal for Trump, the President Wants More." *Wall Street Journal*, 16 December 2019.

Michael C. Bender and Kristina Peterson. "Congress Faces a Tense Agenda, with Little Margin for Error." *Wall Street Journal*, 5 September 2017.

Michael C. Bender. "McConnell and Trump Forge a Bond over Winning." *Wall Street Journal*, 7 November 2018.

Michael C. Bender, Lindsay Wise, Siobhan Hughes, and Rebecca Ballhaus. "How Republicans Scotched the Idea of Witnesses in Trump's Impeachment Trial." *Wall Street Journal*, 1 February 2020.

Chapter 5. Victory Lap

NBC News. "Trump to Utah Governor: 'How's Mitt Romney? You Keep Him, We Don't Want Him.'" YouTube, 10 February 2020.

"Manchester, NH Weather History." Weather Underground.

"Majority Whip Steve Scalise Endorses Trump, Cites Supreme Court Nominees, and Taxes as Key Issues." *The Hayride*, 13 May 2016.

Jenna Johnson. "The Night Donald Trump Became the Presumptive Nominee." *Washington Post*, 4 May 2016.

Jason Scheiber. "GOP Celebrates Trump's Primary Victory." *Union Leader*, 11 February 2020.

@parscale (Brad Parscale). "#1 off the line. The hat that will Keep America Great!" *Twitter*, 24 August 2019, 9:01 p.m.

"President George W. Bush—Campaign Organization, New Hampshire." P2004, Democracy in Action, 24 November 2003.

Tanya Basu. "Trump Says He'll Send Refugees Back to Syria If Elected." *Time*, 1 October 2015.

Greg Miller, Julie Vitkovskaya, and Reuben Fischer-Baum. "'This Deal Will Make Me Look Terrible': Full Transcripts of Trump's Calls with Mexico and Australia." *Washington Post*, 3 August 2017.

Right Side Broadcasting Network. "President Donald Trump Rally LIVE in Manchester, NH 2/10/20." YouTube, 11 February 2020.

"Red Arrow Diner History." Red Arrow Diner, 11 May 2020.

@TrumpNH (Donald Trump NH). "After our amazing event in Windham, Trump stopped by the Red Arrow Diner! credit: @TheBradMielke #nhpolitics #fitn." Twitter, 11 January 2016, 3:13 p.m.

Brad Mielke. "Donald Trump Gets Heckled at New Hampshire Diner: 'Enjoy Your Burger, Racist!'" ABC News, 12 January 2016.

@parscale (Brad Parscale). "So a big test for @bpolitics today. Will they write their boss is a complete racist. This video is horrible." Twitter, 11 February 2020, 8:04 a.m.

@parscale (Brad Parscale). "#BloombergIsARacist." Twitter, 11 February 2020, 9:07 a.m.

Kristine Phillips and Johnson Kevin. "Paul Manafort Was 'a Grave Counterintelligence Threat,' Republican-Led Senate Panel Finds." *USA Today*, 19 August 2020.

"Full Rally: President Trump in Manchester, New Hampshire Night before Primary." *Rev*, 30 July 2020.

Peter Elkind and Doris Burke. "The Myths of the 'Genius' behind Trump's Reelection Campaign." *ProPublica*, 22 June 2020.

Rishika Dugyala. "Here's How Six of Texas' Most Interesting Local Primary Races Turned Out." *Texas Tribune*, 6 March 2018.

Gilbert Garcia. "GOP Chair Launches Congressional Bid, with Help from Parscale." *San Antonio Express News*, 18 November 2017.

Alayna Treene, Jonathan Swan, and Harry Stevens. "Scoop: Inside a Top Trump Adviser's Fundraising Mirage." *Axios*, 5 May 2019.

Jeffrey Jones. "More in the U.S. Say They Are Better Off than in Past Elections." Gallup, 23 March 2021.

"The Bloomberg Billionaires Index." Bloomberg, 2021.

Stephanie Saul and Rachel Shorey. "How Michael Bloomberg Used His Money to Aid Democratic Victories in the House." *New York Times*, 1 December 2018.

Alexander Burns and Jonathan Martin. "Trump's Takeover of the Republican Party Is Almost Complete." *New York Times*, 3 April 2019.

Fredreka Schouten. "First on CNN: How a Bloomberg-Funded Gun-Control Group Helped Turn Virginia Blue." CNN, 6 November 2019.

"Virginia Democrats Take Control of State Legislature for First Time in over Two Decades." Associated Press, 6 November 2019.

Todd Spangler. "Mike Bloomberg Holds 7-Point Lead on Trump in Michigan, Poll Shows." *Detroit Free Press*, 15 January 2020.

"Transcript for the CDC Telebriefing Update on COVID-19." Centers for Disease Control and Prevention, 26 February 2020.

Anna Isaac and Alexander Osipovich. "Stocks Give Up Gains; Treasury Yields Fall." *Wall Street Journal*, 26 February 2020.

Chapter 6. Covid, Part One: Hyperbole in the Time of Pandemic

"Chris Christie Compares Handling Blizzard to Dealing with ISIS." ABC, 25 January 2016.

Daniella Silva. "Trump Defends Throwing Paper Towels to Hurricane Survivors in Puerto Rico." NBC, 8 October 2017.

Matthew Pottinger et al. "The Council on Foreign Relations Holds a Discussion on U.S. Veterans: From the Battlefield to the Home Front—News Event." *Council on Foreign Relations*, 21 October 2014.

Helen Branswell. "CDC Details First U.S. Case of Novel Virus Spreading in China." *Statnews*, 24 January 2020.

Tyler Pager. "Cuccinelli on Rules Rebuff: 'This Is Disgusting.'" *Politico*, 18 July 2016.

Jonathan Swan and Margaret Talev. "Navarro Memos Warning of Mass Coronavirus Death Circulated in January." *Axios*, 7 April 2020.

Michael C. Bender and Gordon Lubold. "On Coronavirus, National Security Threats, O'Brien Picks His Spots." *Wall Street Journal*, 29 April 2020.

Peter Nicholas. "Republicans Defend Trump Aide Who Admitted Telling 'White Lies' on President's Behalf." *Wall Street Journal*, 28 February 2018.

Michael C. Bender. "Trump Finds Loopholes in Chief of Staff's New Regime." *Wall Street Journal*, 5 December 2017.

"Stock Market Performance by President." *MacroTrends*.

Noel Randewich and Saqib Ahmed. "Trump's Stock Market: A Wild Four Years." Reuters, 29 October 2020.

Vibhuti Agarwal and Michael C. Bender. "Trump Kicks Off Two-Day India Visit with Massive Rally." *Wall Street Journal*, 24 February 2020.

Caitlin McCabe. "Dow Industrials Close 1,000 Points Lower as Coronavirus Cases Mount." *Wall Street Journal*, 24 February 2020.

Betsy McKay, Margherita Stancati, and Dasl Yoon. "Coronavirus's Global Spread May Not Be Contained, WHO Says." *Wall Street Journal*, 25 February 2020.

Anna Isaac and Alexander Osipovich. "Stocks Give Up Gains; Treasury Yields Fall." *Wall Street Journal*, 26 February 2020.

"Transcript for the CDC Telebriefing Update on COVID-19." Centers for Disease Control and Prevention, 26 February 2020.

"Donald Trump Charlotte, North Carolina Rally Transcript: Trump Holds Rally Before Super Tuesday." *Rev*, 2 March 2020.

@atrupar (Aaron Rupar). "Trump makes up the word 'vivor.'" Twitter, 3 March 2020, 11:35 a.m.

Aaron Rupar. "Trump Fox News Coronavirus Interview: Trump Spreads Dangerous Misinformation." *Vox*, 5 March 2020.

Daniel Dale and Tara Subramaniam. "Fact Check: From Coronavirus to Kim Jong Un, Trump Makes at Least 14 False Claims in Fox News Town Hall." CNN, 6 March 2020.

Jake Sherman and Anna Palmer. "First in Politico Playbook: Mark Meadows to Leave Congress, plus What McConnell Will Say on Impeachment." *Politico*, 19 December 2019.

"Executive Order, No. 202: Declaring a Disaster Emergency in the State of New York." Governor Andrew Cuomo, 7 March 2020.

"Inslee Issues COVID-19 Emergency Proclamation." Office of the Governor, State of Washington, 29 February 2020.

Joe Hagan. "'Dishonesty...Is Always an Indicator of Weakness': Tucker Carlson on How He Brought His Coronavirus Message to Mar-a-Lago." *Vanity Fair*, 17 March 2020.

Rob Picheta and Arnaud Siad. "Bolsonaro's Visit to See Trump in March Was a 'Corona Trip,' Says Brazil's Former Health Secretary." CNN, 14 May 2020.

@gabstargardter (Gabriel Stargardter). "The guy standing to Trump's left just tested positive for coronavirus, according to Brazilian media. Fabio Wajngarten posted this photo, taken during meetings at Mar-a-Lago, five days ago." Twitter, 12 March 2020, 11:03 a.m.

Angela Ruggiero. "Bay Area Limo Driver Who Died of COVID-19 Tied to Trump's Mar-a-Lago, Claim Alleges." *Mercury News*, 13 August 2020.

@maggieNYT (Maggie Haberman). "Email that just went out from Trump Victory about a donor who was at MAL on Sunday who tested positive for Coronavirus." Twitter, 13 March 2020, 4:29 p.m.

Paul Vigna, Avantika Chilkoti, and David Winning. "Stocks Fall More than 7% in Dow's Worst Day since 2008." *Wall Street Journal*, 9 March 2020.

Haley Byrd, Paul LeBlanc, Lauren Fox, and Kaitlan Collins. "5 Congressmen—Including Trump's Future Chief of Staff and Lawmaker Who Shook President's Hand—to Self-Quarantine after CPAC" CNN, 10 March 2020.

Peter Baker, Maggie Haberman, and Annie Karni. "Trump Floats Economic Stimulus in Response to Coronavirus." *New York Times*, 10 March 2020.

Jeremy Diamond, Kevin Liptak, and Kaitlan Collins. "Deep into Crisis, Trump Demands 'Something Big' on Coronavirus." CNN, 12 March 2020.

@WHO (World Health Organization). "Media briefing on #COVID19 with @DrTedros. #coronavirus." Twitter, 11 March 2020, 12:16 p.m.

"Presidential Actions to Exclude Aliens Under INA § 212(f)." *Congressional Research Service*, 4 May 2020.

"Updated Guidance on Telework Flexibilities in Response to Coronavirus." Office of Management and Budget, 12 March 2020.

Paul Kiernan. "Federal Government Urged to Close Offices to Contain Coronavirus." *Wall Street Journal*, 14 March 2020.

@tomhanks (Tom Hanks). Twitter, 11 March 2020, 9:14 p.m.

@wojespn (Adrian Wojnarowski). "The NBA has suspended the season." Twitter, 11 March 2020, 9:31 p.m.

Andrew Restuccia, Jennifer Calfas, Alejandro Lazo, and Sam Schechner. "Trump Declares National Emergency to Confront Coronavirus." *Wall Street Journal*, 13 March 2020.

Kaitlan Collins and Kevin Liptak. "What Drove Trump's Newfound Somber Tone on Coronavirus." CNN, 18 March 2020.

"Benjamin Robert Hirschmann." Harold W. Vick Funeral Home.

60 Minutes. "COVID-19 Victims' Stories: Ben Hirschmann." YouTube, 26 April 2020.

Chad Livengood. "A Young Man's Death from COVID-19 Leaves Family with Big Questions." *Crain's Detroit*, 9 April 2020.

Chapter 7. Covid, Part Two: Retooling the Reelect

Jedd Rosche. "RNC Chief of Staff Katie Walsh Describes the $175 Million Tool to Win Elections." CNN, 2 November 2016.

Elena Schneider. "ActBlue's Stunning Third Quarter: $1.5 Billion in Donations." *Politico*, 15 October 2020.

Shane Goldmacher. "The $1 Million Upside for an RNC Digital Guru." *Politico*, 18 April 2017.

Peter Elking. "Brad Parscale Won Big in 2016, Can He Win Again as Donald Trump's Campaign Manager?" *Texas Monthly*, 25 February 2021.

Caleb Ecarma. "Trump Throws Full-Blown Tantrum over GOP Ad Criticizing Coronavirus Response." *Vanity Fair*, 6 May 2020.

Leah Asmelash. "Face Masks: Surgeon General Wants Americans to Stop Buying Them." CNN, 2 March 2020.

Donald G. McNeil Jr. "The U.S. Now Leads the World in Confirmed Coronavirus Cases." *New York Times*, 26 March 2020.

Siobhán O'Grady, Rick Noack, Kim Bellware, Meryl Kornfield, and Teo Armus. "As U.S. Coronavirus Deaths Surpass 10,000, HHS Watchdog Says American Hospitals Face 'Severe' Shortages of Equipment, Staff, and Tests." *Washington Post*, 6 April 2020.

Derek Hawkins, Marisa Iati, Hannah Knowles, Simon Denyer, Meryl Kornfield, Timothy Bella, and Jesse Dougherty. "Confirmed U.S. Covid-19 Death Toll Reaches 20,000, Highest in the World." *Washington Post*, 11 April 2020 .

Michael Scherer, Josh Dawsey, Annie Linskey, and Toluse Olorunnipa. "Trump Campaign Concludes There Is More to Be Gained by Attacking Biden than Trying to Promote President's Pandemic Response." *Washington Post*, 18 April 2020.

Michael Scherer and Josh Dawsey. "Trump Campaign Divided over How to Attack Biden amid Worries over Troubling Poll Numbers." *Washington Post*, 2 May 2020.

Maggie Haberman. "Trump, Head of Government, Leans into Antigovernment Message." *New York Times*, 20 April 2020.

Kate O'Keeffe, Michael C. Bender, and Chun Han Wong. "Coronavirus Casts Deep Chill over U.S.-China Relations." *Wall Street Journal*, 6 May 2020.

Shane Goldmacher. "Biden Faces a Cash Gap with Trump. He Has to Close It Virtually." *New York Times*, 31 March 2020.

Michael C. Bender and Ken Thomas. "Trump Makes Push for Seniors as Coronavirus Crisis Erodes Support." *Wall Street Journal*, 1 May 2020.

Michael C. Bender. "GOP Leader Pushes Party to Pursue Suburban Women Like Her." *Wall Street Journal*, 31 October 2020.

Chapter 8. Law and Order

Todd Richmond. "Victim in Police Encounter Had Started New Life in Minnesota." Associated Press, 27 May 2020.

Nicholas Bogel-Burroughs and Jack Healy. "Cup Foods, a Minneapolis Corner Store Forever Tied to the Death of George Floyd." *New York Times*, 15 June 2020.

"Transcript of 911 Call Leading to Floyd's Arrest." Famous Trials.

Richard Feloni and Yusuf George. "These Are the Corporate Responses to the George Floyd Protests That Stand Out." Just Capital, 30 June 2020.

Kim Parker, Juliana Menasce Horowitz, and Monica Anderson. "Amid Protests, Majorities across Racial and Ethnic Groups Express Support for the Black Lives Matter Movement." Pew Research Center, 12 June 2020.

Stephen Losey. "Chief Wright: 'I Am George Floyd,' Promises Review of Air Force Justice System." *Air Force Times*, 1 June 2020.

Danyelle Solomon, Connor Maxwell, and Abril Castro. "Systematic Inequality and Economic Opportunity." Center for American Progress, 7 August 2019.

Elise Gould and Valerie Wilson. "Black Workers Face Two of the Most Lethal Preexisting Conditions for Coronavirus—Racism and Economic Inequality." Economic Policy Institute, 1 June 2020.

"Hospitalization Rates and Characteristics of Patients Hospitalized with Laboratory-Confirmed Coronavirus Disease 2019—COVID-NET, 14 States, March 1–30, 2020." Centers for Disease Control and Prevention, 17 April 2020.

Samantha Artiga, Kendal Orgera, and Anthony Damico. "Changes in Health Coverage by Race and Ethnicity since the ACA, 2010–2018." Kaiser Family Foundation, 5 March 2020.

Brita Belli. "Racial Disparity in Police Shootings Unchanged over 5 years." *Yale News*, 27 October 2020.

John Creamer. "Inequalities Persist Despite Decline in Poverty for All Major Race and Hispanic Origin Groups." U.S. Census Bureau, 15 September 2020.

"Risk for COVID-19 Infection, Hospitalization, and Death by Race/Ethnicity." Centers for Disease Control and Prevention, 23 April 2021.

"Trump Supporter Who Punched Protester: 'Next Time, We Might Have to Kill Him.'" *Inside Edition*, 9 March 2016.

Jeremy Diamond. "First on CNN: Charges Dropped against CBS Reporter, Chicago Police Say." CNN, 17 March 2016.

"On This Day—Jan 14, 1963: Newly Elected Governor George Wallace Calls for 'Segregation Forever!'" Equal Justice Initiative.

Glenn Kessler. "Donald Trump and David Duke: For the Record." *Washington Post*, 1 March 2016.

@MittRomney (Mitt Romney). "A disqualifying & disgusting response by @real DonaldTrump to the KKK, His coddling of repugnant bigotry is not in the character of America." Twitter, 29 February 2016, 1:22 p.m.

"Open Letter on Donald Trump from GOP National Security Leaders." War on the Rocks, 2 March 2016.

"Full Text: Donald Trump 2016 RNC Draft Speech Transcript." *Politico*, 21 July 2016.

Gabriel Sherman. "The Legacy." *New York Magazine*, 10 July 2009.

Ronald Smothers. "Democratic Donor Receives Two-Year Prison Sentence." *New York Times*, 5 March 2005.

Robert Hanley. "Donor Apologized to Sister for Seduction of Husband." *New York Times*, 13 January 2005.

"Livingston, NJ—Bridgewater Inn, NJ." Google Maps.

"Trump National Golf Club Bedminster—Red Bull Motor Inn." Mapquest.

"Political Contributor, Developer Charles Kushner Pleads Guilty to Tax Fraud, Witness Retaliation, and Making False Statements to the Federal Election Commission" [press release]. U.S. Department of Justice, 18 August 2004.

Ronald Smothers. "Democratic Donor Receives Two-Year Prison Sentence." *New York Times*, 5 March 2005.

Mary Clare Jalonick. "White House Adviser Kushner, Senator Talk Criminal Justice." Associated Press, 30 March 2017.

"Attorney General Jeff Sessions Delivers Remarks on Efforts to Combat Violent Crime in St. Louis." U.S. Department of Justice, 31 March 2017.

Jim Salter. "Sessions: Ferguson Emblem of Tense Relationship with Police." Associated Press, 31 March 2017.

Beth Reinhard. "Attorney General Sessions Revives Policy of Tougher Sentences for Drug Offenders." *Wall Street Journal*, 12 May 2017.

Daniel W. Drezner. "The Beclowning of the Executive Branch." *Washington Post*, 31 March 2017.

"Jared Kushner." *Fortune*.

Ben Kesling, Jennifer Levitz, and Scott Calvert. "Charlottesville Victim's Mother Is 'Proud of How She Died.'" *Wall Street Journal*, 13 August 2017.

United States of America vs. James Alex Fields Jr. U.S. District Court, Charlottesville, VA, 27 June 2018.

@Merck (Merck). "Statement from Kenneth C. Frazier, chairman and chief executive officer, Merck…" Twitter, 14 August 2017, 8:00 a.m.

@realdonaldtrump (Donald J. Trump). "Now that Ken Frazier of Merck Pharma has resigned from President's Manufacturing Council, he will have more time to LOWER RIPOFF DRUG PRICES!" Twitter, 14 August 2017, 8:54 a.m. Trump Twitter Archive.

Dan Merica. "Trump Pushes Death Penalty for Some Drug Dealers." CNN, 19 March 2018.

"White House Summit on Criminal Justice Policy." C-SPAN, 19 May 2018.

CNBC. "President Donald Trump Delivers Remarks at Prison Reform Summit— May 18, 2018 | CNBC." YouTube, 18 May 2018.

Linda A. Moore. "Kim Kardashian at the White House: 5 Things to Know about Alice Marie Johnson." *Commercial Appeal*, 31 May 2018.

Rebecca Ballhaus and Louise Radnofsky. "Trump Grants Commutation to Woman after Kim Kardashian West's Appeal." *Wall Street Journal*, 6 June 2018.

Michael C. Bender and Rebecca Ballhaus. "Kelly's Rules for Trump's West Wing: Stop Bickering, Get in Early, Make an Appointment." *Wall Street Journal*, 4 August 2017.

Samantha J. Gross. "At 'Latinos for Trump' Kickoff in Miami, Pence Takes Aim at Democrat 'Socialism.'" *Miami Herald*, 25 June 2019.

Natalie Andrews. "House Passes Criminal-Justice Reform Bill." *Wall Street Journal*, 20 December 2018.

Kara Gotsch. "One Year after the First Step Act: Mixed Outcomes." Sentencing Project, 17 December 2019.

"Secretary DeVos Issues Full Forgiveness of HBCU Hurricane Relief Loans" [press release]. U.S. Department of Education, 14 March 2018.

Collin Binkley. "Trump Signs Bill Restoring Funding for Black Colleges." Associated Press, 19 December 2019.

"America First Policies 2018 990." Center for Public Integrity.

Chandelis Duster and Maegan Vazquez. "A Pro-Trump Group Helped Fund the Nonprofit Holding Cash Giveaways to Black Attendees." CNN, 14 February 2020.

Seth A. Richardson. "Trump Allies Indefinitely Postpone Planned $50,000 Cash Giveaway in Cleveland." Cleveland.com, 29 February 2020.

Bonnie V. Winston and Ronald E. Carrington. "Virginia Union University Rescinds Permission for Outside Group to Use Campus Facility for Trump event." *Richmond Free Press*, 17 January 2020.

Andrew J. Tobias. "IRS Revokes Tax-Exempt Status for Trump Allies' Charity That Organized Cleveland Cash Giveaway." Cleveland.com, 29 August 2020.

Darnella Frazier. Facebook, 26 May 2020.

Paul Walsh. "Teen Who Recorded George Floyd Video Wasn't Looking to Be a Hero, Her Lawyer Says." *Star Tribune*, 11 June 2020.

Scott Calvert and Valerie Bauerlein. "Viral Videos Shape Views of Police Conduct." *Wall Street Journal*, 30 December 2015.

Jeff Wagner. "'It's Real Ugly': Protesters Clash with Minneapolis Police after George Floyd's Death." WCCO, 26 May 2020.

Ben Zimmer. "'Looting': A Term with Roots in Protest and Conflict." *Wall Street Journal*, 4 June 2020.

Newley Purnell and Andrew Restuccia. "Twitter Flags Trump Tweet about George Floyd Protests for 'Glorifying Violence.'" *Wall Street Journal*, 29 May 2020.

"Timeline: How the First Week of George Floyd Protests Unfolded in Richmond." *Richmond Times-Dispatch*, 7 June 2020.

Leah Sottile. "The Chaos Agents." *New York Times Magazine*, 19 August 2020.

Andrew Blankstein and Ben Collins. "Alleged 'Boogaloo' Extremist Charged in Killing of Federal Officer during George Floyd Protest." NBC, 17 June 2020.

United States of America v. Steven Carrillo. U.S. District Court for the Northern District of California, 15 June 2020.

United States of America v. Robert Alvin Justus, Jr. U.S. District Court for the Northern District of California, 12 June 2020.

"Lafayette Square, Washington, DC." U.S. General Services Administration.

"Andrew Jackson Statue, Lafayette Square." White House Historical Association.

Jonathan Lemire and Zeke Miller. "Trump Took Shelter in White House Bunker as Protests Raged." Associated Press, 31 May 2020.

"Updates: Protests against Police Brutality and Social Injustice Continue Tuesday." WUSA, 30 May 2020.

Carol D. Leonnig. "Protesters' Breach of Temporary Fences near White House Complex Prompted Secret Service to Move Trump to Secure Bunker." *Washington Post*, 3 June 2020.

Nate Carlisle. "Man Who Drew Bow and Arrow on Salt Lake City Protesters Is in Jail, Charged with Three Felonies." *Salt Lake Tribune*, 4 June 2020.

Reuters. "U.S. Protests: Man Points Bow and Arrow at Crowd *graphic video*" YouTube, 31 May 2020.

Evan Bush. "Timeline of Demonstrations over the Police Killing of George Floyd." *Seattle Times*, 6 June 2020.

Rio Lancanlale. "Las Vegas Woman Becomes 60th Victim of October 2017 Mass Shooting." *Las Vegas Review-Journal*, 17 September 2020.

"From Unrest to Joy, DC's Week of George Floyd Protests Made Space for a Spectrum of Emotions." WUSA, 6 June 2020.

Peter Hermann, Sarah Pulliam Bailey, and Michelle Boorstein. "Fire Set at Historic St. John's Church during Protests of George Floyd's Death." *Washington Post*, 1 June 2020.

"St. John's Church." National Park Service.

"History." St. John's Church.

William Seale. "Foreword: White House History." White House Historical Association.

Chapter 9. Anarchy and Chaos

"CNN Newsroom." CNN, 1 June 2020.

"Tanker Truck Drives into Minneapolis George Floyd Protesters on I-35W Bridge; Driver in Custody." WCCO, 31 May 2020.

David Schaper. "10 Years after Bridge Collapse, America Is Still Crumbling." NPR, 1 August 2017.

Amber Athey and Vince Coglianese. "Trump Plans to Invoke Insurrection Act to Boot Illegal Immigrants." *Daily Caller*, 16 May 2019.

Vivian Salama. "Exit of Mattis, Last of Trump's 'Generals,' Removes Voice of Moderation." *Wall Street Journal*, 20 December 2018.

"Donald Trump Phone Call Transcript with Governors after Protests: 'You Have to Dominate' & 'Most of You Are Weak.'" Rev, 1 June 2020.

B. Philip Bigler. "Lincoln Memorial." Encyclopedia Britannica.

"Donald Trump Coronavirus Press Conference Transcript May 22: Says Places of Worship Must Open Immediately." Rev, 22 May 2020.

Carol D. Leonnig, Matt Zapotosky, Josh Dawsey, and Rebecca Tan. "Barr Personally Ordered Removal of Protesters near White House, Leading to Use of Force against Largely Peaceful Crowd." *Washington Post*, 2 June 2020.

Paul D. Shinkman. "D.C. Guard Officer 'Deeply Disturbed' by Police Crackdown at Lafayette Square." *U.S. News & World Report*, 27 July 2020.

"Written Statement of Adam DeMarco." U.S. House of Representatives, Committee on Natural Resources, 28 July 2020.

Dalton Bennett, Sarah Cahlan, Aaron C. Davis, and Joyce Sohyun Lee. "The Crackdown before Trump's Photo Op." *Washington Post*, 8 June 2020.

Bloomberg Quicktake: Now. "Trump Says He'll Deploy Military Unless States Halt Violent Protests in Rose Garden Speech." YouTube, 1 June 2020.

Bruce White. "Detail of North Door Carvings." White House Historical Association, 24 February 2017.

Commercial Break. "CNN—Trump Walks to St. John's for Photo Op (June 1, 2020)." YouTube, 1 June 2020.

Tommy Christopher. "Watch: Bible Literacy Champion Trump Hilariously Refused to Name His Favorite Verse." Mediaite, 31 January 2019.

Eric Bradner. "Trump Blames Tony Perkins for '2 Corinthians.'" CNN, 21 January 2016.

CNN. "Donald Trump: I Brought My Bible." YouTube, 26 September 2015.

@JenniferJJacobs (Jennifer Jacobs). "'Pretty great.' Trump told me after visit to St John's church, which suffered a fire last night amid George Floyd protest, He didn't answer our questions on: clear park just for photo op, is this still a democracy, is systemic racism root of problem, will military further inflame." Twitter, 1 June 2020, 7:23 p.m.

@JasonMillerinDC (Jason Miller). "Now we're rolling—this is how we do crowd dispersement, folks. No church fires tonight. The A-Team has been brought in to keep our streets safe. Failed Mayors like Bowser and Frey should have been set up to do this Friday night!" Twitter, 1 June 2020, 6:38 p.m.

@marklevinshow (Mark R. Levin). "The president's walk through Lafayette Park, controlled the night before by rioters, to the burned out St. John's Church, holding his bible in his hand, was truly historic, A fabulous moment of enormous important." Twitter, 1 June 2020, 7:37 p.m.

@hughhewitt (Hugh Hewitt). "Very admirable of @POTUS to demonstrate that the rule of law will not be intimidated by lawlessness." Twitter, 1 June 2020, 7:09 p.m.

Michael C. Bender and Sadie Gurman. "Forceful Removal of Protesters from Outside White House Spurs Debate." *Wall Street Journal*, 2 June 2020.

Beth Reinhard and Reid J. Epstein. "A Pastor with a Passion for Trump." *Wall Street Journal*, 7 April 2016.

"Grassley Releases Review of Tax Issues Raised by Media-Based Ministries" [press release]. U.S. Senate Committee on Finance, 6 January 2011.

Gordon Lubold. "Trump Wanted to Fire Esper over Troops Dispute." *Wall Street Journal*, 9 June 2020.

"President Trump on the Brian Kilmeade Show." Fox News Radio, 3 June 2020.

Corey Dickstein. "Pentagon Leaders Planned to Send Home Active-Duty Troops in DC Area before Reversing Decision." *Stars and Stripes*, 3 June 2020.

Eric Schmitt, Thomas Gibbons-Neff, and Peter Baker. "Trump Agrees to Send Home Troops from Washington, Easing Tensions with the Pentagon." *New York Times*, 4 June 2020.

Isaac Arnsdorf. "Prominent GOP lobbyist Joins Trump Forces in Pennsylvania." *Politico*, 26 April 2016.

"John Bell Hood." National Park Service.

Douglas L. Kriner and Francis X. Shen. "Battlefield Casualties and Ballot Box Defeat: Did the Bush-Obama Wars Cost Clinton the White House?" SSRN, 19 June 2017.

Chapter 10. Juneteenth, Observed

"BOK Center's New Renovations Are Underway." KJRH, 13 September 2019.

"New Public Policy Leadership Department Is 18th in College." University of Mississippi.

@realdonaldtrump (Donald J. Trump). "We had previously scheduled our #MAGA Rally in Tulsa, Oklahoma, for June 19th—a big deal. Unfortunately, however, this would fall on the Juneteenth Holiday. Many of my African American friends and supporters have reached out to suggest that we consider changing the date out..." Twitter, 12 June 2020, 11:23 p.m. Trump Twitter Archive.

Michael C. Bender and Rebecca Ballhaus. "Trump Put Re-Election Prospects Ahead of National Interest, Bolton Alleges." *Wall Street Journal*, 17 June 2020.

"Abbott Launches Molecular Point-of-Care Test to Detect Novel Coronavirus in As Little As Five Minutes" [press release]. Abbott, 27 March 2020.

"Transcript of President Trump's Interview with Wall Street Journal." *Wall Street Journal*, 18 June 2020.

"Top Battlegrounds: Wisconsin, Michigan, Pennsylvania, North Carolina, Florida, Arizona." *RealClearPolitics*.

Michael C. Bender and Catherine Lucey. "Trump Signals Re-Election Bid Will Echo 2016 Themes." *Wall Street Journal*, 18 June 2019.

"Speech: Donald Trump Announces His 2020 Candidacy at a Political Rally in Orlando—June 18, 2019." Factbase.

Rebecca Ballhaus and Julie Bykowicz. "Trump Picks 'Data-Driven' Digital Expert to Run 2020 Re-Election Campaign." *Wall Street Journal*, 27 February 2018.

Jeva Lange. "President Trump Has Already Filed for Re-election. That's Not Normal." *The Week*, 27 January 2017.

Michael C. Bender. "Donald Trump Strikes Nationalistic Tone in Inaugural Speech." *Wall Street Journal*, 20 January 2017.

"Donald Trump Tulsa, Oklahoma Rally Speech Transcript." Rev, 21 June 2020.

Chapter 11. The Last MAGA Rally

Melanie Grayce West. "New York City Kicks Off Covid-19 Vaccine Drive." *Wall Street Journal*, 14 December 2020.

State of Michigan, Office of Governor Gretchen Whitmer. "Executive Order 2020-86: Encouraging the use of telehealth services during the COVID-19 emergency—RESCINDED."

"Telehealth Benefits in Medicare are a Lifeline for Patients during Coronavirus Outbreak." Centers for Medicare and Medicaid Services, 9 March 2020.

@benrileysmith (Ben Riley-Smith). "This is the man at the front of one of the queues for Trump's rally in Tulsa—Mike Boatman. Says he turned up at 2.30am on Monday (FIVE days ago) to get in line. Is his 10th rally. Mike says he misses the president. 1/" Twitter, 19 June 2020, 9:30 p.m.

Amber Phillips. "What Is Antifa?" *Washington Post*, 15 June 2020.

Ken Bensinger and Kadia Goba. "Trump Called the $10 Million a Loan. His Campaign Called It a Donation. Who Paid It Back, and How?" *BuzzFeed News*, 21 October 2020.

@realdonaldtrump (Donald J. Trump). "Almost One Million people request tickets for the Saturday Night Rally in Tulsa, Oklahoma!" Twitter, 15 June 2020, 9:28 a.m.

@parscale (Brad Parscale). "Over 1M ticket requests for the @realDonaldTrump #MAGA Rally in Tulsa on Saturday. Before entering each guest will get: Temperature check—Hand sanitizer—Mask There will be precautions for the heat and bottled water as well." Twitter, 15 June 2020, 10:55 a.m.

David Smith. "Trump Tower Meeting with Russians 'Treasonous', Bannon Says in Explosive Book." *The Guardian*, 3 January 2018.

Sarah Blaskey and Jay Weaver. "He's a Chinese Billionaire and a Member of Trump's Mar-a-Lago. Is He Also a Communist Spy?" *Miami Herald*, 23 July 2019.

"Lady May Yacht for Sale." Boat International.

Michael C. Bender and Beth Reinhard. "'Pollstress' Conway Brings Trump Campaign Experience with Conservative Edge." *Wall Street Journal*, 18 August 2016.

Scott Horsley. "3 Months of Hell: U.S. Economy Drops 32.9% in Worst GDP Report Ever." NPR, 30 July 2020.

Michael Scherer and Josh Dawsey. "Trump Frustrated with Campaign Manager Parscale amid Falling Polls." *Washington Post*, 12 July 2020.

Liz Essley White. "Exclusive: White House Document Shows 18 States in Coronavirus 'Red Zone.'" Center for Public Integrity, 16 July 2020.

@THEHermanCain (The Cain Gang). "We are sorry to announce that Herman Cain has tested positive for COVID-19, and is currently receiving treatment in an Atlanta-area hospital. Please keep him, and all who are battling this virus, in your prayers. Our full statement appears below. Updates to follow." Twitter, 2 July 2020, 1:00 p.m.

Chapter 12. Stepien's Shot

Tom Wilk. "Awash in Washingtons." *New Jersey Monthly*, 17 January 2011.

"About Minebrook." Minebrook Golf Club.

Linda Voorhis. "Bloomingdale Picks GOP for Mayor, 2 Council Seats." *The Record*, 3 November 1993.

Diane Cardwell. "Robert D. Franks, G.O.P. Leader in New Jersey, Is Dead at 58." *New York Times*, 10 April 2010.

David Kocieniewski and Laura Mansnerus. "McGreevey Savors Party's Gains as G.O.P. Reviews Losses." *New York Times*, 6 November 2003.

Andrew Rice. "Most Likely to Destroy a Governor." *New York Magazine*, 18 September 2016.

"Michael DuHaime—Partner." Mercury LLC.

John Holl. "A New Owner for a Hot Political Site." *New York Times*, 11 March 2011.

Ted Sherman. "A Look Back at the Bridgegate Scandal, as Sentencing Approaches…" NJ.com, 28 March 2017.

Amanda Terkel and Sam Stein. "Days of Chaos in Fort Lee during Chris Christie Administration's Traffic Experiment." *HuffPost*, 10 January 2014.

Ted Mann. "Port Chief Fumed over Bridge Jam." *Wall Street Journal*, 1 October 2013.

Shawn Boburg. "For Trump Son-in-Law and Confidant Jared Kushner, a Long History of Fierce Loyalty." *Washington Post*, 27 November 2016.

"Full transcript: N.J. Gov. Chris Christie's January 9 News Conference on George Washington Bridge Scandal." *Washington Post*, 9 January 2014.

Andrea Bernstein. "Here's the Unofficial List of Bridgegate Co-conspirators." WNYC, 30 September 2016.

Nick Rummel. "List of Unindicted Co-conspirators in 'Bridgegate' Kept under Seal." Courthouse News Service, 17 May 2016.

"New Jersey: Public Reacts to Bridgegate Charges" [press release]. Monmouth University, 4 May 2015.

Shelly Banjo, Jordan Fabian, and Nick Wadhams. "Trump Says He's Considering a Ban on TikTok in the U.S." Bloomberg, 7 July 2020.

Ashley Parker and William Wan. "Trump Keeps Boasting about Passing a Cognitive Test—but It Doesn't Mean What He Thinks It Does." *Washington Post*, 22 July 2020.

Matea Gold. "What Is Left Hand Enterprises and Why Did the Trump Campaign Pay It $730,000?" *Washington Post*, 23 June 2016.

Julie Bykowicz. "Trump's Campaign Machine Has Two-Year Head Start." *Wall Street Journal*, 14 April 2019.

Jonathan Lemire. "Trump Wears Mask in Public for First Time during Pandemic." Associated Press, 11 July 2020.

"Rudy Giuliani Campaign Announces Health Care Advisors." PNHP.org, 30 July 2007.

Mike Spies, Jake Pearson, and Derek Willis. "Republican National Committee Obscured How Much It Pays Its Chief of Staff." ProPublica, 21 February 2020.

"General Election: Trump vs. Biden." *RealClearPolitics*.

"Donald Trump Coronavirus Press Conference Transcript July 23: Talks GOP Convention, School Reopening." Rev, 23 July 2020.

Chapter 13. The Trump TV Convention

@realDonaldTrump (Donald J. Trump). "Great Ratings & Reviews Last Night. Thank you!" Twitter, 28 August 2020, 9:56 a.m. Trump Twitter Archive.

Brian Stelter. "Biden Hits Trump Where It Hurts: In the Convention Speech Ratings." CNN, 29 August 2020.

@NewDay (CNN New Day). "Former WH aide @Cliff_Sims responds after President Trump tweets about him while being interviewed on @NewDay: 'Don't matter to me what Donald Trump or anyone else says that I am.' https://cnn.it/2FUEcTT." Twitter, 29 January 2019, 9:00 a.m.

@realDonaldTrump (Donald J. Trump). "A low level staffer that I hardly knew named Cliff Sims wrote yet another boring book based on made up stories and fiction. He pretended to be an insider when in fact he was nothing more than a gofer. He signed a non-disclosure agreement. He is a mess!" Twitter, 29 January 2019, 8:45 a.m. Trump Twitter Archive.

Chapter 14. Hell Week and a Half

"What Are the Dimensions of the Oval Office?" White House Historical Association.

"Slavery and the White House." White House Historical Association.

Christopher H. Sterling. "'The Fireside Chats'—President Franklin D. Roosevelt (1933–1944)." Library of Congress.

"Diplomatic Reception Room." White House Museum.

"Fact Check: Hunter Biden's Military Discharge Was Administrative, Not Dishonorable." Reuters, 1 October 2020.

Ian Schwartz. "CNN's Dana Bash: Debate Was a 'Shitshow.'" *RealClearPolitics*, 29 September 2020.

Erik Wemple. "The Life of Campaign 2016's Substitute Debate Moderator." *Washington Post*, 19 October 2016.

Michael C. Bender. "Here's Who Traveled with Trump on Air Force One This Week." *Wall Street Journal*, 2 October 2020.

NBC News/Wall Street Journal Survey, early October 2020.

Michael C. Bender and Rebecca Ballhaus. "Trump Didn't Disclose First Positive Covid-19 Test while Awaiting a Second Test on Thursday." *Wall Street Journal*, 4 October 2020.

"Donald Trump Duluth, Minnesota Campaign Rally Transcript September 30: Night after First Debate." Rev, 30 September 2020.

@JenniferJJacobs (Jennifer Jacobs). "NEWS: Hope Hicks, who traveled with Trump aboard Air Force One to and from the presidential debate on Tuesday, and to his Minnesota rally yesterday, has coronavirus, sources tell me." Twitter, 1 October 2020, 8:09 p.m.

Annie Karni and Maggie Haberman. "Trump Makes First Public Appearance since Leaving Walter Reed." *New York Times*, 10 October 2020.

"Donald Trump Video Speech Transcript after Release from Walter Reed Hospital October 5." Rev, 5 October 2020.

NBC News/Wall Street Journal Survey, mid-October 2020.

Nick Niedzwiadek. "The 35 People Who Have Tested Positive in the Trump Covid Outbreak." *Politico*, 2 October 2020.

Janet Hook. "Donald Trump Least Popular New President in at Least a Generation, Poll Finds." *Wall Street Journal*, 17 January 2017.

NBC News/Wall Street Journal Survey, January 2018.

NBC News/Wall Street Journal Survey, September 2020.

Chapter 15. Where's Hunter?

"Betting Odds—2020 U.S. President." *RealClearPolitics.*

@atrupar (Aaron Rupar). "'If you fuck around with us, if you do something bad to us, we are gonna do things to you that have never been done before.'—the President of the United States." Twitter, 9 October 2020, 2:05 p.m.

@AmerIndependent (The American Independent). "Trump: 'The first time I ever heard of Black Lives Matter, I said, 'that's such a terrible term,' because it's such a racist term. It's a term that sows division between blacks and whites and everybody else.'" Twitter, 9 October 2020, 2:40 p.m.

Michael C. Bender and Joshua Jamerson. "Trump Plans In-Person White House Event, Rally in Florida." *Wall Street Journal,* 9 October 2020.

"Lindsey Graham Refuses to Take COVID Test for Senate Debate in SC." *Axios,* 10 October 2020.

"Fauci: We Had a Superspreader Event at the White House." *Axios,* 9 October 2020.

Tony Bobulinski, Letter to CEFC China Energy Company Ltd., 1 August 2017, p. 15.

Dennis Haugh. "About." Personal website.

"Trump Calls Giuliani 'Greatest Crime Fighter in Last 50 Years.'" ABC, 16 December 2020.

Rebecca Ballhaus. "Rudy Giuliani Hires Robert Costello to Represent Him." *Wall Street Journal,* 6 November 2019.

"Donald Trump Campaign Rally Sanford, Florida Transcript October 12: First Rally since Diagnosis." Rev, 12 October 2020.

"Donald Trump Rally Des Moines, Iowa Transcript October 14." Rev, 14 October 2020.

Michael M. Grynbaum. "As Trump Flouts Safety Protocols, News Outlets Balk at Close Coverage." *New York Times,* 12 October 2020.

Seema Mehta and Arit John. "The Beach Boys, Tony Lido Isle, $150,000 Tickets: A Peek inside Trump's Orange County Fundraiser." *Lost Angeles Times,* 18 October 2020.

Chris Willman. "Brian Wilson Disavows Trump's Beach Boys Benefit in California (Exclusive)." *Variety,* 18 October 2020.

Sen. Ron Johnson and Sen. Charles Grassley, Letters to Tony Bobulinski, James Gilliar, James Biden, Benjamin Klubes, Preston Burton, George Mesires, and Rob Walker, via email, 21 October 2020.

"Johnson, Grassley Will Interview Former Hunter Biden Business Associate, Request Documents from Other Individuals, Including James and Hunter Biden." Majority Media, U.S. Senate Committee on Homeland Security and Governmental Affairs, 22 October 2020.

"The Second Presidential Debate." *New York Times*, 7 October 2008.

Joel Achenbach and Jacqueline Dupree. "U.S. Tops 60,000 Daily Coronavirus Infections for First Time since Early August." *Washington Post*, 15 October 2020.

"Donald Trump & Joe Biden Final Presidential Debate Transcript 2020." Rev, 22 October 2020.

Mike McIntire, Russ Buettner, and Susanne Craig. "Trump Records Shed New Light on Chinese Business Pursuits." *New York Times*, 20 October 2020.

"Biden to Trump: 'I Have Not Taken a Penny from Any Foreign Source Ever in My Life.'" *Axios*, 23 October 2020.

Chapter 16. Final Stretch

"A Brief History of the Delaware Canal." Friends of the Delaware Canal.

"Randal James Thom Obituary." Tribune Archive.

"2020 General Election." Palm Beach County Supervisor of Elections. Updated 23 November 2020.

Chapter 17. Election Day

"Doral, Florida—Fayetteville, North Carolina—Avoca, Pennsylvania—Traverse City, Michigan—Kenosha, Wisconsin—Grand Rapids, Michigan—Washington, District of Columbia." Google Maps.

Kimberly Truong. "The Mystery of Trump's Bizarrely Long Ties Has Finally Been Solved." *The Cut*, 16 January 2019.

"State Poll Opening and Closing Times (2020)." *Ballotpedia*.

"'Non-Scalable' Fence Erected around White House in Anticipation of Election Protests." *South China Morning Post*, 3 November 2020.

"Gucci Printed Silk-Twill Mini Dress." Net-a-Porter.

John Binder. "Fashion Notes: First Lady Melania Trump Votes in Gucci, Hermès Glamor." *Breitbart*, 3 November 2020.

"D.C. Mayor's Letter to the White House." *Washington Post*, 7 October 2020.

Julie Zauzmer. "D.C. Says 190,000 Have Activated New Coronavirus Contact-Tracing Tool." *Washington Post*, 26 October 2020.

DC Mayor's Office. "Mayor Bowser Provides Coronavirus Update, 10/26/20." YouTube, 26 October 2020.

"8-Ball Corner Pocket, Mr. President." White House Museum.

Jeff Zeleny and Kevin Liptak. "White House Portraits of Bill Clinton and George W. Bush Moved from Prominent Space to Rarely Used Room." CNN, 17 July 2020.

@JHoganGidley (J. Hogan Gidley). "Hey, anyone know if Joe Biden has called a 'lid' yet?" Twitter, 3 November 2020, 7:42 a.m.

Christopher Cadelago. "Trump's Election-Night Claims Color Final Campaign Stretch." *Politico*, 2 November 2020.

Fox and Friends. Fox News Channel, 3 November 2020.

Anna Hirtenstein and Paul Vigna. "Dow Logs Biggest One-Day Gain since July." *Wall Street Journal*, 3 November 2020.

Todd Spangler. "Here's How Biden Beat Trump in Michigan—and It Wasn't Corruption." *Detroit Free Press*, 6 November 2020.

Nathan Denzin. "How a Handful of Counties Turned Out En Masse, Winning Wisconsin for Joe Biden." *Daily Cardinal*, 6 November 2020.

Chapter 18. Acquittal, Part Two: The Insurrection

Amy Gardner, Ashley Parker, Josh Dawsey, and Emma Brown. "Top Republicans Back Trump's Effort to Challenge Election Results." *Washington Post*, November 9, 2020.

Makini Brice and Tom Hals. "Trump Campaign Challenges Election Results in Wisconsin Supreme Court." Reuters, 1 December 2020.

Kate Brumback. "Georgia Again Certifies Election Results Showing Biden Won." Associated Press, 7 December 2020.

@FSPhiladelphia (Four Seasons Hotel Philadelphia at Comcast Center). "To clarify, President Trump's press conference will NOT be held at Four Seasons Hotel Philadelphia. It will be held at Four Seasons Total Landscaping—no relation with the hotel." Twitter, 7 November 2020, 10:45 a.m.

@DonaldJTrumpJr (Donald Trump Jr.). "The best thing for America's future is for @realDonaldTrump to go to total war over this election to expose all of the fraud, cheating, dead/no longer in state voters, that has been going on for far too long. It's time to clean up this mess & stop looking like a banana republic!" Twitter, 5 November 2020, 5:08 p.m.

Katie Benner. "Trump and Justice Dept. Lawyer Said to Have Plotted to Oust Acting Attorney General." *New York Times*, 22 January 2021.

Tom Jackman, Paul Duggan, Ann E. Marimow, and Spencer S. Hsu. "Proud Boys Sparked Clashes during Pro-Trump Rally, D.C. Officials Say." *Washington Post*, 14 December 2020.

Joe Heim and Marissa J. Lang. "For D.C. Protests, Proud Boys Settle in at City's Oldest Hotel and Its Bar." *Washington Post*, 28 December 2020.

@Mike_Pence (Mike Pence). Twitter, 6 January 2021, 1:02 p.m.

Maki Becker. "Rochester Man Charged with Using Police Shield to Break Capitol Window." *Buffalo News*, 15 January 2021.

Ashley Parker, Carol D. Leonnig, Paul Kane, and Emma Brown. "How the Rioters Who Stormed the Capitol Came Dangerously Close to Pence." *Washington Post*, 15 January 2021.

Philip Rucker, Ashley Parker, and Josh Dawsey. "After Inciting Mob Attack, Trump Retreats in Rage. Then, Grudgingly, He Admits His Loss." *Washington Post*, 7 January 2021.

Epilogue

Jo Werne. "Mar-a-Lago; a Decorator's Dream: Refurbishing 58 Bedrooms under One Roof." *Houston Chronicle*, 9 March 1986.

About the Author

Michael C. Bender is the senior White House reporter for the *Wall Street Journal* whose coverage of President Trump has been recognized for its deep sourcing, balance, and valuable behind-the-scenes portraits of Trump's administration and presidential campaigns. Bender was awarded the Gerald R. Ford Foundation Journalism Prize for Distinguished Reporting on the Presidency in 2019 for work that "set a consistently high standard of reporting" and "provided a valuable chronicle of the president, his team, and the movement that has reshaped American politics and national policy." In 2020, he received the National Press Club award for political analysis for a series of stories that detailed the sights, sounds, and inner workings of Trump campaign rallies. Since 2000, Bender has covered local, state, and national politics for the (Grand Junction, Colorado) *Daily Sentinel*, *Dayton Daily News*, *Palm Beach Post*, *Tampa Bay Times*, and Bloomberg News. He joined the *Journal* in 2016 and published more than 1,100 stories about Trump in the next five years. He has also served as an on-air political analyst for CNN. Born and raised in Cleveland with his six younger sisters, Bender graduated from the Ohio State University in 2000 with a degree in history and now lives in Washington with his wife, *Washington Post* White House bureau chief Ashley Parker, and two daughters.